After Adam Smith

After Adam Smith

A CENTURY OF TRANSFORMATION
IN POLITICS AND
POLITICAL ECONOMY

Murray Milgate & Shannon C. Stimson

PRINCETON UNIVERSITY PRESS
PRINCETON AND OXFORD

Library of Congress Cataloging-in-Publication Data

Milgate, Murray.
After Adam Smith : a century of transformation in politics
and political economy / Murray Milgate and Shannon C. Stimson.
        p.   cm.
Includes bibliographical references and index.
ISBN 978-0-691-14037-7 (cloth : alk. paper)
1. Economics—Political aspects—History. 2. Classical school of
economics—History. I. Stimson, Shannon C. II. Title.
HB74.P65M55 2009
330.15′3—dc22   2009016033

British Library Cataloging-in-Publication Data is available

This book has been composed in Sabon

Printed on acid-free paper. ∞

press.princeton.edu

Printed in the United States of America
3 5 7 9 10 8 6 4 2

CONTENTS

PREFACE

THE MUTUAL INTERPLAY between economics and politics is a striking feature of our everyday experience. Whether for good or ill, there seems to be something almost sacred about the names of some of the great economic and political thinkers of the past. They are not infrequently deployed in the arena of current debate and controversy either to legitimate particular ways of thinking about our economic and political circumstances, or to suggest new ways of addressing some of the more challenging difficulties of our own times. Yet this quite understandable appeal to a presumed higher or foundational authority seems to overlook not only the distance that separates us from their original writings (and the problems they faced in their own times), but also the paths that our thinking about economics and politics have travelled in the meantime.

There would be few writers of whom this could more surely be said than Adam Smith. His name is pretty well synonymous with the case for unregulated free markets in every sphere of life in which they operate. Furthermore, the recent collapse of global credit markets, and the turmoil in financial circles and the real economy that has followed in its wake, has seen the name of John Maynard Keynes reappearing in the print and electronic media, as the champion of large-scale deficit spending, to an extent that would have been almost unimaginable twenty years ago. Such appropriations of the past, however convenient they may be to various partisan causes of the present, have a tendency to make us misremember the past, and to encourage us too readily to skip over the conceptual changes that have been wrought on those ideas as they have been handed down to us today. The kinds of things that Smith may have had to say about free markets, or that Keynes may have had to say about government loan expenditure, are not infrequently different from what we may take them to be, and they have certainly been modified and changed by subsequent ideas and events that cannot be put to one side.

The complex connections between liberty, free markets, and social and economic justice, for example, have seen quite radical embellishment since Smith's day. The very conception of civil society that formed the starting point of classical political economy was not only different from that which forms the basis of economic thinking today, but it was altered in their own hands to suit the changing economic circumstances and political aspirations they confronted. We inherit, so to speak, not the original, but the summation of the reworkings to which it has been subjected over time. Prudence, therefore, would seem to suggest that the time may be ripe for an attempt to bring back into sharper focus some of those changes that took place after Adam Smith.

Another example may further illustrate their importance. What might it have been about perfect liberty in commercial relations that attracted Smith and those who came after him? In the middle of the twentieth century, much as now, the answer to this question seemed pretty obvious—it (or "perfect competition," as we have since learned to reconceptualise it) promoted efficiency in the allocation of resources such that all would be fully utilised to the greatest social and individual benefit. Waste of resources, human or physical, would thus all but vanish before our very eyes. So casual has our association of this idea with Smith become, that we have come to think of it as capturing the very essence of the invisible hand. Yet quite apart from the fact that neither analytically nor historically has market competition ever been able to be shown to be capable of delivering such an outcome, it does not accurately reflect what Smith himself seems to have seen as its promise.

On the contrary, when the idea of perfect liberty in commercial relations was introduced by Smith it was because he saw it as being best suited to the development of the division of labour—that is, to increases in the wealth of the nation. It is to its effects on the rate of productivity growth that one should turn for Smith's case for fostering it, not to some putative ability of competition efficiently to allocate a *given* set of resources. To put it simply, the case for capitalism was that it was best suited to promote innovation and technological progress—a claim that might more plausibly find some basis in the historical evidence of the last two hundred years. Freedom of international trade, too, was not advocated because it would lead to a more efficient allocation of global resources, but because Smith claimed that without it the division of labour would be limited by the extent of the market.

In this book we examine one set of conceptual transformations in politics and political economy that took place during a part of what is called the classical period of political economy—broadly from the late eighteenth to the late nineteenth century. In this sense we traverse a similar landscape to that travelled by Elie Halévy in his classic study of philosophical radicalism, but with less an emphasis on the growth and development of ideas and with more an emphasis on moments of conceptual adjustment and change. This, however, is not to beg a comparison with Halévy's book. We would judge our own enterprise to have achieved a measure of success not only if it contributed to a clearer understanding of what the writers of those years actually had to say about politics and political economy but also, and more importantly in a time of economic uncertainty and rethinking, if it contributed to securing a more acute appreciation of the fact that they could not possibly have been saying many of the things that have since been attributed to them.

In the course of writing this book we have received valuable comments from many of our colleagues and friends. Samuel Beer, Ruth Collier, Hannah Dawson, David Lieberman, Ian Shapiro, Elena Wang, and Giancarlo de Vivo read the entire manuscript and offered astute criticisms and suggestions for its improvement. We received valuable comments on earlier versions of individual chapters from Sonja Amadae, Fonna Forman-Barzilai, Geoff Brennan, Michael Gillespie, Alan Houston, Melissa Lane, Doug Long, James Moore, Mike Munger, Michael Rogin, and Andrew Sabl. Jane Gingrich and James Harney provided us with excellent research support at important stages in the development of our work. We would also wish to record our debt to those friends and intellectual colleagues—John Eatwell, Harvey Goldman, Debra Satz, Tracy Strong, Cheryl Welch, Donald Winch, and Giancarlo de Vivo—whose own considerations of these (and many other) topics have been a source of spirited debate, historical criticism, and much common sense. We alone are responsible for any errors that remain.

Our thanks to former students and colleagues of the Committee on Degrees in Social Studies at Harvard University, and its distinguished former chairman, David Landes, under whose leadership this project was originally conceived. Thanks also to the students of Berkeley's Program in the Political and Economic Development of Industrial Societies and its chairman, Brad DeLong; to the Gerst Program in Political and Economic Studies; the Cambridge Seminar on the History of Political Thought; the 2003 Oxford Kobe Seminar on the History of Civil Society and its generous principal originator, Jose Harris; the 2007 UCLA Conference on Common Liberalism sponsored by the School of Public Policy and the Department of Political Science; and the 2008 Liberty Fund Edinburgh Conference on Adam Smith's *Moral Sentiments* and its meticulous organiser, Chandran Kukathas. A special debt of gratitude is owed to the president and fellows of Queens' College Cambridge for their generous support of this project. Acknowledgement is due also to the editors of the *American Political Science Review, Contributions to Political Economy,* the *European Journal for the History of Economic Thought, Political Studies,* and *Public Choice* (and their respective publishers: Cambridge University Press, Oxford University Press, Taylor Francis, Blackwell Publishing, and Elsevier) for permission to incorporate some of our earlier published work in this book.

It is fitting for us finally to acknowledge three individuals, Joseph Duncan and the late Judith Shklar and Joan Robinson, who in their different ways have remained invaluable to all of our work over very many years.

What follows is our attempt to illustrate how some of the mutual inter-actions between economics and politics were played out in the century or so after Adam Smith—and to highlight how, when thinking about politics and political economy, we might fruitfully rethink both the degree of their remove as well as the relevance of their conclusions to our own present concerns.

MM & SCS
January 2009

After Adam Smith

Chapter One

INTRODUCTION

THIS BOOK considers a number of the key political and economic themes and concepts that emerged in the early period of political economy up to the final quarter of the nineteenth century. We trace the manner in which a systematic interrelationship between politics and political economy was developed, altered, and refined in those years. Many writers and many circumstances contributed to the formation and development of politics and political economy. Who these writers were, what contexts might be useful in understanding their ideas, and how those ideas shaped the discourse of politics and political economy form the object of our analysis. That Adam Smith and John Stuart Mill have garnered by far the most attention in this arena—and that the secondary interest in their work shows no sign of diminishing in intensity—goes without saying. Yet there exist only a few substantive attempts either to connect those ideas and arguments about politics systematically to the economic thinking of those two individual writers, or more importantly to trace the interdependent development of politics and political economy in their as well as others hands.

Our interest is to show how, and in what ways, political economists sought to influence and alter the understanding of politics and political life in these years. We are concerned with a *transition* that took place between an eighteenth-century discourse on commercial society and the liberty of trade, and an understanding of these same subjects as they came to be exemplified in later nineteenth-century considerations of both politics and political economy. Our canvass covers the landscape, then, of what is now called classical political economy—and our object is to chart the conceptual transformations in politics and political economy, and the perceived relationships between them, that took place after Adam Smith.

In the years between 1750 and 1870 there appeared a range of efforts to develop a new and sophisticated framework of concepts through which, it was believed, one might secure a better understanding of the commercial and subsequently industrial character of civil society. From these efforts was to emerge not only an identifiable discipline known as political economy but also, in the hands of some, a science of politics. Questions of how and to what effect order and good government, justice and individual liberty, might be enhanced or compromised by the workings of the market were widely canvassed—and the findings of the new discourse of political economy came increasingly to inform (and transform) the answers. Politics and political economy began to be seen as systematically interrelated, and it has remained so ever since.

These developments often overlapped, often drew on each other, and were often forged in the hands of the very same writers. They took shape over time, and by way of mutual theoretical interaction and criticism, as part of an ongoing and sometimes volatile conversation concerning both the nature of market society along with the characteristics of the polity and policies appropriate to it. In these years, political economy was at the epicentre of new and unfolding understandings of society; it could illuminate, it seemed to some, not only the movements in the price of provisions but also the very basis of liberty and progress.

§1. Smith's *Wealth of Nations* and Mill's *Principles of Political Economy* stand, in a sense, at the beginning and the end of the nearly one hundred years of developments that concern us here. Of course, not all issues were treated in the same depth or with the same intentions by Smith and Mill, and not all of their arguments proceeded to entirely satisfactory conclusions. On this point or that, one might more usefully consult Baron Montesquieu or Jean-Jacques Rousseau, Anne-Robert-Jacques Turgot or François Quesnay, or Jeremy Bentham. On yet other points one might wish to look to Immanuel Kant or Edmund Burke, and on still others to David Hume or Adam Ferguson, or Bernard de Mandeville. But what Smith did manage to do in the *Wealth of Nations*, and for the first time, was to examine in a systematic way what much of the earlier literature of political economy had approached in a piecemeal manner—as a set of individual, largely disparate or unconnected economic phenomena and problems. Regardless of his intentions, the effect of Smith's efforts was to provide a deep reservoir of ideas and arguments for later political economists to draw on in framing some of their own concerns, gloss their own interpretations, and against which to provide their own corrections, clarifications, and criticisms as their needs required.

If political economy in the eighteenth century was more than what was to be found in Smith alone—and its conceptual apparatus more extensive and, in places, more developed than it was even in its presentation in the *Wealth of Nations*—then by the middle of the nineteenth century there was little objectively left of Smith's original arguments in the literature of political economy. The ideas and arguments of Thomas Robert Malthus, David Ricardo, and Mill had risen to dominance, and had moved considerations of the interdependence between politics and political economy into new and different directions. Nevertheless, on consulting the vast secondary literature on these subjects one sometimes comes away with the impression that this simple point is often forgotten.

In much of that literature, for example, Smith's name appears again and again; one gets the impression that the relationship he forged between politics and political economy was not only decisive but that it was born fully formed too. In some of that literature, whether from the political Left or Right, it is almost as if all of the essential ingredients of, say, a twentieth-century welfare state or its neoliberal counterpart actually emerged complete in 1776 in the *Wealth of Nations*. Nothing could be more anachronistic and misleading.

Smith invented neither the principle of population nor the doctrine of comparative advantage; he invented neither the theory of the division of labour nor the quantity theory of money; he resolved neither the analytical problem of price determination nor adequately explained the distribution of income between the classes. Smith did not establish the priority of the market over the state nor is he responsible for the reduction of politics to economics. He is not the strictly lineal descendant of John Locke in some putative progression towards modern liberalism, although he certainly integrated considerations of political and economic life into one coherent discourse. He is not the champion of unregulated competition, nor the moral purveyor of possessive individualism, nor the architect of an economic theory of capitalist democracy—not, at least, as these ideas are understood today.

The political economy that forms the subject matter of this book, however, should not be understood as just a body of economic thought and doctrine—although to be sure, there are certain unifying themes and concerns that characterise its landscape, and mark it out from what came before and what followed it. Nor yet should it be understood simply as a catalogue of the diverse, and often conflicting, ideas and arguments produced by a group of thinkers writing on economic affairs between the middle of the eighteenth and the middle of the nineteenth century—although without doubt, those years do broadly define the period of its heyday. Such conceptions, while perhaps well suited to other ends, seem at once too narrow, too self-limiting, and too static to capture its essential character.[1]

---

[1] Ever since Karl Marx (1867, 174–75, 175n) first coined the term classical political economy in the first volume of *Das Kapital*, it has been the subject of many a page of critical analysis, historical interpretation, and theoretical reconsideration. In fact, this literature has become so extensive that it is not unreasonable to ask what value might remain to be extracted from traversing, once again, a terrain already travelled by the classical writers. To this question we will offer in our own defence just two responses: that the time is never unripe for an effort at historical recovery, and that there is at least some novelty in addressing the ways in which political economy informed and transformed politics in this period—be it at the practical, theoretical, or doctrinal level.

Furthermore, the history of the accumulated historical scholarship sometimes seems to be nothing if not a series of grand tournaments between contemporary minds seeking to appropriate the past to various partisan causes of the present. The regularity with which the historians have charged each other with this sort of offence against the past—and in so doing, the regularity with which one encounters implicit claims to be doing better history—may even be an indicator of its ubiquity. Within the doctrinal camp itself, for example, there has been not a little argument about which doctrines actually define the movement in the first place. For their part, more contextual accounts have sought to expose the narrowness, thinness, and (sometimes) ideological biases of doctrinal reconstructions. Within the contextual camp, however, there is always the delicate problem of what context to choose.

A glance at the work of the historians of economic thought, for instance, readily reveals a distinct ebb and flow in their views about these thinkers. On the one hand, some have chosen to cast their political economy as being essentially different from the economics of today. This view stresses discontinuity—not just in economic theory and method but also with respect to the kinds of problems each addresses. On the other hand, there are those who have chosen to accentuate the similarities between them and modern theory and method, and/or between the economic problems faced then and those faced now.

On the first line of argument, while it is true that political economy is said to differ from the economics (and the economic problems) of today, it might yet be said to be either relevant or irrelevant to the present concerns. If different and irrelevant, it might be found to be, say, outdated, wrong, or wrongheaded (or some combination of all three). It might also be, say, that the progress of economic science, and/or the very development of the economy itself, had rendered these ideas and arguments irrelevant to the present concerns.[2] If different and relevant, these thinkers might be shown to have had, for example, a more robust economic theory or have provided invaluable insights (theoretical or practical) now lost.[3] On the second line of argument, an emphasis on continuity customarily goes hand in hand with a quite favourable image of political economy.

In addition to the historians of economic thought, there are also historians who seek to recover a much broader understanding of political econ-

---

[2] Implicitly, John Maynard Keynes made just such a claim when he declared in his *General Theory* that by the "classical" writers he meant everyone (except for the "heretics" and Thomas Robert Malthus) who had written before him.

[3] The considerable body of scholarship due to Maurice Dobb, Ronald Meek, and Andrew Skinner probably falls into this category. One should also mention here those economists who favour taking a more sophisticated view of the broader *intellectual* landscape—and so who worry about accounts that might be said to be overly economistic in outlook.

omy. But the catalogue of their findings is often no less redolent of their current concerns than is that of doctrinal historians. Even among the ever-dwindling ranks of Marxist historians, similar tendencies are apparent. There are some of their number who see political economy as apologetics, and who set out their position against it. Others of their number link political economy to Karl Marx's contributions by way of a rational reconstruction of the analytical connections between them.

§2. We begin with what appears to us today as Smith's political odyssey. We consider his contributions to the discourse of political and economic thought as it has been viewed through a lens provided by the myriad of characterisations of both his personal politics and the politics to which his political economy putatively gave rise. Here we find that a challenging complexity in Smith's own presentation is reflected in wide disagreement among his interpreters as to his contribution—whether theoretical, historical, or ideological. In particular, it would seem that attempts to understand Smith from much later vantage points fail to give sufficient weight to either the process through which his framework of concepts had been transmitted to them or the subtle, but substantial transformations that had been worked on his ideas before they reached them. By attending to those transformations, we may find ourselves in a better position from which to draw out the basis as well as content of Smith's original idea of perfect liberty in both its market and governmental manifestations—and to understand how it was developed and altered after him.

§3. In that task, we first consider the deployment of an older notion of civil society—but in what seems to have been an increasingly distinctive guise—immediately before and after the *Wealth of Nations*. There is a real sense in which it was eighteenth-century political economy that established the presumption that civil society should be conceived as comprising the economic aspect of social life. Still, just what such an economic understanding of civil society entailed, what institutions, social groups, and voluntary associations were taken to be formative of its anatomy, and how civil society itself was thought to relate to the polity all underwent important changes after Smith.

These changes were partly the result of a historical development that saw the mercantile and commercial character of economic society of the eighteenth century give way, quite rapidly, to its industrial counterpart in the nineteenth century. But they were also the result of changes in the approach to the theory of political economy itself that took place over the same period. What began in the writings of Ferguson and Smith as an attempt to outline a picture of civil society more suited to the newly

---

Here one thinks of the works of Edwin Seligman, Jacob Viner, Albert Hirschman, and Donald Winch.

emerging characteristics of an economic world dominated by market exchange, changed over time to become, by the 1870s, a world modelled as
being one of isolated, individual decision making in an austere, putatively
universally applicable context. Civil society was thereby emptied of much
of the earlier social, institutional, cultural, and historical content that it
was initially thought to embody. We present these developments as the
rise and fall of civil society in chapter 3 below.

§4. From the anatomy of civil society, so to speak, we turn to a consideration of its main organs, and the framework of concepts deployed by the
classical political economists to examine them. The relationship between
economic and political life more generally is the subject of chapter 4.
Viewed in perspective, it would appear that Bentham's utilitarian calculator, modified (perhaps) by some of Mill's later moral embellishments, became in the hands of the neoclassical writers of the 1870s not only the
accepted view of the personality of economic man but also the model of
man from which to deduce the very laws governing market exchange and
the distribution of income. Self-interested action, now thought of as constrained optimisation, was to become not only a component part of economic life in civil society but rather its only component. Where once stood
Smith's rich description of morally regulated, prudent behaviour to describe self-interested action—derived from a model of a socially constructed self—now stood a rational calculator of exclusively private costs
and benefits.

§5. The set of organising concepts and themes introduced into political
economy to aid in understanding the operation of the economy—free
competition, the economic machine, natural conditions, and the invisible
hand—form the subject matter of chapter 5.

From this plurality of views, we then consider the more self-consciously
uniform picture of Smith's enterprise created by Dugald Stewart. Stewart
altered the figure of Smith for both political economy and political theory
in decisive ways. He altered Smith's views on the input that political economy might have into both legislative practice and constitutional reform.
Stewart created a figure of Smith for whom political economy was exclusively a science of the legislator, but one that had nothing to contribute
to debates over forms of constitutional order. In Stewart's figure of Smith,
the former could enact progressive reforms without touching on the latter
in revolutionary ways.

§6. Despite Stewart's effort to build a coherent basis for the further
development of a now-Smithian project—one that moved political economy significantly away from Smith's own picture—he was not entirely
successful. When Malthus first entered the conversation (admittedly
anonymously) at the end of the eighteenth century, he reworked Smith's
understanding of the relationships between the wealth of nations and

prosperity and progress in quite fundamental ways. With the introduction of the principle of population, along with the possibility that there might arise in the progress of wealth a general overproduction of commodities, political economy and politics could no longer ignore, or put to one side as Stewart had suggested, the question of the moral integrity of market society. Malthus's interventions cast new and grave doubts on the moral and political content of economic progress itself—doubts that later critics of unbridled market life, as diverse as Marx and John Maynard Keynes, would later seize on. An examination of this reworking as well as its impact on thinking about moral and political reform is presented in chapter 7 below.

§7. We next turn to the so-called philosophic radicals, and the development of the discussion of politics and political economy in their hands. James Mill and the utilitarians were united in adopting Malthus's principle of population, but they differed dramatically from both the economic and political solutions that Malthus thought to follow from it. Mill in particular presented what he took to be a democratic reform of the constitution (expansive in principle, but somewhat limited in application) as the antidote to the imminent difficulties associated with the progress of wealth. Utility and property became, for him, the principal desiderata for constitutional reform. These arguments and how they were played out by the early philosophic radicals are examined in chapter 8 below. Their emphasis on the centrality of individual decision-making capacity in political life introduced a set of ideas that was to leave a lasting legacy.

§8. In political economy, however, other philosophic radicals charted a different course. Among their number—and most opposed to Malthus's own politics, policies, and political economy—was Ricardo. Ricardo, like James Mill, chose to accept Malthus's population principle. But on the question of the possibility of a general overproduction of commodities, he vigorously opposed Malthus on the need for any systematic state action to prevent economic stagnation and decline. He opposed him as well on the more theoretical issues of distribution and growth. Ricardo's interest in politics and the democratic reform of parliament led him to discuss the expansion of the franchise, the secret ballot, and electoral reform in a manner controversially informed by his theory of political economy. Rather than deferring to utility, property, and individual decision-making capacity, as Mill and the utilitarians had done, Ricardo appears to have mapped economic participation directly to political citizenship. While cognisant of the often conflictual character of economic life, Ricardo appears to have been sanguine about its political consequences. The Ricardian basis of an argument for democratic reform in the early decades of the nineteenth century occupies us in chapter 9 below.

§9. Historically speaking, none of these radical reforms proved sufficient to stem the growing dissatisfaction with the apparent mismatch between the theory of market order and its actual operation. Developments in economic and political theory were thought unsatisfactory, or at least insufficient, on the ground. The response was picked up in theory, and in the streets, by a group of utopian and popular political-economic writers. The utopian writers introduced ideas into economic and political discourse that transformed notions of progress into notions of retrogression, translated pragmatic solutions into visionary phantasms, and shifted the political debate from practical policy and incremental improvements to be achieved at the ballot box into systems of ideas within which the conundrums of justice, population, and distribution would all but disappear. The writers of popular political economy, on the other hand, attempted to solve existing inequalities and theoretical incongruities through direct action—namely, social and political revolution. The interventions of these writers, coupled with their effects on the understanding of the political economy and politics of industrial society, occupy us in chapters 10 and 11.

§10. With political economy and politics in some disarray by the 1840s, when John Stuart Mill declared his intention in the *Principles of Political Economy* to provide for his mid-nineteenth-century audience what he claimed Smith had supplied in the *Wealth of Nations* for the previous century, he could not have chosen a more opportune time. Mill's contributions are the subject matter of chapter 12. Mill published his *Principles* claiming not only to be modernising Smith's economic vision but also to be definitively addressing the dissatisfaction of the utopian projectors and the populist critics. He redefined the scope and reach of political economy itself. Mill offered his own creative recapitulation of the relationship between policymaking and economic principles—and between political theory and political economy. When Mill distinguished between arguments for economic liberty and political liberty, and rethought the strict separation between the science of production and the distribution of wealth—a distinction he believed to be a matter of political choice—his thinking reflected the beleaguered state of politics and political economy by the middle of the century.

§11. We conclude by considering two responses to Mill's efforts—responses that framed the debate about politics and political economy thereafter. On one side stands Marx's critique of classical political economy and, on the other, the neoclassical attack on the putative logical shortcomings of the formal economic theorising of the whole of the classical tendency. Both of these critiques were to have profound effects on the subsequent development as well as understanding of the relationship between politics and political economy. A conversation emerged from

Marx's work that was always afterwards conducted outside the mainstream of economics, while mainstream economics was born from the theory of the neoclassical writers. It was at this juncture that the political economy of the classical writers was recast. It was also at this juncture that the real foundations of our current understanding of the market mechanism appear to have been laid down. The journey travelled by political economy and politics after Smith seems at this time to have reached a divide in the road.

Chapter Two

ADAM SMITH'S POLITICAL ODYSSEY

> Tell me, O muse, of that ingenious hero who travelled
> far and wide after he had sacked the famous town
> of Troy. Many cities did he visit, and many were the
> nations with whose manners and customs he was
> acquainted; moreover he suffered much by sea while try-
> ing to save his own life and bring his men safely home.
> —Homer, *The Odyssey*

IN MARCH 2007, the Bank of England issued a new twenty-pound bank-note featuring Smith's image. The image was taken from a likeness of the portrait medallion of Smith (a three-inch bust in two states, done from life) by James Tassie and dated 1787, making Smith sixty-four years of age. It is now housed in the Scottish National Portrait Gallery in Edinburgh.[1] Smith, of course, has not lacked for literary portraitists. If one turns to the literature of political and economic thought, one will find little unanimity as to how we are to render his contribution.

The first such sketch, drawn for a late eighteenth- and early nineteenth-century audience, was provided by Stewart. According to Stewart, Smith's "great aim" was to "direct the policy of nations" towards "unlimited freedom of trade" (1793, 10, 56, 64). It was the policy of laissez-faire, rather than a theoretical account of value, distribution, and growth—subjects that occupied the first two books of the *Wealth of Nations*, but that Stewart scarcely mentions—that Stewart wished his readers to see in Smith. A large part of Stewart's reformulation of Smith can be understood as an attempt to defuse the efforts of either revolutionary admirers such as Thomas Paine or conservatives such as Burke equally to lay claim to Smith's political economic legacy.[2]

---

[1] For a discussion of this particular image, see Buchan (2006, 137). Buchan notes that "both states show Smith in profile, one in modern dress and a bag wig, the other bare-shouldered and bare-headed in the antique manner."

[2] For a discussion of the debate over Smith's putative "revolutionary" or "conservative" credentials that occupied European and British intellectuals in the 1790s, see Winch (1985a) and Rothschild (1992). Smith was not unaware of how his ideas were being read by some in France in the late 1780s. A letter to Smith from the French economist Dupont de Nemours in 1788 concerning constitutional developments in France informed him that more than the French economists, Smith had helped to speed up the useful revolution in France: "Vous

Stewart's sketch provided an influential rendering of Smith in Britain until Mill took up his pen to compose his *Principles of Political Economy* in 1845. Although David Buchanan, Edward Gibbon Wakefield, and J. R. McCulloch had added a few embellishments to the figure of Smith in their editions of the *Wealth of Nations* in 1814 and 1828, respectively (editions of not inconsiderable influence in their day), it was Mill who was bold enough to recast Smith in his own image. Mill thought the *Wealth of Nations* to be "in many parts obsolete, and in all, imperfect," and proceeded to attempt "a work similar in object," but one that was adapted "to the more extended knowledge and improved ideas of the present age" (1871, xcii). Mill painted the picture of a Smith who was less a man of great theoretical insight,[3] than one of sound practical sense and judgment—someone who, when it came to economics, was an all-rounder, with an eye on "practical purposes" rather than "abstract speculations" (1871, xci). Mid-nineteenth-century English pragmatism was thereby given a Scottish ancestry.

In this way, it would seem, the *Wealth of Nations*—a work that had provided the theoretical foundations on which the great writers of the classical school in the first decades of the nineteenth century (Henry Thornton and Francis Horner, and Malthus and Ricardo) were to build, and that had done much the same for Marx a few decades later—had become if not "a very amusing book about old times" (Bagehot 1881, 273), nor one in which "the arguments are not properly clenched" (Stephen 1902, 2:325), nor the "most important book that has ever been written" (Buckle 1873, 1:194), then certainly a work to be valued more for the example it provided of the wide reach of the dismal science, and the value of sound *practical* judgment in the application of economic principles to policymaking.

Alfred Marshall, whose *Principles of Economics* became the standard text for early twentieth-century economics, seems to have thought of the

---

avez beaucoup hâté cette utile revolution, les Économistes français n'y arount pas nui" (*Letter from Dupont de Nemours*, June 19, 1788, in Smith 1976–85, 6:313). Smith added passages to the final 1790 revision of the *Moral Sentiments* that have been described as "remarkably unruffled" despite events in France (Winch 1985a, 233). Smith soberly observed that "it requires the highest effort of political wisdom to determine when a real patriot ought to support and endeavour to reestablish the authority of the old system, and when he ought to give way to the more daring, but often dangerous spirit of innovation" (1759, 231–32). Stewart's reaction was different. Writing his account of Smith's life and writings in 1793 (the same year as the Scottish sedition trials), Stewart chose to quote in full a later passage in those same 1790 additions (1759, 233–34) that when read in isolation, might serve to propagate a more conservative image for Smith.

[3] No doubt with Ricardo in mind, Mill hinted that on that score, others had "equalled and even surpassed" him (1871, xci).

Wealth of Nations in much the same way.[4] "The more one compares him with those who went before and those who came after him," said Marshall, "the finer does his genius appear, the broader his knowledge and the more well-balanced his judgment" (1890, 626). Marshall certainly also linked Smith's name to the doctrine of free trade, but as was his custom, he qualified this strong statement in a footnote (1890, 627, 627n2). Likewise, nothing much was at all said by Marshall of any lasting theoretical contribution that had been made by Smith.[5]

But if there was a broad consensus about the economic legacy of Smith at the end of the nineteenth century—that it was primarily to be located in matters doctrinal rather than matters theoretical—there was less agreement about his intellectual formation. As early as the middle of the nineteenth century, Karl Knies had already suggested that Smith's visits to France and his contact with the physiocrats had been decisive in the composition of the *Wealth of Nations*. By the close of that century, continental (largely German) writers had invented "the Adam Smith problem" (see Oncken 1897, 444), and others had quite seriously accused him, as Edwin Cannan put it, of having "rifled another man's work"—in this case Turgot's *Reflections*.[6] The next century, which witnessed an outpouring of work on that intellectual formation, largely discredited these opinions. Yet there remained a keen interest in Smith's debts to his contemporaries and immediate predecessors.

During the twentieth century, Smith's great contribution to political economy in the *Wealth of Nations* was given an almost bewildering array of readings. More than a half century ago, Ronald Meek noticed that the upshot of such a legion of treatments had been that Whig, Tory, republican, conservative, liberal, and even Marxist political leanings had all been suggested as either the historical or logical complement to the book (1967, 40). Among contemporary economists and political scientists, some form of liberalism has been the most common political mantle associated with Smith. The inadequacy of this perspective to account for his concerns either with the prerequisites of effective citizenship or a more substantive

[4] Somewhat perversely, Marshall refers to Smith as an "English economist" (1890, 626).

[5] Although Marshall cites Smith on upwards of twenty occasions, scarcely one of those references speaks of *theoretical* contributions—except, perhaps, when Marshall draws the parallel between Smith's notion of natural prices and his own long-run normal prices (1980, 289; see also 627).

[6] The "two Adam Smiths" turned initially on the argument that Smith had been inconsistent on the motivations of human behaviour, following first Frances Hutcheson who had rejected the "selfish hypothesis" and later following the neo-Epicureanism of Helvetius by seeing self-interest as the basic motive of human action. Oncken, in contrast, saw the distinction to lie in Smith's differing works, the *Moral Sentiments* and *The Wealth of Nations*, with self-love as the root only of his economic thinking.

politics than often attributed to him has led economists, philosophers, and intellectual historians to argue for the need to revise our understanding of Smith.[7] While their readings of Smith disclose subtle and even distinctive differences, all have been intent on retrieving a better understanding of Smith's political economy. Irrespective of their interpretation, then, they seem to be agreed that Smith's writing has been obscured either by party affiliational renderings of politics in his own time, or nineteenth- and twentieth-century renderings of politics and economics as supportive of laissez-faire capitalism and unfettered free trade.

Smith's political odyssey has thus been a long and contested one. Equally, some of the difficulties of offering a convincing understanding of Smith's political thought have not significantly diminished.[8] Certainly the sense that there is something problematic about the project of recovering his political thought would seem to persist. The effort here is to explore that odyssey, partly in order to chisel away at the interpretive sediment that has built up around the figure of Smith, and partly to consider what, if anything, this distant eighteenth-century thinker might be thought to contribute to our own contemporary political and economic milieu.

DISTINGUISHING SMITH FROM HIS INTERPRETERS

Just why Smith's name has come to be associated with so many political persuasions and partisan causes is a quite complicated matter. But one contributory factor does seem to stand out among the rest: namely, that the characterisation of Smith's politics has largely been left as much to the imaginations of others as to anything to be found in his own published writings. Smith's effort does not seem to have been directed towards presenting a clearly articulated political philosophy or an unambiguously expressed set of political principles.[9]

The earliest efforts of his biographers and friends, for example, deployed Smith's retiring (if not reclusive) personality to account for the lack of any open public declamations by him of his political commitments.

---

[7] See, for example, Winch (1978), Skinner (1979), Haakonssen (1981), Brown (1994), Fitzgibbons (1995), Phillipson (2000), Rothschild (2001a), Fleischacker (2004), Hont (2005), and Robertson (2005).

[8] Duncan Forbes insisted that Smith should be understood as a philosopher "in" rather than "of" politics. As Winch stated, "It would clearly be folly on my part to claim that . . . Smith is a political philosopher in every significant sense of the term. Nevertheless, I do wish to maintain that Smith has a 'politics' which is far from being trivial" (1978, 23).

[9] Direct evidence of Smith's understanding of politics has been characterised as "somewhat scanty" (Winch 1978, 2; see also Skinner 1974, 18; Cropsey 1957, 95, 65; Forbes 1976, 179).

This allowed them considerable scope to supply their own interpretation. The result was confusion, as the outline of Smith's politics provided by Smith's pupil, David Stewart Erskine, the eleventh Earl of Buchan, amply demonstrates:

> [Smith] approached to republicanism in his political principles, and considered a commonwealth as the platform for the monarchy, hereditary succession in the chief magistrate being necessary only to prevent the commonwealth from being shaken by ambition, or absolute dominion introduced by the consequences of contending factions. Yet Pitt and Dundas, praising his book, and adopting its principles in parliament, brought him down from London a Tory, and a Pittite, instead of Whig and a Foxite, as he was when he set out. Bye and bye, the impression wore off, and his former sentiments returned, but unconnected with Pitt, Fox, or anybody else. (cited in Rae 1895, 124)

The effect of these early statements, however, was to be long lasting. Smith's nineteenth-century biographer John Rae, although certainly having the corpus of Smith's work to hand, chose in political matters to follow the unreliable testimony of the Earl of Buchan instead. Smith was portrayed as having been "always theoretically a republican" and as having had "the true spirit of a republican in his love of all rational liberty" (124). In this case, it seems likely that what Buchan and Rae were doing with the term was associating Smith with views of the Whig party. Elsewhere in the biography, Rae presented Smith as a loyal supporter of the "Rockingham Whigs" and "a warm opponent of the North ministry" (378). This same opposition—as expressed in a letter that Smith wrote to Burke supporting Burke's resignation from office over a political dispute within the Whig party[10]—led Burke to describe Smith as a "thorough and loyal Whig" (cited in ibid., 378–79).

It is also important to note that in these loose descriptions of Smith's politics, a contrast was typically drawn with Hume—as, for example, in Rae's claim that "Smith's friendship for Hume never made him Tory" (130). This contrast between Hume and Smith, who were considered to be in agreement on so much else, appears to have rested on the effort of Smith's interpreters and hagiographers to distance him from Hume's equivocal commitments to Whig republicanism (to say nothing of Hume's scathing criticisms of "vulgar" Whig attachments to the "matchless constitution" or his civic republican sentiments).[11]

---

[10] *Smith to Burke*, July 6, 1782, in Smith 1976–85, 259. Burke had resigned as paymaster general on the appointment of Shelburne to succeed Rockingham as prime minister (after Rockingham's death on July 1, 1782).

[11] See Forbes (1975, 182ff; 1976, 195–96) and Moore (1977, 809–39). This said, there are many references of this kind in the *Wealth of Nations*.

There is not a little irony in this characterisation, since Hume was fairly equally critical of Tories and Whigs, and as Duncan Forbes demonstrated, generally chose to characterise himself politically as a sceptical Whig (1976, 181). In fact, it has been due in no small measure Forbes's efforts to relieve Hume of the Tory epithet, and place him squarely in the camp of a sceptical or scientific Whiggism, that led to a reconsideration of the character of the political thought that might be imputed to Smith (1975, 1976). Yet when these efforts turned from the party politics of the day to an examination of Smith's principal published works, commentators differed on which work (or works) they would choose to focus—and their choices often played a role in the differing political characterisations they presented.[12]

The first notable break from a Whig (or Whig republican) interpretation of Smith, that of Elie Halévy, was carried out almost exclusively by reference to the *Wealth of Nations* (1928, 140–41).[13] Halévy embarked on a point by point refutation of the characterisations of Rae. For example, in reference to Smith's purported position as a republican and an admirer of Rousseau, why then, Halévy asked, "did he have such avowed antipathy for the American democracies with 'their rancorous and virulent factions,' which would become 'ten times more virulent than ever' if they were separated?" If, Halévy argued, Smith was a faithful Whig

---

[12] Joseph Cropsey, for example, made no reference to the *Lectures on Jurisprudence* in either *Polity and Economy* or his later article, "Adam Smith and Political Philosophy" (1976). He disagreed with other interpreters of Smith as to which work Smith was referring to at the close of the *Moral Sentiments*, when Smith promised to address "a system of those principles which ought to run through, and be the foundation of law of all nations" in a later effort. As it was the only other work published in Smith's lifetime, Cropsey believed this reference to be to the *Wealth of Nations* (1976, 137). It is now known that what Smith had in mind at the close of the *Moral Sentiments*, however, was almost certainly the compilation of his *Lectures on Jurisprudence*. As others have noted, we have no idea how much of this work was completed in Smith's lifetime, or if it was, whether it was among the papers that Smith demanded to be burnt on his deathbed (Robertson 1983, 459n11). Others, such as Forbes, turned to the *Moral Sentiments* but found the *Lectures* "partial and inadequate," containing many "green plums" of vulgar Whiggism not found in the finished work (1976, 180–81). Still others have embraced the observation of J.G.A. Pocock that an element of the civic humanist tradition "survived and continued to inform political debate in the eighteenth century," and that the Machiavellian language of virtue and corruption as well as "the dangers to moral identity and citizenship posed by advanced commercial society" was reflected in Smith's earlier works. Hence it was believed that a more complete understanding of Smith's intentions in the *Wealth of Nations* might be obtained by constructing a bridge between the *Moral Sentiments* and the *Lectures on Jurisprudence* in developing his understanding of Smith's politics.

[13] Halévy makes one reference to the *Lectures on Jurisprudence* (1928, 89), and one to the *Moral Sentiments*. His citations to the *Wealth of Nations* are to book 5, chapter 3, and book 1, chapter 10.

of Lord Rockingham's party, "he must have been, to use one of Hume's expressions . . . the most sceptical of Whigs," since (following Hume) he expressed scepticism about the absolute inviolability of freedom of the press, and surely "the freedom of the press is perhaps the fundamental point of Whig doctrine" (141). Halévy also remarked on what he took to be the *unrepublican* character of Smith's reproaches of the common people of England for being "so jealous of their liberty, but like the common people of most other countries never rightly understanding wherein it consists. . . . Why so much fuss about general warrants, which are an abuse, it is true, but which will not lead to despotism, and so much indifference about the law of settlement, which paralyses the world of labour" (141).

Halévy concluded by suggesting that democrats—whom *he* (though not others) understood to be synonymous with republicans—and the most conservative of Whigs, such as Sir William Blackstone, denounced standing armies as a threat to liberty by raising the specter of Oliver Cromwell and the Stuarts. In contrast, he pointed out, Smith praised the professional army, which had arisen as a consequence of the division of labour, and which was useful in the rapid civilising of a new country and even in the defence of liberty. The reasoning behind this position was clear, if not unequivocal: a sovereign with a standing army at their disposal could afford to permit that "freedom of expression" that they might otherwise feel too threatening (142; Smith 1776, 5.1:668).

Perhaps more important for those commentators on Smith who were to follow him, Halévy saw Smith as an even greater sceptic than Hume in political affairs. As Halévy noted, "*That Politics may be Reduced to a Science* is the title of one of Hume's *Essays*; but this is not, it appears, Adam Smith's idea." Halevy continues: "As far as concerns the economic and financial legislation of a country, it is possible to proceed scientifically, to lay down principles and draw conclusions, to conceive an organization which is suited . . . 'not to those circumstances which are transitory, occasional, or accidental, but to those which are necessary and therefore always the same.' But it is impossible to proceed in the same way as regards the political organization of a country" (Halévy 1928, 142).

Halévy's effort was more than just a denial of the politics of Whiggism attributed to Smith. He hinted at a deeper schism between economic and political considerations in the *Wealth of Nations*, and attributed this divide to Smith's lack of interest in developing either a science of politics or systematically considering the political implications of his economic theory (142; Forbes 1976, 179–80).[14] Having thus discarded these

---

[14] This imputed split between economics and politics led Halévy to suggest a somewhat paradoxical outcome of Smith's ideas being used to support both radical political conse-

interpretations of Smith's work, Halévy's historical revision focused on its economic component. His reading of the text of the *Wealth of Nations* and its place in the growth of philosophic radicalism established, for Halévy, Smith's economics as "liberal" in that distinctly nineteenth-century sense that remains a staple element of many of Smith's twentieth-century expositors.

While many political and social commentators accepted Halévy's reading of Smith's economics as early or classically liberal, disagreement persisted over the implications of his economic thought for politics (Cropsey 1957; Hirschman 1977). Most have not shared Halévy's idea that Smith had no intention of developing a theory or science of politics. Disagreement continued as to what Smith's intentions were in regard to a theory of politics and its relationship to his economic thinking.

Smith, Liberal Republicanism, and Economic Liberalism

Joseph Cropsey challenged Halévy by suggesting that "it would be incorrect to infer that Smith regarded the political order as unambiguously of secondary importance" until Smith's "political teaching" was explored more thoroughly (1957, 59). Cropsey did not believe that Smith had meant to subordinate the political question of "who should rule" to the economic one of "what is the most productive economy" (59). Although he recognised such subordination in the *Wealth of Nations*, Cropsey made nearly equal use of the text of the *Moral Sentiments* to support an argument that Smith consciously identified the economic order of capitalism with the institutions necessary for political freedom: "To obtain full confirmation in possession and full right to exercise self-preservative powers, what is needed are the institutions of free polity. Examining these, we shall in effect be examining what Smith puts forth as the necessary conditions for the existence of commercial society" (65).

Rather than acknowledge any fissure between Smith's economic and political thought, Cropsey sought to *derive* Smith's political philosophy from the prerequisites of his economic system. At the same time, the arrow of entailment was suggested to run in the other direction as well, and hence Smith's position could be interpreted to mean that "commerce generates freedom and civilization, and at the same time free institutions are indispensable to the preservation of commerce" (95). Another feature of Cropsey's interpretation was to translate Smith's political and eco-

---

quences—"an absolute political liberalism" in the writings of William Godwin and Mary Wollstonecraft—and profoundly conservative political doctrines in the hands of Burke (Halévy 1928, 202, 160; see also Rothschild 1992, 75–76, 83, 88n).

nomic projects into a more contemporary vocabulary, and so he wrote that Smith's subordination of "polity" to the service of "society" and for the sake of "civilization" did not involve an intentional reduction in the importance of political philosophy or "political life" (58, 57):

> Smith's contribution to economics . . . has the character of a description and advocacy of the system now called liberal capitalism; and the ligaments between the economic order and the political system, close under any circumstances, are exceptionally broad and strong in the world as seen and moulded by Adam Smith. The close conjunction of economics to political philosophy, even or perhaps especially if tending toward the eclipse of the latter, is a powerful fact of political philosophy; the men, like Smith, who were responsible for it would have a place in the chronicle of political philosophy on that ground alone. (1976, 132)

A broadly construed relationship between freedom and advancing civilisation were claimed to have been identified by Smith with economic and commercial development. To do so would not be entirely incorrect. Smith used terms such as "free government," "free people," and "every free system of Government" without more explicit conceptual articulation (Forbes 1976, 193). At the very least, it would seem true that Smith's economic principles were not compatible with slavery, since (like Hume's) they required every member of society to be entitled to consideration as an owner of property (see Moore 1977, 111). On Cropsey's account, however, Smith's place in his canon of political philosophy was more than as an advocate of liberal capitalist economics. He was also the advocate of a single form of government to be preferred above all other régimes as truly compatible with such economic principles—"the institutions of free polity," or rather, the "freest republican government," liberal republicanism (1957, 65, 94). In this sense, Cropsey argued that the liberal republican Smith deserved recognition as nothing less than the "architect of our present system of society" (1976, 132).[15]

Cropsey arrived at his account of Smith's political thought—an advocacy that he recognised was not overt but rather implied by Smith's writings—by using two different arguments drawn from each of Smith's two

---

[15] Cropsey presents Smith as in essence a contemporary economic liberal for whom capitalism made freedom in the political sense possible without identifying it *as* freedom. This should not be seen to be the same as the claim made by liberal economists (such as Milton Friedman) that the economy itself is effectively a form of "proportional representation" so that economic and political freedoms go hand in hand (Friedman 1962, 23). For others, critical precisely of this economistic perspective, Smith's place in modern liberalism would be portrayed in equally reductionist terms, but this time as limiting genuine freedom by creating a visionless and sublimated politics (see Wolin 1960).

hand ensured, rather, that "every individual necessarily labours to render the annual revenue *of the society* as great he can" (1776, 4.2:456; emphasis added). In the first work, Smith spoke to concerns over the moral equity of commercial society. In the second, he spoke to the moral reconciliation of self and national interests, but he had nothing to say about the moral or equitable distribution of annual production. Justice, in the *Wealth of Nations*, was concerned with the institutions of the rule of law, the police, and the defence of the citizenry, not with how annual production was distributed.[24]

Winch was not the first to interpret Smith's politics by looking back at it through the lens of civic republicanism. Yet he was the first to characterise so explicitly Smith's attachments to republicanism as an extension of the discourse of civic humanism and republican virtue, and by so doing, to "show that Smith employs a consistent method or style of political analysis in his writings and lectures which cannot be readily encompassed within the categories of the liberal capitalist perspective" (Winch 1978, 26). Smith's politics was separated from epithets such as the nightwatchman state and the "possessive individualism" associated with it through a potentially unsettling suggestion that Smith's politics was more problematic than it had been made to appear.[25]

Winch's argument as to what Smith's politics may have been turned to developments in the philosophy of language being brought to bear on historiographical interpretation by intellectual historians such as J.G.A. Pocock and Quentin Skinner.[26] By studying the arguments that Smith put

[24] This is not to say that Smith did not appreciate that the distribution of income was unequal. He did. Yet when he looked at these inequalities within existing commercial society, and a potential space for politics opened up, he did not fill it. After Smith, others would do so.

[25] For two differing perspectives on Smith's liberal politics at which Winch has taken aim, see Hirschman (1977) and Macpherson (1962). The character of republicanism continues to be contested. Of particular importance is Eric Nelson's argument positing an alternative set of values to those derived from Roman thought—the redistributive as opposed to the accumulative attitude to wealth (2004; see also van Gelderen and Skinner 2005).

[26] Winch's approach was to consider more carefully the contextual political discourse at work at the time that Smith wrote. Although not identical in approach, it is fair to say that Winch's method shared a concern with the interpretation and understanding of speech acts in the history of political thought first discussed by both Pocock and Skinner in the 1960s and 1970s. By exploring the meaning (the illocutionary force) of a theorist's use of language—that is, by considering what a theorist was "doing" when they wrote within a particular contextual framework—a better understanding of the meaning of those utterances might be constructed. Winch was adverting to Pocock's well-known suggestions concerning the relevance of the language of civic humanism, with its notions of virtue and corruption, to the Scottish "conjectural historians of civil society" (Pocock 1975, 458, 498–501; Skinner 1972, 393–408; more recent restatements include Skinner 2002, 1:103–27; Winch 1978, 175).

forward with a view to the presuppositions underlying those contentions at the time—claims cast in a now-unfamiliar language of civic humanism or civic moralism, of neo-Harringtonian or neo-Roman vocabularies of civic virtue and classical republicanism—Winch offered an understanding of what Smith was "doing" in terms of the cultural lexicon of his own time. The result was an interpretation of Smith that did not comport well with a nineteenth- and twentieth-century liberalism, and particularly defied the political vocabulary associated with *homo economicus*.[27]

Smith wrote his accounts of political economy and moral philosophy (among other writings) within the context of the late eighteenth-century "polite" culture of the Edinburgh literati, and in dialogue with the writings of figures such as Hume, Frances Hutcheson, and Ferguson, to name only a few. While Smith's writings did not share Ferguson's "desire to infuse the aristocracy with renewed political zeal as an antidote to the economic specialisation of commercial society," commerce was nevertheless more than simply one stage of the progress of society for Smith. In both the *Moral Sentiments* and the *Lectures on Jurisprudence*, "it [was] a constant cause producing the same effects at all stages"—those effects being luxury, corruption, and the diminution of martial virtue (Winch 1978, 175). By focusing on the areas of greatest weakness in Smith's picture of commercial society in *those* works—the intellectual, social, and martial debilitation of the labouring poor—a space for politics in Smith's thought emerges in the form of the need to create an effective, public-spirited citizenry capable of breaking through the cycle of corruption.

This displaced many of the standing contemporary interpretations of Smith's politics and claimed to recover what Smith was actually doing in work prior to the *Wealth of Nations*. Winch was equally clear that his purpose was heuristic rather than politically didactic or programmatic. That is, it was to displace a contemporary misunderstanding and misuse of Smith, and not to replace it with a new political agenda by extracting a "useable past" (Winch 1978, 5).

POLITICS AND POLITICAL ECONOMY

Smith's political odyssey has since continued, not by displacing the contextual historiography of Winch, but rather by continuing to debate and recast the appropriate context of Smith's political economy, and thus potentially rethink the character, extent, and forward reach of Smith's poli-

---

[27] A contextual historical reading of Smith's politics highlighted the distance, indeed foreignness, of Smith's thinking to present circumstances. At the same time, it challenged the second, related interpretive "myth" that expounding a coherent doctrine, such as the doc-

tics. John Robertson, for example, set aside not only the earlier reduction-ist political readings but at the same time challenged those derived from readings of Smith's moral theory and natural jurisprudence.[28] In other words, he maintained that a grasp of Smith's politics could (and indeed should) be drawn from the systematic considerations of the *Wealth of Nations* alone, where "in formulation and in resolution the problem thus became explicitly and straightforwardly one of 'political economy'" (Robertson 1983, 456).

Several reservations could be raised against deriving Smith's politics in the *Wealth of Nations* from his *Moral Sentiments* and *Lectures on Jurisprudence*. With regard to the connection between the three works it could be argued that it is less Smith's own construction than the imagina-tive work of others. Direct references to the *Moral Sentiments* in the *Wealth of Nations*, or vice versa, are absent.[29] This is perhaps no more than to note that, as does Robertson, the *Wealth of Nations* was a "free-standing" presentation of economic principles, and that confining Smith's understanding of political economy to the civic humanist framework threatens "to liberate Smith's political economy from one interpretive straight-jacket" (namely, liberal capitalism) "only to constrain it with an-other (Robertson 2000, 51).

Robertson's efforts significantly expanded the eighteenth-century con-text in which Smith might be thought to have been working by making a strategic comparison between the Scottish and Neapolitan alternatives to a "common framework of ideas and aspirations" for reform in the eighteenth century (1997, 674). In particular, important political and con-stitutional issues redolent in Smith's political economy could be projected *across* national boundaries, and shown to be of a more common Enlight-enment concern, even as the answers to these problems varied *within* dif-fering national contexts.[30] The context at hand was the experience of life

---

trine of the invisible hand or laissez-faire, was an identifiable intention of Smith's (Skinner 2002, 1:67–76).

[28] Those such as Friedrich Hayek who drew limits on Smith's possible political perspec-tive from his sceptical views on the scope and efficacy of human knowledge are also rejected. The contextual readings of Smith by both Winch and Robertson highlight a basic error in the approach of deriving Smith's politics (or lack of a coherent theory of politics) from arguments based solely on logic. We continue to share with Smith's historical interpreters the view that a definitive understanding of his politics remains both puzzling and problem-atic (Hont 2005, 110).

[29] This, despite the fact that Smith continued the two works until his death. The *Lectures* were never published. The difficulty of contextually analyzing the *Lectures* in terms of ask-ing what Smith was "doing" by writing them may be exacerbated in that they are compiled and collated student notes and recollections of his lectures that he did not himself write.

[30] Robertson's intervention in this area may be understood as part of a critical his-toriographical debate concerning more a national versus universal characterisation of the Enlightenment.

in a nation that had sacrificed its political institutions and independence "in the quest for economic improvement" (1983, 452).[31] According to Robertson, the hopes and misgivings about the trade-off between Scotland's national sovereignty and a place within the larger ambit of Britain's parliamentary sovereignty in the Union of 1706 served to raise the relationship between government and economic progress to the centre of both Smith's historical and theoretical concerns (452). In turn, this focus served to enlarge Smith's theory to one of international scope, while at the same time sharpening his awareness of the limitations and obstacles to any notion of "universal citizenship" within the realities of commercial society (455).[32]

On Robertson's reading of the *Wealth of Nations*, moral and political life in the commercial world was hereafter analyzed with the template of political economy, rather than the other way around. As a consequence, not only had moral philosophy and the historical study of society to take their bearings from political economy, but political and constitutional principles were rendered a branch of it as well (Robertson 2000, 10; 1983, 482). This opened up a space for politics in Smith in those areas where "the relation between government and economic development were problematic" (1983, 460). Two areas of special concern were distributive justice and constitutional change within both Britain's domestic and colonial economy.[33]

In the *Wealth of Nations*, the analysis of the market mechanism that Smith provided suggested that the unimpeded operation of the market would not (as it existed) produce outcomes characterised by distributive justice but rather at best generate dramatic increases in societal wealth (annual production). The question of distributive justice devolved to the political space, as his pointed comparison between the wages of labour under the "genius of the British constitution" and the "scanty maintenance of the labouring poor" under the "mercantile company which oppresses and domineers in the East Indies" illustrated (Smith 1776, 1.8:91).

Smith's analysis in the *Wealth of Nations* was grounded in the analysis of a deepening conflict of interest within commercial society—one that moved well beyond Hume's loose observations of general factional struggle (Robertson 1983, 471). Smith contended that the sources of conflict were deeply embedded in the three great orders: labourers and agriculturalists positioned against employers of stock, merchants, and manufactur-

[31] It was a trade-off that the Neapolitans had made as well.

[32] It was this awareness that, Robertson argued, led Smith to "discard the institutional principles of the civic tradition in favor of parliamentary sovereignty" (455).

[33] As Robertson notes, when the mercantile system "is seen as the outcome of the manipulation of government by the trading interest, it is clear that simply ensuring man's natural economic liberty will not be enough" (461).

ers. It was the task of the legislator, by employing the "wisdom of the state" and a sure sense of balance, to introduce controls over such conflict (471, 461).[34] Robertson concluded that Smith looked "outside" the civic tradition for his constitutional principles, and that "Smith's treatment of the problem of government and economic development cannot be understood if jurisprudential concepts alone are taken to provide the determining framework of his thought" (1983, 457).

Robertson's contextual recovery of Smith's effort to produce a genuinely *political* economy in the *Wealth of Nations* supplied another and important effort to accentuate the significant concern with the politics at the foundation of his work, and raise crucial questions for which Smith does not give us answers: namely, how much and what kinds of control can governments and legislators realistically aspire to have over the economy?[35] At the same time, Robertson noted that when positioned as part of a larger Enlightenment concern with understanding the progress of society the *Wealth of Nations* should be understood historically rather than philosophically—as being adapted to the actual historical circumstances that Smith himself faced. It is difficult not to conclude from this analysis that the forward reach of Smith's *Wealth of Nations*, and with it his politics, was limited by its historical context. It might even prove defensible to claim that Smith had little or nothing to say about what to expect, in terms of the operation of the market or the role for the state in that operation, of the future.

SMITH, GLOBALISATION, AND THE CHALLENGES OF A USEABLE PAST

The effort to appropriate Smith's political economy for use in considerations of our present economic or political life has not greatly abated. The character of a contemporary liberalism—economic, political, or cosmo-

[34] Robertson argued that while individuals may lack the information to "command the economy," the case of government is otherwise. Smith's consideration of the state role in defence provides the exemplary case: "As Smith pointed out, the operation of the division of labour in the organization of defence does not occur in the natural course of economic development: it must be introduced by the 'wisdom of the state.' Far from being guaranteed by the 'invisible hand,' the harmonization of government and economy in commercial society is, Smith believed, the task of the legislator" (471). At the same time, in a more recent book, *The Case for Enlightenment*, Robertson has claimed that at best, Smith thought "legislative initiative on the part of the government should be gradual and piecemeal" (2005, 392).

[35] Robertson concluded: "They advanced good reasons to believe that individuals, even governments, had limited power to affect the course of such development, which worked best when it was the outcome of multiple individual decisions, taken in the self-interested expectation of bettering one's condition on earth. . . . But if the remedies were not to be worse than the existing obstacles, governments would have to learn to act in line

politan—has been formulated in many ways, and often by recourse to numerous citations to the *Wealth of Nations* (and the *Moral Sentiments*). This begs the question of whether and to what degree Smith's writings could possibly present us with a useable past. There has been significant consideration of this question over the last three or four decades. We have been cautioned, quite rightly, that we cannot reasonably interpret authors remote from us in time to be discussing issues of contemporary importance, or to see them as speaking to our own political and economic concerns through the mists of time. Instead, we must be content to do our thinking for ourselves.[36]

Yet the project of appropriating the politics of the *Wealth of Nations* to the consideration of the present has not lost its attractions.[37] For example, the question of whether theories of international trade in the eighteenth century might shed light on the debate over globalisation has recently appeared, and Smith's considerations of the interrelationship between the nation-state and the international economy in the *Wealth of Nations* are being revisited with renewed interest.[38]

The globalisation debate has, of course, raised many issues—concerning free trade; the role of international agencies like the International

---

with public opinion, which itself should be informed by sound principles of political economy" (2005, 405).

[36] See Forbes (1975), Skinner (1969, 1998), Winch (2001), and Haakonssen and Winch (2006). Haakonssen and Winch express the rationale behind this admonition: "In fact, [Smith] has virtually nothing to say about what to expect of the future; and his prescriptions are all 'internalist,' piecemeal, and hedged with qualifying doubt on all sides. For Smith, life is [a] matter of contingency and uncertainty which we negotiate with varying degrees of success, as experience shows and philosophy accounts for" (2006, 388). Forbes had also much earlier cautioned that "it is not appropriate uncritically to translate Smith's policy prescriptions from the eighteenth to the twentieth century—moreover it is quite inconsistent with Smith's own teaching" (1975, 206).

[37] Examples of this proliferate. One has only to look to Ian McLean (2006, with an introduction written by Prime Minister Gordon Brown), Gavin Kennedy (2005, a former Scottish Nationalist Party economics spokesperson), a new edition of Smith's *Wealth of Nations* (2007, introduced by a Tory shadow chancellor, George Osborne), or Deepak Lal (2006) to see how topical Smith has once again become.

[38] One interesting addition to the Smith and globalisation literature has been the contributions of Fonna Forman-Barzalai (2000, 2005). Forman-Barzalai examines Smith's selective use of Stoical thinking, and in particular the Stoical concept of *oikeiosis*—those concentric circles of familial, economic, and political relations combining affectionate self-ownership and other-regarding attachment. She suggests that while Smith rejected an older form of cosmopolitanism, he appears to have "developed a theory of commercial cosmopolitanism to overcome the deficiencies" (2000, 413). On this reading, Smith is seen to share Hume's belief that ties of sympathy dissipate with physical distance, yet in terms of the market "free commercial intercourse among nations" promised to "mitigate conflict among spatially disparate entities, and to generate a tolerable peace in the absence of better motives" (393). For a discussion of Stoical ethics and *oikeiosis*, see Waszek (1984), Annas (1993), Brown (1994), and Long (2007).

Monetary Fund, the World Trade Organization, and the World Bank; "fair" trade; multilateral versus bilateral trade arrangements; tariffs, quotas, and other forms of protection; the consequences of capital account liberalisation and the deregulation of international financial flows; the role of large multinational corporations; the role of nongovernmental organisations; and the eradication of extreme poverty. The list of issues surrounding the globalisation debate is long, and doubtless could be extended beyond those listed here.

One feature of globalisation that many have noticed, however, is the problem posed by the apparent shrinkage of national governmental capacity in the context of a global marketplace.[39] The degree of freedom in policymaking that governments enjoyed under the Bretton Woods system—a system that allowed national governments to pursue Keynesian-style domestic policies to promote full employment and growth (and even to protect their domestic markets from foreign competition) without excessive concern for the reaction of global markets to their local activities—has almost completely disappeared. In its place is a system in which the formulation of national economic policies is constrained by the potential of global markets, and in particular global financial markets, to react in potentially destabilizing ways.

If the globalisation debate is seen as one that pits "nationalists," who claim that economies must operate under the control of national political rule, against "cosmopolitan globalizers," who argue that it is our understanding of political institutions that must give way to (and be shaped by) the seemingly limitless push of a cosmopolitan economy, as one writer has put it (Hont 2005, 155), then it has to be established whether drawing a parallel between these contemporary concerns and those of Smith can stand the test of either historical or theoretical scrutiny. An even stronger suggestion, that Smith's observations on empire along with the political and economic insecurities of long-distance trade are "often identical with our own predicament today" (111), makes still greater interpretive demands on us.[40]

[39] The whole of an interesting collection of papers published by Robert Keohane and Helen Milner in 1996 was devoted to this question; John Eatwell has spoken of the severe constraints it imposed on "the exercise of discretionary policies by national governments" (1996, 24); and Dani Rodrik has recently suggested that "globalization's soft underbelly is the imbalance between the national scope of governments and the global nature of markets" (2007; see also Rodrik 1997).

[40] What are we to make of the claim that Smith's views might be captured in the language of globalisation? Is his idea of trade, both domestic and international, akin to globalisation as we think of it today? Globalisation is not new, but that is not quite the point. A better question to ask might be whether Smith's analysis of international trade has any bearing on our present-day considerations. At least one commentator has suggested that arguing for contemporary globalisation as a "quotidian continuation" of a centuries-old trend of think-

Globalisation has been recognised to be a concept with a considerable history, and the suggestion has been made that it bears comparison to Smith's understanding of international trade.[41] For instance, Emma Rothschild's consideration of the history of the concept of globalisation supports a type of indirect political and economic theorising that does not so much attempt to say precisely how contemporary policymakers should act, as it does to establish the contemporary relevance of Smith's political and economic thinking to them. Quite how we are to negotiate the significance of a deep, contextual consideration of eighteenth-century commercial exchange to today's global economy, though, is really only alluded to.[42]

It might be claimed that in such arguments for Smith's continuing relevance to contemporary economic and political debate, what has been attended to is not so much his relevance to the economic *character* of globalisation but rather his relevance to political *responses* to it. In asking how states are to operate in a world of "imperfect sovereignty and asymmetric information," how national wealth is to be measured "in a world of imputed, invisible, or intra-corporate flows," or how commercial freedom is to be reconciled with other "equally imposing and even more exigent objectives," a set of hugely important questions has been opened up. But there remains the equally formidable challenge of extrapolation to be

---

ing is as simplistic as declaring it to be an utterly new phenomenon (Naim 2004, 2). Better to perhaps recognise that contemporary globalisation has unprecedented features, of which the most important may be generally put as "the greatly expanded options" for individuals and greatly "narrowing the room for maneuvering available to governments"(2). For a discussion concerning Smith's deep ambivalence about the effects of international trading companies, see Muthu (2008).

[41] See Rothschild: "The political ideas of the late 18th century in Europe and North America including ideas of the universal rights of individuals, and of universal freedom of commerce, are at the heart of the modern ideology of 'global market democracy.' These ideas have been associated, at times, with new institutions of international or oceanic political cooperation" (2001b). Globalisation is a distinctly elastic (even indeterminate) concept, but it is thought by Rothschild to entail some of the things that Smith had in mind in theorising international commerce: increased trade, increased flows of capital, and the role of transnational economic and political institutions.

[42] The problem as Rothschild recognises is not one of open or closed markets, or free or protected ones, but rather in the fact that moving too much in one policy direction would create protectionism, while moving too much in another produced reduced national governmental capacity. If the idea that striking an appropriate balance is the task of legislators is reminiscent of Smith, it could only be so in the most general sense, and it remains unclear how extrapolating from his views helps us to think about it. More to the point, modern arguments about globalisation, insofar as they refer to a supposed benefit to openness and liberalization (whether in favour of or opposed to globalisation) presuppose a theory of comparative advantage not advanced until Ricardo—and not fully advanced in its modern neoclassical form until it was possible to imagine, as Léon Walras put it: "The whole world may be looked upon as a vast general market" (1874, 84).

faced if we are to expect that Smith's politics will speak to these questions. The aim of the contemporary retrieval of Smith's politics is without doubt significant if it is to convince us in the most general sense of the value of history in contemplating the conundrums of globalisation. Still, if we are to show that eighteenth-century controversies in political economy sustain a continued or renewed freshness for contemporary economic and political debate, and that in this sense history may be made to speak to present politics, then it would seem that there is more work to be done.[43]

For example, exactly what Smith might have to say to contemporary statespeople and economists is unclear. This may be no more than a reflection of the fact that although Smith was unquestionably concerned with the destabilizing effects of commercial society, a view of the governmental task of balancing political and economic considerations was not consistently developed. There is considerable evidence to suggest that while recognising the need for governmental regulation of the mercantile interest in order to shore up competition, Smith was less clear as to whether the state could or would constrain it (1776, 4.2:470–71).[44] The Wealth of Nations was both critical of the existing state of commercial society, and nuanced and equivocal about the paradoxes associated with commercial advancement as well as the feasibility of either any short- or long-term reform. While concerned with the debilitating effects of commercial society on labourers, Smith acknowledged its potential to support their physical wants to a degree previously unknown.[45] While chastising the mercantile interests for their greedy efforts to influence trade legisla-

---

[43] In particular, Istvan Hont envisaged that by "taking the history of political and economic thought seriously we can see that the globalization debate of the late twentieth and early twentieth-first centuries lacks conceptual novelty" (2005, 155). Hont did not propose to dredge explicit solutions to today's problems from the past: "History cannot be expected to solve the core analytical puzzles of political and economic theory" (156). Rather, he asked a series of questions for economic and political theorists to consider: "If it is right to see the economy as a constitutive part of the remit of modern political theory, in what sense is this so?"; "What precise job does the economy perform for modern politics?"; "Should we assume that a plurality of political visions might suit the integration of politics and the market economy, or should we accept the idea that there is just one privileged state form, the modern representative republic, that has an elective affinity with markets?" (4, 5). He is well aware that these are not new questions.

[44] Smith's most adamant demand in the Wealth of Nations on this point is the following: "Let the same natural liberty of exercising what species of industry they please be restored to all his majesty's subjects, in the same manner as to soldiers and seamen; that is, break down the exclusive privileges of corporations, and repeal the statute of apprenticeship, both which are real encroachments on natural liberty, and add to these the repeal of the law of settlements, so that a poor workman, when thrown out of employment in one trade or in one place, may seek for it in another trade or in another place" (2:470).

[45] See Hont and Ignatieff (1983, 25); Moore (1977, 834–35).

tion in narrow, monopolistic channels, Smith acknowledged that their trade had enriched the country.

Furthermore, Smith was well aware that as actors within the market order, they certainly "knew perfectly" where their self-interest lay, as "it was their business to know it" (1776, 4.1:434). In the *Wealth of Nations*, he wrote that his intention was not "to throw any odious imputation upon the general character of the servants of the East India company" but rather that it was "the system of government, the situation in which they are placed, that I mean to censure; not the character of those who have acted in it. They acted as their situation naturally directed, and they who have clamoured loudest against them would, probably, not have acted better themselves" (4.2:641). The problem was indeed a deeply systemic one that would require considerable political impetus to change. Yet Smith understood that not only "unconquerable" private interests but also "the prejudices of the publick" made the likelihood of establishing unrestrained freedom of trade in Britain equal to that of establishing *Oceana* (4.2:471). It is not entirely surprising, then, that the terms "equivocal," "ironical," "distanced," "internalist," and "piecemeal" have all been used to qualify the politics of Smith's political economy.

We might then ask in what sense "the commercial future that many eighteenth-century observers imagined as plausible has become our historical present" (Hont 2005, 156). We might conclude that we live in a future, imagined or real, informed as much, or indeed more, by subsequent nineteenth-century neoclassical economic thought and practice as it is by the thought of Smith or Hume, and that we understand the conceptual resources of today's economic and political discourse to flow almost exclusively from the marginalist approach to economics introduced in the last quarter of the nineteenth century. Indeed, if the contemporary economic case for liberty is ultimately made in terms of the language of the market, which if left unimpeded by the state is capable of solving a *static* problem of allocating a *fixed* supply of resources, then we have moved well beyond these eighteenth-century thinkers such as Smith. In this sense it might be reasonable to ask whether what we understand today as free market theory—against which a modern form of nationalist-led trade policies might be said to operate—is different in important ways from the eighteenth-century political economy from which it is said to have originated. It might also be well to ask just how that transformation of the conceptual framework of political economy and its relationship to politics that came about *after* Smith took shape.

Chapter Three

THE RISE AND FALL OF CIVIL SOCIETY

Mankind are to be taken in groupes as they have
always subsisted. The history of the individual is but
a detail of the sentiments and thoughts he has entertained in the view of his species; and every experiment
relative to this subject should be made with entire
societies, not with single men.
—Adam Ferguson, *An Essay on the History*
of Civil Society

IN 1767, at the age of forty-four and in the middle of his tenure as the
chair of moral philosophy at Edinburgh that helped cement that institution's international reputation as the seat of the Scottish Enlightenment,
Ferguson published his *Essay on the History of Civil Society*. Much ad-
mired by later classical economists, this work set down in clear and unambiguous terms many of the hallmarks of that tradition. One need only
mention his discussion of the division of labour, the character of economic
progress, and the class structures embedded in the emerging capitalist
economy to appreciate the attractions they found in it. Yet Ferguson's
book also marks the rise of another theme in political economy—one that
has received less attention, but that is of no less significance. That theme
is signalled in the title of the work by the words "civil society," and it is
on the extent to which differing languages and concepts of civil society
might be said to figure in the development of economic thought that we
wish to focus here.

There is a sense, of course, in which this is a tacit history. The vocabulary of political economy came to prefer terms like civilized society,
human society, commercial society, capitalist society, or (much later) market society to describe essentially the same thing. But it is in the language
and theories of political economy that one can find, in the eighteenth
century, the rise of a conceptualisation of civil society differing from an
earlier tradition in which it was thought of as something synonymous
with political society or the system of public government.[1] Equally, it is

---

[1] Jose Harris (2004) contrasts this older idea with the notion of *bürgerliche gesellschaft*,
associated with Georg Wilhelm Friedrich Hegel, in which civil society exists over and
against the state, and in partial independence from it. The latter, she suggests, has almost

in the language of political economy that one can trace the rise and fall of this concept from the early mercantilist writers through to the classical economists, and finally, down to its dissolution in the language of the neoclassical economists of the marginal revolution.

In recognising that the economic system itself established a well-defined set of social relations (mediated through the market), and in attempting to reveal their content and character, civil society and the state were to be cast in a new theoretical light by political economy. While the decisive moment in this project seems to arrive with the articulation of the idea of a self-regulating market mechanism in the economic thought of the late eighteenth century, commercial society itself has a longer history. Across Europe, various forms of market exchange had existed for centuries. But by the eighteenth century something resembling market society in its modern sense—a generalised system of production and distribution organised through markets—had begun to take concrete shape. So much so, in fact, that an idea of civil society entertained in the mind's eye of the political economists of the day (and thereafter) might be said to have existed already in the reality of commercial, financial, and manufacturing activities, especially in England.

Given this, we are compelled to ask why the thoughts of economic writers and thinkers had not turned in that direction earlier than the middle of the eighteenth century. This question brings us to the mercantilists.

MERCANTILISM AND CIVIL SOCIETY

Ever since Eli Heckscher's great work of 1931, mercantilism has generally been employed to describe a loose but identifiable system of ideas dominating English and continental economic discourse from the early seventeenth to the late eighteenth century. Its organising principles—relating power, trade, and treasure to the pursuit of state enrichment and aggrandizement—were conveyed by a number of thinkers (prominent among whom were Thomas Mun in England, Jean-Baptiste Colbert in France, and Antonio Serra in Italy). While divergent in many respects, the literature of mercantilism contains several unifying commitments. First, the accumulation of gold and silver bullion ("treasure") was deemed indispensable to both the wealth of the nation and political power. Second, foreign trade was important as the only source (beyond mines or foreign conquest) of treasure: "we have got no other means to get treasure but

---

no resonance in the language of nineteenth-century Britain. One of the spheres of self-governing associations within Britain that Harris mentions as contrasting with the European state-oriented practice is that of commerce.

by forraign trade" (Mun 1664, 14). Third, the balance of trade was the central economic tool serving the interest of the nation internally and internationally, and it needed to be wielded by the sovereign with the political intention to secure a foreign trade *imbalance*, favouring exports over imports: "we must ever observe this rule; to sell more to strangers than we consume of theirs in value" (8). Finally, the internal organisation of domestic industry fostering the balance of trade must always be hedged with consideration of war. As Mun observed:

> Our *Clothing*, which although it is the greatest Wealth and best Employment of the Poor of this Kingdome, yet neverthelesse we may peradverture employ our selves with better Safety, Plenty, and Profit in using more Tillage and Fishing, than to trust so wholly in the making of Cloth; for in times of War, or by other occasions, if some forraign Princes should prohibit the use thereof in their dominions, it might suddenly cause much poverty and dangerous up-roars, especially by our poor people, when they should be deprived of their ordinary maintenance, which cannot so easily fail them when their labours should be divided into the said diversity of employments. (73)

Although mercantilism is customarily presented as essentially a view of state policy towards the economy, it also embodied an idea of civil society that this convenient characterisation does not seem adequately to capture. Of course, there was a developed body of economic ideas common to mercantilist thinking that consisted of a simple and appealing premise: namely, that national wealth was equivalent to a stock of precious metals (bullion). From this notion arose mercantilism's central dogma, which was disparagingly summed up by Smith as "heap up gold."[2]

The basic case for mercantilist legislation was almost invariably un-derpinned by the application of some variant of the so-called balance of trade doctrine. Under a metallic standard, the trade balance can be repre-sented as b, a quantity of precious metals ("gold"'), with x the gold value of exports and m the gold value of imports. This gives rise to the balance of trade identity: $b \equiv (x - m)$. If mercantilist thinking is reconstructed along these lines, this relation reveals the simplest of all the mercantilist messages: discourage imports and encourage exports. Gerrard de Malynes put it succinctly in recommending that the monarch should not permit "an overbalancing of forreine commodities with his home com-modities or in buying more than he selleth" (1601, 2).

---

[2] Were we to believe Smith, the existence of the entire mercantilist régime would be ex-plained by the way in which sectional interests convinced parliaments (or sovereigns) to enact partial legislation (and this largely by sophistical argumentation). But this seems scarcely accurate—armies, navies, wars, and state building are also good reasons for heap-ing up gold. This last observation raises the question of whether the mercantilists swayed

When a distinction was drawn between raw materials and finished products, the doctrine could be modified so as to argue just the reverse in the case of raw materials: encourage raw material imports and discourage their export. If $b \equiv (x + rx) - (m + rm)$, where rx represents the gold value of reexports of worked up products and rm represents the gold value of imports of raw materials, it had only to be shown that the value of reexports exceeded the value of raw material imports (that is, $rx > rm$) to clinch the case and thereby explain away the apparent paradox. In fact, there is no real need to restrict this reexport version of the balance of trade doctrine to raw materials, since the importation of semifinished products and the subsequent reexport of finished products was just as advantageous to the balance of trade. Viewed in this light, it is hardly surprising to find that mercantilist doctrine proved sufficiently flexible to validate strongly protectionist sentiments when applied by some, or to furnish a case for free trade when applied by others. Almost every shade of opinion on trade seems to have been entertained at one time or another by one or another of the mercantilists.[3]

What is of interest to us here, however, is that implicit and explicit within the literature of mercantilism was the idea that civil society was coterminous with the state, and understood by English mercantilists such as Mun to be a commonwealth. Irrespective of governmental form, mercantilist states needed to be populous in order to supply both the labour and military forces required for the defence as well as acquisition of treasures. The larger the population, the larger the body of labourers, and the more labourers, the higher the production of so-called artificial commodities. In addition, mercantilists relied on state capacity to direct the labouring population of civil society towards balancing the need for so-called natural wealth or agricultural output (consumed largely domestically), and the creation of artificial wealth in the form of tradable commodities.

Mun's discourse is exemplary of the lesson that mercantilism should not be understood as a narrow theory of commerce or trade. Contained within the mercantilist economic literature was a powerful (and to some, rather frightening) normative perspective on the proper character and

---

the state to promulgate legislation in their interests, or whether the state had interests of its own that just happened to be coincidental with those of the merchants.

[3] A related, but distinctive strand in mercantilist thinking was the balance of labour doctrine, which held that $\ell_b \equiv (\ell_x + \ell_{rx}) - (\ell_m + \ell_{rm})$ where ℓ_x is domestic labour embodied in exports, ℓ_{rx} is domestic labour embodied in reexports, ℓ_m is foreign labour embodied in imports to be domestically consumed, and ℓ_{rm} is foreign labour embodied in imported goods to be reexported.

governance of the unequal orders within civil society. Mun actually argued for the utility of poverty within the labouring population, claiming
that "penury and want do make a people wise and industrious" (1664,
73). So committed was he to this singular opinion that he felt that the
subsistence wants of labourers should be minimised—especially their
wants for imported luxury goods. At the same time, though, he maintained that the "pomp of Buildings, Apparel, and the like, in the Nobility,
Gentry and other able persons, cannot impoverish the Kingdome; if it be
done with curious and costly works upon our Materials, and by our own
people, it will maintain the poor with the purse of the rich, which is the
best distribution of the Common-wealth" (60).

At this point it is worth explicitly noticing the view of society that is
deeply embedded in arguments like these. It was not simply that the state
could influence the direction of commercial life but that civil society itself
could not be expected to flourish without the directing force and protection of a sovereign. Whether one considers Mun's mercantilist perspective, Thomas Hobbes's *De Cive*, or Pierre Nicole's *Essais de Morale*, the
need for an authoritarian political order to reconcile people's conflicting
and selfish natures appears to be omnipresent.[4] Moreover, the perspective
at work in these cases is not most effectually captured in the modern
language whereby an authoritarian political order (or state) is seen as
exercising control over an otherwise separate realm of a nascent commercial order. Instead, for both Hobbes and Nicole (and for mercantilists like
Mun), the force of a political "head" must be joined to an otherwise
irrational "body" of human society to form one directed and indistinguishable civil society.

Unquestionably, the capacity of the British state to regulate internal
commerce was, "even at the height of its regulatory activity," a "pale
reflection of its European counterpart" in France (Ekelund and Hébert

---

[4] It is sometimes suggested that in arguing that people's cupidity took the place of human
charity in determining their actions and choices, Nicole had anticipated Smith's observation
in the *Wealth of Nations* to the effect that appeals to the self-interest of others, rather than
to their benevolence, were a surer source of obtaining one's dinner. Yet Nicole's distinctly
darker, Jansenist perspective (that "there is nothing from which greater services can be obtained than from the cupidity of men") is unlike Smith in that he supports a reliance on the
state to regulate people in order to make predictable their commercial interactions. Here is
what Nicole says: "If one leaves cupidity to itself, it knows no limits or measure. Instead of
serving human society it destroys it. . . . A way must, therefore, be found to regulate cupidity, and this consists of the political order, which reins it back by fear and punishment, and
gets it applied to things useful to society. . . . The political order, therefore, is an admirable
invention for procuring, for all, the commodities which the greatest kings could not enjoy,
however many of their officials and whatever riches they possessed, if this order were to be
destroyed" (Nicole 1675, 135–37).

1990, 66).[5] It was, however, sufficient to draw Smith's sharp rebuke a century later; for him, mercantilist regulation was not simply a nonsalutary economic policy but also constituted a political assault on "the boasted liberty of the subject" in sacrifice "to the futile interests of our merchants and manufacturers" (1776, 2:660).

A further taste of this understanding of civil society contained in mercantilist literature may also be extrapolated from British mercantile policy towards the colonies in the eighteenth century. Colonial holdings served both as markets for exports and suppliers of raw materials. Manufacturing was forbidden in most colonies, and commerce between them was controlled by monopoly. Franchises granted exclusive trading rights to particular merchants or groups of them—the East India Company being the famed example. Such mercantilist practices go some way towards explaining the claim that Paine's *Common Sense* can be read as a revolutionary break with the view of civil society as identified with the state.[6] Although sharing the mercantilist viewpoint with regard to trade, Paine's mercantilism was intent on breaking from an old empire to help in the creation of a new one. Indeed, one commentator, John Keane, points to Paine's focus on despotism in support of his argument for recognising a late eighteenth-century transformation in the concept of civil society:

> The transformation and subdivision of the idea of *societas civilis* was stimulated primarily by a specifically *political* development: the fear of state despotism and the hope (spawned by the defeat of the British in the American colonies, as well as by the earliest events of the French revolution) of escaping its clutches. (1988, 65; see also Deane 1989, 37)

It is not surprising, then, to find that when it is rendered in this fashion, Paine's intervention could be seen as marking a watershed on the road

---

[5] Ministers of the British Crown, such as Francis Bacon, lacked the success of a Colbert—who managed to regulate the fabric weavers of Dijon to produce fabric containing neither more nor less than 1,408 threads. The efforts of British sovereigns in issuing internal monopolies on everything from saltpeter, gunpowder, paper, and salt, to alum and soap instead produced a series of common law court decisions transferring the monopoly granting power to Parliament. Robert Ekelund and Robert Hébert claim it was both "its very high degree of centralization and very efficient system of policing, factors that were never so great in England," which made French mercantilism different (1990, 67).

[6] In *Common Sense*, Paine wrote as follows: "Some writers have so confounded society with government, as to leave little or no distinction between them; whereas they are not only different, but have different origins. Society is produced by our wants, and government by our wickedness; the former promotes our happiness *positively* by uniting our affections, the latter *negatively* by restraining our vices. The one encourages intercourse, the other creates distinctions. The first is a patron, the second a punisher" (1776, 231).

towards later, more developed arguments claiming that civil society and political society should be considered as being, at least in part, semiautonomous realms.

POLITICAL ECONOMY, THE INTENTIONS OF STATESMEN, AND CIVIL SOCIETY

The seventeenth-century mercantilist thinkers such as Mun and Colbert theorised state trade policy as a zero-sum game of political will and the brinksmanship of structured imbalance, not just with one state prospering at the expense of others, but also with special groups within the nation (domestic merchants and manufacturers) prospering at the expense of others (domestic consumers and the producers of natural or nonexportable products). While such policies would draw derision from physiocratic writers in the eighteenth century, one mid-eighteenth-century Scottish political economist who still championed mercantilist policies, Sir James Steuart, modified the old mercantilist perception of the character and purposes of civil society. In doing so, he introduced a rather more nuanced view of the role of statesmen in balancing the interests of state and society than had been evident in anything his predecessors had to say. Steuart, conveniently (if a little inaccurately) considered the last of the mercantilists, reaffirmed the earlier state-centred focus on security as the aim of economic policy, and therefore gave preeminent attention to politics and the capacity of the statesman in balancing "work and demand" in the economy:

> This happy state cannot be supported but by the care of the statesman; and when he is found negligent in the discharge of this part of his duty, the consequence is, that either the spirit of industry, which, it is supposed, has cost him much pains to cultivate, is extinguished, or the produce of it rises to so high a value, as to be out of reach of a multitude of purchasers. (1767, 1:195)

Yet Steuart linked his economic policy views to a more progressive one of both civil society and the role of the ideal statesman. As is apparent from the above passage, he achieved this by introducing a concern for greater equity between the orders comprising it. He asserted, for example, that a central question of statesmanship in regulating internal trade was how "to keep the whole of his people constantly employed" and discover "by what means he may promote an equitable circulation of domestic wealth, through the hands of the lower classes, which will prove an adequate equivalent given by the rich, for the services rendered by the industrious poor" (1:276). It was the function of statesmen to mitigate the (supposedly) detrimental effects of the spread of commercial relationships and luxury on civil society through the enactment of sumptuary laws, and by restraining the pace of its development through price controls and taxation: "we must encourage oeconomy, frugality, and a simplicity of manners, discourage the consumption of everything that can be exported, and excite a taste for superfluity in neighbouring nations." In the language of modern economics, Steuart recommended fiscal, monetary, and debt policy "that would counter the stagnation created by the hoarding of the rich" with the explicit intent to "throw it directly into the hands of the industrious, or of the luxurious whom employ them" (Hutchison 1988, 342).[7]

Steuart clearly recognised the dangers of proposing policies that would depend for their success on the judgment of an actual statesman and his ability to see the intentions of his policies fulfilled: "A people taught to expect from a statesman the execution of big plans with impossibility and contradiction, will remain discontented under the government of the best Kings" (1767, 1:13). Thus, his reliance in theory on a benevolent and knowledgeable statesman earned Steuart criticism for a certain lack of realism concerning the character and quantity of knowledge such political stewardship would require. Such a criticism would seem to belie the ideal and hypothetical character of Steuart's virtuous statesman who is motivated not by self-interest but rather only by public spirit (1:145). Steuart was just as clear that the moral character of good action uniformly "consists *in the conformity between the motive, and the duty of the agent*" rather than in consequentialist outcomes (1:142; emphasis added).

Of course, the greater criticism of Steuart's principles of political economy rested on the well-rehearsed charge that it simply lacked "principles." It contained no systematic, general account of the determining factors at work in the economy, no attempt to segregate the fitful and irregular forces at work in commercial society from those of a more regular and persistent character, and no recognition of the possibility that (as the physiocrats soon pointed out) the forces at work in commercial society operated independently of the wills of human beings. In short, the language of self-regulating mechanisms, the methods of scientific investigation, or unintended consequences—all of which might detract from the

[7] As Steuart noted, "Every application of public money implies a want in the state; and every want supplied, implies an encouragement given to industry. In proportion, therefore, as taxes draw money into circulation, which otherwise would not have entered into it at that time, they encourage industry; not by taking the money from individuals, but by throwing it into the hands of the state, which spends it; and thereby throws it directly into the hands of the industrious, or of the luxurious who employ them" (1767, 2:725).

efficacy of or set limits to the role of even the most virtuous statesman—had not yet appeared within the *economic* discourse of civil society. But it was about to do so.

HISTORY, POLITICAL ECONOMY, AND CIVIL SOCIETY

Although Steuart was less than systematic in his account of economic life, he was also developing a historical account of the progress of civilisation entertaining one idea about civil society that would prove to be influential in the more systematic economic and political writings of those who would follow him. This was the idea that it was in civil society that liberty might most seriously be threatened. Raymond Plant (1977) has gone as far as to claim that Hegel actually picked up his conception of the emergence of freedom from Steuart's account of a threefold progress of development in history—from hunter-gatherer society, through to agrarian society, and finally to the commercial society of his day.

Whether or not Plant's assertions for Steuart's lasting influence were entirely accurate, this account of a historical development that reached its last stage in commercial society was certainly characterised by Steuart as constituting a "revolution." Not only did Steuart regard it as a material advance over the agrarian system out of which it developed but also he held that it partook of the character of a social revolution—by replacing "compulsion with inducement" (Plant, 1977, 82). The argument was simple enough. A developing taste for luxuries induced labourers to produce a surplus that could be traded to obtain desired goods beyond subsistence. As the incentive to work increased, the constraints of physical necessity were progressively reduced. This reduction of necessity was the factor that opened the space for greater freedom. Steuart put it as follows: "I deduce modern liberty from the independence of the same classes, by the introduction of industry and circulation of an adequate equivalent for every service." (1:209). Somewhat remarkably, given the kind of arguments for the perfect liberty of commercial relations that were soon to appear in the literature of Scottish political economy, Steuart had demonstrated that in society, individuals were united in greater interdependence without introducing the concept of the division of labour.

Yet a paradox remains at the centre of this conception of civil society. On the one hand, Steuart was implicitly critical of earlier mercantilists, such as Mun, for encouraging statesmen to foster the advantages of imbalanced trade both at home and abroad. It was precisely the statesman's practice of regulating *internal* as well as foreign commerce—action that risked economic hardship and inequity, and posed threats to liberty within the polity—that Steuart attempted to remedy. In part, he did this by urging statesman to better balance "the hands in work and the demand for their labour," and moderate the drive for increasing the treasure of the nation with the aim "to preserve every member of it in health and vigour" (1:195, 236). On the other hand, Steuart also recognised that the employment of the drive for luxury produced its own paradox:

> Luxury still tends as much as ever to the advancement of industry; the statesman's business only is, to remove the seat of it from his own country. When this can be accomplished without detriment to industry at home, he has the opportunity of joining all the advantages of ancient simplicity to the wealth and power which attend upon the luxury of modern states. (1:228)

Thus, while Steuart preferred to use words such as state, society, government, nation, and country as largely interchangeable, he unquestionably remained within the tradition of that earlier concept of civil society that saw it as coterminous with the state.

Ferguson, in contrast, introduced into his account of the progress and manners of commercial nations elements that more recent commentators have suggested are the "first signs of the breakdown of the classical concept of civil society" (Keane 1988, 40). While one may largely agree with the assessment of Nicholas Phillipson that Ferguson was less a political economist than a "moralist who sought to tighten, not loosen the ties which bound political economy to moral philosophy" (1987, 2:301), yet it is useful to explore the effect that Ferguson's economic understanding had on his conception of polity.

Ferguson used the term civil society in differing contexts. In some places, he deployed it to draw a contrast with "rude" or "primitive" settings that, he argued, characterised the "society" of affective ties into which humans were born and from which civil society emerges. On this matter, he was in agreement with Montesquieu. In others, Ferguson used the term to refer to the political organisation of the state: "the dignities, and even the offices, of civil society, were known many ages ago, in Europe by their present appellations" (1767, 79). In this context, he clarified his own position on a debate that had occupied Rousseau in his *Discourse on the Origin of Inequality*—namely, to what extent can one say that civilisation was advancing rather than declining with the emergence of commercial society. Ferguson's answer was that although civilisation was advancing, civil society was declining. His own history of the Roman republic, and his explicit comparisons of Rome and Carthage contained within it, are instructive. According to that argument, Carthage was more advanced both commercially and in the "lucrative arts" than Rome; it was, moreover, superior in every resource except "what is the consequence of public virtue" (Ferguson 1783, 1:88). In the decline of the Roman republic itself, commerce flourished and the "engine of the empire" continued to work, "but these were poor compensations for the want of that vigour, elevation, and freedom, which perished with the Roman republic itself" (6:480).

Ferguson saw that the division of labour posed challenges for public spirit and the disinterested love of the public in "polished" nations (1767, 258–59). As with Steuart's discussion of luxury, the division of labour appeared to Ferguson as both the benefactor of social progress and its worst enemy:

> The separation of the professions, while it seems to promise improvement of skill, and is actually the cause [of] why the productions of every art become more perfect as commerce advances; yet in its termination, and ultimate effects, serves, in some measure, to break the bands of society, to substitute form in place if ingenuity, and to withdraw individuals from the common scene of occupation, on which the sentiments of the heart, and the mind, are most employed. (218)[8]

The problem was not simply that with the expansion of commerce and manufacture, and its accompanying perfection of the commercial arts, a love of luxury and desire for profit developed that morally corrupted people and stifled "the love of perfection," so that "interest cools the imagination, and hardens the heart" (Ferguson 1767, 217). The problem was also with the concomitant withdrawal of individuals from the "common scene" that transformed the whole character of society itself, rendering it a mechanism of multiple and interdependent groups or orders, in which "society is made to consist of parts, of which none is animated with the spirit of society itself" (218). These orders or professions within commercial society then vied within a competitive struggle for profit, luxury, and fame. This was a centripetal struggle fuelled by the propertied classes to create a "change of national manners for the worse" (238). According to Ferguson, that society, together with its approach to government, took on a complex, interdependent, and mechanical character in which repetitive practice was favoured over initiative or change: "The soldier is relieved from every care but that is his service; statesmen divide the business of civil government into shares; *and the servants of the public, in every office, without being skilful in the affairs of state, may succeed, by observing forms which are already established on the experience of others*" (181–82; emphasis added).

Accompanying such a threatened elevation of form and structure over a moral and willed political direction within the social order is the recognition of its accidental character: "The accidents which distribute the

---

[8] By "civilization," Ferguson appears to have intended a concept with a quite specific meaning and one more carefully defined than perhaps any other philosopher of the Scottish Enlightenment—certainly more so than Smith. Duncan Forbes cites Ferguson's discussion of it in *The Principles of Moral and Political Science* (1792): "Civilization . . . both in the

means of subsistence unequally, inclination, and favourable opportunities, assign the different occupations of men; and a sense of utility leads them, without end, to subdivide their professions" (180). It was the very *unintended* arrangement of the system that was seen as problematic, striking at the capacity for an ordered and directed polity.

Ferguson was perplexed (both morally and scientifically), however, about how commercial, political, and cultural relations interact as well as about whether they could really be understood as separable at all. His view was that men are basically social, but that what drew them together was not simply self-interest—indeed, that same self-interest in extreme form had a tendency to tear them apart. Ferguson wrote that "men are so far from valuing society on account of its mere external conveniencies, that they are commonly most attached when those conveniencies are least frequent" (19). He compared the "devoted patriotism of an early Roman" with the "spirit which reigns in a commercial state, where men may be supposed to have experienced, in its full extent, the interest which individuals have in the preservation of their country" (19), and concluded: "It is here indeed, if ever, that man is sometimes found a detached and a solitary being: he has found an object which sets him in competition with his fellow creatures, and he deals with them as he does with his cattle and his soil, for the sake of the profits they bring" (19). If one then asks what exactly civil society was for Ferguson, it is clear that it was neither commercial society nor was it political order per se. Some have argued that Ferguson had a dualistic vision of civil society—as the prerequisite of peace and prosperity, and the harbinger of psychic atomism, corruption, and decline—but that does not seem quite right. It is to mistake what Ferguson said about civilisation for the content of civil society. Instead, for Ferguson, civilisation was about material progress, while civil society was essentially about moral progress. This may explain why he held that moral refinement could have been greater among the Romans than among his contemporaries—and that moral refinement could be found in cultures with quite primitive economic institutions, yet be utterly absent in certain well-developed forms of the modern state.

For Ferguson, the basis of civil society was not the old *raison d'état*, nor rationality (as it was for Locke), nor self-love, nor benevolence. Instead, it was a type of historically observable sentiment to be found in all humankind—a moral sentiment that led people to oppose vice and disorder, and that linked humankind in an aversion to cruelty. Without it, politics would be brutal, and commercial society would ultimately be bankrupt

---

nature of the thing and derivation of the word, belongs rather to the effects of law and political establishment, on the forms of society, than to any state merely of lucrative possession or wealth" (see Forbes 1966, xix–xx).

and morally compromised. There was, of course, an element of modified Stoicism here, but Ferguson was not a candidate for the party of virtue.

This is where his position on unintended consequences takes on an altogether more intriguing character. While he praised the Stoics for believing in providence, and criticised the Epicureans for placing all their emphasis on chance, exactly what Ferguson had to say hinged on the premise that it was just not possible to state in advance what the outcomes of political plans and institutions would be. When he argued that it was the "situation and the genius of a people" that would play into outcomes, rather than the direction of any one individual or their plans—when he famously observed that "every step and every movement of the multitude, even in what are termed enlightened ages, are made with equal blindness to the future; and nations stumble upon establishments, which are indeed the result of human action, but are not the execution of any human design," and that "no constitution is formed by concert, no government copied from a plan" (122–23)—it is important to recognise that he was not uttering what Hayek dubbed the *locus classicus* of the doctrine of spontaneous order.

From that doctrine (and also from Hayek's rendition of it), Ferguson could not be further removed. He maintained single-mindedly that the consequences of chance, and the set of cards a society is dealt (in terms of resources, culture, and institutions), acted to constrain and shape their future possibilities. The fact that all actions had consequences was obvious—some good, and some bad—but no spontaneous order was at work for Ferguson to reconcile them. That reconciliation required politics to protect civil society from the corruption of the commercial order.

Yet it seems fair to suggest, as some have done, that Ferguson (along with others) had contributed in nascent fashion "to a new science of man that focused on the under structure of civil society rather than the narrower institutions of polity":

> In the enlarged framework offered by Scottish inquiry, the deliberate actions of military and political heroes were dwarfed by the unwilled advances of custom, commerce manners, and learning. The consequence was certainly not a loss of interest in politics, but there was a clear sense that the public world no longer represented a sufficient framework of understanding even for the study of politics itself. (Phillips 1996, 306)[9]

The move to a consideration of society in an enlarged framework of systemically interrelated activities of production, distribution, and exchange

---

[9] Pocock has cautioned that historical transformations are not accomplished *seriatum* but that competing paradigms run for periods in tandem. This appears to be the case for the earlier conceptions of polity or civil society as well as emerging conceptions of commercial society in this period.

with its own internal and undirected dynamic was decisive. It ushered in new philosophies of explanation and science to the ferment that was civil society in the eighteenth century.

The metaphor of the imagined machine, with all its Newtonian inflections, served to present the domain of commercial society as autonomous and subject to the operation of regular, persistent, causal processes. Civil society had its own inherent organisation and extrapolitical identity. It is this view that was developed explicitly not only in Smith's writings on political economy but also those on moral theory, jurisprudence, and scientific method.

Before considering Smith's view, though, it might be useful to remark briefly on those of Mandeville—views with which Smith's are often compared, but whose understanding of civil society is significantly different. Despite the effort of commentators to recruit Mandeville as the initiator of a concept of spontaneous order and a precursor of Smith's view of a self-regulating society, such an interpretation remains difficult to sustain.[10] It arises, of course, from a focus on the language of Mandeville's "private vices to public benefit" argument from the *Fable of the Bees* that has been frequently put forward as an early view of causal mechanisms of the market underpinning larger civil society. Yet Mandeville's imputed spontaneous order language needs to be considered carefully. The transformation of these vices to public benefit was undertaken, Mandeville emphasised, with the supervision and experience of statesmen or good politicians—"by dextrous management," as he put it. And he added: "The short-sighted vulgar, in the chain of causes seldom see further than one link; but those who enlarge their view, and will give themselves the leisure of gazing on the prospect of concatenated events, may, in a hundred places see good spring up and pullulate from evil, as naturally as chickens do from eggs" (1714, 123).

This was not, as is so frequently suggested, a systemic argument for that coincidence of public and private advantage—understood as a generalised mechanism of market activity. Indeed, Mandeville was clear that he intended such psychological insights on the power of prodigality and avarice to apply only to the aristocratic and merchant classes, while the labouring classes, on whose poverty the wealth of others depended, were motivated in such a mercantilist analysis by the direct and consequential motivations of destitution.[11] Mandeville's discussion might better be

---

[10] This same reference has been made to support an unfortunate view of Mandeville as the first "laissez-faire" economist.

[11] Smith recognised as much in his critique of mercantilism in the *Wealth of Nations*: "But what improves the circumstances of the greater part can never be regarded as an inconveniency to the whole. No society can surely be flourishing and happy, of which the greater

linked to the long-standing debate over luxury and the role of the statesman taken up by Cesare Beccaria, Hume, Pietro Verri, and Montesquieu
(which Smith chose explicitly to forego, and which cannot be developed
here). Otherwise, Mandeville favoured a host of mercantilist policies that
at the very least, hew his economic thinking quite closely to a concept of
civil society identified with and directed by the interests of the state. For
example, Mandeville spoke of money in the *Fable* as evil, but also as
necessary to the existence and order of civil society.

In rather explicit contrast to both Ferguson and Mandeville, Smith
rarely used the term civil society. He more commonly wrote of civilised
society or human society.[12] Smith did refer to "civil government," where
"order and good government, along with them the liberty and security of
individuals," made possible the progress of opulence, and political economy served as one branch of the "science of the legislator" or statesman
in this pursuit (1776, 1:405).[13] At the same time, however, Smith's description of late medieval history suggested that commerce and manufactures
themselves gradually introduce good order and government as one of
their least observed but most important effects. In both the *Wealth of
Nations* and the *Lectures on Jurisprudence*, Smith was interested in a
philosophical or, as Stewart described it, conjectural history that reveals
the hidden causes of the progress of civilisation from barbarism to its
polished condition in modern times.[14] At the same time, Smith's conjectural history explained the way that individuals acquired moral sentiments within a sphere of what some commentators have referred to as
moral trading.[15]

---

of the members are poor and miserable" (1776, 1:96). On this point, see also Horne (1978,
chapter 4).

[12] After something less than an exhaustive search, we have found only one reference in
the *Moral Sentiments* (1759, 340), and none in the *Wealth of Nations* or the *Lectures on
Jurisprudence*. For "civilized society," see *Wealth of Nations* (1776, 1:376); for "human
society," see *Moral Sentiments* (1759, 85–86).

[13] Smith saw "civil government" as introducing, in the stage of shepherd society, the
protection of private property.

[14] On Smith's use of a conjectural history of society or philosophical history, we note
Winch's insight that much of what has come to be called Smith's four stages of "conjectural
history" is really to be found in the *Lectures on Jurisprudence*. In the *Wealth of Nations*,
Smith dealt more explicitly with only two stages: that of the transformation of civilisation
from feudal to commercial society. But this, Winch suggests, might better be referred to as
an "*actual* history" organized around a particular conjecture concerning what would have
been the "natural" course of development. In making this point, Smith is establishing that
there can be "systems within systems," and that political economy, as the science of the
statesman, needs to comprehend them all.

[15] As Phillipson reminds us, Smith "tells us about the moral progress of individuals who
live in polished societies, who become as skilled in trading sentiments as they are in trading
goods. They are individuals who long for the approval of others but learn the hard way that

In this sense, Smith could write in the *Moral Sentiments* of a "natural state of society" and people's "natural love for society." But he likewise embraced a particular "economy of morals" view of society that was an aggregate outcome of a regard for and relations to others:

> The concern we take in the fortune and happiness of individuals does not, in common cases, arise from that which we take in the fortune and happiness of society. . . . In neither case does our regard for individuals arise from our regard for the multitude: but in both cases our regard for the multitude is compounded and made up of the particular regard we feel for the different individuals of which it is composed. (1759, 89)

In other words, it was not Ferguson's public spiritedness that inspired either the motives for or preserved the general rules of justice. Instead, the good of the whole would be an *unintended consequence* of the individual concerns of its constituent parts.

Smith viewed society as a system, and moral life was also a system. Whether he was considering government and laws, outlining the formation of moral sentiments, or discussing astronomy and the universe—all were presented as systems. In his lectures on the *History of Astronomy*, Smith brought the weight of the analysis of systematic forces to the forefront:

> Systems in many respects resemble machines. A machine is a little system, created to perform, as well as to connect together, in reality, those different movements which the artist has occasion for. A system is an imaginary machine invented to connect in the fancy those different movements and effects which are already in reality performed. (Smith, ca. 1750)

Such systems revolved around connecting principles, and the more sophisticated the system, the fewer and more general the principles. The point was to constrain and simplify our understanding of society for the purposes of better understanding and assisting the continued progress of opulence. The "obvious and simple system of natural liberty" lies at the centre of Smith's account of the market mechanism. According to Smith, it displaces the centrality of both the state and the direct influence of statesmen from this space:

> Every man, as long as he does not violate the laws of justice, is left perfectly free to pursue his own interest his own way, and to bring both his industry and capital into competition with any other man, or order or men. The sover-

---

self-approval brings more contentment than the applause of the world. They are individuals who value propriety" (2000, 80).

eign is completely discharged from a duty, in the attempt to perform which he must always be exposed to innumerable delusions, and for the proper performance of which *no human wisdom or knowledge could ever be sufficient*: the duty of superintending the industry of private people, and of directing it towards the employments most suitable to the interests of society. (1776, 2:687; emphasis added)[16]

How this occurs is really the story of the implications of Smith's political economy for his political thought.

SMITH AND CIVIL SOCIETY, VISIBLE AND INVISIBLE

In examining the relationship between the state and the economic system in this period, Phyllis Deane once argued that the "identification of an analogy between a self-regulating solar system and a self-regulating economy" had to wait until political economists "learned to separate the concept of an economic system—an economy in the modern sense of that term—from the polity in which the contemporary economic problems arose" (1989, 37). A glance at Smith's work in the context of both Newtonian and physiocratic thinking, however, suggests that the logic of Deane's statement should be reversed. It would seem to be rather more accurate to say that identifying the mechanisms regulating social and commercial life came after the political economists had already separated civil society from polity.

Smith's alteration in the conception of civil society rested on a "process of habitual practice," and the illusion of regular and harmonious movement within that process (see also Hume 1777a, 37–41). This is not to say that Smith reduced the concept of civil society to the market but rather that he suggested a vision in which society (in both its commercial and civil perspectives) was created by the same systematic interactions—and that the mechanism of the market lies at its centre (even if it does not comprise the whole of it). Society beyond the market involved the same psychology.[17] As Smith remarked in the *Moral Sentiments*, "We naturally

[16] Later thinkers, such as John Stuart Mill's protégé John Morley, would criticise Smith's view of civil society precisely for its "impoverished moral energy" as demonstrated in his analysis of the stages of society in which every "state of society" is reduced "to a particular stage in the evolution of its general conditions." The result, he argued, was to remove human intention from the motor of society's progress: "the result is that men become spectators of their own affairs and reforming initiative is disregarded" (cited in Burrow 1988, 22).

[17] But see Vivienne Brown (2008), who argues rather that a different concept of agency informs the actors within Smith's moral and commercial spheres.

confound it in our imagination with the order, the regular and harmonious movement of the system, the machine or oeconomy by means of
which it is produced" (1759, 183). In this sense, it has been asserted that
Smith even more than Hume "recognized the limitations of the tradition
of civic concepts" (such as universal citizenship) when confronted with
the reality of commercial society (Robertson 1983, 455).[18] In the *Wealth
of Nations*, Smith finalized this departure from the civil tradition not only
by integrating the analysis of commercial society and politics (and thus
creating his political economy) but also by giving us a new anatomy of
how civil society is constituted and governed.

But it was not until well after Smith that the concept of the self-
regulating market mechanism and its unintended consequences came to
play the much more politically constraining role in the concept of civil
society that modern economists have attributed to them. In the work of
Ricardo, that effort "to separate the concept of an economic system . . .
from the polity" emerges quite clearly (Deane 1989, 36).

RICARDIAN POLITICAL ECONOMY AND CAPITALIST SOCIETY

Ricardo's contribution to an understanding of society along with the
scope and limits of political reform is distinctive. That understanding was
inextricably bound up with the science of a political economy. Indeed,
for Ricardo, the construction of a new political science—one on which a
reformed constitution was to be built—required a more systematic consideration of the relationship between the operation of the mechanism of
the market and political organisation.

Like Smith before him, Ricardo saw society in general (and capitalist
society in particular) as being subject to the influence of certain systematic
forces, more or less regular and persistent in character, and operating
independently of the wills of people. It was, as Ricardo's contemporary
Robert Torrens succinctly put it, "the separation of the community into
a class of capitalists and a class of labourers" in the "more advanced and
complicated stages of society" (1821, 33, 25) that provided the key to
how civil society was to be examined.

The impact of Ricardo's economics on his idea of politics and society
can be measured in two ways. First, in neither his political nor economic

---

[18] According to John Robertson, Hume had already radically altered the "picture" of
what was a historical rather than theoretical consideration, "adapting" its terms to the
"positive pursuit of wealth" (453). In this sense, Robertson suggests, Hume's question was
different from that of earlier civic thinkers in that he asked not what form of government
is best but rather what form of government "would best be adapted to the needs of progres-

thinking was he strictly utilitarian. Second, he was not in the most important respects an individualist. His thought was not utilitarian for the simple reason that in defining the standard of material well-being as aggregate production itself rather than some aggregate of individual utilities, he shifted the focus of analysis away from individual utility maximisers and what would later be called methodological individualism. His thought was also not individualist because his economic analysis focused instead on the conditions of reproduction and growth, where the relevant actors—economic, social, and political—were social classes and not individual agents, and where the relevant categories were objective economic ones rather than the subjective or psychological one of individual utility. This led Ricardo to conceive of the dynamics of society and politics in just the same way as he conceived of the dynamics of economics—namely, in terms of the interplay between these larger group interests.

It was primarily with Ricardo, and his approach to value and distribution, that the idea of class structure became a key economic characteristic of civil society for classical political economy. That this is so was heralded at the very outset of his *Principles of Political Economy* in 1817:

> The produce of the whole earth—all that is derived from its surface by the united application of labour, machinery, and capital, is divided among three classes of the community; namely, the proprietor of the land, the owner of the stock or capital necessary for its cultivation, and the labourers by whose industry it is cultivated. But in different stages of society, the proportions of the whole produce of the earth which will be allotted to each of these classes, under the names of rent, profit, and wages, will be essentially different. . . . To determine the laws which regulate this distribution, is the principal problem of Political Economy. (1821, 5)

Having established that rent was not to be seen as a component part of price (as Smith had thought), Ricardo presented an inverse relationship between the wage and the rate of profit in terms of the labour theory of value. For a given subsistence wage (and a given technology), if natural prices of commodities were determined by the quantity of labour necessary for their production, the rate of profits varied inversely with the *value* of the wage. The value of the wage was the natural price of labour—that is, under the labour theory of value, the quantity of labour required to produce the "food, necessaries, and conveniences . . . essential to him from habit" (93).

---

sive, commercial society" (452). Hume and Smith would offer different answers to this question. For Hume, the answer might lie in some form of republic, but for Smith it was unquestionably parliamentary sovereignty.

In this way, *via* the labour theory (and the consequent relationship between capitalists and workers), the focus of the class structure of civil society became the primary unit of analysis in Ricardo's vision of political economy.[19] This vision had also been present in Smith, but it was not until after Smith that it took such a prominent place within the discipline. Between the time of Smith and that of Ricardo, in fact, since little was made of Smith's labour theory of value, it is hardly surprising that this was so. As Ricardo repeatedly maintained, profits depended on wages, and the interests of landlords were opposed to those of all other groups in society. It would be no exaggeration to say that this was almost the defining feature of what Malthus called the "new" political economy.

But as Ricardo's theory of value and distribution began to be challenged soon after his death, and as his defenders (and one thinks of McCulloch and James Mill here) resorted to ever more elaborate and unconvincing arguments to sustain it, doubts about the adequacy of this characterisation increased. When the neoclassical writers of the 1870s finally dispatched the labour theory of value to the pages of history, Ricardo's characterisation of civil society was replaced by one in which the only relevant feature was the *individuals* who populated it. Explaining the allocation of scarce resources between these individuals rather than the distribution of income between social classes came to dominate the textbooks of economics.

Ricardo's view of society is not marked by the presence of mechanisms that ensure the mutual compatibility of individual interests. Instead, it is one of potential conflict between the productive classes of a capitalist system. He does not use the term civil society anywhere in his work, and his focus on the market mechanism may tend perhaps to isolate society more simply as a generalised structure of class interest standing separate from government. This is the basis of the common view of his work as being that of an economic liberal—and it is to a large extent supported by Ricardo's own writing:

> The desire which every man has to keep his station in life, and to maintain his wealth at the height which it has once attained, occasions most taxes, whether laid on capital or on income, to be paid from income; and therefore as taxation proceeds, or as government increases its expenditure, the annual enjoyments of the people must be diminished, unless they are enabled proportionally to increase their capitals and income. It should be the policy of

[19] Stewart did not even feel the need to mention the labour theory of value in his account of Smith's life and writings.

governments to encourage a disposition to do this in the people, and never to lay such taxes as will inevitably fall on capital; since by doing so, they impair the funds for the maintenance of labour, and thereby diminish the future production of the country. (153)

Ricardo commonly referred to a "state of society" in which labour and specifically "the aggregate sum" of "various kinds of labour" determine the quantity of "other things for which [a commodity] will exchange" (25). In theoretical terms, the good of such a society was reduced in Ricardo's economic thought from the more generalised and politically directed one of an earlier civil society perspective to that of the "representative good" of one or more classes operating within the mechanism of the market. In practical and policy terms, Ricardo became convinced that the general character of society was, in the short run, one of an inherent conflict between the classes, over which the government and the statesman could exercise little or no direct role in ameliorating the "inconveniences." They must rely instead on the long-run workings of the market mechanism.[20] The problem, for Ricardo, was indicative of a disharmony within the system itself:

> I now, however, see reason to be satisfied that the one fund, from which landlords and capitalists derive their revenue, may increase while the other, that upon which the labouring class mainly depend, may diminish, and therefore it follows, if I am right, that the same cause which may increase the net revenue of the country, may at the same time render the population redundant, and deteriorate the condition of the labourer. (388)

While Ricardo too speaks of the progress of society, the character of the laws of the market that regulate that progress take on for him a more fixed and determinate character than they do for Smith. Ricardo writes of the "laws by which wages are regulated," and suggests that "like all other contracts, wages should be left to the fair and free competition of the market, and should never be controlled by the interference of government" (105). He writes of the Poor Laws as opposing the "obvious principles" of political economy, and producing negative conse-

[20] See, for example, Ricardo's argument (in chapter 39 of the revised *Principles*) that the introduction of machinery into the mechanism of the market would have conflictual consequences for society in the short run. In the past, Ricardo had claimed that like Smith, "I thought that the labouring class would equally with the other classes, participate in the advantage, from the general cheapness of commodities arising from the use of machinery. These were my opinions, and they continued unaltered, as far as regards the landlord and the capitalist; but I am convinced, that the substitution of machinery for human labour, is often very injurious to the interest of the class of labourers" (388).

quences that fall outside the control of the political will and capacity of the state:

> The clear and direct tendency of the poor laws, is in direct opposition to these obvious principles: it is not, as the legislature benevolently intended, to amend the condition of the poor, but to deteriorate the condition of both poor and rich; instead of making the poor rich, they are calculated to make the rich poor; and whilst the present laws are in force, it is quite in the natural order of things that the fund for the maintenance of the poor should be progressively increase[d], till it has absorbed all the net revenue of the country, or at least so much of it as the state shall leave to us, after satisfying its own never failing demands for the public expenditure. (105–6)

In Ricardo's *Principles*, the market mechanism is transformed from its imaginative origins in Smith into real, concrete, determinate laws of political economy. Such laws appear to have the certainty of physical laws: "the principle of gravitation is not more certain" than the laws of political economy (see, for example, Ricardo 1821, 108). More important, the principles of political economy (or the laws of the market) now regulate an interlocking mechanism that reaches well beyond particular nation-state borders to form a kind of "international society" in "a system of perfectly free commerce." In this larger international economic order, "each country naturally devotes its capital and labour to such employments as are most beneficial to each. This pursuit of individual [country] advantage is admirably connected with the universal good of the whole. By stimulating industry, by rewarding ingenuity . . . it distributes labour most effectively and most economically; while, by increasing the general mass of productions, it diffuses general benefit, and binds together by one common tie of interest and intercourse, the universal society of nations throughout the civilized world" (133–34). The globalisation of capitalist society had found its first champion.

Ricardo wrote and spoke in favour of measures such as the secret ballot as well as parliamentary and franchise reform. His economic theorising, however, presented a dilemma for any concept of civil society, which on his account was now distinctly separable from politics. Short-run conflicts between classes were thought resistant to political amelioration or interference, while longer-run ones were less obviously so, since beyond the present of commercial society lay its dystopic twin in the form of the stationary state "from which," Ricardo wrote, "I trust we are far distant" (108).

The point at which the understanding of civil society had arrived in the literature of classical economics after Ricardo is well illustrated in the writings of an unlikely pairing: John Stuart Mill and Marx. Although the content and structure of civil society (as well as its problems and their remedies) were seen very differently by each, both had nevertheless come to share the premise that it was the economic element of civil society from which its characteristic features derived.

In the case of Marx, this could hardly be more obvious. One does not need to enter into long disquisitions to prove it, since Marx is best left to speak for himself:

> Assume particular stages of . . . production, commerce and consumption and you will have a corresponding social constitution, a corresponding organisation of the family, of orders or of classes, in a word, a corresponding civil society. Assume a particular civil society and you will get particular political conditions which are only the official expression of civil society. (1846, 136–37)

Yet it is equally true in the case of Mill. When Mill cast his reviewer's eye over the work of perhaps the most celebrated chronicler of civil society, Alexis de Tocqueville, he too concluded that it was the economic organisation of society that established the most significant general characteristics of civil society.

Tocqueville's *Democracy in America* had appeared in two volumes in 1835 and 1840, respectively (the second in a simultaneous English translation by Henry Reeve). Mill reviewed the first volume for the *London and Westminster Review*, and the second volume for the *Edinburgh Review*. Tocqueville's book was a great success, even in the rather insular England of the day. Mill himself remarked at the time that its fame "was as sudden, and as extensive, in this country as in France" (1840, 215). In his more analytical review of the second volume of *Democracy in America*, Mill confronted Tocqueville's presentation of the historical tendencies supposedly at work on civil society—tendencies that Tocqueville associated with the increasing equality of conditions (or what he called "democracy")—and took exception: "Tocqueville then has, at least apparently, confounded the effects of Democracy with the effects of Civilisation. He has bound up in one abstract idea the whole of the tendencies of modern commercial society, and has given them one name—Democracy" (257).

There followed an exercise in reasoning bearing all the hallmarks of his father's mode of argument (and for that matter, of Ricardo's and most of his followers) designed to show that it was from "the tendencies of commercial civilisation" (257) that a proper appreciation of civil society ought to be developed.

It would be no misuse of language to say that the whole thrust of classical economics (and here Marx should be included too) was to reduce the understanding of civil society to its economic foundations. Yet as we have seen, this did not at the same time reduce their perceptions of the content and relevance of civil society itself. It remained the seat of class structures, institutional formations, corporate entities, and all kinds of other voluntary associations. It also remained a powerful source of social and economic problems that stood in need of a remedy. Things were about to take a dramatic turn, though, on that front as well. For the radical overhaul of "economic science" that the marginalist writers were soon to usher in altered entirely this classical picture.

The Marginalisation of Civil Society

It is well-enough known that Ricardo's economic thought was criticised in his own lifetime for its abstract character, generating the remark by Henry Brougham that his views gave the impression of having dropped from another planet. His thinking was criticised after his death as having been able but wrongheaded. But whatever side one takes in the great Ricardo debate, it should not be forgotten that the central focus he had placed on the objective social relations of production and distribution ensured that his economic thought had a theoretical relevance to the conception of civil society in general as well as to the understanding of its actual operation. As we have seen, it did not take someone like Marx long to discover this reservoir of concepts and ideas—and to put it to a more revolutionary purpose.

The classical economists' vision managed to preserve the array of institutions and associations that comprised the social and moral order largely due to the simple fact that landlords, capitalists, and workers were the social categories they identified as actuating the market mechanism. Smith, Malthus, and Ricardo uniformly saw these as the natural attributes of commercial society, and the source, potentially at least, of natural societal fairness. These institutions and associations were also the focus of the economic activities comprising the life of commercial society.

The same cannot be said of the principles of neoclassical economics that were introduced in the marginal revolution of the 1870s. Integral to that change was a shift in the central focus of economic science from production and distribution to exchange—from what some have called the objective conditions of production to the subjective conditions of consumption. Economics moved from thinking of a civil society composed of social classes, professional groups, corporate entities, trade unions, and cooperative societies, to a civil society of isolated individual utility maximisers. Pioneering neoclassical economists such as William Stanley Jevons, Léon Walras, and Alfred Marshall divested their economic theories from direct contact with any socially specific material conditions (other than the existence of well-defined and enforceable property rights) whatsoever.

Homely tales of Robinson Crusoe, allocating his time between work and leisure on a desert island, became the vehicle through which the principles of economics could be illustrated. It would be no exaggeration to say that for many neoclassical writers, Crusoe's desert island was held to be sufficient to capture whatever was essential about the social context within which, as Marshall famously said, people conducted "the ordinary business of life" (1890, 1). Although Marshall stated that it was the task of political economy to study what he called "the social mechanism" (Marshall and Marshall 1881), it is difficult to see what (if anything) "social" was really at work.

In Jevons's *Theory of Political Economy* (1871), to take an early example, it was the constrained optimising behaviour of individual agents (consumers and producers) that *determined* outcomes and market equilibrium. Of course, such agents obeyed a host of "natural" laws—they maximised their utility (profits), were price takers, did not collude, were many, and operated in an environment of freely available information. Still, these were ideal rational actors in a mathematical model of a perfectly competitive market; they were situated, as it were, outside any specific social context. The theory so constructed was also meant to apply, mutatis mutandis, to the rather more complex social reality of Western capitalism of their day.

This decoupling of the analysis of exchange (or better, of allocation) from specific social formations is especially evident in the case of Walras, where the idea that economic science deals in "universals" was brought into sharp relief (1874, 61). This idea contrasts markedly with those of Smith, Ricardo, and Mill—all of whom focused on a specific form of social organisation. Their political economy provided a theory of the operation of "commercial society," "capitalist society," or whatever they chose to call it. They made no claims as to its universal applicability—certainly nothing of the kind that one finds in Walras.

This claim to the universal applicability of neoclassical economics was justified by explicit reference to methodological individualism. By looking at everything from the angle of what modern economics calls microeconomic behaviour, Walras was able to launch a claim that his focus was on the generality of things independent of their specific social setting—a generality so breathtaking that it would, if acceptable, render his economic theory applicable to all humankind throughout all of history. Walras actually divided the whole universe into *persons* and *things* (62) such that the old physiocratic idea that the economy operated "independently of the wills of men" had vanished.

The domain of pure economics was at once strictly limited and dramatically expanded. It was strictly limited because it was now only the relationship between the "wants" of individuals and scarcity of "things" that mattered (65)—no attempt was made (or was thought to be needed) to connect this relationship with the social, cultural, and institutional context in which it was actually situated. It was dramatically expanded, certainly, for the same reason. It all depends on one's point of view.

In a similar fashion, in establishing what he claimed to be the "true system of economics," Jevons simply bypassed Ricardo (the man who, according to him, had shunted the car of economic science onto a wrong track) and appropriated Bentham's utilitarian model of human beings, employing it as the exclusive foundation of a new theory of the market mechanism—one that was radically individualist rather than social in its character. Ronald Meek rather neatly captured the flavour of this change when he said that "the new starting point became, not the socioeconomic relations between men as producers, but the psychological relation between men and finished goods" (1972, 501). By establishing the homogeneity between the elements of cost (interpreted as disutility), Jevons was able to show that the relative prices of commodities were determined by the ratios of their marginal utilities. In a way not open to the Scottish or later classical political economists, this equilibrium condition would soon be shown by other neoclassical economists to involve the proposition that the market mechanism produced an efficient (or optimal) allocation of resources in society and that, for example, involuntary employment "in equilibrium" was impossible. This effectively altered forever the manner in which arguments for and against economic liberty would be constructed. Jevons declared his theory to be "entirely based on a calculus of pleasure and pain," which he described as "the mechanics of utility and self-interest" (1871, 67, 23, 21).

According to a famous remark of Marshall, "political economy or economics is a study of mankind in the ordinary business of life; it examines that part of individual and social action which is most closely connected with the attainment and with the use of the material requisites of well-being" (1890, 1). But when one looks more closely, the "political" was excised from the "economic" just as rigidly by Marshall as it was for others. Consider the following remarks by Marshall: "[Economic study] shuns many political issues, which the practical man cannot ignore: and it is therefore a science, pure and applied, rather than a science and an art. And it is better described by the broad term Economics than by the narrower term Political Economy" (36). Although the question of the universality of economic laws was hedged by Marshall in a way that was not true of Walras, one still finds Marshall urging on his readers the need to understand the "unity in substance, underlying many varieties in form" (2).

Accordingly, free exchange between formally equal individuals became the means through which to secure the most efficient allocation of social resources. The immediate implication of this revolution for the relationship between civil society and the state is a general presumption (indeed a positivist "scientific" basis) for the doctrine of laissez-faire. This is not to say that there was no role for government but rather that there were no values other than efficiency that could establish and direct its activities. The early neoclassical economists did not solve the problem of what is or should be thought of as morally good, nor did they imply any theory of moral or social obligation. They did not suggest which policies would maximise the greatest happiness of the greatest number, but only which ones were Pareto optimal. Only individuals' preferences mattered, and they were not evaluated: *de gustibus non disputandum est.*

All institutional forms in the economy were explained as either exogenous impositions—from the political sphere, for instance—or in terms of individual preferences and technology along with such "natural" phenomena as incomplete information and transactions costs. A thread of anti-institutionalism winds through the marginalist literature, and it was generally replete with references to the "superficial" character of analyses that "do not recede to any theory of utility" (Jevons 1871, xxxi) and the "scientific" necessity of differentiating "purely economic relations" from others—mainly political—"with which they are associated in reality" (Schumpeter 1954, 551).

In its radical individualist programme, neoclassical thought took refuge in explanations of the whole in terms of the behaviour of its individual constituent parts. The satisfaction of individual needs and desires (for utility and profits) were related to one another in a causal time sequence, but there was no sense in which they were "interdependent." They sprung from the individual psychological makeup of agents, and from their "given" and independent preferences. Unlike all earlier economic theories, neoclassical theory lacked any concept of human sympathy (or alternative assumptions as to the social bonds) that might serve as the effective cement of a society.

Chapter Four

ECONOMIC LIFE AND POLITICAL LIFE

The prudent man always studies seriously and
earnestly whatever he professes to understand . . .
steadily sacrificing the ease and enjoyment of the
present moment for the probable expectation of the
still greater ease and enjoyment of a more distant
but more lasting period of time.
—Adam Smith, *Moral Sentiments*

Whilst every man is free to employ his capital where
he pleases, he will naturally seek for it that employment which is most advantageous . . . this restless desire on the part of all employers of stock . . . is then the
desire, which every capitalist has, of diverting his funds
from a less to a more profitable employment.
—David Ricardo, *Principles*

MARX once famously claimed that the economic structure of a society constituted the foundation of almost everything: law, politics, religion, history, and consciousness itself. It was, as he put it, the "real foundation" on which was built a legal and political "superstructure"—and to which there corresponded "definite forms of social consciousness" (1858, 20–21). On his line of thinking, political life was epiphenomenal—reproducing and preserving the social and economic relations of production from which it emerged. Yet Marx was by no means the first, nor the last, to contemplate the relationship between economic and political life. It is a question that goes back at least as far as the ancients—and it has formed the cornerstone of some of the best-known contributions to social and political thought through the ages.[1]

What is of concern to us here, however, is not to delineate what that relationship actually is or even to suggest what it ought to be. Instead, we

[1] In other hands, of course, the same question would appear as one pertaining to the affinities and differences between private and public life; between the baser private interests said to be at work in the market and the public interest that ought to be at work in politics; or between self-regarding and other-regarding action—in short, between private vices and public virtue, as Mandeville memorably put it. In eighteenth-century Europe, it would be fair to say that ethics or moral philosophy was concerned with little else.

are interested in the question of how the relationship has been understood and articulated in the philosophical and scholarly literature—and this in four historical contexts: ancient, mercantilist, classical, and neoclassical. Our primary focus is on the literature of economics, but our historical perspective extends back to the ancients, where the issue of whether there is a recognizably separate "economics" literature is itself a matter of debate. In that sense we shall not hesitate to range across what is normally thought of as "political theory" where it seems appropriate. Although each consideration will have to be brief, we wish to offer a set of vantage points from which to consider the relationship between economic life and political life.

There are a number of ways in which the relationship itself might be construed: with the "economic" as predominant; the "political" as predominant; economic and political essentially independent; the two interdependent but equal; together with the possibility that the two are to be seen as indistinguishable. As we shall see, most of these logical possibilities seem to have figured in the literature at different times.

ANCIENT ECONOMIC AND POLITICAL THOUGHT

To trace the development of ideas regarding ancient *principles* of economics is, according to the conventional wisdom, quite literally to begin with nothing. The first significant body of literature to accumulate on this subject in the last century—and one thinks here especially of Karl Polanyi, Hannah Arendt, and Moses Finley—insisted that no truly systematic reflection on the economy was to be found anywhere in classical antiquity. Finley was perhaps the most unreserved of them all in expressing this opinion. When writing of Aristotle, for example, he was unambiguous: "there is no economic analysis in Aristotle," and "judgments of his performance on that score or attempts to interpret his words so as to rescue them as economic analysis are doomed from the outset" (1987, 113).

This widely accepted feature of ancient thought should, it was then suggested, be understood as the product of some ancient Greek philosophical propensity to merge (or even submerge) economic life into political, social, or ethical behaviour. The concomitance of these elements in a functioning whole of society was thereby said to have masked, for the ancients, the presence of independently recognisable "economic" phenomena in everyday interactions. Finley actually went a little further, arguing that Aristotle "never pretended to examine the price mechanism or any other aspect of market exchange as it was practiced. . . . [H]e was offering a normative ethical analysis: much that went on in practice was unethical on his definition and therefore outside his discourse" (113; see also Finley 1989).

In place of economic principles, then, what is said to emerge in classical antiquity is something else—namely, political or moral philosophy. While it is true that later interpreters of the ancient world (notably Polanyi) discussed at length the nature of exchange in those societies, a consensus does appear to have emerged that holds that such characteristics were "embedded in social and political relationships and could therefore not be examined in isolation" (von Reden 1995, 2).[2]

Of course, no conventional wisdom is without its critics, and there were not a few of them on the question of how far one can discern an analysis of the economy in the writings of the ancients (see, for example, Lowry 1979). Xenophon's *Oeconomicus* has frequently provided the raw material for such endeavours, as has his *Cryopaedia*. In volume 1 of *Capital*, for example, Marx noted Xenophon's discussion of the division of labour in the *Cryopaedia*, and declared it to be as good as anything in Smith (1867, chap. 21, sec. 3). Others have claimed to have found the labour theory of value in Aristotle (see, for instance, Meikle 1979); still others allege to have glimpsed elements of neoclassical price theory (see, for example, Soudek 1952; Gordon 1964). John Ruskin found the other-regarding ethics of the ancients appealing—especially as an antidote to the "ethics" that he (and Thomas Carlyle) associated with utilitarian individualism. It is clear enough, then, that a wide range of conclusions might be drawn regarding the nature of ancient economic *theory*. Rather than therefore adding to these, something might be said about the ancients' understanding of economic *life*, by way of the Greek institution of the *oikos* (household).

In its history of being contrasted with its political counterpart, the polis, the independent claims of the oikos and its ties to another institution, the fledgling city economy, are often overlooked. This would seem to be an important omission, since both the household and city economies of ancient Greece comprised a nexus of relations between persons, determined by moral and political norms. In this ethical context, however, a fundamental distinction can be made between the household economy and the city economy, inasmuch as the former "stood as the natural economy," and "as such was contrasted to the market and the life of unlimited acquisition" (Booth 1993, 7). The Greek household formed the individual building block that all flows of exchange ultimately served: in that sense, the concept of the oikos was basically normative. Analogously, in the

[2] One only has to read a few pages of Polanyi's discussion of the principles of reciprocity and redistribution in *The Great Transformation* to see how far he himself recognised that identifiable economic regularities were at work.

Roman Empire, "the family was the basic social unit through which wealth and status were transmitted" (Garnsey and Saller 1987, 126).

The Greek attitude to the city economy and the acquisitive behaviour with which it was associated was sceptical. In both *Nicomachean Ethics* and the *Politics*, Aristotle held that the property of a household should sustain the life needs of its inhabitants as well as the leisure of its master. Acquisition was thus seen as an appropriate means to these two ends; but acquisition was no longer appropriate when it became an end in itself: "unlimited acquisition, whether for the sake of more wealth alone or . . . the satisfaction of insatiable pleasures, produces a slavish life" (Booth 1993, 51). Acquisitive behaviour was further criticised in that an individual became estranged from ties of *philia* (or mutuality) within their community in the process of accommodating their own self-interest. In essence, as Booth puts it, "the acquisitive life is . . . without a *polis*, because its purpose and specific object, wealth, knows no limits and therefore no community, and as such it is a threat to the community" (53).

Although the concepts of oikos and polis are typically regarded as distinct from one another, then, their fundamental similarity—that both are human communities controlled by rule and subjection—must not be overlooked. In both, as James Booth aptly noted, "rulership is essential," and "it is precisely the proper ranking of rulers over ruled that raises a composite, whether the soul, the household, or the city, above the level of a mere heap, an aggregate, and transforms it into an ordered whole" (40).

Aristotle pointed out that the successful operation of the individual household was not an end in itself but a single piece of a more complex economic puzzle. The self-sufficient behaviour to which each household aspires makes a mere reflection of the city's greater *political* goal of autarky, which one could say embodies the same economising principles as the oikos (albeit on a greater scale). Booth thus summarised it as follows: "However much political rule may differ from that exercised within the household, the two forms of community are united in that they represent ways in which human beings combine to secure for themselves a measure of material self-sufficiency—an answer, in other words, to the scarcity, the grim poverty, which is such a central part of the human condition" (37). In short, the ancients identified a tightly bound economic relationship between human activities in the domestic and political sphere. But does this suggest a priority of one form over the other? Can it be argued that for the Greeks, political life is teleologically prior or foundational to economic life? It might appear so, but we should not overlook other facets of ancient economic and cultural practice that complicate this Aristotelian perspective.

One of these practices is the use of money. Prior to the sixth century, in the period of greatest significance for the polis, the circulation of coin was limited, and it even appears that the Greeks actually had no single word for money sui generis (see von Reden 1995, 173).[3] Yet Aristotle did offer direct commentaries on the function of coinage in an economic transaction—some of which cast doubt on the popular idea that for the ancients, markets were embedded in the polis. These commentaries appear to have led Booth, in his interpretation of Aristotle, to see the polis and the market as *separate* but analogous structures: "both of those latter institutions make equal (the one through the common coin of citizenship, the other through the medium of money) what is unequal" (1993, 40). Furthermore, Sitta von Reden's discussion of Aristotle's works takes a similar stance on the separate functions of the market and the polis, using the representative symbolism of coinage to illustrate this distinction.

For Aristotle, it would thus seem that coinage had a different significance within and outside of the polis. Within the polis, money was seen as an artificial device that created and maintained relationships within the community by setting a uniform standard of value through which people might acquire what they needed. In the *Nicomachean Ethics*, for example, Aristotle wrote that "money has become by convention some kind of representative of demand; and this is why it has the name money (*nomisma*)—because it exists not by nature but by convention (*nomos*)" (2000, 1133 a30–34.1). Likewise, within the context of Roman imperial life under Augustus, coinage served a more propagandistic, political purpose. As Ronald Syme noted in *The Roman Revolution*, when a Roman citizen turned a coin in their palm, "he might meditate on the aspirations or the achievements of the government stamped in some concentrated phrase—*Libertatis P.R. Vindex, Civibus Servateis* or *Signis Receptis*" (2002, 469). Furthermore, Augustus's ultimate triumph, according to Syme, lay in his purported "freeing" of Rome from the tyranny of the consul Antonius, so much so that centuries later "when the phrase *Vindex Libertatis* appears on the coinage, it indicates armed usurpation . . . the removal of either a pretender or a tyrant" (155).

Yet the ancients also seem to have appreciated that the original function of coinage might have existed *outside* of the polis.[4] From their earliest use, as von Reden reminds us, coins facilitated trade between members of neighboring communities, who were not bound by the same political

---

[3] The term *nomisma* meant money, but that word had other common meanings and usages as well (current, regular, and conventional; hence the etymology of the modern term currency). The point is that there was no one word that meant money exclusively.

[4] This is not to say that money did not also have other crucial functions within the polis—not least those relating to the payment of taxes. When taxes are denominated in coin and taxpayers are required to discharge their liabilities in coin, then coinage and the polis become intimately connected. Still, to the extent that private exchanges predate taxes, even when a noncoinage circulating medium was in use, the polis and the market stand as distinctive, conceptually separable institutions.

and moral obligations as members of the same polis or political community. In the context of the intercity market, people were exchanging for commodities rather than for communal relationships. In the absence of communal obligations, exchange could exist as a channel of personal accumulation rather than the communal allocation of resources (von Reden 1995, 186). These two outcomes coexisted in the same economy, like two faces of the same coin, suggesting that the increased circulation of money in exchange for traded goods was somehow involved in the evolution of the market as a separate institution from the polis and thus not one necessarily grounded in political life.[5]

The symbolism of money and exchange seems to have permeated even the most sacred Greek traditions in familiar ways. For example, it was customary in ancient Greece to be buried with a coin under the tongue, as an incentive for the mythological figure Charon to transport the dead across the river Styx and into the underworld (Lowry 1998). This example might be regarded as an instance of economic life providing a foundational framework around which noncommercial aspects of life (if we can call death that) might be constructed.[6]

It would seem, then, that while political life importantly preceded and was foundational to economic life for the ancients, there was more to the story. When considered within certain cultural contexts, economic life sometimes seems to obtain a degree of autonomy and even precedence over politics. If we wish to see a less ambiguous claim for political life dictating the basis of economic life, however, we would have to move far from the ancients to a group of more genuinely economic thinkers of the early modern era: the mercantilists.[7]

THE STATE AND INTERNATIONAL TRADE: MERCANTILISM

What Comte de Mirabeau dubbed "mercantilism" was a rather diverse body of seventeenth-century opinion relating state power to international trade as well as the pursuit of state enrichment and aggrandizement to international trade. In the hands of some mercantilists, of course, it was more than this. Not a few of its architects were deeply concerned with

[5] There is evidence of other types of economic practice—in terms of active credit markets, taxation, and maritime loans—that could be examined or other thinkers who might be discussed, but here we only mean to draw attention to the complexities in the relationship of ancient economic and political life.

[6] For a complex look at coins as cultural and social as well as political signifiers in Greek thought, see Kurke (1999).

[7] We are not suggesting here that a relationship between economic and political life ceased to exist in the near millennium separating these two periods of thought but rather that in the interim, religious life might more accurately be said to have dictated both.

what we might call fiscal politics—linking economic life to the notion of maintaining the state in a condition of perpetual readiness for war. In these manifestations, the state was seen as the central actor, and the capacity of the state to raise revenue that could underwrite military activity was the crucial objective. Where this framework of ideas furnished the rationale for mercantilist policy, mercantilism embodied not just a general preference for "more gold" (national wealth) but also a specific preference for commercial (taxable) activities over private, decentralized market exchange.

In terms of the relation between economic and political life, however, the basic presuppositions of the mercantilist tendency were simple enough. To begin with, the accumulation of gold and silver bullion (or "treasure") served as both the definition of wealth and the explicit tool of economic expansion for purposes of political power. Second, the principal source of such treasure was international trade (see, for example, Mun 1664, 14). The balance of trade—or the "jealousy of trade," as Hume preferred to call it—functioned as an economic means for political ends. Both within and beyond the state, mercantilist doctrine required a sovereign capable of wielding such a tool with both political intent and political acumen in order to secure trade *imbalances* that favoured exports over imports (see Mun 1664, 8). Mercantilism, in this sense, was a classic zero-sum game in which trade was effectively to be conducted on a warlike footing and understood as politics by another means (see Mun 1664, 73).

It is worth noting that mercantilist states might be organised politically in any number of ways—as monarchies, commonwealths, or republics. But whatever their political form, they all placed a priority on fostering population growth in order to supply the personnel necessary for national defence and facilitate that increase in state capacity necessary to produce domestic products for trade. Economic life, in short, was to be conducted so as to serve political ends. Internally, the balance of "natural" wealth (the product of agriculture) to be consumed domestically along with artificial wealth (or tradable goods) was determined by the state, not the market. Mun's *England's Treasure by Forraign Trade* is exemplary of the fact that mercantilism could not be understood as a narrow theory of commerce or trade but rather as an artifact of seventeenth-century statecraft overriding competing religious as well as economic norms. Hence thrift, savings, and parsimony gathered their civic and moral force by virtue of their contribution to state power. At the same time, the human wants of subjects and labourers at subsistence—indeed of the nation generally—should be minimised.[8]

___

[8] Inequality among the orders of society, the minimising of the desire for *imported* luxury goods, and the utility of poverty of the labouring poor could all be justified via the interests of the state (Mun 1664, 73, 60).

The practical scope of the regulatory proposals of English mercantilists (like Mun) was far outstripped by those of their French counterparts (like Colbert). So much so that it was Colbert who drew the brunt of Smith's attack on mercantilism in the fourth book of the *Wealth of Nations*, replete with his insistence that mercantilist regulation should be seen for what it was:—not simply a nonsalutary economic policy but both a political assault on the liberty of subjects and an unjust favouritism accorded to one order of society at the expense of the rest (see Smith 1776, 4.8:660).

Other eighteenth-century Scottish political economists who took up mercantilist policies, such as the Jacobite sympathizer Steuart, adjusted the severity of the need to command the economy in the interest of the state, and placed a greater emphasis on the capacity of the statesman to secure a balance between "work and demand" in the economy.[9] He saw things quite differently from Smith. For Steuart, it was the function of an idealized statesman to ameliorate the negative effects of the spread of commercial relationships by controlling the pace of development through administered (regulated) prices and taxation (1767, 1:336, 276, 279). In this way, Steuart advocated a state-driven macroeconomic strategy designed to "counter the stagnation created by the hoarding of the rich" with the aim of turning that hoarding into productive investment.[10] This was seen, by Steuart, to be at once the route to greater liberty as well as greater security and equality. In a certain sense, then, Steuart's was a more mature mercantilism, where economic life was to be subjected to political control less for the purpose of preparedness for war than for securing economic ends per se.

Steuart's reliance on the political control and coordination of economic activity, internal and external, in his *Inquiry* drew sharp contemporary criticism, principally because it was held to lack practical efficacy. The same ends, it would soon be argued, could be secured by different means. And just as important, a larger attack on Steuart, launched both by his immediate contemporaries (Hume and Smith) as well as modern historians of economic thought, rested on the charge that he had failed to come to grips with any *systematic* understanding of the operation of markets[11]—an understanding that would provide an alternative picture of the

---

[9] "This happy state cannot be supported but by the care of the statesman; and when he is found negligent in the discharge of this part of his duty, the consequence is, that either the spirit of industry, which, it is supposed, has cost him much pains to cultivate, is extinguished, or the produce of it rises to so high a value, as to be out of reach of a multitude of purchasers" (Steuart 1767, 1:195).

[10] See Hutchison (1988, 342); compare Steuart (1767, 2:725).

[11] "Steuart's views on policy followed from his inability to discern, and therefore his unwillingness to rely on, the sufficiently rapid operation of self-adjusting mechanisms in the economies of his day, especially with regard to money and aggregate demand" (Hutchison 1988, 350).

relationship between economic and political life. That insight, in the form of the new language of political economy—namely, the language of the self-regulating market order, science, and unintended consequences—appeared within *economic* discourse in Smith's *Wealth of Nations*. It ushered in yet another understanding of the relationship between economic and political life.

CLASSICAL POLITICAL ECONOMY

With the advent of classical political economy in Scotland in the middle decades of the eighteenth century, especially in the hands of Hume and Smith, the understanding of the relationship between economic and political life was transformed. These writers began to contemplate the idea that forms of trade, or forms of market activity, might actually influence the parameters of government—and not the other way around, as it had been for the mercantilists. This shift in perspective had several distinctive features. It involved the recognition that an autonomous economic sphere was pregnant with normative and moral possibilities. A flourishing economy was desirable independently of its implications for either the state or the polity. This, in turn, went hand in hand with a decidedly individualist turn in classical thinking: the case for a system of "perfect liberty," whether in commercial, constitutional, or institutional arrangements, could now be made essentially (although as we shall see, not necessarily exclusively) in economic terms.

The classical economists raised the question of whether economic progress might of itself be the catalyst for political and constitutional reform. In their contributions, one witnesses the emergence of the idea that commerce, in its quintessentially modern form of the unhindered operation of a freely competitive market mechanism, occupied a position that was understood to have long-term significance for both the development and organisation of political life. One might almost say that Smith's remark that the nation owed its dinner to the self-interest of others, not to their benevolence (1776, 1.2:7)—a remark that had such profound consequences for the subsequent development of economic thought—had greater political import than he could possibly have imagined.

When Smith contrasted constitution making with the "science of the legislator," for which the principles of political economy were indispensable (4.2:468), as a cautious Scot, he had little to say about the former. But his biographer, Stewart, was soon to throw caution to the wind when, during the disturbances of the French Revolution, he argued that *all* that Smith was concerned with was "enlightening the policy of actual legislators" (1793, 55–56). This was an exaggeration to be sure, but not one without some basis in the position that Smith had taken up in the 1770s.

It is beyond debate that Smith believed that three liberties—the liberty of private property, the liberty of trade, and an expanding personal liberty—would go together.

If one turns to Hume, one encounters republican political commitments that were deeper and more explicit than anything to be found in Smith's support for British parliamentary sovereignty. In the *Idea of a Perfect Commonwealth*, Hume argued that with the development of commerce, the role of government could not be limited to securing the personal economic liberty of the individual but ultimately would have to satisfy advancing expectations for fuller participation in political life instead. U.S. constitution makers would later draw on Hume's preference for a government republican in form, but also expansive in its territory so as both to diffuse faction and reap those advantages of scale essential to economic growth.

It seems reasonable to conclude, then, that what one finds in Smith is not only that greater systematization of theoretical thinking about the market mechanism for which he is justly celebrated. One also finds Smith opening up the possibility that there exists a certain priority of economic life (now understood as commerce) over political life (now understood as government), without the complete reduction of either one as foundational to the other.

If this accurately captures the state in which the classical writers of late eighteenth-century Scotland had left the discussion, then when one moves on to the classical writers of the early decades of the nineteenth century, two developments of that earlier discussion appear on the stage. On the one hand, there were those writers whose assertions unfolded along more reductionist or foundational lines—rendering economic life the foundation of political life. On the other hand, there were those writers whose contentions pursued a theme of separability—rendering economic life (and political economy) independent of political life (and politics).

Along the first line of thought, the name of Ricardo inevitably comes to mind. Ricardo appears to have come close to, although perhaps without quite reaching, an understanding of politics as being exclusively contingent on the relations of economic life. His better-known arguments for parliamentary reform (1824a, 1824b), for example, are permeated with the idea that political organisation and political policy ought to be subservient to the needs of the economy—that the interests of *all* the participants in economic life should be represented in government. Even Malthus, whose writings did much to propagate the idea of a separation between the "science" of political economy and the "art" of government, did not seem hesitant to apply his understanding of economic life to questions of constitutional reform in his famous disputes with Ricardo on that subject.

But while Ricardo appears not to have seen any difficulty in reconciling his case for democratic reform with the often conflictual picture of economic life he had sketched, the socialist economists of the 1820s and 1830s took Ricardo's foundational inclinations a little further. Some of their number, like Thomas Hodgskin, went so far as to maintain that political reform could have no efficacy in Britain without a change to the system of private property. It would be Marx, in his critique of Ricardo, who would go on to produce the ultimate reductionist claim about political life.[12]

Along the second line of thought, where the theme of separability begins to appear, it is Mill's *On Liberty* that comes to mind. But there are even stronger examples in the classical literature where separability comes close to becoming a methodological principle. Much of Nassau Senior's methodological pronouncements, despite sharing certain tenets with those of Mill, were grounded on a separation between the domain of economics and that of politics in a manner that prefigures what would later appear more systematically with the neoclassical economists.

For Senior, the task of the economist was to unearth the "laws" or "principles" that governed economic life, to delineate their consequences and advise rather than direct politicians. Although Senior was more certain than Mill regarding the "truth" content of his economic principles (1827, 11), he stuck fast to his rule that while economic science might demonstrate the "true" means to particular ends, it did not speak to the question of establishing or determining what those ends should be. The latter, for Senior, was the exclusive preserve of the politician or statesman.

More recent economic thinkers, not classical in form but who believe themselves to be "Smithian" in inspiration, such as Hayek and Friedman, would deploy an account of the operation of the market mechanism to underpin their own particular visions of the best organisation of political life. In this sense, economic life would not be merely instrumental to politics but instead would be the very substance of it. It would not be just another rational input into the process of political decision making but rather the only way in which that process could be legitimately "free and democratic."

BEYOND THE CLASSICAL ECONOMISTS

Although the growing division within classical economics—between those theorists who saw economic life as foundational to political life, and those who saw the two as partially separable—is significant, it could

---

[12] The transition through Hegel is of considerable importance here. In Hegel's scheme of things, economic and political life are parts of a more expansive conception of human self-

not be said that economic life (in practice or theory) existed for them in total isolation from politics. Even in the work of Mill, where separability best characterises his discussions of individual liberty and distribution, it would hardly be accurate to claim that economic and political life were mutually exclusive for him, or that political life was of no theoretical interest to political economy. When the next generation of economists engaged in the project of constructing a "positive" economic science, however, they seem to have rendered this separation complete. For these writers, not only was economic analysis to be conducted, at its most general level, by treating political parameters as exogenous to the economic model but it was also to be conducted by taking the initial distribution of society's wealth (like individual "talents") as given.

This new generation of economists, whose work comprises the marginal revolution, framed the "economic problem" as the allocation of scarce resources among competing ends. Theirs was a formal model of exchange where free actors, independent of social or political context, sought to maximise their own utility given *any* initial distribution of social wealth. In this world of *abstract* economic life, "isolated exchange" as Carl Menger (1871) called it, political life and politics itself are intentionally excised from the model. It would be wrong to say that political life had thereby been reduced to economic life, but it would not be wrong to say that the same rational action activates both economic human beings and political ones in their separable spheres of activity.

It is not difficult to see how neoclassical economics was able to establish this way of looking at things. The neoclassical economists generalised and mathematically formalised the old Benthamite calculus of pleasure and pain. As Walras was to argue, only the "wants" of individuals and the constraints imposed on them by the scarcity of the "things" they wanted comprised the domain of that science (1874, 62). Practitioners of neoclassical theory, when accused of having thereby substituted a fictitious version of economic human beings for the purposes of economic theory, protested vigorously—but in vain. A good example was Marshall's reaction. In their science, he contended, economists "deal with man as he *is*: not with an abstract or 'economic' man; but a man of flesh and blood . . . who is largely influenced by egoistic motives in his business life . . . but who is neither above vanity and recklessness, nor below . . . sacrificing himself for the good of his family, his neighbors, or his country." Having said this, though, in the very next sentence, when he moved to economic science proper, Marshall conceded that in establishing "their work on a *scientific* basis," neoclassical economists were in fact "concerned chiefly

---

consciousness and reason—one in which the individual human being is mediated with the social whole through the family, economic life, and the state.

with those aspects of life in which the action of motive is so regular that it can be predicted, and the estimate of the motor-forces can be verified by results" (1890, 1.2.s.7: 22; emphasis added).

The removal of any institutional context follows immediately upon this redefinition. If the model of economic science is concerned with the relationship between abstract persons and things, institutional, cultural, and political contexts are irrelevant. That the model deals in the allegedly *universal* categories of "persons" and "things" is the very essence of their claim that economics enjoys the status of a science. The outcomes of the model emerge from the constrained maximising behaviour of *unitary* agents (even if they are sometimes misleadingly described as households or firms). Excluded, and necessarily so, from the model are any of those unique or historically specific entities that had been of relevance to earlier classical political economy—trade unions, banks, monopolies, and the very stuff of political controversy within public life. This move at once severed any connection that economic theory had to past historical circumstances, and permitted its conclusions to range freely over any and all market societies, regardless of their history.[13]

The prioritizing of exchange relations over production relations removed most of the regions of economic life in which politics and political struggles took place, putatively ensuring that economic theory was an "apolitical" enterprise. At the same time, this particular prioritization brought to the fore the subjective psychological conditions surrounding the consumption of commodities and reduced the significance of the objective social conditions of production.

Taking the initial distribution of society's wealth as given prior to exchange, and viewing "factor prices" as consequent on that original distribution (and equal to their marginal productivity), made factor prices the very embodiment of "fair" market prices. And while this may have introduced an implicit norm of justice for some, debate about the inequality in the *prior* distribution was not seen to be within the purview of the economic science, whatever economists might think about it as political individuals. Questions of efficiency were thus separated from questions of equity in a manner that has presented problems that continue to plague present-day economics.

By working with the model of isolated exchange at the most general theoretical level, and imagining it to characterise the essentials of eco-

---

[13] This is not to say that cultural, institutional, and political features could not, and did not, appear in neoclassical writings. They certainly could and did. The key point here, however, is that they appeared at a second (or subsequent) level of analysis, as imperfections or irregularities that modified the conclusions of the more general model when it was being applied to specific, real-world situations.

nomic life, considerable benefits accrued to the neoclassical approach, not least those facilitating its claim to universal applicability and scientific purity. Nevertheless, these did not come without their costs. This strategy had distanced the neoclassical *understanding* of economic life not only from the *concrete* world of economic life but from political life as well. To ameliorate the consequences of the former, an elaborate methodological structure was created to reconnect the abstract with the concrete manifestations of economic life. Marshall was the most ambitious in this regard. He introduced a number of methodological constructs designed to bridge this gap—such as the ceteris paribus argument, the distinction between the long run and the short run, the notion of partial equilibrium, representative firms, and the analysis of market failure.

Thus, all that is salient to concrete economic life appears as neither unimportant nor irrelevant but rather an "imperfection," a market "failure," an "externality," or a "deviation" from the norm. This kind of conceptual language, which cast much in concrete economic life as somehow pathological, had the effect of encouraging the propensity among neoclassical economists to view the world as in need of being reshaped according to the norm. Ironically, however, it was through this route that unexamined political commitments would sometimes be reintroduced into neoclassical reasoning. George Stigler first noticed this tendency when he observed that while the *"attitude"* of economists towards monopoly was "strongly influenced" by *"technical"* neoclassical price theory, their actual "support for pro competitive policies" was due instead "to the strong *virtues* [they] attach to competitive markets" (1982, 9; emphasis added).[14] It would appear that John Bates Clark's famous interventions in the U.S. antitrust debates in the last decade of the nineteenth century strongly advocating greater competition were marked by just this propensity.

As to the separation of abstract economic life from political life, the neoclassical economists encountered yet another problem relating to unexamined political commitments—a problem that interestingly, Bentham thought (probably wrongly) had plagued Smith. In his *Writings on the Poor Laws*, Bentham all but accuses Smith of failing to distinguish between the *necessity* of what might be termed the "hand of government" in practical affairs and the role of an "invisible hand" in the systematic account of the operation of the market—a charge that would later be levelled directly against the neoclassical economists by Keynes (Bentham 2001). Paradoxically, where Bentham had thought that the principle of

[14] This studied attitude to the relation between abstract neoclassical theory and practical policy led Stigler to lament that in the area of monopoly, no contemporary (vide neoclassical) economist had "any professional knowledge on which to base recommendations which should carry weight with a skeptical legislator" (1982, 6).

utility would serve to connect economic theory to the visible "hand of the legislator" (and so solve the problem he saw in Smith), the neoclassical economists generalised that utilitarian calculus *within* the model of isolated exchange in a way that, if anything, made the disconnect a permanent part of their theory. This intrinsic gap between theory and practice only further strengthened the neoclassical economists' general presumption favouring their conception of the invisible hand.[15]

But there is one last area of interest that should not be passed over in any discussion of the relationship of economic theory to economic and political life: namely, contemporary constitutional economics. This approach represents a halfway house between the view of the early classical writers (that economic and political life were interdependent) and that of the neoclassical writers (that economic and political life were separable). It also brings into sharper relief how one might think about the relationship between that theoretical actor, homo economicus, and any particular political or legislative policy. James Buchanan has, in fact, claimed that constitutional economics "is more closely related to the work of Adam Smith and the classical economists than its modern 'non-constitutional' counterpart" in "orthodox" (neoclassical) economics (1989, 79).

The focus of constitutional economics, as Buchanan has described it, is to "explain the working properties of alternative sets of legal-institutional-constitutional rules that constrain the choices and activities of economic and political agents, the rules that define the framework within which the ordinary choices of economic and political agents are made" (79). He contrasts this with standard neoclassical analysis that, he holds, "attempts to explain the choices made by economic agents, their interactions with one another, and the results of those interactions, *within* the existing legal-institutional-constitutional structure of the polity" (80; emphasis added). Yet it should be noted that in being understood to operate at a "higher level" than orthodox neoclassical economics—precisely because it concerns itself with alternative sets of higher-order rules—constitutional economics, no less than its neoclassical counterpart, claims to have "nothing to offer by way of policy advice to political agents who act *within* defined rules" (80; emphasis added).[16]

It is also on this account that Buchanan derives a more direct connection between the field of constitutional economics and the classical project

---

[15] It is through this route that the idea that if one does not know what to do, one should do nothing (a familiar theme of Hayek) entered into economics. There is thus less in Smith than in Bentham's caricature of him to support this view.

[16] It might be noted that Buchanan also sees an obvious aim of classical economics as offering an explanation of how markets operate absent any extensive political direction, by which he means governmental direction. It is in this way that he sees the neoclassical and classical projects to be related.

of Smith. He characterises Smith as a systematizer whose project in the *Wealth of Nations* was to compare alternative institutional structures. That is, Smith modelled "the working properties of a non-politicized economy, which did not exist in reality," and compared that model to a "highly politicized" one that did—mercantilism.[17] Buchanan argues that Smith's project of "comparing alternative institutional structures, alternative sets of constraints within which economic agents make choices," was lost in the late nineteenth and first half of the twentieth century (see 80–81). Under these conditions, the historical error of identifying any success or failure *within* a particular structure of constraints (for example, whether the failures of laissez-faire or command economies) persisted. The result was that when set against idealized criteria, such as "efficiency" and "justice," markets failed as did politics (81). This tournament of finger-pointing could only be remedied, according to Buchanan, by a return to Smith's project, which he identifies as constitutional political economy, suitably updated of course in a modified language of public choice.[18]

As a founder of constitutional economics as it emerged in the 1970s, Buchanan has been careful not to claim too much for its programme. Its ideological preferences for liberty, peace, and prosperity are openly expressed. The achievement of these ends requires attention to "the ultimate selection of a set of constraining rules within which ordinary social interaction takes place." Still, what is of interest here is that Buchanan sees the analysis of this set of constitutional rules—which presumably means the laws of both the market and politics—as constitutional *economics*. This choice implies an identity between economic and political decision making—homo economicus and *homo politicus* become one and the same.

This should not be at all surprising, since Buchanan claims that constitutional economics shares a central methodological presumption with both classical and neoclassical economics: that "only individuals choose and act. Collectivities as such neither choose nor act, and analysis that proceeds as if they do is not within the accepted scientific canon" (83). The additional and distinct methodological principle of homo economicus he draws explicitly from Hume's remark in *Of the Independency of Parliament* that "in constraining any system of government, and fixing

---

[17] This, in essence, is what Mill said in his own *Political Economy* about the socialist critique of capitalism: that it compared the advantages of an abstract theory with the problems of an actual capitalism.

[18] As it emerged from public choice theory, Buchanan claims that the focus of constitutional political economy is on "predictive models of political interactions" (82). Yet Buchanan also claims that constitutional political economy is broader than public choice (he calls it more "imperialistic") in its focus on the "comprehensive structure of political rules" and "predictive models of interaction" (82).

the several checks and controls of the constitution, each man ought to be supposed a knave, and to have no other end, in all his actions, than private interest" (1752b, 117–18).

If one continues reading this passage, though, it can be seen that this opening statement is rhetorical rather than didactic, and the politics that Hume articulates is one of factional allegiance and group dynamics rather than privately interested individual decision makers. The passage may be quoted in full:

> It appears somewhat strange, that a maxim should be true in *politics*, which is false in *fact*. But to satisfy us on this head, we may consider, that men are generally more honest in their private than in their public capacity, and will go to greater lengths to serve a party, than when their own private interest is alone concerned. Honour is a great check upon mankind: But where a considerable body of men act together, this check is, in a great measure, removed; since a man is sure to be approved of by his own party, for what promotes the common interest; and he soon learns to despise the clamours of adversaries. To which we may add, that every court or senate is determined by the greater number of voices; so that, if self-interest influences only the majority, (as it will always do) the whole senate follows the allurements of this separate interest, and acts as if it contained not one member, who had any regard to public interest and liberty. (43)

Despite recognising the importance of constitutional rules and political structures in a way that the neoclassical economists had not, however, some of the earlier problems persist. If political life has not been set to one side, then its terrain appears to have been colonised by homo economicus in terms of both the character and the content of decision making. It would appear that constitutional economics illustrates just how difficult it is to escape from the separability that the neoclassical economics introduced in the late nineteenth century.

Chapter Five

THE ECONOMIC MACHINE
AND THE INVISIBLE HAND

Who wonders at the machinery of the opera-house
who has once been admitted behind the scenes?
—Adam Smith, *History of Astronomy*

Human society, when we contemplate it in a certain
abstract and philosophical light, appears like a great,
an immense machine.
—Adam Smith, *Moral Sentiments*

ROBERT BOYLE, justly famous for many things, once likened the eye of a
fly to an ingeniously produced machine. In saying this, although perhaps
without knowing it, he had given expression to a worldview that by then,
had come to be shared by the scientific community. It was a worldview
that had developed and flourished in the works of some of the greatest
minds of the age. Theirs are names to conjure with: Copernicus, Kepler,
Galileo, Descartes, Huygens, Leibniz, and Newton. It was a simple and
powerful worldview—namely, that the varied phenomena of nature were
linked and organised by discoverable common forces, and that the whole
might be thought of as system resembling a machine. Newton famously
summed it all up with an analogy about clocks.[1] On such presuppositions,
classical mechanics was perfected.

Looking back, it is clear enough now that it was on quite similar presuppositions and often with an explicit acknowledgment of the achievements of Newtonian mechanics that classical political economy was constructed. If the movement of objects in the physical world was governed
by hidden regularities, and if that world might be imagined as working
rather like a machine, it did not take long for political economists to begin
to explore the inner workings of the social world using a similar analogy.
What began with Smith's celebrated references to Newton's principle of
gravitation in his analysis of natural prices was echoed in John Stuart

---

[1] Descartes had gone so far as to suggest that a good training for spotting the hidden
mechanisms at work behind natural phenomena was to have had some practical experience
of constructing automatons.

Mill's pronouncements about the scope and method of political economy nearly a century later.

That a science of political economy that might be built along lines similar to those of classical mechanics was the immediate product of an Enlightenment project—and both its original architects and subsequent developers were all quite self-consciously engaged in that project. To the extent that they were, it is safe to say that the foundation of political economy involved a purposeful enterprise and that it was not just happenstance. That foundation was contrived and conducted by a well-defined group of eighteenth-century writers in Scotland and France.

The Economic Machine

The idea that society was governed by the operation of certain forces, more or less regular in their operation (and more or less objective), and that acted automatically to produce determinate outcomes, was among the more novel inventions of eighteenth-century political economy. It created the speculative space for a *general* account of the operation of the market mechanism, rather than piecemeal or *particular* accounts of isolated economic phenomena. This train of thought entailed two closely related presuppositions.

The first was that something actually existed that one might properly call the market mechanism. As Smith put it when speaking about the physical universe, the "co-existent parts of the universe, are exactly fitted to one another, and all contribute to compose one immense and connected system" (1759, 7.2:1.37).

The second was the idea that philosophical investigation should proceed by understanding a distinction between appearance and reality. To see the system clearly, to understand it rightly, one must look beyond mere appearances that only serve to obscure the real picture. The task of the political economist was, so to speak, to reveal what otherwise might have remained hidden. Smith was quite insistent on this philosophical claim:

> Nature, after the largest experience common observation can acquire, seems to abound with events which appear solitary and incoherent with all that go before them . . . by representing the invisible chains which bind together all these disjointed objects, [philosophy] endeavours to introduce order into this chaos of jarring and discordant appearances. (1750, 46)

The point was put with equal force by the physiocratic philosopher Pierre-Paul Mercier de la Riviere when he asserted that "knowledge permits us to penetrate beneath the surface of things" (1767, 99). In fact, this distinction between appearance and reality was essential to the whole foundation enterprise of these early economic thinkers.[2]

There is an important sense in which it can be said that when Smith and the physiocrats sponsored the introduction of these ideas, the mechanical analogy that Newton had deployed to such great effect in the study of nature had at length found its way into the study of economic society.

The mechanization of the world picture, in both its natural and social dimensions, was thereby completed.[3] The metaphor through which this world picture was transmitted to subsequent generations of economists was that of the economic machine. The introduction of the economic machine into economic thinking transformed the landscape of political economy just as decisively as the introduction of machine production transformed the landscape of the actual economy.[4] Moreover, the introduction of the notion of the economic machine into the discourse of political economy went hand in hand with the articulation of two other conceptual tools: a definition of the market economy, and a distinction between regular and irregular modes of operation of the economic machine.

Smith's understanding of commercial society was, at one level, obvious enough: market exchange. But one needs to be rather more precise than this. Strictly speaking, the presence of socially organised exchange (markets in the broadest sense) does not seem to be the key characteristic of what the classical political economists had in mind when they spoke of modern commercial or market exchange. Socially organised exchange of one kind or another appears to have been a fairly common feature of most human societies throughout much of human history. Wherever it occurs, exchange is an institutionally embedded activity of individuals or groups of individuals (see Polanyi 1944). It uniformly involves something one might call a market, as fairs, trading places, cultural celebrations or

---

[2] Smith speaks of Ptolemy as having been first to distinguish between "the real and apparent motion of the heavenly bodies" (*Astronomy*, 1750, 59–60). In the *Wealth of Nations*, think of Smith's discussion of real and nominal price. The sources of this kind of claim are many: the ancients, the Bible (veils of ignorance), and Newtonian mechanics.

[3] We have borrowed this terminology from that classic work in the history of science written by Eduard Dijksterhuis (1959).

[4] The trope (of likening the economy to a machine) was deployed in the name of working a scientific revolution in economics. The basis of this revolution in thinking about the economy was to be rational argument. Actual machines were deployed in the name of an industrial revolution in production. The basis of this revolution in economic activity was the rational organisation of production. Economy in thought (rationality) also seems to be analogous to the idea of the economy in production that was achieved by machines (via rationalisation). This eighteenth-century analogy persists to the present day; one still encounters it in phrases like "price mechanism" and "market mechanism."

ceremonies, and bazaars are all markets where exchange of one kind or another takes place.

The common feature of such institutionally mediated exchange is, of course, that it functions to ensure that society's material products are distributed between the members (individuals and groups) of that society in such a manner as to underwrite the continuance of the given or existing relations of social life that define the society in question. Gift exchange is a good example of this.

Market exchange in commercial society also does this, but how markets preserve the organisation of social production is the key to understanding their operation. A market economy is a generalised system of production, distribution, and exchange organised through markets. Markets exist not only for all commodities (including capital goods or produced means of production) but also for labour (and land).[5] Thus, Smith speaks of "every improved society" as being one where land "has all become private property" and capital "has accumulated in the hands of particular persons" (1776, 1.6:67–68). It is especially worthwhile to note Smith's remark that "the accumulation of stock must, in the nature of things, be previous to the division of labour" (2:277). As Marx would later put it, this primitive accumulation of capital represented nothing other than the transformation of human labour into a commodity.

This brings us to the distinction between persistent forces and those fitful and irregular ones of a more temporary nature. In modern jargon, the same idea is captured in the familiar distinction between the long run and the short run. On this point, there is no better place to start than with Smith:

> The natural price . . . is, as it were, the central price, to which the prices of all commodities are continually gravitating. Different accidents may sometimes keep them suspended a good deal above it, and sometimes force them down even somewhat below it. But whatever may be the obstacles which hinder them from settling in this centre of repose and continuance, they are constantly tending towards it. (1.7:75)

But what keeps market prices continually gravitating towards their natural level, as Smith put it? In answering this question, Smith introduced

---

[5] It would be misleading simply to call this system "the institution of private property" (as John Stuart Mill and Walras would subsequently do) without further elaboration. For that would fail to record what was new and distinctive about the *social* character of the régime of private property. Like exchange, there had always been private property but there had not always been capitalism. Forms of property relations vary. Of course, different definitions of "class" emerge from each here—contrast Mill (and later Max Weber) with Marx.

another conceptual innovation that would enable him to define quite pre-cisely an abstract object of analysis.[6]

Free Competition, Self-Interest, and Rational Action

It was one thing to argue that market economies were governed by the working of certain systematic and persistent forces, more or less regular in their operation. It was quite another to go on to recognise (and spell out) what those forces might actually be. One might even go so far as to assert (as John Stuart Mill did much later) that it is on the concept of competition that any specific claim that political economy might have to scientific status ultimately rests:

> Only through the principle of competition has political economy any preten-sion to the character of a science. So far as rents, profits, wages, prices, are determined by competition, laws may be assigned to them. Assume competi-tion to be their exclusive regulator, and principles of broad generality and scientific precision may be laid down, according to which they will be regu-lated. (Mill 1871, 2.4.1:147)

According to Smith, the economic machine was set in motion, so to speak, by the forces of competition. The force of competition is a ubiquitous feature of market economies. In fact, it is the motor that drives economic variables towards their natural levels.

The working of free competition, then, or "perfect liberty in commer-cial relations" as Smith called it, was essential for the attainment (on aver-age, over the long run) of natural prices, and thus for the smooth and effective operation of the economic machine. If we leave aside for the present the problem of monopoly, it is worth observing that free competi-tion did not require a particular market structure to be in place, as was to become the case, for example, with the assumption of perfect competition required by Marshall and other later nineteenth-century neoclassical writ-ers when they spoke of long-run normal prices. Instead, in this eighteenth-century context, perfect liberty in commercial relations appears to have referred to the absence of state regulation (or other interference) in those commercial transactions (absent the granting of monopoly privileges)

---

[6] For the present, we are concerned only with the methodological status and conceptual content of the idea of "natural prices." We are not concerned with the *theory* that was deployed to explain their magnitude. On that subject, the labour theory of value takes on central importance. The issues for the transformation of political economy and politics that hinge on the development as well as criticism of the labour theory of value will be the subject of later chapters.

where individuals were seeking to place their accumulated capital to the most advantage. If one thinks of this in more modern terminology for the moment, this is equivalent to saying that no one-to-one mapping between the degree of competition and the structure of the market (or between the degree of competition and the number of firms in the market) seems to have been present in Smith's mind when he first articulated this central organising principle.

The next point to mention in the present context is the idea that aggregate social outcomes were at once the product of the action of individual interests and yet not necessarily the same as those intended by individual actors. As Mirabeau put it, "[The] whole magic of well-ordered society is that each man works for others, while believing that he is working only for himself" (1763, 70). As Smith remarked a decade or so later, "It is not from the benevolence of the butcher, the brewer, or the baker, that we expect our dinner, but from their regard to their own interest" (1776, 1.2:26–27). The same idea gained expression in the *Wealth of Nations* again and again: "A revolution of the greatest importance to the public happiness, was in this manner brought about by two different orders of people, who had not the least intention to serve the public" (3.4:422).

Or elsewhere:

> Every individual is continually exerting himself to find out the most advantageous employment for whatever capital he can command. It is his own advantage, indeed, and not that of society, which he has in view. But the study of his own advantage naturally, or rather necessarily leads him to prefer that employment which is most advantageous to society. (4.2:454)

> [An individual] neither intends to promote the public interest, nor knows how much he is promoting it. By preferring the support of domestic industry to that of foreign industry, he intends only his own security; and by directing that industry in such a manner as its produce may be of the greatest value, he intends only his own gain, and he is in this, as in many other cases, led by an invisible hand to promote an end which is no part of his intention. (4.2:456)

But one should not confuse this general idea of unintended consequences with the idea of either "unforeseen" consequences (as regrettably is often done) or that the outcomes that tended to be produced by the market mechanism were uniformly to the good. That latter leap in particular, as some of the above passages well illustrate, depends on adding to the general idea that outcomes of individual actions might be independent of the wills of human beings—a theory of economic functioning.[7]

---

[7] It is also important to distinguish the idea of unintended consequences from the idea that the economic machine operated "independent of men's wills." Some remarks on con-

Of course, the problem of understanding the springs to action occupied much scholarly and speculative attention in the eighteenth century. The great ethical debates of that century took place between the advocates of the need to inculcate a disinterested spirit of civic or public virtue in order to ensure the orderly conduct of public affairs, and those who sought to show that self-interested action was all that was required. Moral philosophy, as it was called at the time, was almost exclusively concerned with charting this terrain. Smith's *Theory of Moral Sentiments* can, in a certain sense at least, be understood as an attempt to recapture the moral high ground for self-interested action that had been given up by the likes of Mandeville and Hume a little earlier.

The related question in political economy at that same time was how interests were formed, and in particular, whether they stemmed from something called "human nature" or had some other basis in the social circumstances in which individuals conducted their daily lives. As Smith said about the division of labour, "It is the necessary, though very slow and gradual, consequence of a certain propensity in human nature . . . the propensity to truck, barter, and exchange one thing for another" (1776, 1.2:25).

Whatever its source, the rational character of action based on interest was a key element of Smith's argument. By rational, he appears to have meant that calm, calculated, self-conscious adaptation of action in the pursuit of those interests (whatever their origin). In Smith, this idea enters the stage in the "prudent" person. This persona (this modern self) appears first in *Moral Sentiments*:

> The prudent man always *studies seriously* and earnestly to understand whatever he professes to understand. . . . In the *steadiness* of his industry and frugality, in his *steadily* sacrificing the ease and enjoyment of the present moment for the probable expectation of the still greater ease and enjoyment of a more distant but more lasting period of time, the prudent man is always both supported and rewarded by the entire of the impartial spectator. . . . [P]rudence, when carried to the highest degree of perfection, necessarily supposes the art, the *talent*, and the habit or disposition of acting with the most perfect *propriety* in every possible circumstance and situation. (1759, 213–16; emphasis added)

Later, in the *Wealth of Nations* we encounter the "frugal" man: "The principle which prompts [the frugal man] to save, is the desire of bettering our condition, a desire which, though generally *calm and dispassionate,*

---

tracts in Hume and Smith illustrate this; but François Quesnay says it most distinctively: "[Price] is far from being . . . a value which is established by agreement between the contracting parties" (1765, 90).

comes with us from the womb, and never leaves us till we go into the grave" (1776, 341; emphasis added). A few pages further on, Smith speaks of the "*uniform, constant,* and *uninterrupted* effort of every man to better his condition" (343; emphasis added). Finally, even in the famous invisible hand passage, the idea of the rational pursuit of interest by individuals is everywhere apparent: "Every individual is *continually exerting* himself to find out the most advantageous employment for whatever capital he can command. It is his own advantage . . . which he has in view. But the *study* of his own advantage naturally leads him" (454; emphasis added). There will be cause to return to the normative and economic consequences of such actions later. For the present, it is necessary only to stress their rational character—namely, the supposition of the *systematic adjustment* of means to ends by individuals engaged in the business of making a living.[8]

Systematic Adjustment, Natural Conditions, and "Gravitation"

Economists today tend to speak of the systematic adjustment brought about by the market mechanism as a tendency towards equilibrium. Indeed, equilibrium is one of those concepts that could scarcely be more central to economic theory. From what appears to have been the first use of the term in economics by Steuart in 1769, down to the present day, equilibrium analysis (together with its derivative, disequilibrium analysis) has been the foundation on which economic theory has been able to build up its not inconsiderable claims to "scientific" status. Yet despite the persistent use of the concept by economists for over two hundred years, its meaning and role has undergone some quite profound modifications over that period.

At the most elementary level, the term equilibrium is spoken about in a number of ways. It may be regarded as a "balance of forces," as it is, for example, when used to describe the familiar idea of a balance between the forces of demand and supply. Or it can be taken to signify a point from which there is no endogenous "tendency to change"; stationary or steady states exhibit this kind of property. It may also be thought of as that outcome that any given economic process might be said to be "tending towards," however, as in the idea that competitive processes tend to pro-

---

[8] For an interesting argument to the effect that there might be differing conceptions of agency at work in Smith's *Moral Sentiments* and his *Wealth of Nations*, see Brown (1991, 1994, 2008).

duce determinate outcomes. It is in this last guise that the concept seems first to have been applied in economic theory.

Equilibrium is, as Smith might have put it (though he did not use the term), the centre of gravitation of the economic system; it is that configuration of values (relative prices) towards which all economic magnitudes are continually tending to conform.

There are two properties embodied in this original conception, and one that is not, which when taken into account begin to impart to it a rather more precise meaning and a well-defined methodological status. Into the first group of properties enters the formal definition of "equilibrium conditions" and the argument for taking these to be a useful object of analysis. Into the second enters the question of the normative characteristics of these conditions.

There are few better or more appropriate places to isolate the first two properties of equilibrium in this original sense than in chapter 7 of the first book of Smith's *Wealth of Nations*. The assertion there consists of two steps. The first is to define "natural conditions":

> There is in every society . . . an ordinary or average rate of both wages and profits. . . . When the price of any commodity is neither more nor less than what is sufficient to pay . . . the wages of the labour and the profits of the stock employed . . . according to their natural rates, the commodity is then sold for what may be called its natural price. (1776, 72)

The key point here is that natural conditions (read: equilibrium conditions) are associated with a general rate of profit—that is, uniformity in the returns to capital invested in different lines of production under existing best-practice techniques. In the language of the day, this property was thought to be characteristic of the outcome of the operation of the process of "free competition."

The second step in the argument captures the analytical status to be assigned to natural conditions. As we have seen, the natural price was "the central price, to which the prices of all commodities are continually gravitating" (75). This particular "tendency towards equilibrium" was held to be operative in the *actual* economic system at any given time. It is not to be confused with the familiar question concerning the stability of competitive equilibrium in modern analysis. There the question about convergence to equilibrium is posed in some *hypothetical* state of the world where none but the most purely competitive environment is held to prevail. It is also essential to observe that in defining natural conditions in this fashion, nothing has yet been said (nor need it be said) about the forces that act to determine the natural rates of wages and profits, or the natural prices of commodities.

Natural conditions so defined and conceived are the formal expression of the idea that certain systematic or persistent forces, regular in their operation, are at work in the economic system. Smith's earlier idea, that "the co-existent parts of the universe . . . contribute to compose one immense and connected system" (1759, 7.2:289), is translated in this later formulation into an analytical device capable of generating conclusions with a claim to general (as opposed to a particular or special) validity. These general conclusions were customarily referred to as "statements of tendency," "laws," or "principles" in the economic literature of the eighteenth and nineteenth centuries. This neither implied that these general tendencies were swift in their operation nor that they were subject at any time to interference from other obstacles. Like sea level, natural conditions had an unambiguous meaning, even if they were subject to innumerable crosscurrents.

To put it another way, the distinction between general and special cases (like its counterpart, the distinction between equilibrium and disequilibrium) refers neither to the immediate practical relevance of these kinds of cases to actual market conditions, nor to the prevalence, frequency, or probability of their occurrence. In fact, as far as simple observation is concerned, it might well be that special cases would be the order of the day. John Stuart Mill expressed this idea especially clearly when he held that the conclusions of economic theory are only applicable "in the *abstract*"; that is, "they are only true under certain suppositions, in which none but general causes—causes common to the *whole class* of cases under consideration—are taken into account" (1836, 144–45).

To unearth these regularities, one had to enquire behind the scenes, so to speak, to reveal what otherwise might remain hidden. In short, equilibrium, to revert to the modern terminology for a moment, became the central organising category around which economic theory was to be constructed. It is no accident that the formal introduction of the concept into economics is associated with those very writers whose names are closely connected with the foundation of "economic science." It could even be argued that its introduction marks the foundation of the discipline itself, since its appearance divides quite neatly the subsequent literature from the many analyses of individual problems that dominated prior to Smith and the physiocrats.

Ricardo later spoke of fixing his "whole attention on the permanent state of things" that follows from given changes, excluding for the purposes of general analysis "accidental and temporary deviations" (1821, 88). Marshall, though substituting the terminology of "long-run normal conditions" for the older natural conditions, excluded from this category results on which "accidents of the moment exert a preponderating influence" (1890, vii).[9] Not only was the status of equilibrium as the centre of gravitation of the system (the benchmark case, so to speak) preserved but it was defined in the manner of Smith as well.

From a historical point of view, the novelty of the arguments introduced in the eighteenth century by Smith and the physiocrats is not their recognition that there might be situations that could be described as natural but rather that they associated these conditions with the outcome of a specific process common to market economies (free competition) and utilised them in the construction of a general economic analysis of market society. Earlier applications of "natural order" arguments were little more than normative pronouncements about some existing or possible state of society. They certainly abstained from making "scientific" use of the idea of systematic tendencies, even if it may have been involved. This is particularly apparent in the case of the natural law philosophers, but is also true of thinkers such as Locke and Hobbes. Even Hume, who for all intents and purposes had in his possession many elements of Smith's position, was not prepared to admit that thinking in terms of regularities, however useful it might prove to be in dispelling theological and other obfuscations (and thus in advancing "human understanding"), was anything more than a convenient and satisfying way of thinking. The question as to whether the social and economic world was actually governed by such regularities, so central to Smith and the physiocrats, simply did not concern Hume.

Yet the earlier normative connotations of ideas like natural conditions, natural order, and the like quite rapidly disappeared when the terminology was appropriated by economic theory. Nothing was good simply by virtue of its being natural. This, of course, is not to say that once the theoretical analysis of the natural tendencies operating in market economies had been completed, and the outcomes of the competitive process isolated in the abstract, an individual theorist might not at that stage wish to draw some conclusions about the desirability of its results—a normative claim, so to speak. But such statements are not inherent to the concept of equilibrium; they are value judgments about the characteristics of its outcomes.

Contrary to a view sometimes expressed, even Smith's use of deistic analogies and metaphors in the *Theory of Moral Sentiments*, in which we

[9] It is worth noting that on this matter, later neoclassical writers followed suit. John Bates Clark, for instance, held that "natural or normal" values are those to which "in the long run, market values tend to conform" (1899, 16)—and Jevons, Walras, Eugen von Böhm-Bawerk, and Knut Wicksell had all adopted the same procedure. The primary theoretical object of all these writers was to explain that situation characterised by a uniform rate of profit on the supply price of capital invested in different lines of production.

read about God as the creator of the "great machine of the universe" and encounter the invisible hand, is no more than the extraneous window dressing that surrounds a well-defined *theoretical* argument based on the operation of the so-called sympathy mechanism. As W. E. Johnson noted when writing for the original edition of Palgrave's *Dictionary*, "The confusion between scientific law and ethical law no longer prevails," and "the term normal has replaced the older word natural"—to be understood by this terminology as "something which presents a certain empirical uniformity or regularity" (1899, 139).

While natural conditions or long-run normal conditions represent the original concept of equilibrium utilised in economic theory, Mill's *Political Economy* seems to have been the source from which the word equilibrium gained widespread currency. More significant, however, is the fact that in Mill's hands, the meaning and status of the concept undergoes a modification. While maintaining the idea of equilibrium as a long-period position, Mill introduces the notion that the equilibrium theory is essentially "static." The relevant remarks appear at the beginning of the fourth book: "We have to consider the economical condition of mankind as liable to change . . . thereby adding a theory of motion to our theory of equilibrium—the Dynamics of political economy to the Statics" (1871, 4.1:421). Since Mill retained the basic category of "natural and normal conditions," his claim had the effect of adding a property to the list of those associated with the concept of equilibrium. Over the question of whether this additional property was necessary to the concept of equilibrium, however, there was to be less uniformity of opinion. Indeed, this matter gave rise to a debate in which almost all theorists of any repute became contributors at one time or another (until at least the 1930s). The problem was a simple one: are natural or long-period normal conditions the same thing as the "famous fiction" of the stationary or steady state. Much hinged on the answer; a "yes" would have limited the application of equilibrium to an imaginary stationary society in which no one conducts the daily business of life. In the final analysis, the answer seems to have depended rather more on the explanation given for the determination of equilibrium values than on the concept of equilibrium proper.[10]

It seems to be the case that the status of equilibrium in economic analysis has been transformed quite fundamentally since its introduction in the late eighteenth century. From being based on the idea that market societies were governed by certain systematic forces, more or less regular in their operation in different places and at different times, it now seems to be

---

[10] It was not until the 1930s that the issue seems to have been resolved to the general satisfaction of the profession. But then its resolution required the introduction of a new definition of equilibrium.

based on the opinion that nothing essential is hidden behind the many and varied situations in which market economies might actually find themselves. In fact, it appears that these many cases are to be thought of as being more or less singular from the point of view of modern theory. From being the central organising category around which the whole of economic theory was constructed, and therefore the ultimate basis on which its practical application was premised, equilibrium has become in certain circles a category with no meaning independent of the exact specification of the initial conditions for *any* model. Instead of being thought of as furnishing a theory applicable, as Mill would have said, to the whole class of cases under consideration, it is increasingly being regarded by theorists as the solution concept relevant to a particular model, applicable at best to an extremely limited number of cases.

Although the plethora of equilibrium models with which most theorists now deal are technically more sophisticated than has ever been the case, modern opinion is not a little reminiscent of the state of affairs in economics prior to the advent of its systematic study in the hands of Smith and the physiocrats. Yet to what extent this represents a measure of progress will have to await the judgment that is handed down in the future by those who require of economics something as simple, though elusive, as a few tolerably satisfactory solutions to the problems that confront modern market economies.

THE INVISIBLE HAND

No single aspect of Smith's writing attracted more attention and commentary in the twentieth century than the invisible hand.[11] It has been presented by some economists as his most famous dictum, christened by Paul Samuelson as "the invisible hand theorem," and said by Kenneth Arrow and Frank Hahn to be "the most intellectually important contribution economic thought has made to the general understanding of social processes" (1971, 1). Philosophers such as Niklas Luhmann and Robert Nozick have subjected its philosophical origins and implications to analysis. Nor has it lacked critics. On both sides, however, there remains considerable disagreement as to the significance to be attached to a metaphor mentioned only three times in the body of Smith's work.

It has been suggested, for example, that Smith was less than serious in his use of the metaphor, and that his reference to the invisible hand may

---

[11] See Stefan Andriopoulos, who suggests that it was "not before the first decades of this century that the 'invisible hand' was assigned the status of 'very often quoted' or 'celebrated' in the histories of economic thought" (1999, 751–52).

be at best equivocal—by turns a trope, a "mildly ironic joke," or also a serious and nonironic comment on the idea of order without design (Rothschild 2001a, 116, 135). One reason to think that Smith dismissed any serious consideration of an invisible hand principle or theorem is his understanding of the weight that should be attached to the intentions of individual agents (ibid., 123). Yet to suggest that Smith *could not* have used the metaphor seriously *because* to do so would have placed him in conflict with several of his "most profound convictions about individual sentiments, individual responsibility, and the intentions of individual merchants" (ibid., 136) would seem to solve a puzzle by dismissing it.[12] To note Smith's opposition to the Stoical idea of the futility of life, for example, does not necessarily imply a belief that through intention, people could do all things. Nor would it justify the claim that the market mechanism would best be understood as achieving the intentions entertained by the actors in it. Indeed, it is not perhaps "un-Smithian" (ibid., 134) to think that individuals could act so as to promote an end that was no part of their intention. It would seem that we need other ways to understand this metaphor.

One suggestion is that a literary context might be the most appropriate one for understanding its meaning. Emma Rothschild suggests Shakespeare's *Macbeth* with its "bloody and invisible hand" or Ovid's *Metamorphoses* as likely candidates. But there are no compelling contextual reasons to link these literary manifestations of the invisible hand (except that these books were owned by or may have been known to Smith) to Smith's particular use of it.[13] James Buchan has suggested another literary resource in Daniel Defoe's *Moll Flanders*, in which we encounter Moll complaining that "a sudden Blow from an almost invisible Hand, blasted all my happiness" (see Buchan 2006, 2). This too might have been a reference that Smith knew.

---

[12] The value of Rothschild's argument at another level, though, is apparent when balanced against muscular theistic efforts insisting that "Smith's universe is logically dependent upon a divine invisible hand" (Hill 2001, 2). Rothschild has produced valuable evidence against earlier and alternative efforts to interpret the invisible hand as either an "expression of Smith's faith in Stoic providence" or his acceptance of the Christian theistic cosmology thought to underpin Newtonianism with its finger of god. Still, there is no necessary inconsistency in employing the metaphor of the invisible hand to illuminate the fact that the outcomes produced by the market mechanism are independent of the wills of human beings, while at the same time recognising, as John Robertson has pointed out, that "far from being guaranteed by any 'invisible hand,' the harmonization of government and economy in commercial society is, Smith believed, the task of the legislator" (1983, 471). Such an analysis suggests different principles of harmonisation at work in ordinary commercial life and the pursuit of political ends.

[13] For a consideration of the relationship of theatre and theatricality to political economy, see Hundert (2000, 31–47).

This metaphor had clearly existed as part of a framework of concepts that had featured in more systematic approaches to philosophical and scientific enquiry for more than a century. Joseph Glanvill included references to an invisible hand in his *Vanity of Dogmatizing* (1661), and Joseph Spengler has noted that it not only formed part of a "climate of opinion" attempting to make apparent the "hidden processes of Nature" but was also known to Smith (1975, 394). Focusing on this context of traditions of scientific enquiry, and looking to Smith's other known reference to the invisible hand in the *History of Astronomy*, suggests that a seriousness of purpose might stand behind Smith's use of this locution in his accounts of natural philosophy, political economy, and moral life.

In his discussion of natural philosophy in the *History of Astronomy*, Smith considered primitive man's observations of nature. He argued that such a man overlooks many "smaller incoherences" in his experience of nature because he has "no inclination to amuse himself with searching out what, when discovered, seems to serve no other purpose than to render the theatre of nature a more connected spectacle to his imagination" (1750, 48).[14] The more "magnificent irregularities" of nature (he mentions thunder, lightning, meteors, and eclipses) cannot escape his notice, but "his inexperience and uncertainty with regard to everything about them, how they came, how they are to go, what went before, what is to come after them, exasperate his sentiment into terror and consternation" (48).

Smith claimed that these passions necessarily suggest "opinions to justify them." Since they "terrify" primitive man, they *must* "proceed from some intelligent, though *invisible* causes, of whose vengeance and displeasure they are either the signs or the effects" (48; emphasis added). This is why Smith was able to conclude that we find origins of polytheism and "vulgar superstition" ascribing "all the irregular events of nature to the favour or displeasure of intelligent, though invisible beings, to gods, daemons, witches, genii, fairies"—that is, to "the *invisible hand* of Jupiter" (49; emphasis added) . More ordinary events ("fire burns, and water refreshes") may be understood by cause and effect (that is, by "the necessity of their own nature," as Smith puts it) rather than by recourse to the extraordinary or the speculative.

Smith's reference to Nicolas de Malebranche in these passages is illuminating, as Malebranche clearly prefigured Hume's argument that the necessary connections of cause and effect are not the product of sense or reason but a habit confirmed by observing events constantly conjoined.

---

[14] Phillipson suggests that Smith, like Hume, "thought it absurd to expect ordinary men to see that the prosperity and preservation of the state required any diminution of the powers, privileges and immunities of [their] own particular order of society" (1981, 191).

Indeed, Smith makes Malebranche appear to share a Humean sceptical explanation of people's belief in gods and "invisible causes"—that is, as compensatory efforts to settle the uneasiness of mind brought on by such terrifying ruptures in common experience.[15]

If this indicates a seriousness of purpose behind Smith's use of metaphors like the invisible hand in his discussion of natural philosophy, then the same seriousness of purpose can also be shown to exist in his use of it in political economy. The context in which this is best seen is his discussion of Quesnay. Here both his respect and disagreement with Quesnay are revealing.[16] While Smith's admiration of "the profound and original author of the *Economical Table*" was great, he (as well as Hume) rejected the Malebranchean occasionalist cosmology that underpinned Quesnay's system.[17] The key element of occasionalist thought (that is, that material bodies are conceived of as "passive agents" unable to move themselves and thus moved only by a divine force) appears in Quesnay in the form of the doctrine of the exclusive productiveness of agriculture. Nature, not human activity, is the ultimate foundation of productivity. This being so, the imagery that Smith used in his critique of the "man of system"— who thinks that men are like "pieces upon a chess-board" with "no other principle of motion besides that which the hand impresses upon them"— might be applicable to this mistaken cosmology (1759, 6.2.2:234).[18]

The question of how individual wills and government policy might be thought to coincide in what Smith called the "game of human society" leads us directly back to the context of Smith's understanding of the invisible hand. Smith's perspective on the development of science is of the gradual regularization of systems through the constraint and ordering of observation—revealing to people those once apparently "hidden chains of events" that connect them (Smith 1750, 48). The invisible hand is, then, what people would recur to in order to explain such events *if* they did not

---

[15] Smith makes reference to this same passage from Malebranche's *Recherche* in *The Moral Sentiments*, and there introduces his other "mental construct," as Phillipson has described it: the impartial spectator (1981, 186). Forbes left undeveloped a "suspicion" that "Malebranche had more to do with some aspects of Smith's philosophy than is commonly appreciated" (1975, 194). Without suggesting in any way what Forbes's view may have been, we develop here our own suspicion that his claim was correct.

[16] It is well to remember Stewart's claim in his account of Smith's life that had Quesnay lived until 1776, Smith would have dedicated the *Wealth of Nations* to him (1793, 48)

[17] On the relationship between Quesnay and Malbranchean ideas, see Spiegel (1983; see also Whatmore 2002).

[18] There is a debate about whether Smith had anyone in mind when he spoke of "the man of system." Whoever that individual may or may not have been, however, there is little doubt that the imagery Smith used in his criticism of him applied to physiocracy and its mistaken cosmology as well.

understand the character of those hidden chains. In a nearly complete rendition of the Humean argument on the progress of cause and effect, Smith writes:

> The supposition of a chain of intermediate, though invisible, events, which succeed each other in a train similar to that in which the imagination has been accustomed to move, and which link together those two disjointed appearances, is the only means by which the imagination can fill up this interval, is the only bridge which, if one may say so, can smooth its passage from the one object to the other. . . . Such is the nature of this second species of Wonder, which arises from an unusual succession of things. The stop which is thereby given to the career of the imagination, the difficulty which it finds in passing along such disjointed objects, and the feeling of something like a gap or interval betwixt them, constitute the whole essence of this emotion. Upon the clear discovery of a connecting chain of intermediate events, it vanishes altogether. What obstructed the movement of the imagination is then removed. (42)[19]

For Smith, philosophy was "that science which pretends to lay open the concealed connections that unite the various appearances of nature"—it admits us behind the scenes of the imaginary construct (whether to Newton's universe conceived of without need for recourse to theism or the machinery of the market). By rendering the whole "consistent and of a piece" (1750, 50–51), by revealing what otherwise might have remained hidden, we could conclude that when Smith argued that an individual who acts intending his own gain "is in this, as in many other cases, led by an invisible hand to promote an end which was no part of his intention," he was explaining how common men might perceive and speak of the mechanism of market as being veiled.[20] Generally speaking, ordinary people would not pause (or even care, as might philosophers) to see behind the curtain or consider the causal links of the market mechanism.

---

[19] This reference to the reality behind the curtain at the opera is congruent with both Macfie's and Spengler's arguments that Bernard le Bovier de Fontenelle had made "invisible hand" references to the Paris opera's "Engineer in the Pit," who ran the *deus ex machina* contrivance with its "wheels and movements" never seen on the stage. Smith refers to Fontenelle in the *Moral Sentiments* (1759, 125) and was known to own a 1752 edition of Fontenelle's work, *A Week's Conversation on the Plurality of Worlds* (1728). It is Ian Ross's view that Smith took the metaphor of the invisible hand from the *Meditations* of Emperor Marcus Aurelius Antoninus on the "immense connected system" of nature (1995, 167; see also Spengler 1975, 394).

[20] The language of invisibility or veils appears in many discrete historical contexts, and remains a common rhetorical device used in politics and political economy to this day. Veils of ignorance or religion are thought to obscure the reality that science or systematic thought exposes.

The economic machine is created by their habits and expectations, but it in turn creates and shapes the regularities of society.[21] But for most ordinary people, the invisible hand would turn out to be enough to explain those regularities.

Understood in this way, the three different occasions on which Smith uses the invisible hand are only superficially dissimilar.[22] Whether he was elucidating the behaviour of individuals in commercial society in the *Wealth of Nations*, "proud and unfeeling landlords" in the *Moral Sentiments*, or the more primitive men of the *History of Astronomy*, he was summarising order retrospectively perceived. Smith was not offering a proof of either providential order or design. The test of a metaphor could not be *empirical* in that way. Rather, the test of such a rhetorical device must lie in the answer to the Humean-inspired question, "Does it provide a comprehensive, coherent and attractive image of the functioning of the social 'machine' or 'system,' assembled from component ideas that will be familiar and comfortable to its intended audience, and framed in terms compatible with communally accepted standards of propriety?" (Long 2002, 25). In each case Smith appears to believe that it would.[23]

Concluding Observations

Having explored what Smith himself may have intended by the use of the invisible hand as a metaphor, and its role in his understanding of the operation of commercial society, it is useful to chart its life independent of Smith's thinking. In modern economics, the invisible hand took a rather long time to appear on the scene. More than one hundred years after Smith first used the expression, it failed to be noticed, discussed, or the now-famous passage from the *Wealth of Nations* (1776, 4.2:456) even

---

[21] One could agree with J. R. Lindgren's suggestion that the "invisible hand" was "a rhetorical device which Smith invented in order to communicate with men who unlike himself, took no notice of the interests and motives of the members of society" (1969, 912). The invisible hand does not "create" order; it rhetorically summarises an argument already made about how order is perceived. Smith's model for enquiry is this language, rather than Newtonian mechanics per se. See also Brown (1994).

[22] In the *Wealth of Nations*, Smith's use of the metaphor appears in the story of the maximisation of the public interest; in the *Moral Sentiments*, it appears in the near-equal distribution of the necessities of life; in the *Astronomy*, it can be seen in the explanation of events in nature.

[23] Smith does not suggest that such an affirmative answer should be relied on as a certainty, just as he does require or assert the "natural harmony" of the market "as a fact." Indeed, many passages within his work—such as that in the *Wealth of Nations* that argues that the interests of merchants "is always in some respects different from, and even opposite to, that of the public"—confirms that it is not (see 1776, 1.11:267, 4.2.21:462).

cited by Rae in his monumental biography of Smith that appeared in 1895. Although Edwin Cannan added an index entry to the phrase in his 1904 edition of the *Wealth of Nations*, indicating that there was, by then, some significance being attached to the expression among the ranks of English-speaking Smith scholars. Yet the phrase still did not appear in the index to Edwin Seligman's edition of the *Encyclopedia of the Social Sciences* of 1934.[24]

The idea of the invisible hand, now attributed to Smith, seems also to have occurred in the 1880s in the hands of Menger. In his second book, *Investigations into the Method of the Social Sciences & Etc.* (1883), written in the throes of the celebrated *Methodenstreit* with the younger German Historical School led by Gustav Schmoller, it would appear that Menger had read into Smith's turn of phrase a coded reference to one of his own (and subsequently distinctly Austrian) favoured notions: that of an "organic" or "spontaneous" order emerging as the "unintended consequence" (another potent idea for the Austrians) of the individual pursuit of self-interest. In the hands of Ludwig von Mises and later Hayek, the idea of "spontaneous order" took on an altogether more potent contemporary political significance.

The key moment, however, seems to have arrived around the middle of the twentieth century, by which time the phrase had become directly associated with the formal relations that exist between Pareto efficiency and competitive equilibrium within neoclassical economics. While it was never far beneath the surface in the Lange-Hayek debate over central planning versus the market, one may take as a measure of its degree of circulation in this guise Samuelson's formative textbook, *Economics: An Introductory Analysis*. In its first edition, Samuelson unambiguously associated the invisible hand with the efficiency of perfectly competitive equilibrium (1948, 36). Samuelson's student readers, who must by now number in their many hundreds of thousands, have largely followed suit ever since.[25]

---

[24] Interestingly, the phrase is indexed in the late 1960s' successor to Seligman's *Encyclopedia* (the *International Encyclopedia of the Social Sciences*), though not really with great prominence. There, it appears to be associated with Debreu and Arrow's then recent successful demonstration of the optimality of Walrasian general equilibrium. It was not until the publication of the *New Palgrave Dictionary of Economics* in 1987 that the invisible hand warranted a separate entry (Eatwell, Milgate, and Newman 1987, 3:997–99).

[25] When Samuelson's textbook reached its twelfth edition in 1985, William Nordhaus became its coauthor. The list of its translated editions is too long to reproduce. It reached its eighteenth edition in 2005. Although the best of his student readers, like Samuelson himself, recognised just how little comfort this association of the invisible hand with the efficiency of perfectly competitive equilibrium could actually give to those who wished to argue that "any interference with free competition by government was almost certain to be

While these conceptual changes to his putative economic message took place more than a century after Smith, others occurred much earlier. Some of the most significant of these changes began to emerge in the eighteenth century itself. The rendition of Smith offered by the "charismatic and influential" professor of moral philosophy at Edinburgh between 1785 and 1810 (Phillipson 1987, 497)—namely, Stewart—involved a re-working of the figure of Smith as part of a forward-looking project de-signed to reformulate the content and boundaries of the discipline itself.

---

injurious" (Samuelson 1948, 36), there can be little doubt that the invisible hand was not to be understood as Pareto efficiency.

Chapter Six

THE FIGURE OF SMITH

I should be reluctant to expose Smith's errors before
his work has operated its full effect. We owe much at
present to the superstitious worship of Smith's name;
and we must not impair that feeling, till the victory
is more complete.
—Francis Horner, *Memoirs
and Correspondence*

CONSIDER THE FIGURE OF SMITH: architect of economic liberalism, champion of free trade, founding father of economics, advocate of the benefits of unregulated competition, prophet of fiscal responsibility and monetary restraint, and perhaps above all, defender of the freedom of the individual to pursue their own economic self-interest without interference from government. It is not difficult to believe that at the bicentenary of the publication of the *Wealth of Nations*, Stigler quipped that Smith was alive and well, and living in Chicago (see Meek 1977, 3). At the same time, however, Winch was moved to remark that since economists were not always reliable authorities about their own past, their retrospective image of Smith might be seriously faulty (1976, 71). Yet it would be an error to protest that the figure of Smith is entirely remote from the original subject. It is not that it is completely unrecognisable; nor is it, as some have maintained, its opposite.

The difficulty with the figure of Smith lies elsewhere. It is rather that it accentuates certain features at the expense of others, and that it does so in ways that seem to both narrow the scope of Smith's vision into the workings of the market mechanism and reduce his legacy. Over time, the subtleties of the original arguments seem to have been lost, important analytical and practical insights appear to have been forgotten, and the complexities and inconsistencies of Smith's own reasoning have been put aside in the interest of disseminating a more coherent, less cautious, and less problematic image than its original.

Many have expressed unease with this development (Viner 1927; Skinner 1978, 77), sometimes even suggesting that the figure of Smith differs from the genuine article in ways that correspond closely to the ideological preoccupations of those who invoke it (Winch 1985a, 1985b, 1990).

There is an ever burgeoning literature that seeks to recover a more faithful, accurate, and relevant understanding of Smith. Its interpretive project has been to reveal a more useful or historically accurate version of what Smith had to say. Unluckily, however, having charted Smith's odyssey, there would appear to have been a startling number of different Smiths in eighteenth-century Scotland.

This state of affairs begs a series of questions concerning the historical process through which the figure of Smith was forged. Influential though the *Wealth of Nations* itself was in ushering the figure of Smith onto the stage of British political economy (as, indeed, was reference to Smith in parliamentary debate by North, Pitt, and others), it is well-known that the *Edinburgh Review* played a decisive part in transmitting and publicising an identifiable body of "Smithian" principles embodying many of the familiar sentiments of economic liberalism now associated with the figure of Smith.[1] It was the immediate influence of Stewart that provided both the source of that doctrine's most basic principles and the impetus for its propagation.[2]

Stewart's role in shaping the figure of Smith has not been entirely neglected by earlier writers, but his input was customarily cast as part of an

---

[1] Ricardo registered his own attraction to the early economic articles in the *Edinburgh Review* (1951–73, 7, 246). On the importance of the *Edinburgh Review*, Bagehot (1855) should be read together with Stephen (1878). Clive (1956) remains invaluable, supplemented by Hollander (1928), Semmel (1963a), and Fontana (1985).

[2] The economic literature on Stewart is rather small. A representative sample would include J. Hollander (1928), Spiegel (1983, 288), O'Brien (1975, 14–15), S. Hollander (1987); Schumpeter (1954), and Phillipson (1981, 19). S. Hollander (1973) and Pribram (1983) are silent on the subject. There is a concise summary of Stewart's work and its impact in Phillipson (1987, 4:497), and significant discussion of Stewart will be found in Halévy (1928). Winch has drawn attention to Stewart's importance in a number of contexts (Winch 1978, 1983; Collini, Winch, and Burrow 1983, chap. 1). For more recent contributions, see Berg (1980), P. Jones (1983), Fontana (1985), and Rothschild (1992). Davie (1961) provides an account of the position that Stewart occupied in Scottish intellectual life around the turn of the century, and Haakonssen (1984) has examined Stewart's role in the transformation of Smith's moral philosophy.

The impact of Stewart on the Edinburgh reviewers was direct and powerful; as John Clive put it, Stewart was their "principal preceptor" (1956, 108). The three projectors who launched the *Edinburgh Review* in 1802—Sidney Smith, Francis Jeffrey, and Francis Horner—had all passed under Stewart's tutelage. In the first decade of the *Edinburgh Review*, 412 of the 623 articles that appeared were written by one or another of Stewart's Edinburgh students (compare *Wellesley Index* 1966–89, 1:430–50). If the Edinburgh reviewers were distilling the opinions of some academic scribbler of a few years back, it was Stewart's opinions that they were airing (see Cockburn 1856, 109–10; Horner 1843, 1:245, 298–99, 331–32). James Mill, although by then a confirmed utilitarian and dissenter from Stewart's brand of Scottish moral sense philosophy, could yet write to Macvey Napier in 1821 praising Stewart's lectures and declaring that his own "taste for the studies which have formed my favourite pursuits" had been formed under Stewart's influence (quoted in

oral tradition whose impact could only be guessed at, and the concrete details of which were imperfectly catalogued (see, for example, Hollander 1928). More recently, others have explored the subject in a way suggesting that greater attention should be paid to Stewart's "transmutation of the inheritance" (Collini, Winch, and Burrow 1983, 27; see also Winch 1978, 24–26, 186; Winch 1983; Rothschild 2001a; Jones 2004).[3] What remains less well documented are the specific embellishments that the figure of Smith acquired in Stewart's hands, and the primary channels through which Stewart conveyed the figure of Smith to the generation of classical economists who dominated the opening decades of the nineteenth century.

ECONOMIC LIBERALISM AND THE THEORY OF VALUE

The central elements of Stewart's version of Smithian economics are relatively easy to isolate. His account of the *Life and Writings of Adam Smith* (1793) contained all the essential ingredients. This essay was influential enough in itself, quite apart from the impact of Stewart's celebrated Edinburgh lectures.[4] It was included in the 1795 edition of Smith's *Essays on Philosophical Subjects* and in the fifth volume of Stewart's own influential edition of Smith's *Works* of 1811–12.[5] It also constituted Stewart's translation of Smith for a new generation of political economists and practicing politicians.[6]

Bain 1882, 16; Collini, Winch, and Burrow 1983, 61). See Napier (1879, 2–7, 24ff). On this indebtedness, see also Mill (1829, 1:4; 1808b, 44) and De Marchi (1983).

[3] It should be noted that the inheritance Winch speaks of Stewart altering was the philosophical and political "findings and methods of inquiry" of such European thinkers as Quesnay, Turgot, Mirabeau, Campomanes, Beccaria, and Gaetano Filangieri. We do not wish to implicate Winch in the analysis of Stewart's "transmutation" of Smith's economics offered here.

[4] Within an influential coterie of former students these lectures were legendary (see Stewart 1854–60, 8:ix; Mackintosh 1832; Horner 1843; Cockburn 1856). John Veitch, the author of the *Memoir of Dugald Stewart*, went so far as to claim that Stewart furnished a perfect example of the solitary thinker whose views finally came to rule the world (1860, 10:liv; see also Leslie Stephen's entry on Stewart in the *Dictionary of National Biography*).

[5] See the editorial notes to the Glasgow edition of Smith (1795, 29). Just how standard an account this essay had become (among the educated classes, at least) is illustrated by the fact that when John Ramsay McCulloch reviewed Ricardo's *Principles* for the June issue of the *Edinburgh Review* for 1818, Stewart's memoir of Smith was cited in terms that suggested its wide currency (1818, 33).

[6] Stewart's role as a translator is emphasised by Winch (in a context different from the one presently at hand) when he notices that Stewart's "transmission and application of accepted principles to new problems . . . entailed transmutation of the inheritance" (Collini, Winch, and Burrow 1983, 27). In another context (the theory of jurisprudence), Haakons-

The first thing to record about Stewart's *Life and Writings of Adam Smith* is how little space is given to Smith's purely theoretical contributions to economics contained in the first and second books of the *Wealth of Nations*. In fact, only eighteen of the ninety-five pages of Stewart's essay are devoted to a discussion of the *Wealth of Nations* itself, and scarcely any of these deal with the analytical core of Smith's contributions to the theory of value, distribution, growth, or technological change. Instead, most are concerned with "remarking in general terms" on what Stewart claimed was the "great and leading object" of Smith's work: namely, to reveal the universal benefits of perfect liberty in commercial relations, and promote economic policies designed to secure it.[7] The overwhelming emphasis of Stewart's essay was on the presentation of a programmatic model of laissez-faire. Stewart's message was that Smith had established a science whose laws dictated that in market economies, intervention was not only unnecessary but positively harmful to the wealth of the nation. "The great aim of Mr. Smith," Stewart argued, was to "direct the policy of nations with respect to one most important class of its laws, those which form its system of Political Economy" (1793, 10:56). With this claim, a philosophy of economic policy rather than the details of a theory of the operation of the market mechanism was established as the distinguishing feature of the figure of Smith.

As to what the content of that philosophy might be, Stewart was as certain as he was assertive: "unlimited freedom of trade" was "the chief aim of [Smith's] work to recommend" (10:64; see also 1809–10, 9:3). Despite Smith's own more cautious reflections on this and other policy questions (see, for instance, Smith 1776, 4.2:467–69, 471), Stewart heralded free trade as that "liberal principle" that on the authority of Smith, should exclusively "direct the commercial policy of nations" (1793, 10:62). According to Stewart, to draw any other lesson from the *Wealth of Nations* was uniformly the consequence of failing to either see clearly behind the "obscurities" of Smith's original arguments or appreciate the "inconclusiveness of his reasonings" about certain subjects (10:95). With

---

sen has remarked that Stewart effectively "reconstituted" Smith's argument (1984, 212). But for a different opinion of the relationship between Stewart's teachings and the doctrines of Smith, see Clive (1956, 128n4) and Dobb (1973, 39, 39n).

[7] As if to explain his neglect of theory, Stewart claimed that "the fundamental doctrines of Mr. Smith's system are now so generally known, that it would be tedious to offer any recapitulation of them in this place" (1793, 10:60). Cockburn remarked that Stewart's treatment of political economy in the lectures "certainly did not involve his hearers in its intricacies" (1856, 109). Stewart himself also provided an ex post facto reason (1793, 10:87, 87nG) that implied that it had something to do with reaction to the French Revolution (on this matter, see also Hollander 1928; Winch 1978, 186; Rothschild 1992).

the assistance of this device—of classifying any turn in Smith's own argument that might suggest a different understanding of his political economy as a mere ambiguity or infelicity—Stewart ensured that the figure of Smith was associated with the doctrine that "the most effectual plan for advancing a people to greatness, is to maintain that order of things which nature has pointed out, by allowing every man, as long as he observes the rules of justice, to pursue his own interests in his own way, and to bring both his industry and his capital into the freest competition with those of his fellow citizens" (10:60).[8]

While the image of Smith as the uncompromising advocate of laissez-faire turned out to exert a strong and continuing influence on the classical economists, and as decisive as this affirmation of economic liberalism proved to be to the development of the figure of Smith, the agenda that Stewart had drawn up possessed another significant feature. A consideration of the theory of value was placed very much in the background, in contrast to the priority that Stewart accorded to the propagation of economic liberalism. So striking is this feature of his account of Smithian economics that it might even be said that the absence of any sustained attempt to develop the theory of value prior to Ricardo, despite the unsettled state in which Smith had left it, can be explained by Stewart's decision to downgrade its significance.

The idea of promoting economic liberalism without a secure foundation in the theory of value may seem strange to the modern eye. After all, the idea that the market mechanism produces an efficient or optimal allocation of resources—the scientific basis of laissez-faire—is conventionally derived from a theory of value (that is, the formal determination of relative prices by the mutual interaction of the forces of supply and demand). It was, in fact, the provision of this foundation by the marginalist writers of the late nineteenth century that gave to economic liberalism many of its most distinctive features, not least its connection to a form of "possessive individualism" wherein the rational calculation of maximum utility/profits is undertaken by individual price-taking agents. This model of individual action, so closely tied to late nineteenth-century advocacy of laissez-faire, resembles but is nonetheless distinct from Smith's less formal comments concerning the "uniform, constant, and

---

[8] This particular formulation of the doctrine of economic liberalism is not founded on any version of utilitarian individualism. The incorporation of utilitarian elements into arguments associated with the figure of Smith (and economic liberalism) took place at a later date in the hands of writers of the Benthamite persuasion—a trend that did not reach its fullest development until the last quarter of the nineteenth century in the work of the marginalist school.

uninterrupted effort of every man to better his condition" (Smith 1776, 2.3:343). Indeed, it is not possible to derive a formal proposition concerning efficiency in the allocation of resources from the adding-up theory of value to which Smith is commonly thought to have subscribed.[9] Moreover, the absence of this formal proposition in the classical period made the connection between the science of political economy and the doctrine of economic liberalism problematic—and it made it perfectly possible to contend that there was nothing in the science of political economy that *necessarily* supported laissez-faire or economic liberalism. This is perhaps nowhere better illustrated than by the fact that at this time, it was equally possible for radical detractors of the market mechanism to draw on political economy for arguments in support of their case (see, for example, Hodgskin 1827).

An indication of just how important avoiding questions relating to the theory of value was to Stewart's activities on behalf of the figure of Smith may be provided by two episodes in which the theory of value was raised before Ricardo: the debate surrounding Lauderdale's *Public Wealth*, and Horner's excursion into the theory of value in his review of Canard's *Principes d'économie politique*. In both of these instances, the fragility of the figure of Smith in the face of the opening up of the theory of value to closer scrutiny was starkly revealed. On this subject, neither the figure of Smith nor its supporters could be made to speak with an unequivocal or consistent voice.

When Lauderdale's *Public Wealth* appeared in 1804, it proved to contain a withering charge of confusion and inconsistency against Smith. There was no opinion, Lauderdale argued, "that has been anywhere maintained on the subject of the sources of national wealth, which does not appear to have been adopted in different parts of the Inquiry into the Wealth of Nations" (1804, 116; see also 169, 169n). Contrary to Smith, Lauderdale maintained that exchangeable value was determined by the relation between the scarcity and the utility of commodities, saving was not universally conducive to economic growth, and capital (as well as land and labour) was an "original source" of value.

Faced with this fusillade, the figure of Smith was in need of defenders, and they quickly materialised in the persons of Henry Brougham and James Mill. Their reactions to Lauderdale reveal just how far they were prepared to go to repudiate criticism of Smith. They also reveal, however,

[9] Contrary to this commonly held view is that of Samuel Hollander, who argues that Smith had in place all of the basic elements of general equilibrium theory (see, for example, Hollander 1973, 19–22).

the inability to eliminate the underlying problem with Smith's theory of value that Lauderdale had highlighted.

Mill, ever the polemicist, suggested that "the name of Dr Smith is so high that it becomes an object of vanity to find defects in his writings" (1804, 10). Brougham was even more forthright, declaring that Lauderdale's book comprised "a collection of propositions, all of them either self-evident or obviously false" (1804, 346). It seems apparent that even if Brougham and Mill succeeded in salvaging the figure of Smith from disparagement with this defence, they had hardly removed the underlying theoretical problem. Indeed, their own lack of success in providing anything more effective on the subject of value (and sometimes making things worse) appears to confirm the wisdom of Stewart's policy to avoid it. Interestingly, even though Stewart's own observations on Lauderdale's book were more measured than either those of Brougham or Mill, they were no less effective in deflecting the propagation of any fundamental doubts about the figure of Smith. Lauderdale's book, Stewart told his Edinburgh students, deserved "serious examination" because it opened up "some very original views" on a topic "equally interesting and abstruse" (1809–10, 9:459), but the *Wealth of Nations* still provided "the Code which is now almost universally appealed to, all over Europe, as the highest authority which can be quoted in support of any political argument" (9:458).

The second example of how vulnerable the figure of Smith might become in the face of deep interrogation on the subject of value is supplied by Horner's review of Canard's *Principes* (1803a), in which Horner took strong exception to the argument that the exchangeable value of commodities was determined by the amount of labour embodied in their production (and incidentally, to Canard's use of algebra). Horner indicated that Smith, too, had made the same mistake, giving rise to "great obscurity" in much of what "that profound author" had to say on the subject of price (61). According to Horner, Smith's obscurity was due to his failure to be clear on the distinction between labour commanded and labour embodied as measures of value (61).

Following Smith (and Stewart 1809–10, 8:353), Horner (1803a, 62) correctly pointed out that these two *measures* only coincide in that state of society previous to the accumulation of capital. Like Smith, Horner concluded that the labour theory of value was problematic outside some early and rude state of society. Unlike Smith (who opted for adding up the component parts of price), however, Horner offered in its place an elementary discussion of the movement of market prices around their natural level, an epistle to the fact that value was "relative," and the conclusion that the value of one commodity was the quantity of any other commodity for which it was exchanged. This left serious problems, in that all he could say was that the exchangeable value "of any two commodities is liable to vary with the variation of four circumstances, and will depend upon the combined variations of all. These four circumstances are, the demand and the supply of the one commodity, and the demand and supply of the other" (63.). Although the context is different, we find again the dilemma encountered by Mill and Brougham in their attempt to defend Smith against Lauderdale's attack. Having opened up the theory of value and exposed its unsettled character, they were unable to resolve the problem.[10]

The time would come, of course, when the theory of value would assume a dominant place as the cornerstone of economic liberalism. But the time would only be right once the liberal credentials of the figure of Smith were unassailable. To expose errors before that goal had been secured would threaten its realisation. For individuals so directly involved in this project, Stewart and Horner showed remarkable insight into the strategy that lay behind it. They were quite prepared to concede theoretical difficulties and/or obscurities in Smith, but only insofar as it was prudent to do so. In each case, care had to be taken to stress that such admissions did not compromise what Stewart had called in his essay "the great aim of Mr Smith." When it came to value, therefore, where Smith was at his least explicit and where his defenders proved incapable of finding a remedy, silence was expedient.

The Relation between Economics and Politics

Nevertheless, having the figure of Smith speak with the unequivocal voice of economic liberalism without a basis in the theory of value was not the only attribute that Stewart added in the essay. He also directed attention to what he claimed was the correct Smithian position on the relation between political economy and politics. Stewart maintained that if the science of politics was concerned with designing an ideal constitution of political society, as it had been in the hands of writers like Montesquieu and James Harrington, then a "Smithian" economics would have nothing to contribute to its enterprise. Stewart made this point directly and forcefully: "Smith, Quesnay, Turgot, Campomanes, Beccaria, and others, have aimed at the improvement of society—not by delineating plans of new

[10] Horner, recognising that "there is less chance of being led into false opinions by the 'Wealth of Nations' than by almost any other book on that kind of philosophy" (1843, 1:245), never wrote another word on the subject of value.

constitutions, but by enlightening the policy of actual legislators. Such speculations, while they are more essentially and more extensively useful than any others, have no tendency to unhinge established institutions, or to inflame the passions of the multitude" (1793, 10:55–56). Plans for new constitutions, then, were projects to which economic science neither could nor should aspire.

The suggested alternative idea was that social progress was best secured by attending to legislation rather than plans for new constitutions; while Scottish political philosophy had certainly tended in directions from which Stewart's position is not an entirely unwarranted development, it is doubtful if anyone would have gone as far as Stewart in its application.[11] For in forging his version of Smithian economics, Stewart had deployed a new view of the science of politics. It is to this view of politics and its relation to economics that we now turn.

The science of politics, Stewart claimed, should aim exclusively at reducing "the principles of legislation" to a science (1792–1827, 2:230; see also 231)—a reductionist conception of politics that was articulated in his *Life and Writings of Adam Smith*:

> In prosecuting the Science of Politics on this plan, little assistance is to be derived from the speculations of the ancient philosophers, the greater part of whom, in their political inquiries, confined their attention to a comparison of the different forms of government, and to an examination of the provisions they made for perpetuating their own existence, and for extending the

---

[11] This opinion was not new. Alexander Pope had given it the status of a poetical maxim, "For forms of government let fools contest, Whate're is best administer'd is best" (1733, 3:123–24). The question had been the subject of Hume's discussion of whether "politics may be reduced to a science"; but Hume's argument was more concerned with the dangers attendant on the fact that "plans of new constitutions" had increasingly become matters of factional rivalry than it was with rejecting the value of a speculative science of politics per se. Indeed, in the "idea of a perfect commonwealth," a plan of a new constitution was formulated in such characteristic Humean style that it may have left his readers wondering whether the whole subject really might just be "useless and chimerical" after all (1777a, 514). Smith had also contemplated the matter; but while some of his more disparaging remarks about the man of system (1759, 6.2:233–34) lend superficial support to Stewart's position, it would be difficult to prosecute the case that Smith sanctioned Stewart's wholehearted disapprobation for plans of new constitutions (see, for example, 1776, 5.3:934). In the *Moral Sentiments*, moreover, Smith claimed that nothing tended "so much to promote public spirit as the study of politics, of the several systems of civil government, their advantages and disadvantages, of the constitution of our own country" because "political disquisitions, if just, and reasonable, and practicable, are of all the works of speculation the most useful" (1759, 4.1:186–87). Stewart's intervention consisted in making the avoidance of constitutional questions an *invariable* principle, while at the same time eliminating the qualifications attached to earlier opinions of Hume, Smith, or Ferguson.

glory of the State. It was reserved for modern times to investigate those universal principles of justice and of expediency, which ought, under every form of government, regulate the social order. (1793, 10:54)[12]

Stewart's emphasis on the value of expediency to political development and political stability (something so reminiscent of what John Stuart Mill would say decades later) is central to the understanding Stewart's politics. Although broadly congruent with Hume's often repeated preference for "such gentle alterations and innovations as may not give too great disturbance to society" (1777a, 514), it is also indicative of Stewart's commitment to a vision of the constitution as something at once organic and mechanical. His frequent allusions to the "machine of government" is an example of the influence this particular conception of the constitution exercised over his mind (1792–1827, 2:227; 1809–10, 8:354). Given this framework of concepts, Stewart was led almost inexorably, it would seem, to the conclusion that "the perfection of political wisdom consists not in incumbering the machine of government with new contrivances to obviate every partial inconvenience, but in removing, gradually and imperceptibly, the obstacles which disturb the order of nature" (1792–1827, 2:238).[13]

It remained for Stewart to show that such a process would be conducive to progress, and for this task he deferred to an organic conception of political development:

Of the governments which have hitherto appeared in the history of mankind, few or none have taken their rise from political wisdom, but have been the gradual result of time and experience, of circumstances and emergencies. In process of time, indeed, every government acquires a systematical appearance; for, although its different parts arose from circumstances which may be regarded as accidental and irregular, yet there must exist among these parts a certain degree of consistency and analogy. (2:224)

At the same time, this argument provided Stewart with a case against "visionary schemes" in politics. If constitutions were essentially the product of organic social development, the result of accidents of history, experience, and laws, then it was folly to attempt to design one from scratch.[14]

---

[12] Joseph Cropsey's argument that during this period, economics tended to eclipse political philosophy, certainly finds resonance in Stewart's argument (1976, p.132; see also 1957; 1979).

[13] Compare Hume: "It is not with forms of government, as with other artificial contrivances; where an old engine may be rejected, if we can discover another more accurate and commodious, or where trials may safely be made, even though the success be doubtful" (1777a, 512).

[14] Although Smith often presented a picture of political development as the outcome of the operation of unintended consequences, he did not (as we have already noticed) fully

Indeed, Stewart thought he had established with this contention the grounds of his own redefinition of the science of politics as being exclusively about "the art of legislation" (2:220).[15]

In view of these ideas, it is hardly surprising that Stewart confessed himself to being unreservedly in favour of "mixed government" in his political economy lectures (1809–10, 9:352). Nor was it only a matter of political prejudice that led him to refer to the British constitution as "our happy constitution" (8:28). In a letter to Lord Craig at the height of the Terror in France (and in the face of growing British working-class support for the republican sentiments then customarily equated with Jacobinism), Stewart nailed his political colours to the masthead at a time when he found his own credentials being called into question (see Cockburn 1856, 67). Yet he did so by deferring to his political principles; for rather than entering into a diatribe against republicanism (of the kind to be found in certain parts of Burke's writings), Stewart instead invoked his preexisting argument advancing the merits of gradual over rapid political change to establish his opposition to the "mischiefs to be apprehended from the spirit of innovation, and from sudden changes in established institutions" in France—a view that was associated with the figure of Smith.[16]

This move by Stewart, albeit only a step towards establishing the independent province for positive economics, was decisive. In the enterprise of creating and shaping a scientific community of economists, Stewart's simultaneous disavowal of any pretensions that economists might have had towards grander political designs together with his strong affirmation of their monopoly over legitimate speech on economic subjects was a nec-

---

subscribe to the idea that constitutional speculation was an entirely "useless and chimerical" exercise.

[15] "The necessity of studying particular constitutions of government, by the help of systematical descriptions of them, (such descriptions, for example, as are given of that of England by Montesquieu and Blackstone), arises from the same circumstances which render it expedient . . . to study particular languages by consulting the writings of grammarians. . . . [But] the nature and spirit of government, as it is actually exercised at a particular period, cannot always be collected; perhaps it can seldom be collected from an examination of written laws, or of the established forms of a constitution" (2:225).

[16] By way of proof of his convictions, Stewart offered the following evidence: "I have concluded my course with a set of Lectures on the English Constitution, the peculiar excellencies of which I have always enlarged upon in the warmest and most enthusiastic terms" (1854–60, 10:lxxiv). Rothschild has argued that many of Stewart's apprehensions about the consequences of Smith's name being associated with French revolutionary sentiments were well-founded (see 2001a, 52–71). Whether or not there was a real or imagined foundation for Stewart's apprehensions, he clearly entertained them. Others of Stewart's contemporaries used Smith's work to either support or oppose those events as their needs required (see Jones 2004). Our concern is as much with how far Stewart's reworking of Smith should be regarded as a forward-looking project of forming the content and boundaries of a discipline, as it is with reaction to the French Revolution.

essary prerequisite (compare Berg 1980, 37). Stamping such opinions with the authority of Smith's name was both convenient and consonant with establishing a more coherent foundation for the new science of political economy.

Nowhere is this strict separation between the traditional domain of the science of politics and that of the new science of political economy more apparent than in Stewart's discussion of the physiocrats. As many have recognised (see James Mill 1818a; Tocqueville 1858, 159), the physiocrats had managed to combine an economic philosophy of liberty of trade with a political philosophy of despotism. Stewart believed that the "theory of government" inculcated by the physiocrats was of "the most dangerous tendency, recommending in strong and unqualified terms an unmixed despotism, and reprobating all constitutional checks on the sovereign authority." To Quesnay, Stewart attributed a despotic maxim according to which it was a "fundamental principle" that "the sovereign authority, unrestrained by any constitutional checks or balances, should be lodged in the hands of a single person" (1792–1827, 2:240, 240n1; emphasis omitted; reproduced in 1809–10, 8:307–8).

The difficulty to which this gave rise was both theoretical and practical. On the one hand, it was essential to show that there was no necessary connection between the liberal economic doctrines of the physiocrats and their putative illiberal politics. On the other hand, there was an added imperative that derived from a more immediate practical consideration: namely, the need to prevent critics of the liberal system of political economy that Stewart advocated from dismissing it as being too dangerously linked to the perceived political tendencies of the physiocrats.[17] Fortunately for Stewart, his resolution of the theoretical point also provided the legitimation of economic science that he felt was required.

Stewart's resurrection of the physiocrats was straightforward.[18] It relied on applying the dictum that economic science had nothing to contribute to "plans of new constitutions" already articulated in his presentation of Smith. Accordingly, Stewart was able to look favourably on the service of the physiocrats to economics (and especially on what he claimed was

---

[17] On the practical importance of this point for Stewart, see the remarks by Veitch (1860, 10:ln4). See also Stewart's own note (added in 1810) where Stewart explained that the reason for his focus on general matters in that place was because "it was not unusual, even among men of some talents and information, to confound, studiously, the speculative doctrines of Political Economy, with those discussions concerning the first principles of Government which happened unfortunately at the time to agitate the public mind" (1854–60, 10:87).

[18] Of course, one could hardly say that discussions of physiocratic economic theory were common events in British economics circles of the day. The two notable exceptions to this rule (Lauderdale 1804; James Mill 1818a) both passed through Stewart's lecture room.

their single overriding aim of "enlightening the public on questions of political economy") while at the same time rejecting their dangerous political tendencies (see 1815–21, 1:380–81). As he would later caution the audience at his Edinburgh lectures on political economy, "Wherever I have mentioned the system of the Economists in terms of approbation, I would be understood to refer solely to their doctrines on the subject of *Political Economy* proper" (1809–10, 8:307).

This last statement, as already mentioned, was not unrelated to Stewart's fears that revolutionary French plans of new constitutions might find their way to Britain. The final sentence of the passage just quoted makes this sufficiently clear.[19] Still, it seems evident that Stewart's conceptual separation between economic science and the science of politics reached well beyond the exigencies of particular historical circumstance, and that his effort to bring Smith along in his enterprise was a pedagogical exercise in disciplinary legitimation (see Berg 1980, 35, 37).

The opinions that Stewart attributed to Smith and the physiocrats on the question of the relation between political economy and politics turned out to be his own. The figure of Smith was systematically remodelled by Stewart to suit a now familiar, but at the time quite new conception of the place of economic science in the world of politics. Stewart's *Lectures* opened with the unequivocal claim that the aim of economics is "to enlighten those who are destined for the functions of government" (1809–10, 8:17). Likewise, the idea that economics does not (and should not) speak to questions of constitutional design but only to those of legislation (and economic legislation at that) gained full expression in the *Lectures*. Towards the end of the course, Stewart insisted again that "the science of Political Economy, much more than the theory of government, is entitled in the present circumstances of mankind, to the attention of the speculative politician" (9:400–401). Furthermore, this theme was given a new twist; for while Stewart advocated the strict separation between economic science and the science of politics when the latter was construed broadly as dealing with the constitution of political society, that separation was allowed to lapse when the science of politics was construed more narrowly as treating only legislative matters.[20]

---

[19] On this point, see Winch (1978, 186). In his *Memoir of Dugald Stewart*, Veitch remarked that for Stewart it was necessary "to vindicate a place for Political Economy, to reiterate, enforce, and carry out, in detailed application to existing circumstances of society, the doctrines of Smith" (1860, 10:li). For an attempt to interpret Stewart's effort to "redefine" Smith's views on politics and political economy almost exclusively as part of a conservative reaction in Britain to the French Revolution, see Rothschild (1992) but also Winch (1985a).

[20] Horner applauded this view (1843, 1:131).

Indeed, Stewart argued that in the department of politics concerned with legislation and policy, economics not only could but should speak. It provided the rational yardstick against which the suitability of legislation was to be measured. The grounds on which Stewart claimed that economic science was decisive in this sphere were familiar. According to Stewart, since both economic science and legislation were concerned with the happiness of the nation, then (in this narrow arena at least) economics had a direct and active role to play in politics. Not content to let the case rest on the proposition that it was on "the particular system of political economy which is established in any country, that the happiness of the people immediately depends," Stewart took the claim a step further and held that it was only "from the remote tendency that wise forms of Government have to produce wise systems of Political Economy, that the utility of the former" actually derived (1809–10, 8:21–22). At a stroke, political economy, which for Smith had been a "branch of the science of a statesman or legislator" (1776, 4:428), had been given an altogether more significant priority.

Since by the "system of political economy" Stewart meant nothing other than the framework of laws governing economic life—where, for him, laissez-faire should rule—it is apparent that Stewart drew no distinction between the goals of economics and those of politics when the latter was narrowly conceived as lawmaking. The idea was not just that legislators *could* listen to economic advice but that they *should* do so. Stewart was adamant about this, going as far as to assert that "what I would chiefly rest my hopes upon, in looking forward to the future condition of mankind, is the influence which the science of Political Economy . . . must necessarily have, in directing the rulers of nations to just principles of administration, by showing them how intimately the interests of government are connected with those of the people, and the authority which this science must gradually acquire over the minds both of the governors and the governed" (1809–10, 9:399–400; emphasis omitted).

According to Stewart, the proper place of economists in the world of politics did not simply involve passively tendering advice and letting politicians decide whether to take it. This idea, which would involve a more thoroughgoing separation between economics and politics, only gradually emerged later in the classical period. Stewart's sentiments were codified in the course of his consideration of what Burke had called one of the "finest problems in legislation" (1795, 4:278). As far as Stewart was concerned, the solution to Burke's legislative problem—"to ascertain what the State ought to take upon itself to direct by the public wisdom, and what it ought to leave, with as little interference as possible, to individual discretion"—was one of the principle objects of the science of political economy (1809–10, 8:16–17). Evidently, Stewart did not merely think that economic science *contributed* to this legislative problem; he thought that it actually *solved* it.

It is worth noting that this argument required a new view of the relation between constitutional questions and economic science. This was furnished by the subsidiary claim that legislation was actually *more* important to human happiness and social progress than the constitutional forms of government. Stewart even contended that the appropriate laws would spontaneously generate the kind of political society one might desire on their own account. On this line of reasoning, there is a priority of laws over constitutions as well as systems of political economy over forms of government.[21] Stewart maintained that forms of government were "of trifling moment" in comparison to systems of political economy (1809–10, 8:22; see also 18, 21). This particular opinion provided Stewart with the rationale he needed for the order of treatment of the two subjects adopted in his *Lectures*: "Of the two branches of Political Science, the Theory of Government and Political Economy, the latter is that which is most immediately connected with human happiness and improvement and is therefore entitled, *in the first instance*, to the attention of the student" (8:24; see also 21, 23).[22]

By removing consideration of forms of government from the domain of political economy, Stewart was quite self-consciously attempting to shape a discipline bearing the imprimatur of Smith, whose credentials made it essentially conservative of the existing political order of things. Viewed from this perspective, his intervention seems to have been among the first of many subsequent moves by economists to make the conclusions of economic theory (like those of the natural sciences) independent not just of politics but (later in the nineteenth century) also of psychology, history, institutions, and even social structures. Furthermore, it appears to be the first systematic and sustained attempt by a fellow economist to disseminate an image of Smith (and the discipline he founded) exclusively associated with the idea that in almost all imaginable situations, markets know best. This may help to explain why the figure of Smith can at once be seen as "conservative" and an "economic liberal." Stewart's view of politics fashioned Smith in Stewart's own image, against radical reform of the British constitution and simultaneously in favour of gradual change in economic policy.

---

[21] The fact that this argument embodies a presumption in favour of moderate reform and gradual adjustment over radical reform and rapid change corresponds fairly well with Stewart's own ideological sympathies.

[22] Compare Charles James Fox, who was clear about what he thought of this line of thinking: "How vain . . . how idle, how presumptuous is the opinion that laws can do everything! And how weak and pernicious the maxim founded upon it, that measures, not men,

Since Smith's actual views on the role of government vis-à-vis the market were "nothing if not complex" (Skinner 1990, 239; see also Skinner 1979; Viner 1927; but compare Rosenberg 1979, 20), it is necessary to turn to Stewart's longer disquisitions on Smith's economic theory in the Edinburgh lectures to reveal how he was able to have the figure of Smith he was shaping in the essay conform to those more complex ideas.

MONEY, MACHINERY, AND THE SOCIAL QUESTION

In order to render both economic liberalism as well as the priority of economics over politics congruent with particular details of Smith's economic theory, Stewart deployed two different strategies, the results of which were the same. In certain cases, Stewart provided "Smithian corrections" to Smith, while in others (where the original had little or nothing to say) he offered "Smithian extensions" of Smith.

Such theoretical corrections are especially conspicuous in Stewart's monetary analysis. On almost every detail, Stewart's account of Smith is far removed from the *Wealth of Nations*. Bentham was invoked to "correct" Smith's opinion that the regulation of money interest rates might be conducive to the wealth of the nation. Steuart was invoked to "correct" Smith's version of the real bills doctrine. George Berkeley and Isaac de Pinto were invoked to bring to the fore the possibility that variations in the velocity of money's circulation might significantly alter the standard conclusions of the quantity theory. The actual experience of the British economy under the Bank Restriction Act was invoked to highlight the incompleteness in Smith's analysis of the possibility of the overissue of paper currency. Taken together, these corrections to Smith (independently of whether or not one regards them as improvements in monetary theory) modified much of the concrete monetary analysis found in the original.

One version was carried directly into the public domain by Horner. It was Horner who had brought Henry Thornton's classic *Paper Credit* to the attention of the readers of the *Edinburgh Review*, and who eight years later had moved in the House of Commons for the establishment of a select committee to enquire into the depreciation of the paper pound. Together with Thornton and William Huskisson, Horner was the joint author of the *Bullion Report* (1810), the document that set the parameters of monetary debate in Britain for at least the next century.[23] Further-

---

are to be attended to" (1808, 38). It might be added that Fox's observations were quoted by Stewart against himself (1809–10, 8:26).

[23] When speaking of the report and its main arguments, Horner wrote to Stewart that he was confident the matter would be settled "agreeably to *our* views" and every day he heard

more, while Horner's monetary analysis was a version of his master's, Lauderdale's equally influential contributions to the monetary debates of the day (1805, 1812, and 1813) were an almost exact replica of them. Both Horner and Lauderdale had followed Stewart to the letter in rejecting Smith's idea that paper currency could never be issued to excess. They both differed from Smith in his apparent conviction that the "Daedalian wings of paper money" would carry it swiftly back to the banking system on the first sign of any overissue (see, for example, Smith 1776, 2.2:321ff). But only Lauderdale had followed Stewart into the finer points of the analysis of the role of the banking system in precipitating the events with which the Bank Restriction Act is now uniformly associated. Stewart's original argument—namely, that the discretionary credit policies of the banking system, combined with antiusury laws that precluded a rise in money interest rates, had produced a crisis of overinvestment through the creation of "fictitious capital" (accumulated without that reduction in consumption required for "real" accumulation)—not only became Lauderdale's own but has since become the basis on which any claim Lauderdale may have to distinction in the history of economics is often made to rest.[24]

On public finance, on the other hand, Stewart followed more closely in the footsteps of Smith. Smith's own emphasis on fiscal responsibility, easy taxes, and the night watchman state were the staple of Stewart's economic liberalism. Nevertheless, even here Stewart introduced an interesting embellishment and omitted one characteristic feature of his predecessor's argument. In his treatment of public expenditure in the *Lectures*, Stewart began by echoing Smith's words from the fifth book of the *Wealth of Nations*—namely, that he considered it to be axiomatic that there existed certain necessary expenses of the "sovereign or common-wealth" (compare Smith 1776, 4.9:688, with Stewart 1809–10, 9:211). Yet before entering into a consideration of proposals concerning the appropriate methods of financing such public expenditure (taxation and/or borrowing), Stewart made two significant movements away from Smith.

The first was an amendment to the list of the necessary expenses of the state. Smith had divided necessary expenditures into the categories of national defence, the administration of justice, public works, and public education, and maintaining "the dignity of the Sovereign." Stewart, on

---

of "converts" (1843, 2:38). The fact that Stewart himself was critical of the report (1809–10, 8:appendix 2) need not detain us here.

[24] Stewart's monetary analysis was given a whole new lease on life in the early 1930s when many of its essential ingredients were taken up (quite explicitly) by Hayek in his theory of industrial fluctuations (see Hayek 1935, 20–21). For the details of the correspondence between Stewart and Lauderdale on this subject, see Stewart (1809–10, 8:431–52).

the other hand, deleted all reference to education and added explicitly, and as a separate category, support of the "Religious Establishment." Smith had dealt with this last matter under the more general rubric of public education. But in that context, he had sharply distinguished it from the education of the nation's youth in the basic skills of literacy and numeracy. Smith's suggestion for the establishment by the state of "little schools" for the young in each district or parish, at which attendance might even be made compulsory, fell unambiguously into that category (1776, 5.1:785). Furthermore, when Smith did come to discuss the specific question of the state funding of religious institutions, he was less than wholehearted in his support for it. While Smith had conceded that the expense of the institutions for "religious instruction" might "without injustice, be defrayed by the general contribution of the whole society," he had immediately added that such expense "might perhaps with equal propriety, and even with some advantage, be defrayed altogether by those who receive the immediate benefit of such education and instruction, or by the voluntary contribution of those who think they have occasion for either the one or the other" (5.1:815).

The second departure from Smith occurred in the explanation of the necessity of public expenditure. As is well-known, Smith had explained the necessity of public expenditure (in the fields he had allowed in the fifth book of the *Wealth of Nations*) by deferring to his celebrated four-stages account of the progress of society (see especially 1776, 5.1:669–70, 694–95, 707, 709, 722–23; see also Meek 1967). In this manner, Smith had effectively argued that it was only in the stage of commercial society that the state would be required to take on itself the functions he had articulated. In Stewart's account, what has since come to be regarded as one of the hallmarks of earlier Scottish opinion (not just of Smith) was entirely omitted. Stewart seems to have been content to ascribe the necessity of these functions to the mere existence of political society itself. As Stewart put it, it was evident that "in *every* political community, there are variety of expenses which must be necessarily incurred by the sovereign for the public service" (1809–10, 9:210; emphasis added). While the disappearance of Smith's four-stages theory from the discourse of classical economics is a fact that cannot be denied, there is no evidence that Stewart's departure from it in this context acted as the spur. Nevertheless, it does appear to represent one of the first concrete signs of its demise.

On the social question, Stewart focused on two themes that were to become the central focus of the British classical economists ever after: the Poor Law question, and the machinery question. The Poor Law question, of course, was hardly new to economists. But Stewart's opening remarks in the *Lectures*—that he sought to use his discussion of poor relief to

furnish a "striking illustration" of the general "danger of multiplying un-
necessarily the objects of the law, by attempting to secure artificially, by
the wisdom of man, those beneficent ends which are sufficiently provided
for by the wisdom of nature" (9:255)—seems to have staked out the well-
known (and often criticised) position adopted by most of the classical
economists on this subject—a position that culminated in the Poor Law
Amendment Act of 1834.[25] With Frederick Morton Eden as his guide,
Stewart led his pupils towards thinking in terms of institutional remedies
for poverty—remedies that involved some combination of charity (workhouses), self-help (friendly societies, benefit clubs, and even savings
banks), and moral education.[26] The trend in Stewart's thinking about the
poor became conventional wisdom among the later classical economists.
Moreover, Stewart was the first classical economist to incorporate Malthus's arguments on this subject into the core of economic analysis.[27]

Stewart's consideration of the machinery question in his Edinburgh lectures sponsored the addition of that particular subject onto the agenda of
classical economics. It also provides a good example of Stewart's strategy
of providing Smithian extensions to Smith. In the *Wealth of Nations*, the
machinery question had scarcely appeared at all, and most of the pre-
Smithian treatments of the subject were less than substantial.[28] But the
machinery question did not simply appear on Stewart's agenda by virtue
of the fact that it presented an interesting theoretical lacuna that Smith
had left largely unexamined. That is only a part of the story. For the
machinery question had already been taken onto the streets and become
a matter of practical political struggle well before the turn of the century.
This particular impulse towards examining the machinery question seems
to have been decisive; in the *Lectures*, Stewart referred to the disturbances
in Lancashire (in the early 1780s), "occasioned by the introduction of

[25] In his discussion of the Poor Laws and the laws of settlement, Smith had concentrated
almost exclusively on the barriers to the mobility of labour that went along with these
measures (1776, 1.10:152–57); it would be difficult to produce evidence of any systematic
application in Smith's own writings of Stewart's *general* maxim (which is, admittedly, essentially Smithian) to the *particular* question of the poor.

[26] For Stewart, the point of educating the masses was not for "the discovery or embellishment of natural genius" but as "the best security for the morals and good order of the
community" (1809–10, 9:341).

[27] Stewart referred to the first *Essay* (Malthus 1798a), which had been published anonymously; Malthus did not put his name to the *Essay* until the 1803 edition (Stewart 1809–
10, 8:202–3; see also the editorial annotations accompanying 203, 64).

[28] For example, Montesquieu's brief remarks on the subject (1748, 2:9), of which much
has been made by some, hardly qualify him as the sponsor of the question (though Stewart
does refer to them; see 1809–10, 8:190). Josiah Tucker, however, does have a greater claim
to priority in opening the debate, but not, it would seem, any claim with respect to adding
it to the classical economists' agenda.

Sir Richard Arkwright's machinery," to motivate his students to take the matter seriously (1809–10, 8:325). It was as much from this source as from any theoretical development by Smith that the machinery question seems to have captured Stewart's attention.[29]

With the well-known exception of Ricardo, Stewart's opinion on the effects of the introduction of machinery laid down the party line for later classical economists. Here, a Smithian extension of Smith was called for, and Stewart's argument was straightforward and successful. The introduction of machinery, since it economised on the use of labour, might adversely affect particular workers, but not workers in general, and even then, only temporarily and not permanently. "It is hardly possible to introduce suddenly the smallest innovation," Stewart wrote,

> without incurring some inconveniences. But temporary inconveniences furnish no objection to solid improvements. Those which may arise from the sudden introduction of a machine cannot possibly be of long continuance. The workmen will, in all probability, be soon able to turn their industry into some other channel; and they are certainly entitled to every assistance the public can give them, when they are thus forced to change their professional habits. (1809–10, 8:193)[30]

Yet even such temporary dislocation was held by Stewart to be a less than insurmountable problem, and certainly not one requiring the intervention of government. Whenever the introduction of machinery in a given industry was accompanied by increased sales (due to the reduction in its supply price), any initial decline in employment accompanying the introduction of machinery would be more than offset by the rise in output required to meet the greater demand (the latter being, in its turn, caused by the decreased costs of production consequent on the use of machinery). With a statement of what amounted to Say's Law before Jean-Baptiste Say, Stewart held that the "mechanical abridgement of labour" released a "quantity of manufacturing capital" that augmented "the funds des-

---

[29] This is not to deny that in his discussion of Smith's treatment of the division of labour, Stewart found no purely theoretical reasons to focus on the use of machinery as the principal source of improvements in productivity. Stewart chided Smith for having focused almost exclusively on the productivity gains accruing to the application of increasingly specialised labour to productive activity at the expense of an adequate discussion of machinery. On this, see Stewart (1809–10, 8:315, 331–32). Indeed, Stewart went so far as to propose to his students that the phrase "economy of labour" might be better adapted to the analysis of productivity change than was Smith's "division of labour" (8:332).

[30] Stewart also recommended that when judging the usefulness of "mechanical contrivances" in agriculture, "it is absolutely necessary to abstract from the *individual* hardships that may fall under our notice, and to fix our attention on those *general* principles which influence the national prosperity" (8:131; emphasis added).

tined for the maintenance of labour," which in turn, could not "fail to find immediate employment either in extending the scale of old establishments, or in striking out new channels of industry" (8:194–95). In this way, Smith's brief original remarks on machinery, that "all such improvements in mechanicks, *as enable the same number of workman to perform an equal quantity of work*, with cheaper and simpler machinery than had been usual before, are always regarded as advantageous to every society" (1776, 2.2:287; emphasis added), were dramatically transformed. Of course, the practical effect was salutary. Armed with Stewart's rendition of the machinery question, political economists and actual legislators entered the debate with rational and scientific arguments to reject the threatening voice of workers who found themselves increasingly dissatisfied with the effects of machinery on their own well-being.

It is worth stating, though, that while the figure of Smith handed down to the next generation was more or less deliberately reinvented, there always remained a certain ambivalence in Stewart's attitude towards Smith. The operation on which Stewart had embarked was a delicate one. A remodelling of Smith could be carried only so far before it amounted to a repudiation, and given the legitimacy that the figure of Smith was meant to lend to the science of political economy, that prospect continually haunted Stewart. This is why one frequently encounters recapitulations in the *Lectures* to the effect that all the lecturer had actually intended was to illustrate some "elementary principles" that would "facilitate and assist" his pupils in their reading of the *Wealth of Nations*.[31] That such exhortations often come at the end of some long disquisition that by its conclusion had so significantly altered Smith's argument as to make it almost unrecognisable, exemplifies the tensions inherent in the enterprise. Nevertheless, however delicate the operation, it proved to be a success.

The Scope and Method of Political Economy

We have already indicated that while the particular events of the 1790s doubtless had their effect, it is also the case that Stewart's interventions were driven by a dynamic internal to the science of political economy itself. That dynamic expressed itself in the drive to delineate the scope and method of a newly emerging discipline. Stewart's contribution to this

---

[31] These remarks are taken from the end of Stewart's discussion of monetary theory (1809–10, 8:425); but see also those that follow his discussion of the division of labour (8:326).

enterprise is perhaps the most fully developed example to be found in the whole of the classical period prior to John Stuart Mill.

The question at issue was exactly how one should go about applying the conclusions of economic science to practical matters of legislation. As Stewart correctly recognised, economic science itself dealt in *general* principles, with cases in which none but the most persistent and systematic factors are at work. As he put it in his political economy lectures, in theoretical investigations, it was "proper to abstract" from "merely accidental circumstances," and this was, he claimed, "for the same reason, that in studying the theory of mechanics, we abstract from the effects of friction, the rigidity of ropes, and the weight of the materials of which the machines are composed" (1809–10, 8:336). Legislation and policy, on the other hand, dealt with *special* problems, with cases in which a multitude of particular factors will be at work. As Stewart reminded Lauderdale in 1811, "There are few, if any, political maxims, which admit, like the axioms of mathematics, of a literal and unqualified application in all imaginable combinations of circumstances," and he continued,

> [Maxims] are, in general abbreviated, and consequently loose statements of important conclusions, adopted by their conciseness to serve as aids to the memory; but requiring, when they are assumed as principles of reasoning, the exercise of our own common sense, in supplying those indispensable conditions and exceptions, which are to be collected from their spirit rather than from their letter. (8:445–46)

Stewart's own resolution of this methodological conundrum was set out in his *Philosophy of the Human Mind*. The basic argument was that in order "to proceed with safety in the use of general principles, much caution and address are necessary, both in establishing their truth, and in applying them to practice" (1792–1827, 2:206). In conformity with his overarching strategy of associating the figure of Smith with everything he said, Stewart elsewhere indicated that this practice represented the "characteristical excellence" of Smith, who had abstracted "entirely from the ideal perfection to which it is possible things may have a tendency" and adapted "his speculations to the present state of this part of the world" (1809–10, 8:305). What is revealing about this modern idea is that Stewart appears to have believed that caution was called for not only on methodological grounds but also political ones as well.

This methodological imperative has become part of the conventional wisdom of economics. The relation between its theoretical and applied branches continues to be seen almost exactly as Stewart formulated it. Stewart put it this way: "As all general principles are founded on classifications which imply the exercise of abstraction, it is necessary to regard them, in their practical applications, merely as approximations to the truth" (1792–1827, 2:213). There is nothing in this claim that would strike a contemporary economist as being remarkable; nor, for that matter, is there much in it that would not have been familiar to anyone who has studied the progress of eighteenth-century Scottish philosophical speculation. What is new is Stewart's direct and explicit application of the idea to the question of the use and/or abuse of economic science.

The other theme in Stewart's argument for the exercise of caution in the application of general principles had nothing to do with methodological practice. According to Stewart, caution had another virtue in that it reduced what he perceived to be the political dangers associated with any overly "rash application of general principles" (2:219). Without due attention to the restricted domain of the application of general principles, the world might come to be ruled by visionaries with radical plans for political change. As Stewart observed: "Sanguine and inconsiderate projects of reformation are frequently the offspring of clear and argumentative and systematical understandings, but rarely of comprehensive minds" (2:238).

This sentiment corresponded to the received opinion in the circles of moderate reform of the day, which held the idea that readjustment rather than radical restructuring offered the most suitable route to political improvement. It appears to have been the case that while Stewart was anxious for economists to be admitted into the world of politics, he was equally keen that they should not bring with them any ideas and assertions that might be radically disruptive of the existing state of political society. In short, the economist who put into effect Stewart's proposed code of practice could safely be admitted into the corridors of power as reformers, not as subversives.

As to why Stewart found it necessary to supplement his methodological discussion with a crusade of this kind, the answer appears to have resided in the complex and shifting British reaction to events that were taking place across the channel. In particular, it sprang from the manner in which British opinion had implicated the ideas of the physiocrats in those upheavals. By the middle of the 1790s, the physiocrats were so widely held to have been disreputable that the science to which they contributed had increasingly come to be regarded with deep suspicion in what were otherwise widely different political camps. Faced with this climate of opinion, economic science had to reclaim the middle ground, and Stewart went out of his way to establish its respectability. "The general conclusion to which these observations lead," he wrote in his *Philosophy of the Human Mind*, "is sufficiently obvious; that the perfection of political wisdom does not consist in an indiscriminate zeal against reformers, but in a gradual and prudent accommodation of established institutions to the varying opinions, manners, and circumstances of mankind" (2:229).

CONCLUDING REMARKS

In an essay titled "On the Definition of Political Economy; and on the Method of Investigation Proper to It" that appeared in the *Westminster Review* in 1836 (but was written in 1829)—an essay that stands as exemplary of a vision of economic science that the classical economists had largely come to share—John Stuart Mill presented the growth of the discipline in organic terms. According to Mill, economics had not emerged because economists had first measured out the "ground for intellectual cultivation" and subsequently "begun to plant it." On the contrary, as far as Mill was concerned, "facts classed themselves," "discoveries were gathered in," and truths "agglomerated," and all of this without the need for "intentional classification." In much the same way as Mill thought that the modern market economy took shape as the unintended consequence of the rational pursuit of individual self-interest (without the intervention of any human wisdom, as Smith might have put it), the science that studied that economy evidenced the same general pattern of development. Delimiting the province of economics, codifying its territorial boundaries, was (for Mill) like building the walls around an already existing city (1836, 120).

However appealing this picture may be, and however revealing it is of the general tenets of Mill's own epistemology, the role of Stewart in the propagation of Smithian economics would appear to undermine its faithfulness as a representation of what actually took place. For there can be no doubt that Stewart was quite self-consciously engaged in a project of erecting the walls of a city whose architecture and citizenry were at that time scarcely more than those of some imagined community of the future. A monument was certainly to stand in the central square of the city—the statue of Smith—but that monument was carved by Stewart with features that would ensure it embodied only those representations and called up only those associations conformable to his own vision of economic science.

Chapter Seven

POPULATION AND POLITICAL ECONOMY

The bursting of a flower may be trifle. Another will
soon succeed it. But the bursting of the bonds of society is such a separation of parts as cannot take place
without giving the most acute pain to thousands: and a
long time may elapse, and much misery may be
endured, before the wound grows up again.
—Thomas Robert Malthus, *Essay on Population*

THE INTRODUCTION of the principle of population into British political
economy in the late 1790s marked the most significant transformation
that occurred in the subject as it moved into the nineteenth century. It
could not have been more influential—not only for the political implications of political economy but also for the understanding of its social and
moral content. Where once the populousness of a nation was thought of
as a measure of its health, as a beacon of its prosperity and fecundity, the
principle of population called this into question.[1] Furthermore, it sent a
new and ominous message concerning the subsistence wage. The natural
wage rate would now be established by biological necessity rather than
by convention. A certain degree of optimism about the possibilities for
unlimited growth and progress turned instead into an uneasy pessimism.
The connecting tissues of an older agrarian society had been severed, and
nothing seemed to be offered in its place. The moral integrity of society
was under threat. For the first time, instead of being seen as a discourse

---

[1] While Hume's "On the Populousness of Ancient Nations" seems to suggest "the happiness of any society and its populousness are necessary attendants" as a general rule, Malthus
culled it for its historical evidence, and frequently criticised and revised the character of
Hume's causal claims (see Eugene Rotwein's comments in Hume [1955, 116]). For example,
Malthus claimed in the *Essay on Population* that

> Hume, in his essay on the populousness of ancient and modern nations, when he inter-
> mingles, as he says, an inquiry concerning causes, with that concerning facts, does not
> seem to see with his usual penetration, how very little some of the causes he alludes to
> could enable him to form any judgment of the actual population of ancient nations. If
> any inference can be drawn from them, perhaps it should be directly the reverse of
> what Hume draws, though I certainly ought to speak with great diffidence in dissenting
> from a man, who of all others on such subjects was the least likely to be deceived by
> first appearances. (1826, 1:24)

of enlightenment, political economy began to be viewed as a dismal science. It became the subject of derision. Malthus was at the forefront of this change.

Smith occupied a preeminent place in Malthus's thought and writing on morals, politics, and political economy. Whether serving as the anvil in forging Malthus's attack on the speculative visions of William Godwin and Marquis de Condorcet ("phantom[s] of the imagination" [1803, 1:316], as he called them) in the first *Essay on Population*,[2] or as his point of departure in writing the *Principles of Political Economy* essentially as a critical commentary on Ricardo's "new political economy," Smith's orienting influence is apparent. This is not surprising. Though not a consummate theorist, Malthus was consistently a reactive and critical thinker, and throughout his life the work of Smith remained vital and transformative in his enterprise.

Despite Smith's formative influence on Malthus's work, however, this is not how many of his readers have tended to see their relationship.[3] When Malthus chose in the pages of the *Quarterly Review* for 1824 to claim Smith as his ally in an emerging divide between "old" and "new" political economy, James Mill returned fire in the pages of the *Westminster Review*, arguing "that the difficulty of reconciling Mr Malthus and Adam Smith is insuperable" (1824b, 215). Then as now, when the debate was joined, Malthus was required to carry a twin burden.

On the one hand, in Smith's own time, the *Essay on Population* was seen as opposing Smith's political economy with a "dismal science"—and as functioning as a "de-moralizer" of an existing "moral economy."[4] In the twentieth century, beginning with Polanyi, commentators on the

---

[2] This remained true in each of its subsequent three editions (1803, 1806, and 1807)— until Robert Owen replaced Godwin as the focus of Malthus's attention in the third chapter of the third book of the 1817 edition (see Malthus 1803, 1:333). Malthus's writings exist in several scholarly editions. When we refer to the *Essay on Population* in the edition compiled by Patricia James (taken from the 1803 edition of the original with the variora of 1806, 1807, 1817, and 1826), we shall cite it as follows: (Malthus 1803). When we refer to the edition compiled by E. A. Wrigley and D. Souden edition (taken from the 1826 edition), we shall cite it as: (Malthus 1826). When we refer to his *Principles of Political Economy* in the edition compiled by John Pullen (taken from the first edition of 1820), we shall cite it as: (Malthus 1820). When we refer to the edition of the *Principles* compiled by Wrigley and Souden (taken from the posthumously published edition of 1836), we shall cite it as: (Malthus 1836).

[3] One might think here of nineteenth-century critics like Carlyle, Marx, McCulloch, and John Stuart Mill, or twentieth-century critics like Polanyi, E. P. Thompson, and Gertrude Himmelfarb.

[4] The classic statement of this came from Carlyle. In the twentieth century, E. P. Thompson's most influential work (1971) highlighted a deep vein of social injustice in the treatment of the English working class in this period. The force of Thompson's critique of political economy was that it had replaced a moral one.

Smith-Malthus debate persistently maintained this focus on the *Essay on Population* in order to highlight Malthus's moral impoverishment of Smith's political economy through the introduction of a "naturalism" understood as a kind of crude biological reductionism.[5]

On the other hand, it has also been suggested that Malthus's political economy presented a more extreme version of Smithian concepts such as the invisible hand (hidden hand of providence) and, in his opposition to the Poor Laws, laissez-faire.[6] Although it is recognised that this was not perhaps Malthus's own perception of his enterprise, it has been argued that in his hands, "more harshly than Smith, more practically than Mandeville," private virtue had become "apparently pernicious" and "vice a source of benefit" (Burrow 1988, 59).[7] Opinion remains sharply divided over whether Malthus's effort in the *Essay on Population* should be understood as a direct challenge and subversion of the more optimistic perspective on social and commercial development present in Smith (Himmelfarb 1983), or an actual defence of Smith's moral and political economy from the critique levelled by Godwin (Winch 1993). To answer this question, it is necessary to consider Malthus's method of approaching political economy.

THE INTRODUCTION OF METHOD: THE *CRISIS* AND THE *ESSAY ON POPULATION*

The Crisis (1796), Malthus's first though unpublished work, was inspired by not one but two unsettling experiences: the continued political threat to Britain of the effects of an imploding French Revolution and war with France, and the visible "distresses and dissatisfactions" of a growing and

---

[5] See, for example, Polanyi (1944, chapter 10) and Himmelfarb (1983, chapter 4). For an alternative reading, see Winch (1993, 1996). Wrigley has written on the pitfalls of drawing an extreme distinction between the interests of Smith and Malthus in the limits to growth, and the implications of "population, resources and environment, a viewpoint they shared with David Ricardo" (1989, 30–48).

[6] Central to the entire debate is the putative separation between political economy and moral philosophy that Malthus is said to have introduced by grounding the former on the drives of human biology, rather than the efficacy of human will and reason or governmental direction. It is in this sense that Malthus is believed to have "naturalized" laissez-faire, and destroyed the integrity of moral and economic life that Smith had defended as both necessary and thus possible. For an analysis of the romantic connection made between Malthus's political economy and natural theology by influential clerical economists such as Thomas Chalmers, see Hilton (1977, 303–14).

[7] Burrow adds: "In embracing Political Economy and defending Malthus, the Philosophic Radicals accepted the doctrine of unintended consequences in economic life as one of their chief defining characteristics, and so won a large part of their reputation for being harsh, unfeeling, and coldly mechanical" (59). Certainly, his theory of population is read by many

increasingly impoverished rural labouring class at home.[8] These difficulties were being dramatically brought together in his mind by a series of events involving the splits and defections occurring in the Pitt administration in opposition to the war, and the repression and high taxation that resulted from it, and the simultaneous political debate engendered by "Mr. Pitt's Poor Law Bill." "Where are we to look for principles that may save us?" Malthus asked (James 1979, 52).

The title reflects Malthus's general approach of focusing on and reacting to perceived ruptures in the general chain of experience—ruptures that whether they are to be experienced in our understanding of how the universe should operate or how the system of political economy should operate (or indeed as Smith noted, how a card game should be played), are bound to engender frustration on the part of the observer and a search for "new principles" by which to resuture those gaps in our understanding. The concerns are redolent of those of Hume and Smith.[9]

At the time, Malthus had no systematic answer to this question.[10] To address the immediate political crisis that events in France had engen-

---

to have exceeded Smith's reliance on "unintended consequences," to serve as a veritable "test case" for that "doctrine" (59).

[8] Patricia James notes that at the close of the eighteenth century, "the poor of England were near starvation" and their condition in 1800 was to be exacerbated by another late harvest (1979, 86).

[9] The traditions of Humean naturalism and Newtonism were shared in differing degrees by Smith and Malthus. Malthus was interested in reducing the complexity of natural phenomena to an explanatory number of principles, without, however, erring on the side of being too reductionist. He was always finding multiple causes that needed to be accounted for. Indeed, as will be discussed later, Hume is his constant guide, not only on the fundamental question of "causality" in the science of political economy but also on the methods and use of history in forming generalisations from evidence as well as generating revisable principles, and the fundamental psychology of habits, constraints, anticipations, and conventions of the market mechanism. Malthus takes Hume to have stated clearly the belief that people must be encouraged to want and possess not only the "power to produce" but also "the will to consume," and it is an important element in his consideration of effective demand (see Malthus 1836, 9). Of course, being Malthus, he does find points in Hume to disagree with. For example, he notes in the *Essay* that "some of the causes which Hume produces are in the same manner unsatisfactory, or rather make against the inference he has in view than for it." For example, Malthus felt both Hume and Robert Wallace gave too much weight to "the prevalence of the small pox, and other disorders unknown to the ancients . . . as an argument against the populousness of modern nations" (2:152). Malthus does take a more Humean picture of natural laws and what they are—habitual regularities in no sense "determinist" and fit only for *comparison* with Newton's "laws" (see 1820, 13). See also Smith's discussion of the "discomfort, eventually even violent disorder" of the mind, when customary connections of events and expectations are broken (ca. 1750, 44).

[10] It should be noted that prior to Malthus, Bentham had considered the question of pauperism and apparently hoped to do so on the same scale as his prison reform. His *Pauper Management Improved* appeared in 1797, but after Malthus's *Essay* appeared nothing more from Bentham was forthcoming (see Poynter 1969, 107). Bentham's later *Theory of Legisla-*

dered in Britain, he proposed a purely practical solution—"the revival of the true Whig principles in a body of the community sufficiently numerous and powerful [the gentry] to snatch the object of contention from the opposing factions" (James 1979, 50). On the question of the means by which the crisis of the rural poor was to be alleviated, Malthus was more circumspect, supporting the Pitt proposal for continued parish relief but registering uncertainty about the principles that supported it. Acknowledging the growing number of indigent labouring poor in England, Malthus had at this point nothing systematic to say and could only comment in passing:

> On the subject of population, I cannot agree with Archdeacon Paley, who says, that the quantity of happiness in any country is best measured by the number of people. Increasing population is the most certain possible sign of the happiness and prosperity of a state; but the actual population may only be a sign of the happiness that is past. (cited in Empson 1837, 469–506)[11]

When Malthus turned to Godwin's essay on "Avarice and Profusion" in *The Enquirer* (1797) together with his *An Enquiry concerning Political Justice and Its Influence on Modern Morals and Happiness* (1793), he found just such an opportunity to offer a systematic analysis of the political and economic crises he was observing. Godwin's was in his opinion, however, a deeply flawed and—in the context of the times—unsettling proposal to connect a theory of people's perfectible nature to a principle of diminishing population, and enunciate a root and branch reform of

---

tion (1802) and *Constitutional Code* (1830) contained some brief discussions of the pauper question but nothing more. J. R. Poynter, however, claims that Bentham's consideration of paupers before Malthus, probably in response to the scarcity of 1795, did produce a series of timely essays, including the *Independent Labourer*, three *Essays on the Poor Laws*, and the two larger works, *Pauper Systems Compared* and *Pauper Management Improved*, "interrupting their composition" in 1797 to write his *Observations* on Pitt's Bill (1969, 107). Bentham apparently blamed George III for the fact that nothing "institutional" had come of this work: "But for George the Third, all the paupers in the country would, long ago, have been under my management." (108). What is perhaps interesting about Bentham's plans and Malthus's own priorities and methods is how vastly different they are—with Malthus's rejection of workhouses as morally corruptive being only one point in contrast.

[11] The reading of Malthus as a Paleyite Utilitarian presents complexities. Unquestionably, larger utility understood in terms of the larger interests of the nation is at work in Malthus's thought, as is the understanding of the market mechanism as a system in which both individual and class interests confront one another in the form of wages, profits and rent and are reconciled in the prices of commodities. Equally clearly, Malthus shared certain moral and religious perspectives with Paley. However, on the issue of population, Malthus could not be characterized as a Paleyite Utilitarian since it is clear that he looked at the same phenomena as Paley, did the numbers, but came up with quite different views. In addition to Boyd Hilton (1988), there are two additional studies of the relationship of Malthus's evolving economic, social and moral thought and Paley's theodicy (Winch, 1996 and A.M.C. Waterman, 1991).

both the constitution and the advancing commercial society over which it governed. In what might be described as Godwin's futuristic utopia of enlightened rationalism, reason would so triumph over selfish interest—"mind over matter"—such that

the men therefore whom we are supposing to exist, when the earth shall refuse itself to a more extended population, will probably cease to propagate. The whole will be a people of men, and not of children. Generation will not succeed generation, nor truth have, in a certain degree, to recommence her career every thirty years. Other improvements may be expected to keep pace with those of health and longevity. There will be no war, no crimes, no administration of justice, as it is called, and no government. Every man will seek, with ineffable ardor, the good of all. (James 1979, 59–60)

If Godwin's claims appeared to Malthus wholly lacking in either empirical or genuine logical thought, and his "beautiful system" was a mere "phantom of the imagination," it nevertheless provided him with the impetus for "a candid investigation of these subjects, accompanied with a perfect readiness to adopt any theory, warranted by sound philosophy" (1826, 1:64–65, 60). In short, his *Essay on Population*:

It is a perfectly just observation of Mr. Godwin, that "There is a principle in human society by which population is perpetually kept down to the level of the means of subsistence." The sole question is, what is this principle? Is it some obscure and occult cause? Is it some mysterious interference of heaven, which at a certain period, strikes the men with impotence, and the women with barrenness? Or is it a cause open to our researches, within our view, a cause, which has constantly been observed to operate, though with varied force, in every state in which man has been placed? Is it not a degree of misery, the necessary and inevitable results of the laws of nature, which human institutions, so far from aggravating, have tended considerably to mitigate, though they never can remove? (1:70)

GODWIN, SMITH, AND THE *ESSAY ON POPULATION*

The *Essay on Population*, which Malthus chose to publicly acknowledge some five years after its original publication in 1798, is his most lasting contribution to the economic, moral, and political thought of his own period. While Malthus published only one edition of his *Principles of Political Economy* during his lifetime,[12] he produced six editions of the

---

[12] The second 1826 edition, with his substantial changes all but complete, appeared shortly after his death.

Essay on Population, continuously expanding and revising it to nearly four times its original length, and offering that "collection of a greater number of facts in elucidation of the general argument" that he acknowledged in his original preface remained to be supplied (1826, 1:i). In the course of these revisions, he even changed the subtitle, erasing mention of Godwin and Condorcet. The revised text of the 1803 edition effectively announced Malthus's enlarged and modified views of the population principle. So great were the changes that some have been led to regard them as effectively separate works (1:8).[13] The work became—next to Smith's *Wealth of Nations*—the most widely read economic treatise of the time. It made Malthus "England's foremost living political economist" until the publication of Ricardo's *Principles of Political Economy* in 1817 (Semmel 1963b, 7). It certainly made him, forever, the person who the critics most loved to hate.

Malthus's original *Essay on Population* was accused of combining the twin faults of being unoriginal as well as empirically unsupportable.[14] Undoubtedly he was not the first to examine either increasing population or the growth of pauperism. Equally, however, he was the first to attempt to consider as a matter of science how they might be systematically related and related in a particular way. He used this systematic relationship to destroy utterly what he took to be the fatuous optimism of Godwin's belief in the perfectibility of human beings. He jettisoned Godwin's Rousseauist-inspired idea that the source of society's woes was to be found in the institutions of government and commercial society.

---

[13] The subsequent (second through sixth) editions then "remained recognizably the same" (8). James says of this second edition that it is so different from the first, it is difficult to believe they were written only five years apart: the basic population principle remains the same, and "a few passages from the first edition appear verbatim in the second, but one's general impression is that these two books are the work of two different men" (cited in Malthus 1803, 1:81).

[14] While his numbers (and proportionate ratios) purporting to describe Britain's demographic problem may have been ultimately wrong, his intuitions of the situation were in an important sense profoundly right (Malthus 1798a, 22). Although the exact character and causes (increasing birth versus declining mortality rates) of Britain's population "crises of the last quarter of the 18th century is still subject to debate, the reality of it is not in question." According to one source,

From 1760 to 1801 English agriculture was unable to keep pace with the growth of population; domestic agricultural output grew by an average of only 0.44 percent per year, while population increased by an average of 0.83 percent per year. It was a Malthusian crisis. Yet growth rates accelerated to a still higher level. The population of great Britain doubled, from 10.7 to 21 million, between 1801 and 1851, a growth rate of 1.36 percent per year. How could this unprecedented swarming of people on a small offshore island be made consistent with a rising standard of living? It was impossible on the fixed area of English cultivable land, whatever miracles English technological progress in agriculture might accomplish. (B. Thomas 1986, 70–171)

Malthus's critique here is fundamentally a methodological one, claiming that however admirable, Godwin simply lacked sufficient logic, empirical or historical evidence, proper inference techniques, and causal principles to prove his claims:

> The system of equality which Mr Godwin proposes, is, without doubt, by far the most beautiful and engaging of any that has yet appeared. An amelioration of society to be produced merely by reason and conviction, wears much more the promise of permanence, than any change effected and maintained by force. The unlimited exercise of private judgment, is a doctrine inexpressibly grand and captivating, and has vast superiority over those systems where every individual is in a manner the slave of the public. The substitution of benevolence as the master-spring, and moving principle of society, instead of self-love, is a consummation devoutly to be wished. In short, it is impossible to contemplate the whole of this fair structure, without emotions of delight and admiration, accompanied with ardent longing for the period of its accomplishment. But, alas! That moment can never arrive. The whole is little better than a dream, a beautiful phantom of the imagination. These "gorgeous palaces" of happiness and immortality, these "solemn temples" or truth and virtue will dissolve, "like the baseless fabric of a vision," when we awaken to real life, and contemplate the true and genuine situation of man on earth. (1826, 1:64–65)

Godwin's supposition of a radical break between how a person is and what they will come to be was an obvious problem for Malthus. For Malthus, Godwin had forgone the connecting logic of Hume—no unbroken chain of cause and effect. This meant that Godwin's claim was merely speculative (or even, "spectoral"), or as Malthus put it, "little better than a dream." It was but a "phantom of the imagination" in that it had no direct relationship either to people or society as they existed.

The problems inherent in Godwin's analysis were for Malthus primarily flaws in his method of enquiry: "He has not proceeded in his inquiries with the caution that sound philosophy seems to require. His conclusions are often unwarranted by his premises. He fails sometimes in removing the objections which he himself brings forward" (1826, 1:64). While the "spirit and energy" of Godwin's "beautiful system" were praiseworthy, Malthus claimed that the result of such reasoning about human perfectibility and population (as both Godwin and Condorcet were proposing) was not sound philosophy, and as such, it was potentially dangerous to the proper conduct of a human science: "Improbable and unfounded hypotheses, so far from enlarging the bounds of human science, they are contracting it; so far from promoting the improvement of the human mind, they are obstructing it: they are throwing us back again almost into the infancy of knowledge" (1:60). But Malthus thought that the damage done was not only to weaken the foundations of a Newtonian method in human science. He also considered it dangerous to the psychology and expectations of ordinary people, who might act on the "illusion" of such false causal chains and believe incorrectly that "everything appeared to be in the grasp of human powers." The practical effects of such "mentally intoxicated" people, in Malthus's view, would be to disrupt the conduct of British social and political life (in a particularly French way) (1:60–64).

In the *Essay on Population*, Malthus linked together the elements of science he found missing from Godwin—namely, a causal explanation, a fundamental principle motivating the whole (his principle of population), and evidence of "invariable experience" (1826, 1:62). The second edition contained much more of the historical and comparative cultural data that Malthus felt compelled to supply in order to support the polemic of the original work. But he did not engage in theoretical or conjectural history, or propose a theory of the stages of development of society. Instead, he brought to bear evidence for the application of his principle of population from many more cases drawn from both the ancient and modern world. Malthus's use of history mirrored that of Hume (to whom he specifically refers).[15] Like Hume, Malthus sought to avail himself of the widest possible repository of experiences on which to ground any generalisation. History provided, for Malthus, a sufficient quantity of experiments on which to frame reliable propositions and isolated those regularities of human behaviour that came to function as connecting principles of human nature (1803, 1:292–93).[16]

The population principle was cast in the form of a Humean law—it required not only an understanding of the principles of human nature but also that there be a high degree of "constant conjunction" between such principles and specific, discrete sets of historical conditions. This is what the historical cases were intended to provide.[17]

While the basic claims concerning the causes and the effects of the principle of population remained unchanged, the 1803 edition proposed a

[15] Malthus lists Hume's *Of Commerce, Of the Populousness of Ancient Nations*, and *Of the Rise and Progress of the Arts and Sciences*.

[16] For example, after an extensive canvassing of a "statistical account" of Scotland and Ireland, he concludes: "All the checks to population which have been observed to prevail in society, in the course of this review of it, are clearly resolvable into moral restraint, vice, and misery." In support, Malthus quotes Hume that "of all sciences, there is none where first appearances are more deceitful than in politics (2:185). Critics of Malthus accused him of piling up evidence. This would be fundamentally to misunderstand his scientific method.

[17] In this sense, Malthus's use of history eluded both Ricardo and Keynes. For example, Ricardo complained that he was himself only concerned with England whereas Malthus drew generalisations looking at Ireland, the United States, India, and China (1820b, 346). Keynes criticised Malthus for trying to make his theory "more realistic" by "burdening" it with "historical details" (see Skidelsky 1992, 413).

significant revision to the preventive checks to population by way of the explicit development of the concept of moral restraint as the most effective "voluntary" and "prudential check to the growth of population" (Malthus 1803, 1:16).[18] Some would assert that this revision effectively amounted to a recantation of his original argument that people's natural propensity to reproduce was unable to be checked except by pestilence (death and disease). Whether seen as a fundamental revision (and concession to Godwin), or the enhancement of a position already implicit in the first edition, moral or prudential restraint must be added to the other explicit features that Malthus introduced into the classical description of market society.[19]

SMITH IN THE *ESSAY ON POPULATION* AND MALTHUS'S *POLITICAL ECONOMY*

Malthus's fundamental disagreements with Godwin drew explicitly on a view of human science and a method of enquiry appropriate to it. He publicly endorsed the opinion that Smith's *Wealth of Nations* had "done for political economy, what the *Principia* of Newton did for physics" (1824, 257).[20] He explicitly traced this approach to Hume. Smith had presented society as "an imaginary machine." Science, according to Smith, took the form of a "systematical arrangement of different observations connected by a few common principles" and succeeded (as Newton had done) in "connecting all together in the same chain" (1750, 66–67).[21] Malthus's writing, too, is replete with machine analogies.

---

[18] While many have suggested that this concept, introduced in the 1803 edition, was new, Wrigley argues that it was present in 1798 and was not quite as novel as Malthus was himself to claim in the edition of 1803 (in Malthus 1826, 1:78). The suggestion of moral restraint is certainly there in the first edition, but it also seems correct to note that the greater emphasis on the operation of the preventive mechanism (as opposed to the positive checks) not only in recent English history but also "modern Europe" was thought by Malthus to be the "most powerful of the checks" (1803, 1:305). Malthus concluded this by the use of the newly available 1800 census data by Rickman, but also by reference to additional historical studies that would support his Humean approach to the use of history (2:185).

[19] According to A.M.C. Waterman, "moral or prudential restraint" was interpreted by critics following Robert Southey as Malthus's retreat from the "negative polemic" against Godwin and represented a reopening of "the possibility of continuous improvement in the human condition" (1991, 140). In relation to Smith's conception of market, Malthus himself saw this merely as an adjustment. Yet in several ways, what moral restraint entails is the most serious departure from "the master," as it impinges on the fundamental integrating mechanisms on which Smith relies for an image of societal order absent design and independent of the wills of men.

[20] Malthus is here quoting and agreeing with J. R. McCulloch's assessment of Smith.

[21] That is, neither Smith nor Malthus believed that the laws of a human science were identical in their character to Newton's laws, as Malthus stated explicitly in the *Principles*:

Malthus imagined market society as a machine, and placed the principle of population—understood as a set of complex relations and practices between land, food, and numbers of people—at its center. It was "the masterspring and moving principle of society" (Malthus 1803, 1:316). In this, he generalised a causal claim of body over mind: "The first great awakener of the mind seems to be the wants of the body" (1826, 1:124). These references to machines were sometimes quite general, as when he referred (as Smith had done before him) in the *Principles of Political Economy* to the earth as resembling a machine:

> The earth has been sometimes compared to a vast machine, presented by nature to man for the production of food and raw materials; but, to make the resemblance more just, as far as they admit of comparison, we should consider the soil as a present to man of a great number of machines, all susceptible of continued improvement by the application of capital to them, but yet of very different original qualities and powers. (1820, 184)

What Malthus meant by this was a complex system of causal factors whose effects needed to be understood. This becomes clear when he then makes the comparison between real and imagined machines:

> The machines which produce corn and raw material, on the contrary, are the gifts of nature, not the works of man; and we find, by experience that these gifts have very different qualities and powers. The most fertile lands of the country, those which, like the best machinery in manufactures, yield the greatest products with the least labour and capital, are never found sufficient, owing to the second main cause of rent before stated, to supply the effective demand of an increasing population. (185)[22]

Having followed Smith so closely in his critique of Godwin's optimistic fantasy, Malthus must have encountered an unhappy surprise when he realised that (contra Smith) the growth of the wealth of the nation was not inconsistent with the expanding poverty of a significant part of it.

The study of the laws of nature is, in all its branches, interesting. Even those physical laws by which the more distant parts of the universe are governed, and over which, of course, it is impossible for man to have the slightest influence, are yet noble and rational objects of curiosity; but the laws which regulate the movements of human society have an infinitely stronger claim to our attention, both because they relate to objects about which we are daily and hourly conversant, and because their effects are constantly modified by human interference. (1820, 1:13)

[22] Malthus's view of the machine is more complex than the claim of his work as mechanistic normally implies. In contrast, if one turns to Malthus's contemporary, Ricardo, one will find there a rendering of Smith's idea of the economic machine as something more concrete, deterministic, and applicable.

The professed object of Dr Adam Smith's inquiry, is, the nature and causes of the wealth of nations. There is another inquiry, however, perhaps still more interesting, which he occasionally mixes with it; I mean an inquiry into the causes which effect the happiness of nations, or the happiness and comfort of the lower orders of society, which is the most numerous class in every nation. I am sufficiently aware of the near connection of these two subjects, and that the causes which tend to increase the wealth of a state, tend also, generally speaking, to increase the happiness of the lower classes of the people. But perhaps Dr Adam Smith has considered *these two inquiries as still more nearly connected than they really are; at least, he has not stopped to take notice of those instances, where the wealth of a society may increase (according to his definition of wealth) without having any tendency to increase the comforts of the labouring part of it.* (1826, 1:107; emphasis added)[23]

While Malthus stated clearly in this passage that he was not to be understood as wishing to enter into a philosophical discussion of the meaning of happiness, he did assert that whatever it was, it certainly included health along with a "command of the necessaries and conveniences of life" (1:107). With this addition, however, he had driven a wedge between the concepts of wealth and happiness—and had directly confronted those passages of the *Wealth of Nations* that might have tended either to conflate them or have implied that there might be no trade-off between them.

But if the principle of population thus distanced Malthus from Smith, in almost all of Malthus's other writings on political economy, and especially in his disagreements with Ricardo (and the adherents of what Malthus dubbed the "new" political economy), he presented himself as a faithful disciple of Smith (and the "old" political economy). While on some subjects this case would be difficult to prosecute (and here, one thinks especially of his contributions to monetary theory during the Bullion Controversy and his position on the possibility of a general overproduction of commodities),[24] and on others it is less so.

For example, on the subject of value and distribution, there is more than a little truth in Malthus's claim. In the *Quarterly Review* for 1824, he maintained, like Smith, that in the presence of positive profits, exchangeable value was no longer determined by the quantity of labour employed to obtain them. In *The Measure of Value* (Malthus 1823) he

---

[23] As Henry George later wrote: "It is this very fact—that want appears where productive power is greatest and the production of wealth is largest—that constitutes the enigma which perplexes the civilized world, and which we are trying to unravel" (1926, 150). Of course, George did not feel Malthus had correctly unravelled it either, seeing the cause to be more "in the maladjustments of men."

[24] In these two contexts, Malthus neither applied established quantity theory arguments nor did he rule out the possibility of general gluts.

maintained, like Smith, that labour commanded would thus be the appropriate measure of value. In the *Principles of Political Economy* he maintained, like Smith, that the rate of profits was determined by the "competition of capitals." On all of these matters, he was at odds with Ricardo and aligned with Smith.[25]

To say this is, however, only to affirm that the relationship between Smith and Malthus is a subtle and variable one. That Malthus always deferred to the writer he called "the master" is evident enough. That he also held the *Wealth of Nations* in such esteem that he was offended when Ricardo chose to depart from it in his *Principles of Political Economy* is apparent. But that the reality of the theoretical and conceptual linkages between Smith and Malthus on two key topics in political economy—population and progress—are less secure, is also certain.

Passion, Moral Restraint, and Unintended Consequences

There is another link that is sometimes made between Malthus and Smith: the role of unintended consequences: "Nothing can tend so strongly to bring theories and general principles into discredit as the occurrence of consequences, from particular premises, that have not been foreseen" (Malthus 1836, 12). Yet in the body of Malthus's own writings with regard to the market system there is significant resistance to the use of unintended consequences as a theoretical or practical mechanism of explanation.[26] Malthus discusses the pitfalls, moral and economic, of consequences *unforeseen* in the chain of cause and effect related to population growth:

> From the inattention of mankind hitherto to the consequences of increasing too fast, it must be presumed, that these consequences are not so immediately and powerfully connected with the conduct which leads to them, as in other instances; *but the delayed knowledge of particular effects does not alter their nature*, or our obligation to regulate our conduct accordingly, as soon as we are satisfied of what this conduct ought to be. (1803, 2:88; emphasis added)

What appears to be unintended—and for the moral theorist, then, unaccountable—is on closer examination merely unforeseen. It is the result of ignorance or inattention to the consequences of their own action. People are not relieved of moral accountability for their actions when the nexus between cause and effect is close. Smith had also placed accountability "to

[25] This is not the place to examine in detail how successful Malthus was in defending these positions against Ricardo and the writers of the new political economy. These are fully and definitively discussed in De Vivo (1984).

[26] Winch has argued that "unintended consequences play a much larger role in Smith's explanations of social outcomes than they do in Malthus's" (1993, 247).

God and his fellow creatures" at the centre of an individual's character as a moral being (1976–85, 6:52). Although not entirely successful, Malthus appears to be at pains to avoid the appearance of moral muddle introduced in this context by direct resort to an argument of either unintended consequences or, as we shall see, the invisible hand.

When the nexus between cause and effect is more distant, Malthus adds that "it has not been till after long and painful experience that the conduct most favourable to the happiness of man has been forced upon his attention" (1803, 2:88); again, not unintended but unforeseen, and thus in principle, foreseeable. The workers' moral responsibility for their actions in exercising moral restraint therefore lies at the heart of how Malthus saw the population problem. In other words, as Malthus developed his argument, the solution to the problem of population as he perceived it was either prudence or pestilence. The positive or involuntary checks to population growth in the forms of misery, death, and disease involved painful experience. Although their causes may seem to people at times inexplicable, Malthus does not take that fact to be indicative of a need to rely on Providence as an explanatory device. The will of "Inscrutable Providence" is unknowable to us. As such, it could never be included in a scientific analysis of the imaginary machine of the market. At best, it could be rationalized as a signal to people of the need to pay attention to the larger and *foreseeable* consequences of their actions (see Malthus 1803, 2:228, 249).[27]

In this way, Malthus could be said to have developed the causal logic of the principle of population very much in Humean terms. Hume had argued in the *Treatise of Human Nature* that passions directly arising from the "natural impulses of instinct" were "perfectly unaccountable" (1739–40, 439). Among these passions Hume included hunger and physical desire or lust. In themselves morally neutral, they "produce both good and evil, and proceed not from them, like the other affections" (439; see also 1748, 301). These passions involve a direct attraction to objects, and are irreducible to other elements. Eating and procreative sex are not pursued rationally, "for" pleasure. They are not rationally self-interested passions in that sense, though pleasure certainly may follow in their wake. In recognition of this, Hume contended that instinct might impel someone to repeatedly, and with complete foreknowledge of the consequences, to adopt a course of action detrimental to themselves: "Men often act *know-*

---

[27] On Malthus's account, we are not beguiled by nature; nature assists us with information in the form of reactions to our actions, which over time, even the least attentive can recognise. This would seem to make the claim that only "a providential view of history could moralize unintended consequences" perhaps true but less applicable to Malthus's own thought than to later forms of "Malthusianism" (Burrow 1988, 66).

ingly against their interest, for which reason the view of the greatest possible good does not always influence them" (1739–40, 418; emphasis added). The choice to constrain such instincts through reason is thus a moral choice.

For this reason alone, it might be thought to be inappropriate for *any* type of argument based on unintended consequences. Yet such an instinct could be subjected to rational control. This is what makes such voluntary, preventive, and accountable control worthy to be called "*moral restraint.*" As Malthus noted, "The preventive check, as far as it is voluntary, is peculiar to man, and arises from that distinctive superiority in his reasoning faculties which enables him to *calculate distant consequences*" (1803, 1:16; emphasis added).

SMITH, MALTHUS, AND THE INVISIBLE HAND

In emphasising the role of experience and consequences foreseen in acting accountably within his vision of market society, Malthus had placed himself somewhere in the middle between Godwin and Smith. Malthus gave greater stress than Smith had done to human agency in the successful operation of the market, while rejecting the more radical position of utopian reformers (such as Godwin) for whom reason was an efficacious tool in the perfectibility of human beings.[28]

For Malthus, the capacity to calculate distant consequences and form reliable plans for the future is a fundamental part of the formation of moral character, or prudence (1820, 251). The need to calculate distant consequences is also an important part of the ordinary operation of commerce. For example, an emphasis on the certainty of expectation would seem to accompany the principle of supply and demand on which Malthus's mechanism of the market depended. Often, for Malthus, it is the probable expectation of what cannot as well as what can be done that operates to prevent the perception of unhappy surprises in the system's ebb and flow of cause and effect that comprises supply and demand.[29]

---

[28] As one commentator has noted, he "did not soften this vision with allusions to 'the hidden hand of providence' in the manner of Mrs. Marcet, which may be why his commitment to laissez-faire remained shaky" (Hilton 1988, 70). James went further to suggest that Malthus "was at heart a paternal interventionist" (1979, 313).

[29] "To know what can be done, and how to do it, is beyond a doubt, the most valuable species of information. The next to it is, to know what cannot be done, and why we cannot do it" (1820, 17). One example of this is to be found in Malthus's (anonymous) "Investigation of the Cause of the Present High Price of Provisions." Written in the politically volatile context of the 1800 grain shortage, Malthus argued using the principle of supply and demand that the cause of the high prices distressing the poor was real shortage, and not, as

If the invisible hand was absent in Malthus's discussions of the market mechanism, however, reference to it was appearing in the works of evangelical or Christian economists such as Thomas Chalmers.[30] Indeed, by 1800, Stewart was openly critical of Malthus for not mitigating those "gloomy inferences" surrounding his political economy, by including references to an economy of nature in which its "self-correcting function" would be "asserted and explained, both in political economy and social ethics" (cited in Waterman 1991, 113–14). It seemed to many that insofar as the logic of an invisible hand was linked to an assertion about both growth and human progress within a system of natural liberty, Malthus's principle of population stood in apparent tension with it.[31] It is in this context that Malthus's language in the defensive 1806 appendix to the *Essay on Population* appears most reminiscent of Smith's metaphor.

In an effort to defend the economic core of his principle of population from religious critics (who claimed that it contradicted "the original command of the Creator"), Malthus repeated Smith's insight: that self-love is a more powerful and original passion than benevolence for humankind. When it comes to one's own survival, or that of one's family, "the great author of nature" has not left our actions to be governed by "the cold and speculative consideration of general consequences." "By this wise provision," Malthus claimed, "the most ignorant are led to promote the

---

was being claimed, selfish speculation on the part of corn dealers. While expressing support for the justices who, "very humanely, and I am far from saying improperly," increased the level of parish relief to the poor as wage support for the purchase of corn in a rising market, Malthus refused to condemn those dealers who chose in the short term to hold back corn from sale. He maintained that those dealers who kept back corn "undoubtedly consulted their own interest; but they, as undoubtedly, *whether the intention was there or not is of no consequence*, consulted the true interest of the state: for, if they had not kept it back, too much would have been consumed, and there would have been a famine instead of a scarcity at the end of the year" (1800, 9; emphasis added). Malthus's language deliberately sets aside issues of intended or unintended consequences, as he now saw the question as one purely of economic analysis of the laws of supply and demand, which for him lay at the core of the operation of the market mechanism.

[30] Waterman notes that the Smithian idea of an invisible hand was given "theological significance" by Christian political economists (1991, 150).

[31] Stewart's own position, as expressed in his *Elements of the Philosophy of the Human Mind*, was that when primitive man "follows blindly his instinctive principles of action, he is led by an invisible hand, and contributes his share to the execution of a plan, of the nature and advantages of which he has no conception." It is difficult to see how such a providentialist rendering of "instinct" could but controvert the import of the *Essay on Population* (Stewart 1792–1827, 248). According to Waterman, the task of reconciling Malthusianism with the self-correcting function of nature "constituted the programme of Christian Political Economy" (1991, 114). Boyd Hilton has distinguished Malthus's economic thought from those of the Evangelical economists such as Chalmers, who "rested firmly on providentialism" and were anxious to "show the hand of God at work in the economic operations of society" (1988).

general happiness, an end which they would have totally failed to attain if the moving principle of their conduct had been benevolence" (1803, 2:214, 214n19–20).

In following Smith, Malthus avoids actual reference to the invisible hand, and renounced any suggestion that his argument gave "the slightest sanction" to Mandeville's logic of the unintended consequences relating vice to virtue. Quite to the contrary, Malthus presented it as a case in which a positive passion, that of parental love, has caused positive effects—namely, the survival of the species. Malthus was quite aware (like Hume) that instincts were capable of producing positive or negative consequences. Accordingly, that this same passion, "which under proper regulations is the source of all honorable industry," when "pushed to excess . . . becomes useless and disgusting, and consequently vicious."[32] Moral restraint was prudential, not blind. It was providential restraint. It was a vehicle to tip the scales against a dismal social prognosis contained in the unrestricted operation of the law of population. It was human (and Humean) foresight of the likely consequences of cause and effect set against human passions. Malthus wished to promote it as a capacity within the reach of ordinary people, whom he believed were in principle capable of understanding the principles of a developing science of political economy—not opaque, but visible.[33]

This points to a basic revision that Malthus made to Smith's political economy. Writing nearly a quarter century after Smith, and from within a more fractious political and economic context, Malthus could no longer make use of the invisible hand (nor indeed, could any other classical economist) as Smith had done—as a felicitous metaphor for informing ordinary people's perceptions of market society. Instead, Malthus argued that "political economy is perhaps the only science of which it might be said that the ignorance of it is not merely a deprivation of the good, but produces great evil." He proposed in the 1803 edition of the *Essay on Population* that Smith's suggestion to teach "the elementary parts of geometry

---

[32] At another point in his analysis of Malthus's revision of the *Essay on Population*, Waterman argues based on this passage that under the pressure of Stewart's "ideological programme" Malthus "formulated an 'invisible hand' theorem" by discussing moral restraint in terms of individuals deferring marriage out of *self-love* in order to achieve *target* income, thereby restricting the supply of labour, raising price, and thus bringing about the unintended consequence that "actual income from labour is brought nearer *target* income" (1991, 143).

[33] This is not to suggest, with Samuel Hollander (1989), that Malthus's Christianity is irrelevant to his economic thinking, nor is this point intended as a disagreement with assertions made by Winch that for Malthus, the invisible hand—if he had employed it—could only be that of the Christian deity" (1993). It is to suggest that for methodological reasons, however, Malthus had no need to recur to it in order to explain the working of the market mechanism.

and mechanics" in parish schools should be amended to include "the simplest principles of political economy." Malthus continued, "I cannot help
thinking that the common principles by which markets are regulated
might be made sufficiently clear to be of considerable use. . . . It is certainly a subject that, as it interests the lower classes of people nearly,
would like[ly] attract their attention" (1803, 2:152, 152n10; see also
O'Brien 1975, 272).

While less than sanguine in 1803 about whether this goal could be
accomplished, some two decades later Malthus remarked on the great
strides that had been made on this project:

> It is particularly gratifying to me, at the end of the year 1825, to see that
> what I stated as so desirable twenty-two years ago, seem to be now on the
> eve of its accomplishment. The increasing attention which in the interval has
> been paid to the science of political economy; the lectures which have been
> given at Cambridge, London, and Liverpool; the chair which has lately been
> established at Oxford; the projected University in the metropolis; and, above
> all, the Mechanic's Institution, open the fairest prospect that, within a mod-
> erate period of time, the fundamental principles of political economy will,
> to a very useful extent, be known to the higher, middle, and a most important
> portion of the working classes of society in England. (1803, 2:152n10)[34]

In Malthus's opinion, for moral and political as well as economic reasons,
it was both necessary and possible that the principles of the market mechanism be broadly understood by those who participated in it. In large part
this was so because he believed that individuals, government, and societal
institutions were to be held morally accountable for the practical consequences of their actions. For this reason, the chains of cause and effect in
the machine of the market had to be open to inspection by everyone.
Contrary to those who feared the politically incendiary consequences of
educating the labouring classes, Malthus called such arguments illiberal
and feeble. The labouring classes needed a clear-eyed appraisal of the
"real nature of their situation" (2:154).

---

[34] Malthus's commitment to education is important. This was clearly Malthus's aim not
only in writing a treatise on *Definitions in Political Economy* along with rules to guide
political economists in the use of their terms but also in his belief that the community needed
the help of educational institutions to promote their shared understandings and expectations for the science.

Chapter Eight

UTILITY, PROPERTY, AND POLITICAL
PARTICIPATION

In all questions of political change, there are two dangers, of an opposite direction, to be considered. The
first is the danger of doing too little; the second that of
doing too much. The first is by far the most common
error; as timidity is a much more universal and powerful source of human misery than rashness; although the
evils produced by the second, are much more simultaneous, and, for the moment, much more formidable.
—James Mill, "Emancipation of Spanish America,"
Edinburgh Review

BETWEEN 1751 AND 1806, the population of England nearly doubled.[1]
This dramatic demographic change presented new challenges both to political economists and political thinkers within the nation. An earlier confidence in the connection between a growing population and rising economic prosperity—a confidence that the *Wealth of Nations* was taken to
reinforce—subsided. In its place arose growing fears of the social, civil,
and political dangers that might be posed by a restless labouring population. In the hands of some, the Malthusian principle of population provided an analytical framework from which to consider these economic,
moral, and political consequences.[2] It highlighted both a challenge to the
moral integrity of modern society, and doubts as to whether hoped-for
economic growth and social progress was sustainable. It suggested possible solutions by way of prudential checks and Poor Law reform. Yet the
Benthamite principle of utility provided another analytical framework
and a set of suggested solutions. The earliest and best-known suggestions
for reform from this perspective came from James Mill.

[1] See Wrigley and Scofield (1981, 208–9). Their estimates have the population of
England growing from a total of 5,772,415 to 9,267,570. By 1820, the combined population of England, Scotland, and Ireland was 20.6 million (in Western Europe, only France
was more populous).

[2] See, for example, Place (1822). See also the earlier and formative findings of
Eden (1797).

While it would be something of an exaggeration to say that a great controversy rages over Mill's role in the movement for democratic reform in Britain during the first three decades of the nineteenth century, it is certainly true that sharp divisions exist over exactly how that role is to be cast. According to some, Mill was quintessentially the spokesperson for the political demands of the middle classes, the advocate of a reform of Parliament designed to make it representative of the interests of private property.[3] According to others, Mill was more the democrat he often declared himself to be, the advocate of a reform of Parliament designed to make it more broadly representative of "the people."[4] Doubtless, these divisions persist because so much is at stake. The democratic commitment of those varieties of liberalism that find their basis in utilitarian theory is ultimately in question. This is perhaps why commentators on Mill's politics seem to agree on one thing at least: that we cannot have it both ways, and that it is necessary for us to locate Mill's politics squarely in one or other of these putatively opposing encampments.

The possibility that Mill's politics might have embraced each of these opinions has not, of course, been entirely overlooked. But those who have travelled this interpretive path have almost uniformly reached the conclusion that Mill was either inconsistent or confused, or both.[5] The appeal

[3] Thus, for example, Asa Briggs remarked that the "paeans of praise" for the middle ranks of society that arose during that time "were echoed even more eloquently and certainly more permanently by James Mill in his famous *Essay on Government*" (1956, 68–69). Winch's editorial annotations to Mill's *Selected Economic Writings* note that "for all his talk of 'the people,' Mill's view of the working-class movement was basically paternalistic; their best fate was to be guided, and perhaps ultimately assimilated, by their immediate superiors" (cited in Mill 1966, 202; see also 13, 196, but compare his remarks in Collini, Winch, and Burrow 1983, 101). See also Grampp (1948, 728); Gay (1984, 40). The charge that Mill was the champion of the interests of the middle classes against those of the working class was regularly brought against him by contemporary working-class radicals; see Thompson (1984, esp. 31–33, 56). For Mill's opinion of one of their number (Thomas Hodgskin), see his *Letter to Brougham*, September 3, 1832, in the Brougham Papers, University College, London, Mss. 10765; quoted in Robbins (1961, 135).

[4] See, for example, Hamburger (1962, 188ff); Burrow (1988, 40); Ryan (1984, 113). Alan Ryan argues that

identifying James Mill as the uninhibited apologist for capitalism that he has retrospectively been claimed to be ought to reflect on the fact that Mill's own view of what had to be avoided at all costs was what he called the unhealthy condition of the large manufacturing districts, where an impoverished work force confronted a harsh, selfish and money-grabbing group of employers. If democracy and property were to be compatible, the distribution of property had to be such that it diffused rather than provoked the class war. (1984, 113)

[5] Elie Halévy claimed that in the essay on *Government*, Mill "was obliged to be careful concerning both the publisher who printed it, and the public to whom it was addressed," and that Mill "explicitly adheres in it neither to the principle of utility nor to the democratic idea" (1928, 420). See also William Thomas, who remarked that "a document which af-

of this line of interpretation is that it at least allows one to avoid the intellectual gymnastics seemingly so common in those readings that would have us paint Mill's politics in either black or white. For unlike them, on this alternative reading one is able to admit all of what Mill actually had to say on the subject of politics, rather than having to find reasons why one might legitimately put to one side those of his remarks that do not blend neatly into whichever representation of Mill's politics is being fashioned.[6]

We wish to suggest and explore another interpretive strategy. Mill's contributions to the science of politics—"that master science," as he once called it (1818a, 708)—might be more satisfactorily understood when due account is taken of the fact that in presenting his vision of a reformed polity, Mill found it necessary to provide a mapping from the principles on which representation was made to rest, to the actual conditions of the societies in which those principles were to be applied. The "philosophical Mill" and the "polemical Mill" appear as characters in this drama in essentially the same costumes they have worn in previous renderings of Mill's politics. The difference, however, is that on the reading we propose, it is necessary to neither elevate the one over the other, nor see them as appearing as representations of some basic or underlying inconsistency of thought. In what follows, we shall attempt to document how, beginning and ending with a framework of concepts in which utility and knowledge were the desiderata for political participation, Mill was led (for reasons both theoretical and practical) to associate property with the requisite capacity for political judgment.

THE PRINCIPLES OF REPRESENTATION

When Mill opened the entry on *Government* for Macvey Napier's supplement to the 4th, 5th, and 6th editions of the *Encyclopedia Britannica* with the assertion that "the whole science of human nature must be explored, to lay a foundation for the science of politics" (1820a, 3), it was for him no recently formed opinion. In a review of Gaetano Filangieri's *Science of Legislation* for the September issue of the *Literary Journal* as far back as 1806, Mill had already revealed his preference for a maxim he there

fords quotations to support all these interpretations must either be very rich in matter or very confused in argument," and claimed that the essay on *Government* does indeed contain "two mutually contradictory positions" (1969, 250–51).

[6] Terence Ball dismissed the charge of inconsistency by claiming that it stems from an "anachronistic" reading of Mill (in Mill 1992, xxi). According to Ball, when Mill referred to the "middling rank," he did not intend to identify the "middle class." Rather, he had in mind that older eighteenth-century Scottish notion of "rank"; see also De Marchi (1983) and Haakonssen (1985).

attributed to Filangieri: that "political laws are ultimately founded on certain fixed principles, derived from the nature of man . . . [and] according as laws coincide with these principles they are good, according as they discord with them they are bad" (1806c, 228). Whether or not the "fixed principles" concerning the "nature of man" to which Mill subscribed in 1806 were derived from utilitarian philosophy or the Scottish moral-sense tradition of Reid or Stewart, it is clear that by the time of the essay on *Government*, the principles of representative government, according to Mill's plan for a new constitution, were to be derived from nothing less than the application of the utilitarian theory of choice and action to politics.[7] Mill spared his readers the journey into the details of that theory in the essay on *Government* itself, remarking only that "to understand what is included in the happiness of the greatest number, we must understand what is included in the happiness of the individuals of whom it is composed" (1820a, 3), and that "the lot of every human being is determined by his pains and pleasures; and that his happiness corresponds with the degree in which his pleasures are great, and his pains are small" (4).[8]

Mill's rendition of the utilitarian theory of human nature began with a model of man as an essentially aggressive and domineering pleasure seeker who, if unchecked, would "as a law of human nature . . . take from others anything which they have and he desires" (1820a, 8). Or as he put it the essay on *Jurisprudence*, "As every man desires to have for himself as many good things as possible, and as there is not a sufficiency of good things for all, the strong if left to themselves, would take from the weak everything, or at least as much as they pleased" (1820b, 4). In this way, it was on the presumption that "there is no limit to the number of men whose actions we desire to have conformable to our will" (1820a, 11) that Mill grounded his contentions for both the actual need for and the

---

[7] An earlier perspective holds that Mill began as a devotee of the Scottish moral-sense view, having attended Stewart's moral philosophy lectures in Edinburgh in the 1790s and converted to utilitarianism only after his meeting with Bentham in 1808. As Halévy put it, "Bentham gave Mill a doctrine, and Mill gave Bentham a school" (1928, 251; see also 154, 249–50; see also Winch's comments in Mill 1966, 7). In support of this interpretation, Halévy offered three of Mill's articles for the *Literary Journal* (1806b, 1806c, 1806d) that are said to be fully conformable to the Scottish tradition of moral sense, alongside his article on Spanish America for the January issue of the *Edinburgh Review* in 1809, and his review of Stewart's *Elements of the Philosophy of the Human Mind* for the *British Review* in 1815, both of which are said to embrace the utilitarian position (see 1928, 257; see also Winch's comments in Mill 1966, 7, 7n). Another possible interpretation is that the seeds of Mill's later devotion to utilitarian philosophy might well have been planted thanks to an encounter with Filangieri in 1806. Filangieri was himself heavily indebted for his arguments to the Italian utilitarian Beccaria (see Mill 1806c).

[8] Mill's more substantial thoughts on this subject came nine years later, in the form of the second volume of his *Analysis of the Phenomena of the Human Mind* (1829).

necessary structure of government. Inevitably, this led him to a conception of civil government in which the state was at once a human institution rooted in individual aspirations towards political liberty and a potential usurper of that very liberty. Utility thus explained the origin of government, and mandated that its powers over individuals should be kept limited and small.

According to Mill, all the "difficult questions of Government relate to the means of restraining those, in whose hands are lodged the powers necessary for the protection of all, from making bad use of it. Whatever would be the temptations under which individuals would lie, if there was no Government, to take the objects of desire from others weaker than themselves, under the same temptations the members of the Government lie, to take the objects of desire from the members of the community, if they are not prevented from doing so" (5). This conception of a political world in which power must constantly check power led Mill to reject in principle the three "pure forms" of government: democracy (the many), aristocracy (the few), and monarchy (the one), or any theory of a mixed or "balanced" government of all three.[9] No set of powers so aggressively construed could possibly be expected to compromise:

> The Democracy or the Community have all possible motives to endeavour to prevent the Monarchy and Aristocracy from exercising power, or obtaining the wealth of the community, for their own advantage: The Monarchy and Aristocracy have all possible motives for endeavouring to obtain unlimited power over the persons and property of the community: The consequence is inevitable; they have all possible motives for combining to obtain that power, and unless the people have power enough to be a match for both, they have no protection. (1820a, 16)

It was on the basis of this demonstration, and the corollary that any interest not congruent with those of the community was "sinister," that Mill constructed his theory of representative government. In achieving representative government, the "real object to be aimed at in the composition of the legislature," he argued, was "to prevent the predominance of the interest of any individual or of any class; because if such interest

---

[9] This, too, it should be said, was an opinion of Mill's; the review of Filangieri in 1806 well illustrates his attachment to it. For example, in one place he writes (approvingly) as follows: "Montesquieu said that fear was the principle in a despotic government, honour in a monarchy, and virtue in a republic. Our author shows that these are only modifications of the same principle, the love of power" (1806c, 231). The idea is reminiscent of Hume's remark that "political writers have established it as a maxim, that, in contriving any system of government, and fixing the several checks and controls of the constitution, every man ought to be supposed a *knave*, and to have no other end, in all his actions, than private interest" (1752c, 42), which Mill brought to his own defence in the *Fragment on Mackintosh* (1835b, 279–81).

predominates . . . it will be promoted at the expense of the community" (1826e, 781; see also Hamburger 1963, 22). The only form of government that would check the tendency of the monarchy or aristocracy to domineer was one that placed the power of government (identified as the legitimate power to check) in the community. Yet the people themselves (democracy) could not be entrusted to exercise these powers, therefore they must be handed over to a "body of men, called Representatives" (1820a, 18).[10] The question still remained as to how these representatives themselves were to be prevented from domineering; "*quis custodiet ipsos custodes?*" (1835d, 15). Mill's answer was twofold. On the one hand, short but unspecified terms of office would, he claimed, ensure that representatives identified their own interests with those of the community (1820a, 18). On the other hand, Mill maintained that it was necessary to limit and shape the character of the *electors* eligible to choose such representatives, to those whose interest could also be ascertained to be identical to that of the community. The mechanisms for this second and more formative political task were the secret ballot and education.

In the *Parliamentary Review* of legislative activity during the sessions of 1826–27 and 1827–28, Mill contributed a review essay on "Constitutional Legislation" in which he asserted that the prevailing system of open voting promoted the corruption of politics in at least two ways. First, it obviously enhanced the ability of the wealthy to give a veneer of electoral legitimacy to their own sinister interests by exerting pressure on those beneath them to cast votes in their support: "If the poor man cannot conceal from the rich man how he votes, the rich man knows to a certainty when his price commands his commodity, and he can make sure of it" (1827, 365). Second, the open system was necessarily morally corruptive of the poor, since "the voter, whether he be a good man, or a bad man, would, if he followed his own inclination, vote differently from the mode in which influence is exerted to induce him to vote." The consequence for the citizen, Mill argued, was that if "he is a bad man, and disregards a promise, he votes as he pleases, knowing he may do so with impunity; and his promise passes for nothing. If on the contrary we suppose that he is a good man, the good man knows that it is a bad thing to make a bad promise; but a worse thing to keep it" (365).[11] Either way, the virtue of the would-be voter was impuned.

---

[10] Mill's argument ran as follows: "A whole community would form a numerous assembly . . . [and] all numerous assemblies are essentially incapable of business . . . where the assembly is numerous, so many persons desire to speak, and feelings, by mutual inflammation, become so violent, that calm and effectual deliberation is impossible" (6).

[11] For an expanded discussion of the morally corruptive effects of the open vote system, see Mill (1830, 8–10).

In Mill's hands, the secret ballot became the single most important weapon against rule by the wealthy. "The ballot, and that alone, can enable [the people] to choose, and render the British constitution in reality what it now is only in pretence" (1830, 13). Elsewhere, with greater rhetorical flourish, Mill wrote: "Make voting secret, and who will pay for a vote which is of no value, when it cannot be known? Make voting secret, and who will incur the expense of bringing distant voters to the poll, who may all vote for the opposite party?" (1827, 362). Mill continued to place faith in the secret ballot, even as late as 1835, as that element of democratic reform most necessary to secure good government (1835a, 203–4; see also 1830, 1).[12] On a theoretical level, this is not surprising, since the secret ballot goes well with the fear of corrupted interests so strongly expressed in all of Mill's political writings. Without electors whose choices can be made independently, there could be no checking of the influence of "sinister interest" in the constitution (Halévy 1913–32, 1:12; see especially the discussion of corruption on 8–10). Secrecy, Mill believed, would ensure independence. Unfortunately, the secret ballot alone could not prevent the rise of another equally sinister interest: the poor. Here Mill's answer was not to "check" but rather to educate it.

"The virtue of the people, you say, is weak. Unhappily it is so, deplorably weak," Mill wrote in the July issue of the *Westminster Review* for 1830 in an article on the ballot. Its improvement required more than franchise or electoral reform, however; an indispensable component to Mill's parliamentary reform proposals was a plan of education. The details of that plan are of less importance to this discussion than is its unambiguous purpose: to create a community of shared (common) interest out of individuals whose interests could be understood as neither naturally nor originally coincident nor bound up with those of others. When one turns to the essay on *Government*, the paramount necessity of the existence of such a coherent moral and political "community" in order to make his proposal for a reformed government "representative" through the "identity of interests between ruler and ruled" becomes clear. Referred to by Mill as an "exposition of the Elements of Political Knowledge," the essay on *Government* isolated middle-class morality as the most important component of political knowledge available to the masses. Consonant with his general and rather sketchily crafted argument in the essay on *Education* for the supplement to the *Encyclopedia Britannica*—that the foundation of mental life is grounded on associations (mental sequences)—it was necessary for political knowledge and effective political

[12] Indeed, some have gone so far as to claim that the utilitarians "put all their eggs in one basket"—and perhaps the wrong basket at that—namely, the secret ballot. See Thomas (1969, 284); see also Carr (1971, 553–80).

participation that the individual develop the correct associations or "primary habits" of mind.[13] The appropriate habits or associations for the labouring classes were to be formed through their assimilation of the moral norms and values of that "virtuous and intelligent rank." The middle rank, which according to Mill, "gives to science, to art and to legislation itself, their most distinguished ornaments . . . advice and example" (1820a, 32), became for him a vanguard in the formation of those opinions identified with the interests of the community.[14]

In the earlier essay on *Government*, these same norms provided the foundation of the community and enabled its constituents to identify as representatives, those individuals whose interests were consonant with it. Here, the discussion of creating a genuine community of interest that could safely select representatives who conveyed its virtues into politics, replaced any direct discussion of the more familiar radical proposals for "universality, equality, annuality and secrecy."[15] Despite Mill's allegiance to "the plebian, the democratical" (1830, 6), he effectively did little more for the theory of representation in the essay on *Government* than to substitute a "new virtualism" for the old. It was Mill's continued willingness to view the labouring class as a threat, and at times to envisage their principal political role as being one that should be exercised *outside* of government, poised and ready to check the sinister interests of "their Rulers" (1820a, 19), which led Bentham to characterize Mill's democratic commitments as equivocal.[16] Whether Bentham's assessment was accurate or not, Mill's characterisation of the actual political function of even an expanded electorate remained reminiscent of an eighteenth-century vision of popular protest.

In shifting the focus of achieving "good government" away from the virtue of the representative and placing it instead on that of the commu-

---

[13] The relevant passages may be found in Mill (1818b, 71–99, esp. 93–96; see also 1829).

[14] Not all democratic reformers had such sanguine views of the middling rank. Percy Bysshe Shelley, for one, suggested that they "poisoned the literature of the age in which they lived by requiring either the antitype of their own mediocrity in books, or such stupid and distorted and inharmonious idealisms as alone have the power to stir their torpid imaginations. Their domestic affections are feeble, and they have no others. They think of any commerce with their species but as a means, never as an end, and as a means to the basest forms of personal advantage" (1819–20, 29). Mill developed his argument on the middling rank as vanguard in his review of Samuel Bailey's *Publication of Opinions* (1826b; see also 1806a; 1812; 1813; 1826d, 263; 1835d, 23).

[15] Indeed, as William Thomas has noted, "At a time when moderate radicals were becoming more hesitant and popular radicals more extreme about the traditional radical demands for universal suffrage, shorter parliaments and the ballot, the *Essay* managed to evade all three" (1969, 257).

[16] "He argues against oppression less because he loves the oppressed many, than because he hates the oppressing few. He fights for the people—[not] that he cares for the suffering

nity of electors, Mill's theory of government took at best only a dubious step towards modern representative democracy. It ensured that his approach to expanding the franchise was almost wholly negative; so much so that when applied, it proved to exclude from the franchise all but the "aggregate males" of the community who could meet the "identity of interest" criterion (Mill 1820a, 21).[17] In contrast to visions of representation that might have placed a value on bringing into government the existing diversity of interests (especially class interests) present in the community, Mill's theory continued to stress commonality and uniformity. The question that Mill had not yet answered in any satisfactory or modern way, however, was exactly who it was among "the people" that made up this community.

Mill's starting point in the consideration of the extent of the franchise once again bears all the hallmarks of utilitarianism. He set out to determine the capacity for political decision making on the premise that what was required for good political choice was the full knowledge of one's own interest and the wherewithal to act rationally on it. Mill then resolved the problem that individuals might entertain mistaken views of interest in a typically utilitarian manner—education was the answer. Maintaining that the "evils which arise from mistake are not incurable" because "if parties who act contrary to their interest had a proper knowledge of that interest, they would act well," Mill concluded that all that was necessary was knowledge; "knowledge, on the part of those whose interests are the same as those of the community, would be an adequate remedy." For Mill, of course, knowledge was "a thing which is capable of being increased" (1820a, 29; see also 1826d, 268). At issue here is both what *type* of knowledge is necessary to politics, and the relationship between that knowledge and political stability. As to the type of knowl-

---

people, but that he cannot tolerate the suffering-creating rulers." See also Bowring's editorial annotations to the correspondence with James Mill, in *Works*, 1838–43, 10:432.

[17] It is worth noting that while Mill professed a desire to see the interest of the community expressed in politics, the community was, for him, one marked by shared, even homogeneous interests, and it existed more as an abstract ideal to be realised (constructed) in the future. This may help to explain the occasional expressions of frustration by John Stuart Mill, who shared his father's hope for the construction of this ideal community of interest, at the slow progress being made towards it during his own lifetime:

In England, it would hardly be believed to what degree all that is morally objectionable in the lowest class of the working people is nourished, if not engendered, by the low state of their understandings. . . . Few have considered how anyone who could instil into these people the commonest worldly wisdom—who could render them capable of even selfish prudential calculations—would improve their conduct in every regulation of life, and clear the soil for the growth of right feelings and worthy propensities. (1845, 511; on this point, see also the discussion in Coats 1967, 152–53)

edge required beyond the practical instruction to be derived from observing the operation of the "political machine" (1835d, 23), Mill adverts to the customary utilitarian conception of knowledge as individual mental capacity developed through formal education. On this line of argument, education "is the means which may be employed to render the *mind* . . . an operative cause of happiness" (1818b, 41).

Once more, the utilitarian model of an individual is placed at the centre of Mill's argument. If individuals are seeking to act in ways that promote their own interest (that is, if utility is their objective), they must possess full information not only of the alternatives available to them but also of the utility they will derive once a particular course of action has been chosen. "Good choice" mandates the full knowledge of possibilities *and* consequences. Appropriately enough, in the essay on *Liberty of the Press* for the *Encyclopedia Britannica* supplement, the case was made in unambiguous terms: "The very foundation of a good choice is knowledge. The fuller and more perfect the knowledge, the better the chance . . . of a good choice" (1821, 19). Years later, in the *Analysis of the Phenomena of the Human Mind*, Mill would return to the same theme: "for the most perfect performance of acts of prudence, the greatest measure of knowledge is required" (1829, 2:282–83).

As to what this type of knowledge had to contribute to political stability, Mill's answer was as consistent as it was unequivocal: educated individuals would come to see their own interests as being in conformity with those of "the community." Knowledge made things safer; its absence threatened political stability. Moreover, if education failed to suffice to bring an individual's interests into conformity with those of the community, discipline would be required. So much so, in fact, that since "there are some minds with which you cannot be sure of being able in every case to bring evidence, as it were, in contact," it would be necessary to arm magistrates "with a coercive power" (1818a, 717).

Having deduced from the principle of utility the proposition that representative democracy was the only means of securing good government, and having shown that "intellectual aptitude" among the voting public was the only prerequisite to the choice of suitable representatives, Mill turned his attention to the question of the property qualification.[18] The argument ran as follows. First, take a high qualification; this must be

[18] As if to highlight the point that representative democracy was the only means of securing good government, Mill titled the sixth section of *Government*, "In the Representative System *alone* the Securities for good Government are to be found" (1820a, 16, emphasis added). We borrow the term intellectual aptitude from Bentham's *Plan of Parliamentary Reform* (1817, 3:522), as did Mill somewhat later in his *Analysis of the Phenomena of the Human Mind* (1829, 2:181–83).

rejected because it would yield just another form of aristocratic or oligarchic government. Next, consider a low qualification; this, too, must be rejected. A "very low qualification is of no use, as affording no security for a good choice beyond that which would exist if no pecuniary qualification was required" (1820a, 22), since the votes of the propertyless would be so few as not to disturb the interest of the rest of the "community." Interestingly, however, in the essay on *Government*, Mill did not quite conclude that "therefore" no property qualification was necessary to good government.

Instead, Mill posed a rather different question. If one thought that such a qualification was needed, on what principle might it be determined? On the argument that it was "not easy to find any satisfactory principle to guide us in our researches" (1820a, 23), Mill acquiesced to the property qualification, but with the proviso that it be fixed at a level ensuring the inclusion of "the majority" of the community. It seemed to Mill "hardly necessary" to "carry the analysis of the pecuniary qualification" any further. That said, two features of this claim should be kept in mind. The first is that Mill still maintained the primary principle of his science of politics: that it was "the interests of the community" that had to be conveyed into politics, not the "interests of property." At the same time, however, Mill conceded that a secondary *association* between the possession of property and the interests of the community might exist. Such an association would allow a subset of the community—the property-owning middle class—to convey the interests of all safely into government. In this sense, property for Mill appears as a proxy for the community interest, and not as the dominant vehicle of political exclusion.[19]

This is not to say that Mill did not articulate a principle of exclusion. In casting his philosopher's eye across the list of names of potential electors, Mill constructed an interesting exclusionary criterion. "One thing is pretty clear," he asserted: "that all those whose interests are indisputably included in those of other individuals, may be struck off without inconvenience" (1820a, 21). It was thanks to this particular criterion, that women and "children" (with the age of forty being Mill's preferred boundary between minority and majority [22][20]) were struck off Mill's electoral register.

Several points can be made about this argument. In the first place, confining ourselves to matters of logic for the moment, Mill's exclusionary rule fits uneasily within the utilitarian calculus. The application of utility

---

[19] This position might be contrasted with that of the Whig reformers of the day; see, for example, Jeffrey (1809, 1819); Mackintosh (1818, 1820).

[20] The supposed security to good government afforded by this qualification was, according to Mill, that "men of forty have a deep interest in the welfare of the younger men."

theory to any problem of choice requires (among other things) the assumption that agents possess the capacity to choose, and that they have
full information as to the possibilities and consequences of their actions.
Models of rational self-interest, in other words, assume not just rationality but also knowledge. When addressing the problem of who should be
excluded from the electoral register, it was therefore logical to check that
each of these requirements were met by voters. Thus, in certain parts
of the essay on *Government*, Mill was led quite consistently to advance
education as a criterion against which to judge the suitability of electors.
The associated idea that when one agent's interests were "included" in
another's, utility theory mandated the exclusion of one or another of
them, however, is false. Under a simple majority-rule voting procedure,
in a society that consisted of more than two individuals, even if a woman
whose interests were supposedly included in those of some man had *identical* preferences to that man, political choice would in general fail to
satisfy Mill's utilitarian criterion of the greatest aggregate utility.[21]

The logic that inspired Mill's new virtualism, which sits so uneasily
within the body of his utilitarian thought, comes out particularly clearly
in a short exchange between Ricardo and Mill on the publication of Mill's
History of British India, where Mill seems to have applied it to determine
the mode of government best suited to that colony. Ricardo had read
Mill's book when it appeared in late 1817, and had discussed it in correspondence with both Mill and Malthus. At the outset, Ricardo expressed
his doubts to Mill as to whether "the Government and laws of one state of
society" were well "adapted for another state of society."[22] This, Ricardo
correctly noticed, was "one of the great difficulties of the science."[23] His
doubts arose from an obvious consideration—namely, that the "people
of England, who are governors, have an interest opposed to that of the
people of India, who are the governed, in the same manner as the interest
of a despotic sovereign is opposed to that of his people."[24]

---

[21] There is no reason to expect this to be the case, and if it is not, then the implications
for the logic of Mill's argument might be even more damaging than in the case where it is.
One famous attack on Mill's assertion about disenfranchising women—namely, that contained in William Thompson's *An Appeal of One-Half the Human Race, Women, against
the Pretensions of the Other Half, Men*—relied almost entirely on establishing the absence
of an identity of interest between the sexes. Thomas discussed Mill's argument for the disen-
franchisement of women and children on these grounds, but does not explore the logical
difficulty (1979, 128). See also Claeys (1989, 173).

[22] *Letter to Mill*, December 18, 1817, in Ricardo (1951–73, 7:22). Unless otherwise indicated, all subsequent references to Mill's correspondence are to that part of it contained in
this edition of Ricardo.

[23] Ibid., 7:229.

[24] *Letter to Mill*, December 30, 1817, 7:239.

Furthermore, since the British public's general apathy towards the administration of India was taken as a given by Ricardo, he held that even the "outside" check of public opinion at home was not likely to be "very active and will therefore not much tend towards the correction of abuses" in colonial administration.[25] He was led, therefore, to wonder whether the "salutory dread of insurrection" was all that remained to check "misrule and oppression" in that country.[26] Ricardo, though, then proceeded to put his finger squarely on the problem with Mill's new virtualism: "Are we to fix our eyes steadily on the end, the happiness of the governed, and pursue it at the expense of those principles which all men are agreed in calling virtuous? If so might not . . . [any] . . . ruler, disregard all the engagements of his predecessors, and by force of arms compel the submission of all the native powers of India if he could show that there was a great probability of adding to the happiness of the people by the introduction of better instruments of government?"[27]

No reply to these queries from Ricardo is extant. But the correspondence between the two surrounding Mill's *History of British India* speaks directly to the questions Ricardo raised, and it aids in clarifying the character of Mill's thinking on these points. In his first letter praising Mill's performance, the ever modest Ricardo declared that he was now "anxiously disposed to understand" the science of legislation, and that he entertained "sanguine expectations" as to the "practicability of improvements in legislation."[28] To this, Mill replied that he had no doubt that "we shall now understand one another" on that subject, and asserted that "the ends are there, in the first place, known—they are clear and definite," and that it remained only "to determine the choice of means."[29] In saying this, of course, Mill was no more than repeating the method that he applied in legitimating representative government in England; it was the necessary means to the greatest happiness. In India, for Mill at least, the means would be different. When Ricardo politely enquired of Mill as to

---

[25] Ibid.

[26] *Letter to Mill*, January 6, 1818, 7:241.

[27] Ibid., 7:241–42. The difficulty that Ricardo foresaw, then, was precisely a problem at the core of Mill's theory of representation. Furthermore, when that theory was grounded in the theory of utility, the problem took the form of having to determine "how to balance one object of utility against another" (7:242). Stimson and Milgate (1993, 905) mistakenly claimed that Ricardo's argument here involved a recognition of the problem of interpersonal comparisons of utility. We wish to thank Giancarlo De Vivo for pointing out the error of interpretation.

[28] *Letter to Mill*, December 18, 1817, 7:229, 228. This, it would seem, was no mere intellectual curiosity; negotiations were already under way with Lord Portarlington for what was to become Ricardo's seat in the House of Commons.

[29] *Letter to Ricardo*, December 27, 1817, 7:234–35.

what one should do when exclusive focus on the ends led, as it did in the case of India, to the justification of an imperial despotism, Mill was silent.

Mill's silence on this crucial question was fortunate. If the essay on *Government* is to be taken at its word, which purports to show that only representative government is sanctioned by the principle of utility, then the idea that the government of India could be safely entrusted to the members of the Imperial Parliament at Westminster would seem to contradict his best-known contribution to the science of government. If, on the other hand, one seeks to rescue him from contradiction by reminding ourselves that the principle of utility sanctions only a government representative of those capable of knowing what is in their own best interest and acting on it, and that in nations like India this might be a few (or none), then it would appear that we might have plunged him into a deeper quagmire. For in that case, the theory of representative government as a government of the "democracy or community" would seem to be fatally compromised.[30]

John Stuart Mill delivered the utilitarian theory of government from this impasse (compare Thompson 1976, 25–27). The younger Mill freely abandoned the claim that the principle of utility sanctioned only equal representation (even at home), and without a second thought declared that the ignorance of savages rendered enlightened imperial rule superior to a "native despotism" (1861a, 409). But if James Mill was silent on the relation between utility and self-rule in India in his correspondence with Ricardo, he had not always been so reluctant in expressing the implications of his science of politics when it was to be applied to "underdeveloped" political cultures. In an article on Spanish America in the *Edinburgh Review* in 1809, the elder Mill was as clear as his son was to be some sixty years later. Proceeding on the familiar premise that the "ignorance and irritability" of "the people" might "be worked upon by men of evil intentions," Mill held that in the project of establishing the conditions for political liberty in Spanish America, "as much as possible should be done *for* the people—but nothing *by* them" (1809, 304–5).

In conformity with his well-established prerequisite of appropriate aptitude, Mill asserted that there was "one danger in rendering the basis of representation too wide"—namely, that "you incur the inconveniences of

---

[30] Ricardo appears to have seen this particular matter (which concerns the logic of Mill's argument) rather differently. On reading Mill's essay in summer 1820, Ricardo wrote to Mill saying that he found it "a consistent and clear development of your own views" (*Letter to Mill*, July 27, 1820, 8:211). Two years later, he sent a copy of the essay to Hutches Trower, recommending it as "an excellent article and well reasoned throughout" (*Letter to Trower*, January 25, 1822, 9:154). For a more detailed discussion of Ricardo's politics and its relation to James Mill, see Milgate and Stimson (1991b, esp. 3–6, 21–23, 63–65, 69–70, 92–93, 96–99, 121–22).

the ignorant and precipitate passions of the vulgar" (308).[31] In Mill's hands, the task of settling on a stable equilibrium between the level of knowledge attained by the general public and the extent of representation became (and remained) the central problematic of the utilitarian theory of government. In all Mill's discussions of the principles of representation, the idea was neither abandoned, compromised, nor obscured. However unacceptable his argument might seem today, or however comforting it might be to endorse some (but not all) of its aspects, it does violence to the historical record to attribute a contemporary disquiet over such matters to some putative problem with Mill's own contribution to the science of politics.

Representation in Practice

When one pauses to consider just how many of "the people" of Britain would have been enfranchised under Mill's suggested scheme in the essay on *Government*—that is, if one makes a rough estimate of the number of names that would have appeared on his electoral register for Great Britain and Ireland—the result turns out to be interesting. Taking the demographic profile for Great Britain and Ireland for 1820, the year that Mill's essay appeared, the number of males aged forty or above was approximately 2.1 million, or 10 percent of a total population of about 21 million (see Mitchell 1988, 9–10). Assuming that the then existing electorate numbered approximately 500,000 adult males, a little arithmetic yields the conclusion that had all of Mill's forty-year-old-plus men been enfranchised, the scheme would have quadrupled the electoral franchise.

Some appreciation of the kind of adjustment in the electoral franchise that the practical adoption of Mill's scheme would have entailed can be gauged by recalling that when parliamentary reform finally did arrive in 1832, Whig reformer Lord John Russell estimated that if enacted, his bill would add about 500,000 voters to the electoral rolls of a kingdom of some 24 million inhabitants (and this, it should be emphasised, under a "man of property" franchise, where one attained majority status at age twenty-one and not forty).[32] Had his estimate been accurate, the First Reform Bill would have roughly doubled the existing electoral franchise. As it turned out, the net addition to the franchise was a little over 300,000 (see Halévy 1913–32, 3:27, 27n5). An actual expansion of the elective

---

[31] Mill then referred his readers to Bentham's *Fragment on Government* for further enlightenment on the subject.

[32] See his speech in the House of Commons, March 1, 1831, reprinted in Black (1969, 70).

franchise on Mill's scheme would therefore have been seven times greater than that eventually secured under the 1832 Reform Bill.

The comparative statistics, however, tell only part of the story of the distance that separated the Whig and Radical reformers of the day. It has to be remembered that for most of the Whig reformers, the First Reform Bill stood at the end of the road to democracy, while for the Radicals, it marked only its beginning. Thus, for example, as home secretary in Lord Melbourne's cabinet, Lord Russell declared at the opening of Parliament after the 1837 general election (in the speech that earned him the nickname "Finality Jack" in radical circles) that the wide scope of the constitutional readjustment worked by the First Reform Bill was acceded to by his Whig colleagues precisely because it was meant to be final.[33] On the eve of the Chartists' decade, which was so greatly to alter the political landscape of Britain, it is remarkable that the political leadership of the day believed the distance thought left to be covered after the First Reform Bill was only negligible.

As far as Mill was concerned, the practical reform of the franchise accomplished in 1832, while tending in the right direction, was a mere "crumb of reform" (1835d, 12). In the four years that remained of his life after the enactment of the First Reform Bill, Mill steadfastly ridiculed the idea that the act of 1832 could be thought of as a final measure. Declaring it to be the work of "half-and-half reformers," he continued to play out the central themes of his science of politics against a new backdrop. Nothing had been done to remove the abuses concomitant on the open-voting system (14–15; 1835a); the House of Lords remained a seat of aristocratic power with the ability to subvert the wishes of the House of Commons (1836a, 297–301); the "injustice and oppression" of sinecures and other forms of political privilege remained in place (293–94); the religious establishment remained intact; and even the House of Commons itself still needed to be "chosen by the people, not nominally, as, to a great degree, it is at present, but actually, and in truth" (1835c, 51). In short, the British electoral reform of 1832 provided none of the securities to good government that Mill had long demanded.

Another arena in which Mill deployed his theory of government was in his reflections on the popular disturbances of the day—especially those at St. Peters Fields, Manchester. Mill addressed the events of Peterloo in the essay on *Government* itself. His remarks are sufficiently important to reproduce in full:

> What signify the irregularities of the mob, more than half composed in the greater number of instances, of boys and women, and disturbing for a few hours or days a particular town? What signifies the occasional turbulence of

---

[33] On the nickname, see Walpole (1889, 1:289–90); Wallas (1925, 366).

a manufacturing district, peculiarly unhappy from a very great deficiency of a middle rank, as there the population almost wholly consists of rich manufacturers and poor workmen; with whose minds no pains are taken by anybody; with whose afflictions there is no virtuous family of the middle rank to sympathize; whose children have no good example of such a family to see and to admire; and who are placed in the highly unfavourable situation of fluctuating between very high wages in one year, and very low wages in another? It is altogether futile with regard to the foundation of good government to say that this or the other portion of the people, may at this, or the other time, depart from the wisdom of the middle rank. (1820a, 32)

While this should not be taken to indicate that Mill wished to deny democratic citizenship to the working class, these remarks are indicative of the character of Mill's argument *for* enfranchising them. For example, consider the remarks about needing to educate people to correct opinions, and about having them emulate those "virtuous families of the middle rank" that Mill advocated. It was essential for Mill to show that most of the time, most of the people "continue to be guided by that rank." It is also worth noticing that Mill claimed that these instances of popular unrest should, in fact, be regarded as an "exception" to the "rule" that the people *were* capable of judging. Indeed, Mill argued that these exceptions actually *proved* the rule: since there were so few of these protesters (measured against the whole population), "therefore" most must have been guided by those middling ranks of people of good sense. What is of importance here is that the practical locus of reform was tied to the people, while the locus of the theoretical contention remained where it always had been—with appropriate knowledge, the interests of the community, and the standard-bearers of those interests.

Knowledge and Property: The Political Community

It is evident, then, that whether in the context of his philosophical or practical discourse, Mill uniformly advocated a government representative of a political community whose boundaries were to be drawn up according to one and only one criterion: knowledge. In this way, Mill's argument shifted the focus of deciding the question of who should vote from its traditional eighteenth-century domain of inherent personal character with its origins in birth, rank, or breeding.[34] Instead, Mill located it

---

[34] On this particular subject, Burke claimed that "men are qualified for civil liberty, in exact proportion to their disposition to put moral chains upon their own appetites; in proportion as their love of justice is above their own rapacity; in proportion as their own soundness and sobriety of understanding is above vanity and presumption; in proportion as they are more disposed to listen to the counsels of the wise and good, in preference to the flattery

squarely in the domain of the human mind—"the eye of plain reason" (1814, 2). The capacity to judge correctly one's own interest and act on it was all that was required. Rationality replaced reputation as the single most important qualification for citizenship.

In introducing this idea, Mill had brought the doctrine of the equality of people into the science of politics in a way not open to the old virtualists among Mill's Whig contemporaries and predecessors. Unlike the virtues of the "great orders," in which eighteenth-century thinkers had placed so much faith, rational thought and action was potentially within the grasp of all. Even so, Mill's argument retained some vestiges of that earlier discourse. There still remained "the community" of shared and common interest of which government alone was to take heed. Nevertheless, since it was Mill's conception of rational action that informed his understanding of the nature of such a community, much of what has previously been regarded as either confused or contradictory in Mill's politics falls readily into place. Given Mill's particular characterisation of rational action, equality and political liberty came to fit easily with middle-class commitments to capitalist accumulation along with their associated elevation of the values of frugality, prudence, and financial foresight. In this way, property should be understood as a "signifier" of appropriate knowledge, not a substitute for it. It was, so to speak, the enabling clause of Mill's science of politics, not its primary principle.

Among the most conspicuous instances of the association that Mill drew between appropriate knowledge and middle-class understandings are those one encounters in his contributions to economic debate; and within that particular subset of his work, there are few sources more revealing of the general trend in Mill's argument than his *Elements of Political Economy*. Mill's description of accumulation in the *Elements*, for example, bears all the hallmarks of his method of drawing out this association.

Proceeding along lines made familiar by Smith and Ricardo, Mill asserted that the "augmentation of capital" was "everywhere exactly in proportion to the degree of saving," and that "the amount of that augmentation, annually, is the same thing with the amount of the savings, which are made annually" (1826a, 218). With savings behaviour "therefore" holding the key to economic growth and prosperity, and with this requiring individual choices as to the allocation of current income between present and future consumption, Mill saw the whole matter as resolving itself into a simple problem of the felicific calculus—of balancing

---

of knaves" (1839, 3:326). Wherever intellectual aptitude was appropriate to informed choice, there was just no need to put "moral chains" on one's own "appetites."

a present sacrifice (disutility) against a future benefit (utility).[35] But this was a matter, of course, that had always hinged (for the utilitarians) on individual knowledge. The more thorough the knowledge, so the argument ran, the more likely a time preference favouring the long view over the short. In his economic writings, Mill was fond of calling this the "disposition to accumulate" (1817a, 2:92, 93; 1826d, 262), and its utility to society was paramount.[36] As he put it in his rarely consulted essay on *Banks for Savings* for the supplement to the *Encyclopedia Britannica*, "Human happiness is prodigiously improved by reserving for future use a proportion of the command which . . . a man may possess over the means of enjoyment" (1817a, 92). The idea that appropriate knowledge was requisite to inculcating this propensity to save was, in fact, among the oldest of all of Mill's political maxims.[37]

It was when Mill turned his attention to discovering the existing seat of this knowledge that he was led to the middling classes, or as he called them, the capitalists (1826d, 263). It was at this point that property entered his discussion of democratic reform. Viewed from this perspective, Mill's frequent references to the value to society of "many people of small to middling fortunes" in whom the "disposition to accumulate" was strong were derivative of his idea that utility and knowledge were central to democratic political participation, and not in contradiction to it.

While it is easy enough to understand why his working-class radical detractors should have found in that clause grounds sufficient for their determined opposition, it is imperative that Mill's position not be con-

[35] The claim that savings behavior is key involves Say's Law: "whatever is saved from annual produce, in order to be converted into capital, is necessarily consumed" (Mill 1826a, 326; see also 325). The point, then, is that capital accumulation actually requires not only that individuals save some portion of their current income but that they also invest those savings. Say's Law, in this domain of its application, conveniently allowed Mill to sidestep the relation between saving and investment. Terence W. Hutchison referred to Mill's development of Smith's idea that saving is investing as "ambiguous but dogmatic rigmarole" (1967, 398)

[36] Incidentally, disposition to accumulate was a phrase that John Stuart Mill would deploy years later in his own *Principles of Political Economy* in order to make exactly the same argument (see, for example, 1871,1.11.§1–§2).

[37] See, for example, Mill's discussion of "frugality and industry" in his review "Colquhoun's System of Education for the Labouring Poor" (1806a, 528–9, 533). See also Mill's discussion of the relation between "prudent" action—which, for him, involved a present sacrifice for a future gain—and knowledge in *Analysis of the Phenomena of the Human Mind* (1829, 2:282–83); his discussion of the importance of education in fostering "foresight" and "self-command" in the essay on *Benefit Societies* for the supplement to the *Encyclopedia Britannica* (1817b, 263); and his discussion of the need for designing a system of education to inculcate "temperance" (i.e., "the steady habit of resisting a present desire, for the sake of a greater good") in the essay on *Education* for the *Britannica* supplement (1818b, 104).

founded with that of other middle-class reformers of the day. Unlike his philosophic Whig contemporaries (and the authors of the Reform Bill of 1832), for Mill the ownership of property itself had nothing to do with establishing what James Mackintosh called "moral trust" in his speech in the debate over the Reform Bill in 1831.[38] Indeed, how much closer Mill's politics stood to that of his working-class radical detractors (and how distant it was from that of even the most advanced Whigs) may be measured by the fact that many of those theorists articulating the political aspirations of the working class actually took up Mill's principle (appropriate knowledge) and simply deployed it more aggressively to make their case for the inclusion of all adults into the political nation, without the need for a property qualification.

On the philosophical plane, Mill had begun from a model of people quintessentially utilitarian in constitution. Starting with individual agents, it was to his account of the science of human nature that he turned in the quest for a science of politics suitable for the modern world. To make the case for the inclusion of larger numbers into the political nation according to this line of reasoning, all that needed to be established was that individuals had the capacity to judge their own interests, and that they were unencumbered in their ability to act on them. But if Mill was an individualist in this philosophical arena, he was neither automatically nor necessarily a democrat in the political one. On that subject, everything turned on the question of judging when (or if) individual capacity had reached an acceptable standard. This criterion proved to be sufficiently malleable to allow him to appear either expansive and democratic, or narrow and elitist, as the case required.

Had Mill considered the relationship between different interests as being shaped by deep-seated class antagonisms rather than individual interests—as not a few of his contemporaries were actually doing—one might wonder whether the transition he was able to make between wider and narrower visions of franchise reform would have been quite so seamless.[39] Instead of finding that whenever appropriate aptitude prevailed,

---

[38] On the floor of the House of Commons, on July 4, 1831, Mackintosh referred to property as constituting "a moral trust," and as "the nourisher of mankind, the incentive of industry, the cement of human society" (1836, 2:385).

[39] Mill did not apply the utilitarian model of choice and action (the model he so consistently used when discussing political action) to a discussion of economic behaviour. Such an application of the utilitarian calculus to economic behaviour had not been made by anyone at the time (and would not be made for another half century). Moreover, according to Mill, political economy at the time provided a definitive and final account of economic behaviour that did not draw on this model (see, for example, Mill 1836b, 554, 556, 565). The younger Mill, however, later entered into just such applications of utilitarianism to economic choice, and we shall see below with what consequences for the conceptual transformation of politics and political economy.

the different interests of all might be accommodated within a stable and fully participatory democratic polity—and that only where appropriate knowledge did not prevail did conflict remain (and might a stable polity thus require a restriction of the franchise)—he would have found class conflict to be an essential feature of civil society. He would then have had to face the problem of determining how to address the question of mapping a fundamentally fractured community to the franchise in an entirely different way. But he did not.

Ricardo, however, saw the economic fault lines of civil society in those very terms of deeply etched class antagonisms.[40] Yet he imposed no property qualification on his case for an expanded franchise; indeed, he appears to have been sanguine about proposing quite extensive franchise reform. Others who recognised the antagonism within the working classes to the rights of property saw this as sufficient reason to deny them the vote. Still others—and one may think of Thomas Hodgskin, John Francis Bray, and Alexander Gray—deployed the class antagonism suggested by the labour theory of value, not in order to derive the need for a property qualification, but in order to provide an argument for the revolutionary transformation of the régime of private property itself.

---

[40] Ricardo could therefore claim that "the interest of the landlord is opposed to every other class in the community" (1820b, 116–17), and elsewhere, that the rate of profits depends on real wages (1821, 143–44), and yet contend for an extension of the franchise "to every class of the people" (1824b, 503).

Chapter Nine

ECONOMIC OPINION ON
PARLIAMENTARY REFORM

The grand cause, good government, is always present
to my mind, but I hope it will have a better champion
in the House of Commons. In every argument with my
friends I do what I can to maintain the cause of truth,
as far as I can see it, and frequently flatter myself that I
am successful. I am quite sure that the good cause is advancing, though at a very moderate step, and all we
can hope to do in our time is to help it a little forward.
—*Ricardo to James Mill*, August 30, 1823

WHEN SMITH had written elliptically of the importance of "general principles" to the "science of the legislator" (1776, 4.2:468), Stewart took him
to mean that the science of political economy furnished those general
principles. As a result, Stewart concluded that while the findings of political economy might be used as a guide to economic policymaking, they
had nothing to say (especially in the aftermath of the French Revolution)
about the constitution of political society. This conception of the relationship between economics and politics has been handed down to practicing
economists pretty well intact—despite the fact that Smith's economics has
since been used to buttress cases for a wide variety of forms of political
organisation (from neoliberalism to social democracy, and almost everything in between).

In Smith's own time, the physiocrats were exemplary of just how far
the science of the legislator was separated from constitutional politics
proper. For the physiocrats appear to have seen little conflict between the
prolongation of the political order of the *ancien régime* in France and the
implementation of essentially the same philosophy of economic policy
advocated by Smith—namely, perfect liberty in commercial relations. As
Tocqueville noticed, although the physiocrats "were all in favour of the
free exchange of commodities and a system of *laissez faire* and *laissez
passer* in commerce and industry," nevertheless "political liberty in the
full sense of the term was something that passed their imagination or was

promptly dismissed from their thoughts if by any chance the idea of it occurred to them" (1858, 159).[1]

In the history of economics, there have been notable uses of political economy to address questions of political and constitutional order. One would almost certainly wish to single out Mill and Marx in the nineteenth century, and Schumpeter, Hayek, and Friedman in the twentieth. Whatever one may think about the political arrangements advocated by any of these economists, one thing is certain: that each has utilised his account of the operation of the market mechanism to underpin a particular vision of the ideal organisation of political society. For all of them, political economy was not just another rational input into the policymaking process but was also one of the building blocks of the science of politics itself. Doubtless, tolerably convincing cases could be made for the addition of other names to the list of economists whose work might warrant inclusion in this particular category.

Ricardo, however, would probably not be a name most would think to include on such a list. The customary image of Ricardo is of the pure economic theorist, at work on his theorems, and supposedly concerned only with "directing government to right measures."[2] In fact, even in this sphere Ricardo has often been accused of being too much the pure theorist—so much so that Schumpeter actually called the habit of applying too readily the conclusions of abstract economic models directly to practical economic policy questions the "Ricardian Vice." Yet notwithstanding this

---

[1] Smith's own attitude to the physiocratic system was interesting. He recognised it as "the nearest approximation to the truth that has yet been published upon the subject of political economy" (1776, 4.9:678), and praised it for (among other things) "representing perfect liberty as the only effectual expedient for rendering ... annual reproduction the greatest possible" (ibid). Compare the attitude that Stewart took with respect to the physiocratic system (an attitude in which Stewart implicated Smith).

[2] Ricardo was, *tout court*, the leading political economist of his day. Perhaps for this reason, he has had, and indeed continues to have, both sharp critics and hagiographers, and those who simply agree with Marshall that Ricardo occupied "so important a place in the history of economics" that any misunderstanding of him "must necessarily be very mischievous" (1890, 503). When raising the broader social and political aspects of his writing, the disagreement has been equally sharp. Hutchison's opinion concerning Ricardo's social and political views expressed the conviction that he was lacking in "sophisticated" or independent thought, and merely repeated James Mill's coaching in an unabridged form (1953, 81; 1994). Others have disagreed, offering different readings of the content and character of Ricardo's writing on both economic and political subjects (see, for example, Blaug 1958; Fetter 1975, 1980; Gordon 1976; Grampp 1948; Milgate and Stimson 1991b; Fenn 1992; Dixon 2008). Our own earlier contribution to this discussion mined "a very shallow textual vein" (Hont 1994, 341). In both that earlier work and this, it might be said that when examining the historical context of economic and political reform in this period, the interest of Ricardo's writing on these subjects rests less on the total amount written than on understanding the larger question of what he might have been doing when he wrote.

conventional image, Ricardo did address some of the broader constitutional questions of his day, and he did so by bringing to bear the conclusions of political economy. As he declared to the electors of Westminister
in 1823, "The only remedy for the national grievances" was "a full, fair,
free, and equal representation of the people in the Commons' House of
Parliament" (1951–73, 5:484). In the course of making the case for a
democratic reform of the British constitution, Ricardo effectively introduced into the discourse of political economy another way of using some
of its more familiar concepts—the role of economic classes, the antagonism between the interests of those classes, and the relationship of both
to economic prosperity and political stability. In offering an economic
interpretation of politics, Ricardo did not turn to the utilitarian model of
individual choice and action, as Bentham and James Mill had done, but
rather to political economy, and in particular, to his own fundamental
transformation of Smith's account of value and distribution as he had
found it in Book 1 of the *Wealth of Nations*.[3]

When Ricardo entered Parliament (for the Irish pocket borough of Portarlington) in 1819, the 658 county, borough, and university members of
the House of Commons were returned at septennial general elections by
an all-male electoral body that amounted to scarcely more than 2.5 percent of the population. In the counties, the franchise extended only as far
as the celebrated forty-shilling freeholder. In the boroughs, the franchise
was more heterogeneous but scarcely more extensive. It ranged from the
potwalloping and scot-and-lot boroughs at the more "democratic" end
of the spectrum, through corporation boroughs, and right down to the
pocket and rotten boroughs at the other.[4] The system was unequal, it was
subject to abuse.[5] Its legitimacy had also come under siege from the people. The great public protests of Ricardo's day uniformly included on their
agenda a demand for parliamentary reform. It was against the theoretical

---

[3] That revision arose from what Ricardo referred to as Smith's "original error respecting
value" (*Letter to Mill*, December 1816, in Ricardo 1951–73, 7:100; unless otherwise indicated, all subsequent references to Mill's correspondence are to that part of it contained in
this edition of Ricardo)—namely, the error that Ricardo perceived had taken place when
Smith had abandoned the labour theory of value outside the "early and rude state of society" (when positive profits had emerged), and had moved instead to an "adding-up" theory
of value (retaining only labour commanded as the *measure* of value). Subject to what Ricardo called "exceptions," he argued that the relative quantities of labour embodied continued to determine relative prices even when the rate of profit was positive.

[4] See T.H.B. Oldfield's *Representative History* (1816), which remains the classic account
of the inequalities and abuses of the unreformed House of Commons, for both detailed
electoral statistics and the definitions of the (then) prevailing franchise.

[5] Bentham's remark to the effect that if he had £10m or £20m he would "buy liberty
with it for the people" (1817, 3:486) is perhaps indicative of just how far an actual market
for votes had developed under the old electoral system.

and practical foundations of this system of representation that the early philosophic radicals, led by Bentham and James Mill, waged their campaign for parliamentary reform. It was into this campaign that Ricardo injected a distinctively economic approach to politics.[6]

THE QUESTION OF THE FRANCHISE

If government was to be representative of public opinion in a directly democratic way, as Ricardo had proposed, then the question immediately arose as to the extent of the enfranchisement thereby mandated. As a rule, in addressing the question of who should vote, or what amounts to the same thing, the question of political citizenship, the philosophic radicals with whom Ricardo was most closely associated spoke in voices adjusted to suit the circumstances. At bottom, of course, it was a matter of principle and had to be dealt with as such. Bentham seems to have been the only one to have realised this, and he paid the price of going out on a limb with his motto of "Universality, Equality, Annuality, Secrecy." But in many instances, especially in the context of actual political struggles where there was a real possibility of securing a measure of parliamentary reform, a note of expediency regularly entered the discourse of philosophic radicalism. Mill's essay on *Government* seems to stand as exemplary of it.[7]

Ricardo was no exception to this rule. Although he did declare himself against any piecemeal approach to reform on the floor of the House of Commons in 1823, when he was faced with the charge that democracy was an avatar of the end of civilisation, Ricardo spoke in an accommodating voice. Thus, one can find him talking of securing "unbiased good sense" among electors, enfranchising only "the reasonable part of the country," getting "all the wisdom and virtue of the country to act in Government," and taking "precautions" in "bestowing the elective franchise."[8] In his speech to the House of Commons on Lord Russell's motion for a reform of Parliament in 1823, Ricardo even invoked the authority

[6] Although this discussion will not exhaust everything that Ricardo had to say about politics, it is indicative of a distinctive strand of early philosophical radical thinking about parliamentary reform and its relationship to classical political economy (see Milgate and Stimson 1991b).

[7] It has been claimed that Mill never really addressed the question of enfranchisement at the level of principle at all. Halévy went so far as to argue that Mill's case for representative government "is the argument of a lawyer rather than of a philosopher" (1928, 421).

[8] *Letter to Trower*, March 22, 1818, 7:260; see also *Letter to McCulloch*, January 17, 1821, 8:336; *Letter to Trower*, November 2, 1818, 7:320; *Letter to Trower*, December 20, 1818, 7:366, 368.

of Montesquieu to support his faith in "the people," and bolster his main conclusion "that instead of selecting demagogues and disturbers of the peace, as was unjustly apprehended, the people, if left to the unrestricted exercise of their choice, would act wisely and prudently."[9]

But it is one thing to have to meet political adversaries head-on in parliamentary debate (and the direct involvement of the philosophic radicals in daily politics helps to explain why they devoted so much attention to the moral character of electors in that particular context), and it is quite another to settle the issue of the extent of the franchise on the basis of theoretical principles. What is decisive about Ricardo's contribution to that more theoretical project is that he resolved the question of the franchise in a way that set him apart from not only James Mill but also John Stuart Mill (whose best-known intervention in the debate came some forty years after Ricardo's death).

As we have seen, James Mill's starting point in the consideration of the extent of the franchise bore all the hallmarks of utilitarianism. He set out to determine which individuals in the existing population possessed the capacity for political decision making on the premise that what was required for sound judgment and good political choice was the full knowledge of one's own interest and the wherewithal to act rationally on it. Mill then resolved the problem that individuals might be mistaken about their long-term interests in a straightforward manner. Education was the answer:

> The evils which arise from mistake are not incurable; for, if parties who act contrary to their interest had a proper knowledge of that interest, they would act well. What is necessary, then, is knowledge. Knowledge, on the part of those whose interests are the same as those of the community, would be an adequate remedy. But knowledge is a thing which is capable of being increased. (1820a, 29)

At issue here, of course, is both what type of knowledge is necessary to politics, and Mill's conception of the relationship between improved knowledge and political order. On this subject, Mill adverted to the customary utilitarian conception of knowledge as individual mental capability, developed through education. According to this line of reasoning, education is "the means which may be employed to render the *mind*, as far as possible, an operative cause of happiness" (1818b, 41), and improved education becomes instrumental to "adopting the best means" to achieve that end.[10] The benefit of this to society is established courtesy of the

---

[9] *Speeches and Evidence*, April 24, 1823, 5:289.

[10] In *Schools for All*, Mill writes of an aim "to extirpate . . . ignorance by the force of education, and to plant knowledge in its stead" (1812, 126).

familiar argument that if each individual secures the maximum amount of happiness possible, then the happiness of the nation (which is simply the aggregate of the happiness of the individuals who compose it) would also attain its maximum.

This claim bears a strong family resemblance to that which John Stuart Mill would develop decades later. If individuals are seeking to act in ways that promote their own interest (that is, in the pursuit of happiness/utility), they must possess full information not only of the alternatives available to them but also of the utility they will derive once a particular course has been chosen. This last requirement is the key to the problem of "error," for even if one knew all of the possibilities, one might still not know the consequences (in terms of utility) of different actions. In their customary fashion, both of the Mills thus transformed the question of the extent of the franchise into a question about the extent of individual knowledge of consequences. If individuals had the knowledge, so the argument ran, they would not choose to elect "demagogues and disturbers of the peace" as it would be contrary to their interests to do so.[11]

Ricardo, on the other hand, seems to have embarked on a somewhat different course on his journey towards this same destination. He did not begin with the isolated utility maximiser, who needed "knowledge" of the possibilities and consequences (in terms of "happiness") of choice and action in order to secure his goals. Nor was his an argument where the greatest good of society was discussed in concepts directly connected to the proposition that the best of all possible worlds would be the aggregate outcome of the efficient pursuit of individual utility maximisation. For these reasons, Ricardo was not led to the question of judging the capacity for political decision making on the part of the potential electorate in quite the same way as Mill. Though good government was that which secured the greatest good, the key to the novelty of Ricardo's contention was that he developed an alternative standard against which to measure the greatest good.[12]

The starting point of Ricardo's argument is the familiar premise (dating back to Quesnay and Smith) that the material prosperity of the nation depends on "the quantity of commodities annually produced" (1821, 277; see also 279), or what amounts to the same thing, the "annual produce of the industry of the country."[13] Good government, he claims, attends to material prosperity. Quite apart from the most obvious difference

---

[11] This feature of the argument allowed the Mills, by turns, to be educational reformers, supporters of the political emancipation of women, and advocates of plural voting.

[12] See *Letter to Mill*, August 4, 1822, 9:213.

[13] See *Letter to McCulloch*, 8:399.

between this standard of well-being and that of "general" utility (namely, that the former is directly quantifiable while the latter is not), the significance of focusing on material prosperity is that it leads Ricardo to formulate the question of the capacity of the electorate to decide in economic terms. Rather than insisting that individuals know their own interests, then, Ricardo is led to consider whether social groups know how material prosperity is best secured and whether they act in ways generally conducive to its improvement.

According to Ricardo, there are two ways of looking at annual production that need to be carefully distinguished in any discussion of material prosperity (1821, 273–88): gross versus net product. On the one hand, material well-being can be considered simply as the total quantity of commodities produced; on the other, it can be considered as the quantity of commodities produced after allowance had been made for that part of the whole that goes to replace the commodities used to produce it (which, for Ricardo, included wage goods). Different judgments might be rendered as to the state of material prosperity according to whether one focused on gross or net product. As Ricardo observed in a celebrated passage, Smith "constantly magnifies the advantages which a country derives from a large gross, rather than a large net income" (347), whereas the "real interest of the nation" is more closely connected to net product and its disbursement (348).

Many familiar Ricardian themes are contingent on focusing on net product and its distribution between profits and rent. To begin with, the claim that an increase in net product acts as a spur to economic progress follows from Ricardo's recognition that profits are the ultimate source of revenue for accumulation—that is, for future reproduction on an extended scale.[14] Since increased reproduction entails a greater volume of employment for wage labourers, "the labouring class have no small interest in the manner in which the net income of the country is expended" (392). Furthermore, the idea that the use of these surpluses for the purchase of luxuries acts as a drag on the rate of growth rests on this proposition, so that workers "must naturally desire that as much of the revenue as possible should be diverted from expenditure on luxuries"

[14] Hence the argument that "the wealth of a country may be increased in two ways: it may be increased by employing a greater proportion of revenue in the maintenance of productive labour . . . or it may be increased, without employing any additional quantity of labour, by making the same quantity more productive" (1821, 278). It is perhaps worth observing that when Marx decided to substitute the term surplus value for the phrase net product, the accumulation process described here by Ricardo was given a whole new social significance, for it enabled Marx to portray it as the process of extracting (absolute and relative) surplus value.

(393).[15] The proposition that "there are no taxes which have not a tendency to lessen the power to accumulate" (152) is one of its corollaries, since "the power of paying taxes, is in proportion to net, and not in proportion to gross" product (349).[16] Lastly, the idea that restrictions on the free trade in corn are detrimental to the nation, perhaps the most well-known of all Ricardian doctrines, also rests on the proposition. That story is simple enough. A rise in the price of corn consequent on restrictions on its importation has the effect of driving cultivation onto less fertile lands, thereby raising the rents received by landlords at the expense of the profits in general. The effect of the fall in profits is to reduce the power to accumulate.

Some less well-known Ricardian themes, however, are contingent on focusing on gross product. In particular, the idea of wealth—or riches, as Ricardo customarily refers to it—is to be understood as referring to gross rather than net product. Riches, argues Ricardo, depend on the "abundance" of commodities produced (1821, 275), so that if one is, for example, comparing the wealth of the nation at two different points in time, or comparing the wealth of two different countries, then it is to the gross product that he recommends we turn. This helps to explain why Ricardo became sceptical as to the universally beneficial effects of the introduction of machinery on the economic state of the nation that although always accompanied by an increase in net product, may be associated with a decrease in gross product. When the task is to understand the potential for future growth (that is, to judge the prospects for economic progress), Ricardo invariably consults net product. When the task is concerned instead with assessing the existing state of the nation, Ricardo consults gross product.

The originality in his mode of addressing the suffrage question is, then, apparent: Ricardo made the question of the degree of the franchise turn on the relationship between democratic participation and material well-being. The link Ricardo thereby established between the suffrage question and material prosperity entailed a relationship between his politics and economics of a rather more compelling nature than simply that political

[15] The point that had to be understood, according to Ricardo, was that while "all the productions of a country are consumed . . . it makes the greatest difference imaginable whether they are consumed by those who reproduce, or by those who do not reproduce another value. When we say that revenue is saved, and added to capital, what we mean is, that the portion of revenue, so said to be added to capital, is consumed by productive instead of unproductive labourers" (151, 151n*).

[16] Ricardo reminded McCulloch in 1820 that "it is only because taxation interferes with the accumulation of capital, and diminishes the demand for labour, that it is injurious to the working classes" (*Letter to McCulloch*, March 29, 1820, 8:168–69). See also Ricardo (1820b, 381–82).

economy aids in "directing government to right measures" (though it would certainly be quite useful in that arena as well).[17] The science of political economy thus became in Ricardo's hands the stablemate to the "science of politics" itself.

The idea that the general question of political organisation could be analysed from an economic point of view was stated quite explicitly by Ricardo in the first of his two discourses on politics, *Observations on Parliamentary Reform*: "Although it may be true that the country has flourished with a House of Commons constituted as ours has been, it must be shown that such a constitution of it is favourable to the prosperity of the country" (1824b, 499). In setting himself the task of defending an argument for democratic politics on the grounds that it tended to promote material prosperity, Ricardo stands in contrast to James Mill, who as we have seen, made the extent of the franchise turn on the relationship between his more directly individualistic premises of democratic participation and rising individual "mental qualities" or improved "levels" of personal development.[18] This contrast is brought into sharp relief when one looks at how Ricardo went about making the case that workers had the capacity for political decision making. For here, Ricardo's argument not only challenged the basis of the older doctrine of virtual representation (even in the attenuated form that was retained by Mill) but also brought forward the value of public opinion in a manner different from James Mill.[19]

THE POLITICAL CAPACITY OF THE WORKING CLASS

There are a number of quite striking examples of this, but perhaps one of the clearest is closely bound up with Ricardo's theoretical volte-face—the revision of his opinion on the subject of the effects of the introduction of machinery.[20] Indeed, the fact that the value of the common opinion of

---

[17] Thus, Paul Samuelson's claim that the classical economists "lived during the industrial revolution, but scarcely looked out from their libraries to notice the remaking of the world" could be rethought (1978, 1428).

[18] A distinction should be noted between James Mill and John Stuart Mill, on the one hand, and between James Mill and Ricardo, on the other. James Mill's essay on *Government* contains both approaches to securing the greatest good. At one point, he speaks (reminiscent of Ricardo) of interest as the "greatest possible quantity of the produce of his labour" (1820a, 5), while at another, he speaks of it as "preference" in a manner more like his son.

[19] This would seem to fit well with Coats's observation that Mill had a "tendency to give priority to moral . . . considerations, over merely economic ones" (1971, 13).

[20] The story of this change of opinion is well-known. For further details, the reader may consult the editorial introduction to Ricardo's *Works and Correspondence* (1951–73, 1:lvii–lx).

workers was confirmed by the observation that workers correctly comprehended the effects of the introduction of machinery was not lost on Ricardo.[21] He went out of his way to say so in the new chapter on machinery in the third edition of the *Principles*: "The opinion entertained by the labouring class, that the employment of machinery is frequently detrimental to their interests, is not founded on prejudice or error, but is conformable to the correct principles of political economy" (1821, 392).[22] Ricardo's reasoning on the subject is simple enough; "as plain as any proposition in geometry," as he told McCulloch. When the introduction of machinery (which is *always* associated with an increase in net product) is accompanied by a decrease in gross product, it will be "very injurious to the interests of the class of labourers" (1821, 388), and what is more, it will diminish "the means of enjoyment of some one, or more, classes of the community."[23] He reiterated the claim on the floor of the House of Commons in May 1823, declaring that machinery "must, in some degree, operate prejudicially to the working classes."[24]

But while the reasoning is straightforward, its interpretation has turned out to be rather more problematic. The interpretive question is this: To what context does the argument apply?

One line of thinking has been that Ricardo's argument refers to the immediate or temporary effects of the introduction of machinery, and that the difficulty is therefore likely to be short-lived. This was certainly the construction that John Stuart Mill put on it nearly thirty years later:

> All increase of fixed capital [machinery], when it takes place at the expense of circulating, must be, *at least temporarily*, prejudicial to the interests of the labourers. . . . Nevertheless, I do not believe that as things are actually transacted, improvements in production are often, if ever, injurious, even temporarily, to the labouring classes in the aggregate. (1871, 1.6:§2, §3; emphasis added)

This construal of Ricardo's meaning is given increased credibility by some remarks he makes at the end of the same chapter to the effect that "the

---

[21] Nor was it lost on Malthus, who wrote that "you have used one expression which is liable to be taken fast hold of by the labouring class" (*Letter to Ricardo*, July 16, 1821, 9:18). McCulloch also saw the political implications, and seems to have become almost apoplectic when he read the offending chapter: "If your reasoning . . . be well founded, the laws against the Luddites are a disgrace to the Statute book. Let me beg you to reconsider this subject" (*Letter to Ricardo*, June 5, 1821, 8:385).

[22] In contrast, as late as 1846, Brougham was still trying to attribute "the rage against machinery" to "ignorance of economical science" (quoted in Brinton 1949, 33–34). Ricardo's statement suggests his disagreement with Brougham.

[23] *Letter to McCulloch*, June 18, 1821, 8:388.

[24] *Speeches and Evidence*, December 16, 1819, 5:303.

statements that I have made will not, I hope, lead to the inference that machinery should not be encouraged" (1821, 395). Any deleterious effects attributed to the introduction of machinery by Ricardo would then be taken to refer exclusively to short-run disequilibria and the problems involved in making a transition from the old to the new equilibrium.

If this reading is accurate, then Ricardo's claim would hardly be supportive of the need to place value on the common opinion of the labouring classes, for in this instance, it would confirm instead that their opinion was shortsighted. Indeed, were this to be the case, the proposition would furnish the basis for an assertion (such as Mill's) that demonstrated that *no* weight should be attached to the opinion. A longer view would be what was called for.

There are good grounds for taking up an alternative reading. In the first place, Mill's interpretation, as just outlined, seems to reduce to an argument about the effects of machinery essentially equivalent to the one that Ricardo had actually held *before* he declared himself to have changed his mind.

That earlier contention was set out by Ricardo in his speech to the House of Commons in December 1819, in the debate over a motion to establish a select committee to enquire into certain "plans" of Robert Owen—a debate in which the question of the effects of machinery had arisen. At the time, Ricardo had held that while "it could not be denied that, on the whole view of the subject, . . . machinery did not lessen the demand for labour," it might be "mis-applied" in a particular industry.[25] Ricardo recognised that this might occasion an overproduction in that *particular* industry (together with a *temporary* dislocation of the worker). But he had then maintained that this effect could neither be general nor lasting. The *British Press* report of this part of Ricardo's intervention actually makes him sound just like Mill:

> [Mr. Ricardo] never could think that machinery could do mischief to any country, either in its immediate or its permanent effect. Machinery, indeed, in one way might be carried too far, that is where it is employed in the manufacture of a particular commodity, as for instance, in the manufacture of cotton, but where the individual extended it too far it would not repay him, and he would be soon obliged to reduce it, or employ it in another channel.[26]

Still, if we are to believe Mill, it is this kind of argument that is also to be found in the new chapter on machinery. When it is recalled that the later argument (of 1821) was heralded by Ricardo as a great "change of

[25] Ibid., 5:31.
[26] *Works and Correspondence*, 5:31, 31n1.

mind"—and this quite explicitly (both in the third edition of the *Principles* and on the floor of the House of Commons)—it is difficult to believe that Ricardo would be offering exactly the *same* claim he had made *before* his change of mind.

Theoretically speaking, a tolerably convincing case can be made out to the effect that the new assertion is actually an exercise in comparative statics rather than an analysis of temporary effects consequent on the need to make the transition to a new equilibrium. For not only are exercises in comparative statics the staple of Ricardo's technique of theorising (as he was wont to put it, they allowed him to emphasise the permanent effects of changes), but it is clear that they are exactly what Ricardo engages in his famous numerical example in the machinery chapter.[27] If it is an exercise in comparative statics, then the opinion that the demand for labour may fall consequent on the introduction of machinery is not shortsighted.

The above should not be taken to imply that before his change of mind on the subject of machinery, Ricardo had given any less weight to the opinions of the labouring classes. In fact, the reverse seems to be true, but he had done so on different grounds. In the parliamentary session of 1819, Ricardo had voted against the Six Acts that were promulgated after the Peterloo massacre, and in speaking against one of them (the Seditious Meetings Prevention Bill) on the floor of the House of Commons on December 6, 1819, he made it perfectly clear that he was not in favour of such opinions but rather for having them better represented in that very body.[28] What is more, he had made a similar argument in correspondence with Hutches Trower two months before that renders visible the basis of this earlier contention:

> One word on the Manchester proceedings. . . . I hope that no law can be produced to justify the violent interference of magistrates to dissolve a meeting of the people, the avowed object of which was to petition legally for a redress of real or imagined grievances. If the right to petition is only to be exercised at the discretion of magistrates, or of any other body in the state, then it is a farce to call us a free people. These large assemblages of the people are to be regretted—they may in their consequences be productive of mischief, but if the security of our freedom depend[s] on our right to

[27] *Letter to Malthus*, January 24, 1817, 7:120.

[28] Speeches and Evidence, December 6, 1819, 5:28–29. When Ricardo had spoken in the new chapter on machinery of not being aware of needing to retract anything he had published on the subject, he must not have had clearly in his mind the following passage from the *Essay on Profits*: "The effects on the interest of [the labouring] class, would be nearly the same as the effects of improved machinery, which it is now no longer questioned, has a decided tendency to raise the real wages of labour" (4:35).

assemble and state our wrongs, which in the absence of real representation I believe it does, then we must patiently suffer the lesser evil to avoid the greater.[29]

Here the argument seems to rest on a direct correspondence between genuine representation and the actualisation of political freedom. Ricardo's reference to the grievances as being "real or imagined," as if the verdict might go either way, may indicate the weight he was placing here on a purely political assertion. It did not matter whether the complaints were real or imagined; inadequate representation precluded the opinions from being registered as they should be registered if freedom was to be secured as justice mandated. Once Ricardo had availed himself of his newly established theoretical principle on the effects of machinery, which confirmed the grievance to be real and not imagined, the result only strengthened the basis of his support for the representation of common opinion by giving it an additional grounding in his economics in a manner it had not enjoyed before.

In many other instances, Ricardo speaks of the common opinion of workers as being in conformity with the "correct principles of the political economy" and so, as he argued, the interest of the community as a whole, in many other cases. "The working class," he once wrote to Francis Place, "are often cruelly calumniated."[30] Another example of his confidence in the opinion of workers came in his opposition to a proposed act (in 1823) to increase by statute the number of apprentices taken on board all vessels of the Merchant Marine. Ricardo spoke against this measure in the House of Commons on three separate occasions (March 13 and 24, and April 18, 1823), each time making the point that the proposed act was drafted only in the interests of employers, and that they sought only to lower wages.[31] He urged the honourable members opposite to consult the seamen, who would be able to acquaint them with the real motive and true effect.[32] Furthermore, the relative frequency with which Ricardo cites in-

---

[29] *Letter to Trower,* September 25, 1819, 8:80.

[30] *Letter to Place,* September 9, 1821, 9:54.

[31] *Speeches and Evidence,* 5:273, 276–77.

[32] It is worth noticing here that there is a striking passage in a letter to James Brown, written during the stagnation of 1819, which seems at once to reinforce the opinion that Ricardo was very much concerned about the condition of the working class, and also to place in a clearer light his alleged tendency to focus exclusively on long-run rather than short-run effects. The remark, it should be noted, is made in the context of a discussion of the effects of introducing one of Ricardo's favourite policies—a freer trade in corn:

We all have to lament the present distressed state of the labouring classes in this country, but the remedy is not very apparent to me. The correcting of our errors of legislation with regard to trade would *ultimately* be of considerable service to all classes of the

stances like these, where workers came to form the correct opinion (that is, an opinion conformable to the interest of the nation), suggests that they were not necessarily a special or limited class of cases.[33]

The one notable exception to this rule seems to have been Ricardo's position on the old Poor Laws, to which he was fervently opposed.[34] The problem here, of course, is not so much that this opposition diminishes his credentials as being a "friend to the poor" (1821, 106–7). It would be difficult to prosecute that case, given that Ricardo was the first to admit the misery that labourers experienced in times of depression, and his insistence that any project for the removal of existing legislation had to be slow and gradual. Rather, the problem is that Ricardo spoke with such conviction of the need to "teach the labouring classes that they must themselves provide for those casualties to which they are exposed," that one is led to wonder why it was that the poor themselves did not learn that the Poor Laws ran directly counter to the principles of political economy (at least, that is, in the version they were enunciated by Ricardo), and so to their own (and the nation's) interests.[35]

Ricardo does, however, provide us with a clue as to the resolution of this paradox. As it turns out, it is a clue that might be just as helpful in explaining the rule as it is in explaining the exception. According to Ricardo, the failure of the poor to comprehend the "pernicious tendency of these laws" was the direct consequence of their having lived for too long within a culture, itself the immediate product of those laws, where social norms and values were such as to render it impossible for them even to begin to do so. The Poor Laws had "been so long established," maintained Ricardo, that "the habits of the poor" had been "formed upon

---

community, but it would afford no immediate relief. . . . [T]he derangement which such measures would occasion in the actual employment of capital, and the changes which would become necessary, would rather aggravate than relieve the distress under which we are now labouring. (*Letter to Brown*, October 13, 1819, 8:103; emphasis added)

[33] Thus, in *Parliamentary Reform*, Ricardo spoke of an unjustified "presumption of mistaken views of interest" entertained by the ruling classes with respect to their inferiors (1824b, 502).

[34] One other case where Ricardo berated the opinions of workers—namely, the Spitalfield silk weavers (whose employment contract was underwritten by special legislation)—does not seem to stand as a glaring exception to the rule. Ricardo's argument here was that the Spitalfield weavers enjoyed their local privileges at the expense of weavers in other parts of the country. That is, what Ricardo opposed was the idea that the interests of a faction of a class should be allowed to dominate the interests of the class as a whole.

[35] *Letter to Trower*, January 26, 1818, 7:248. The parallel passage in the *Principles* runs as follows: "By impressing on the poor the value of independence, by teaching them that they must look not to systematic or casual charity, but to their own exertions for support, . . . we shall by degrees approach a sounder and more healthful state" (1821, 107).

their operation" (1821, 106). This idea—that character and culture were closely related in this way—differed hardly at all from that of a much more famous friend of the poor, Owen. In his *New View of Society*, Owen had argued that "the direct and certain effects" of the Poor Laws were to "injure the poor," because "they prepare the poor to acquire the worst habits, and practice every kind of crime" (1816, 141–42). Nevertheless, it must be said that on the general question of the poor—that is, their economic position rather than their political one—Ricardo advanced not far beyond the opinions of other reformers. Here, the influence of Malthus's principle of population seems to have been the decisive factor in shaping his views. So wedded was he to this, that he proposed no policies that might alleviate the sufferings of the poor if, on that principle, they would contribute to further population increase.[36]

If the exclusion of the poor from normal economic life was utilised in this manner by Ricardo to sustain his well-known position on their general incapacity for citizenship in the prevailing economic circumstances, it seems natural enough to look to the inclusion of others in economic life (and especially of workers) to illuminate his more general point about the extensiveness of the reasonable part of the country. Since workers certainly did not acquire it from books or schools, the only possible forum left where they might have developed their capacities was in the school of life. While Ricardo would not have differed with Jane Marcet, author of the popular *Conversations on Political Economy*, over her idea that "a more general knowledge of political economy" would be productive of "no trifling good" (Marcet 1821, 11), and while he even applauded her own efforts to make the science more widely available, it is perfectly clear that his confidence in the reasonable people was not premised on their first having undertaken a formal course of instruction in the science.

At this juncture, it is instructive to return for a moment to the contrast between Ricardo's arguments for the enfranchisement of the working class and those of James Mill. In the essay on *Government*, Mill had also considered the question of how far one might extend the franchise in the face of existing instances of popular protest and unrest among the labouring classes. He, too, considered the value of the common opinions of the

---

[36] Thus, while Ricardo actually funded the establishment of a school on Lancasterian principles for both boys and girls in Minchinhampton in 1816, he declined a request to contribute the sum of £50 to a scheme that Brougham had launched for the schooling of the poor in London if the daily programme entailed feeding the children. James Mill hastily wrote back to Ricardo, urging him to fund the London project, since Brougham had never intended actually to feed the children (see *Letter to Mill*, December 12, 1818, 7:360, and subsequent correspondence).

labouring classes as they were expressed in the selfsame gatherings that
Ricardo had defended in Parliament (before Mill's essay appeared) and
had none too elliptically alluded to in the chapter on machinery.

> What signify the irregularities of the mob, more than half composed in the
> greater number of instances, of boys and women, and disturbing for a few
> hours or days a particular town? What signifies the occasional turbulence of
> a manufacturing district, peculiarly unhappy from a very great deficiency of
> a middle rank, as there the population almost wholly consists of rich manu-
> facturers and poor workmen; with whose minds no pains are taken by any-
> body; with whose afflictions there is no virtuous family of the middle rank
> to sympathize; whose children have no good example of such a family to see
> and to admire; and who are placed in the highly unfavourable situation of
> fluctuating between very high wages in one year, and very low wages in an-
> other? It is altogether futile with regard to the foundation of good govern-
> ment to say that this or the other portion of the people, may at this, or the
> other time, depart from the wisdom of the middle rank. (1820a, 32)

While this should not be taken to indicate that Mill wished to deny democratic citizenship to the working class, it does suggest that Mill's argument
for enfranchising them differs from anything deployed by Ricardo.[37]
There is nothing in Ricardo, for example, about needing to educate people
to correct opinions or about having them emulate those "virtuous families
of the middle rank" that Mill advocates. Ricardo simply held that these
individuals were to be represented as a matter of principle. For Mill, it
was essential to the argument to show that most of the time, most of the
people "continue to be guided by that rank" (1820a, 32).[38] Nothing of
this kind seems to have been present in Ricardo's argument.

There is another feature of Mill's reasoning on this subject that should
not be allowed to pass without comment, since it further highlights the
contrast with Ricardo. Mill claimed that these instances of popular unrest
should, in fact, be regarded as an exception to the rule that the people

---

[37] Although, since Mill does remark that better than half of the mob were "women and
boys," they would all be disqualified on the grounds of age and gender by Mill in any case,
despite their riotous assembly. Indeed, was not "males over the age of forty" Mill's electorate (1820a, 22)?

[38] There would seem, therefore, to be some truth in the judgment passed (in the context
of another of Mill's essays) by one historian on Mill's "democratic" thought: "[Mill] was
championing certain 'outs' who wished to get in. He was no defender of liberty or equality
in the abstract. The lower class, 'brutalized,' undiscriminating, the prey of violent demagogues, in his opinion obviously could no more be trusted than the aristocracy. Clearly the
article [on the *Edinburgh Review* in 1824] was never written by a thorough-going democrat" (Nesbitt 1934, 42).

were capable of judging. Already, one might note, his reasoning is in contradistinction to that of Ricardo, for whom these protests represented the expression of a "correct" and not "mistaken" opinion. Like a good lawyer not satisfied with the brilliance of their performance, Mill next proceeds to assert that these exceptions actually *prove* the rule (1829, 32–33). Since there are so few of these protesters (measured against the whole population), clearly most of the population are guided by those middling ranks of people of good sense. Interestingly enough, for Ricardo, not only was such guidance unnecessary but it might turn out to be counterproductive too. As we have already seen, Ricardo was well aware that individuals belonged to particular social classes and that class interests diverged; what he wanted from democracy was the representation of these interests, not the elimination of all of them save those of the middle class.

This confidence in the capacity of members of the working class to come to correct conclusions on matters concerning the well-being of the nation pervades Ricardo's politics, and it is uniformly informed by an appeal to the "science of political economy." This helps to explain why Ricardo's proposals as to the extent of the suffrage stand much closer to those originally expounded by Bentham (universality) than to those proposed by either James Mill or, in his later writings, John Stuart Mill. And what applied to workers applied also to disenfranchised small manufacturers, and for the same reason—they, too, were capable of forming political opinions conformable to the interests of the nation: "The reasoning by which the liberty of trade is supported, is so powerful, that it is daily obtaining converts. It is with pleasure, that I see the progress which this great principle is making amongst those whom we should have expected to cling the longest to old prejudices" (1816, 70). In this pamphlet, Ricardo goes on to discuss the example of a group of Gloucestershire clothiers who petitioned Parliament in 1816 for the removal of the Corn Laws. The petition offered a quid pro quo, suggesting that the dismantling of the protection of agriculture could be accompanied by the removal of the protection enjoyed by the clothiers' own industry, which Ricardo warmly commended. Now it is of the first importance to notice that on Ricardo's argument, these sections of the population were to be represented not because they numbered among those good and virtuous people of the middle rank (as Mill might have put it). Instead, their claim to representation as formulated by Ricardo was no different from that of workers: a capacity for judgment congruent with both their own and the community's interest in economic prosperity.

The sword of participatory democracy was double-edged, however. Not only did Ricardo wield it so as to construct a positive case for thoroughgoing parliamentary reform but he used it to construct a negative case against existing constitutional arrangements as well. One might almost say that in doing so, the distance between Ricardo's theory of value and distribution and that of Smith is mirrored in the distance between their respective visions of the need for constitutional reform. The basic claim, of course, was also the standard fare of philosophic radicalism: participatory democracy was the nation's only security against the domination of politics by sinister interests. In developing it, though, Ricardo mobilised the science of political economy for political ends in a manner not attempted by the other philosophic radicals of his day.

THE CONSTITUTION OF THE MONETARY AUTHORITY

Exemplary of this particular use of an economic argument for democratic participation is Ricardo's assault on the conduct of monetary policy by successive Tory governments prior to their move to restore specie payments in 1819. Commencing with the Bullion Controversy of 1809–11, Ricardo had consistently maintained that bankers and, more especially, the directors of the Bank of England had been pursuing their own interests in direct opposition to, and at the expense of, the national interest. The actual space for the exercise of these sinister interests, according to Ricardo, had been opened up by a complex combination of circumstances, the precondition for which had been Parliament's act to suspend specie payments in 1797. By removing this legislative restriction on the Bank of England's ability to issue paper currency, while still allowing it to enjoy an effective monopoly of note issue, this act had set in motion a sort of self-reinforcing vicious cycle. Remembering that it was always open to the bank's directors to augment their profits by issuing paper currency (in the form of loans at interest or the discounting of bills) in excess of the underlying monetary base (gold stocks), and remembering too that these overissues, as they were called, were (according to standard quantity theory conclusions) inflationary, a situation had arisen whereby the interest of the community (price stability) was opposed to the interests of the monetary authorities (bank profits). The problem was, then, that the monetary authorities had the power to act on their interests, while the community was powerless to stop them.

Given Ricardo's self-confessed delight at attacking the Bank of England ("I always enjoy any attack upon the Bank," he once confided to Malthus), it is not surprising that he entered the fray with vigour.[39] Against the above-mentioned (and other) illiberal practices, Ricardo mustered a number of arguments.

---

[39] *Letter to Malthus*, September 10, 1815, 6:268–69.

In the first place, he mounted a moral crusade (one that had been suggested to him by James Mill) against the bank being allowed to appropriate to itself the profits derived from the use of the deposits of public funds. The public, on Ricardo's thinking, was in "justice" entitled to remuneration, while the bank was in "gratitude" bound "voluntarily to relinquish to the state, the whole benefit" (1816, 93) derived from these deposits.[40] Ricardo calculated that from this source, the bank had secured for its own benefit (between 1806 and 1816) some £3.8 million in profits directly at the expense of the public. He was especially outraged that the bank (that is, the owners of bank stock) was actually claiming a *right* to these purloined profits under its charter: "Is it not lamentable to view a great and opulent body like the Bank of England, exhibiting a wish to augment their hoards by undue gains wrested from the hands of an overburthened people?" (1816, 93).[41] Ricardo repeated essentially the same argument in Parliament years later, although he does appear to have toned it down a little by attributing the conduct of bank's directors rather more to their "error" of "not knowing how to manage [their own concerns] upon true principles" than to moral turpitude.[42] *Hansard* reported him as follows: "With regard to the directors, he was willing, at all times, to give them full credit for honesty of intention; but he could not help thinking, that they had at different times involved the country in considerable difficulties."[43]

The directors' retort was that they were legitimately judged in their conduct by the proprietors of bank stock at regular intervals (elections took place annually), and that this method of judgment was to be preferred to "all the theories of modern philosophers on the subject."[44] That a director should have preferred this mode of assessment is not at all

---

[40] Writing to Malthus in the period leading up to the publication of this pamphlet, Ricardo stated: "I think the Bank an unnecessary establishment getting rich by those profits which *fairly* belong to the public" (*Letter to Malthus*, September 10, 1815, 6:268; emphasis added).

[41] This particular argument was suggested to him by Mill, and indeed Ricardo seems to have copied it word for word from Mill's letter into the text of his pamphlet. Mill had written: "Hold up to view unsparingly the infamy of a great and opulent body like the bank, exhibiting a wish to augument its hoards by undue gains wrested from the hands of an overburthened people" (*Letter from Mill*, January 3, 1816, 7:5). Ricardo was not alone in this crusade, and as Frank Whitson Fetter noted in his *British Monetary Orthodoxy*, "Men who were far apart on most points were in agreement that someone was making too much money from the paper money system" (1965, 70).

[42] *Speeches and Evidence*, March 8, 1822, 5:143. He added that "the directors had convinced him by their conduct that they did not know what they were about" (5:144).

[43] *Speeches and Evidence*, March 8, 1822, 5:143.

[44] These are the words of one Mr. Pearse, himself a bank director. They are cited by Piero Sraffa in the editorial apparatus attached to Ricardo's speech (1951–73, 5:143).

surprising. One would hardly expect those to whom bank profits were being distributed as dividends to vote out the current directors in favour of others whose actions might better conform to Ricardo's code of conduct; it would be against their own interests to do so. Furthermore, this was not the only argument forwarded by the bank against its critics. It was also maintained that the bank's policy, far from being detrimental to the national interest, was actually conducive to it. This claim rested on the articulation of a relation between economic activity, credit creation, the supply of money, and the price level that differed from the one offered by Ricardo. Grounded on the real-bills doctrine, the bank's basic case was that its own activities had been dictated entirely by the needs of trade, so that its issue of paper money was not (and according to some of its more extreme proponents, could not be) in excess. Since this claim was to gain influential political support at the time (in the person of Nicholas Vansittart at the Exchequer) as well as important theoretical support some twenty years later in the debate surrounding the Bank Charter Act of 1844 (in the persons of Thomas Tooke and John Fullarton), it is clear that the moral condemnation of the Bank of England had its limitations.[45]

Ricardo's second line of attack saw him deploy an argument bringing forward the value of free information as a check to what he saw as the existing abuses of the bank: "The public attention has been lately called to the affairs of the Bank; and the subject of their profits is generally canvassed and understood" (1816, 114). While both of these challenges were not without their own force, it is well to note that they had both been suggested to Ricardo by Mill. Ricardo's third avenue of attack, however, appears to have been utterly original to him. In it, he maintained that popular sovereignty, and not simply a change of economic policy nor a sacking of the bank's current directors (nor even threats to remove its existing charter), was the ultimate channel through which such abuses could permanently be checked. *Hansard* reported the speech in which Ricardo made this argument as follows: "[Mr. Ricardo] did not think this a question only between the Bank and ministers . . . , but rather between ministers and the Bank on the one side, and the country on the other."[46]

---

[45] This is not the place to explore the theoretical issues at stake in these debates, except to say that everything hinged on the domain of applicability of the quantity theory of money, and specifically, whether its conclusions could be applied to the short run as readily as they could be applied to the long run. The quite different assessment of the Bank of England's policy that the anti-Ricardian theory mandated was nicely summarised by Tooke: "The Bank, on the contrary, was enabled, by the Restriction Act, to relieve the distress. . . . The Directors extended their discounts very considerably in 1810; and . . . they thus only filled the vacuum in the circulation" (1848, 123).

[46] *Speeches and Evidence*, May 24, 1819, 5:9–10.

With this assertion, of course, Ricardo immediately distanced himself from both the Whigs and the Tory liberals (like William Huskisson), and this despite the fact that all three of these groups favoured roughly the same change of policy (control over excessive note issue). Unlike Ricardo, the two existing parties (and here one should also include the majority of Tories who had sided with Vansittart against the Bullion Report in 1811) appear to have seen the underlying issue as exclusively one about the appropriate design of monetary policy. Whatever their position on that score, they uniformly saw the question entirely as a matter "between ministers and the Bank." For Whigs, who regularly criticised the Tory government's lax financial policies, a sufficient solution was that Tory ministers be replaced by Whig ministers. For the Tory liberals, the solution was the resumption of specie payments—a measure they succeeded in carrying in 1819. But Ricardo had introduced an entirely novel idea concerning the ultimate check on the conduct of monetary policy, for that check was to be exercised by the country itself (or more accurately, "the reasonable part" of it), and not just by the theories of the political economists as imbibed by the legislators. The idea of this kind of direct public involvement in politics was (and remains) remarkable. It contrasts sharply with both the traditional Benthamite confidence in professional expertise in government, and the more modern Schumpeterian theory of democracy that gives similar primacy to elites in policymaking and relegates the people to simply choosing among elites. This is not to say that Ricardo failed to appreciate the value of expert advice in the formulation of government policy; his own contributions in that regard are sufficient to dispel that inference. What appears to have been the case, rather, is that the requisite knowledge for useful inputs into politics was not seen by Ricardo to have been the exclusive preserve of experts.

It is impossible to leave this subject without remarking that certain modern quantity theorists seem to have taken an altogether different route to the solution of the conduct of monetary policy. Some of their number have preferred to advocate drawing up and enacting a strict set of rules—sometimes legislative rules of self-command (like balanced-budget amendments), sometimes quantitative controls on bank reserves (such as monetary base controls), and sometimes both—on the presumption that these fixed rules will act to direct the conduct of monetary policy into "scientifically correct" channels. To be sure, still others of their number have taken the free banking route of having no monetary regulation at all, not even of note issue—no central bank, no lender of last resort. Yet the impulse behind these strategies turns out to be essentially the same; the idea is to remove from the hands of politicians all "technical" decisions concerning the regulation of the currency.

In the present context, what is interesting about both of these contemporary approaches is the fact that they go directly against the course of action advocated by Ricardo. While his approach was to seek to place the conduct of monetary policy squarely within the political arena, contemporary quantity theorists seem to want to do just the opposite. In either of its contemporary manifestations, the campaign is for the complete removal of the formulation of monetary policy from the sphere of political discourse. It is tempting to speculate as to whether such attempts may be due in part to the fact that (unlike Ricardo), these modern exponents of the quantity theory lack the confidence that public opinion will uniformly be led to see the desirability ("scientific correctness") of quantity theory recommendations. But in that event, their democratic commitment comes to its limit when faced with the prospect of their favourite theories being exploded in the domain of public opinion.

DEMOCRATIC REFORM AND PUBLIC EXPENDITURE

Should it be thought that Ricardo's argument against the Bank of England was merely an isolated instance of the idea that effective economic decision making at the level of government was not only a matter of getting the policy right but also intimately bound up with the democratic or undemocratic constitution of political society itself, it is worth remarking that this theme appears again and again throughout his thinking about politics. Another example of its influence is to be found in Ricardo's famous campaign against government loan expenditure, and in particular, against the burden of a national debt that by 1820 was in excess of £800 million.[47] Ricardo's "wild sort of notion," as Mallet called it,[48] involved a proposal to pay off the whole of the national debt by means of a once-and-for-all tax on property, a capital levy, so that "by one great effort, we should get rid of one of the most terrible scourges which was ever invented to afflict a nation" (Ricardo 1951–73, 4:197).[49] When he set out the details of the plan in 1820, Ricardo's idea seems to have been that the debt would be retired over two or three years. By 1823, he was advocating

[47] See Hargreaves (1930, table B, 292); Mitchell (1988, table 11.7, 601).

[48] See the editorial annotations in Ricardo (1951–73, 8:147, 147n1).

[49] Ricardo had given the idea an airing in 1817 in the *Principles* (1821, 248) and floated it again in the House of Commons in 1819 (*Speeches and Evidence*, December 24, 1819, 5:38) before it appeared in the supplement to the *Encyclopedia Britannica* in 1820. The fact that Ricardo's proposed tax was not to be levied on those "whose incomes are derived from wages or salaries" (*Letter to McCulloch*, September 15, 1820, 8:238) caused some critical comment at the time, and warrants mention here only insofar as it speaks to the caricature of Ricardo as the class enemy of the wage earner.

that it be retired over "two, three, six or twelve months."[50] It goes without saying that Ricardo's plan did not receive a particularly auspicious reception in the circles that counted:

> As it usually happens I am attacked by the most opposite parties. By some stockholders I am accused of not doing justice to them, by suggesting that they are not fairly entitled, in ready money, to £100, for £100–3pc[ts], but to the market price of £100 stock, £70. By another party—the landholders, I am accused of wishing to give the lands of the country to the stockholders, and it is more than hinted at that I have an interested view in making the proposal.[51]

Ricardo was not slow in realising where the problem lay. It was one thing to have diagnosed the burden of the debt, since as far as he was concerned, it "destroyed the equilibrium of prices, occasioned many persons to emigrate to other countries, in order to avoid the burthen of taxation which it entailed, and hung like a mill-stone round the exertion and industry of the country."[52] But it was quite another to expect that an unrepresentative legislature would ever see any such plan through to its completion: "The most serious obstacle which I see against the adoption of the plan is the state of representation in the House of Commons, which is such as to afford us no security that if we got rid of the present debt, we should not be plunged into another."[53]

---

[50] *Speeches and Evidence*, March 11, 1823, 5:271. The poet Percy Bysshe Shelley, interestingly enough, had the same thought in 1820; see his unpublished *Philosophical View of Reform* (1819–20, 34–37).

[51] *Letter to Trower*, December 28, 1819, 8:147.

[52] *Speeches and Evidence*, June 9, 1819, 5:21. A quite different stand on the prospect of redeeming the national debt was taken by Piercy Ravenstone (Richard Puller), who declaimed that to

> destroy it could only enter into the head of a cold-blooded and wrong-headed political economist, who, shut up in his closet, lost in abstraction . . . has cast away all sympathy with his fellow-creatures, and with the frenzied zeal of a madman is ever eager to pursue his favourite scheme, reckless of the havoc he is dealing around him, and seeing no way to possible good but through certain evil. (1824, 60)

[53] *Letter to Trower*, December 28, 1819, 8:148. It might be noted that in his essay on *Colony* for the supplement to the *Encyclopedia Britannica*, James Mill had made a similar point:

> If it be objected . . . that this propensity of governments to spend may be corrected, we answer, that this is not the present question. Take governments as, with hardly any exception, they have always been (this is a pretty wide experience); and the effect is certain. There is one way to be sure, of preventing the great evil, and preventing it thoroughly. But there is only one. In the constitution of the government, make the interest of the many to have the ascendancy over the interest of the few, and the expence of government will not be large. (1817c, 264)

Of course, there were also deep theoretical issues at stake in the economic debate over the effects on prosperity of government loan expenditure. Malthus, for one, had built up an argument (though he was not always as consistent as he might have been) to the effect that if the capital of the country was not always fully employed, there would be both scope for a productive contribution of government deficit expenditure to national prosperity and a positive danger of inducing a contraction of economic activity if the debt were to be annihilated overnight. In a long passage at the end of his *Principles of Political Economy*, Malthus stated that argument with considerable clarity:

> If there could be no sort of difficulty in finding profitable employment for any amount of capital, provided labour were sufficiently abundant, the way to national wealth, though it might not always be easy, would be quite straight, and our only object need be to save from revenue, and repress unproductive consumers. But, if it appears that the greatest powers of production are rendered comparatively useless without effectual consumption, and that a proper distribution of the produce is as necessary to the continued increase of wealth as the means of producing it, it follows that, in cases of this kind, the question depends upon proportions; and it would be the height of rashness to determine, under all circumstances, that the sudden diminution of the national debt and the reduction of taxation must necessarily tend to increase the national wealth, and provide employment for the labouring classes. (1820, 411)[54]

In this line of thinking, Malthus was followed by William Blake (not the poet, but a friend of Ricardo who, like him, was a member of the London Geological Society and the Political Economy Club). In 1823, Blake had published *Observations on the Expenditure of Government*, in which he had claimed that the mistake of the orthodox Ricardian view lay in its supposition that "the whole capital of the country is fully occupied; and, secondly, that there is immediate employment for successive accumula-

---

[54] The analytical problem with Malthus's argument was that he often seemed to apply this to the long-run equilibrium of the system, whereas his framework of concepts (which included Say's Law) meant that its domain of applicability was restricted to short-run disequilibrium. Some of the consequences of this inconsistency for the robustness of Malthus's contention and its contribution to Ricardo's victory over Malthus in the theoretical debate (so lamented by Keynes) are examined in more detail in Milgate (1982, 46–57). Nor should it be forgotten that these underlying theoretical differences were reflected in the diagnosis each gave for the economic difficulties that confronted the economy after the war. Malthus, for his part, thought that loan expenditure had greatly contributed to economic expansion during the war, and attributed the economic downturn to other causes; Ricardo denied the former, and attributed the latter (in part, at least) to the burden of taxation imposed by the need to finance such a large debt (see Ricardo 1951–73, 2:451–52).

tions of capital as it accrues from saving" (1823, 54; also in Ricardo 1951–73, 4:340.).[55] To these two names, one could also add those of Lauderdale and the Birmingham economist Thomas Attwood.

Nevertheless, despite the existence of alternative views, it would be true to say that at the time, Ricardo's opinion represented the conventional wisdom on the subject among the classical economists. McCulloch, for example, wrote a long and unfavourable review of Blake's pamphlet in the *Scotsman* for April 12, 1823, and the teenage John Stuart Mill performed a similar service for the Ricardian orthodoxy in the *Westminster Review* for July 1824 (1824, 47), so it was natural enough for Ricardo to have assumed the veracity of his argument, as even Trower agreed with him on this point.[56] What stands him apart from the rest of his colleagues is that he turned to the constitution of political society as the chief obstacle to the adoption of the "right" policy.

In this context, it is also worth observing that Ricardo came to oppose the sinking fund for what appears to have been much the same kinds of reasons—namely, the inadequacy of political controls over its misapplication. Without a democratic polity (and perhaps even with one—a point on which Ricardo does not explicitly speculate in this case), there was no guarantee against the use of the sinking fund by the government to finance current public expenditures in a way that instead of contributing to the repayment of the national debt (the purpose for which the fund was designed), actually acted to increase it. On this point, Ricardo had ample evidence in the behaviour of successive Chancellors of the Exchequer (and in the policies of Vansittart in particular) both during and after the Napoleonic Wars, and he was quick to deploy it in his essay on the funding system for the *Encyclopedia Britannica* (1820a, 152–53).[57] In no small measure, this explains why Ricardo became sceptical that there were any

[55] Ricardo made extensive notes on Blake (reproduced in 1951–73, 327–52). Unlike Malthus, however, Blake seems here to have recognised explicitly that the difficulty arose precisely because new saving might not automatically find its way into investment in the short run (that is, he seems to have seen that it was when it was applied to short-run analysis that Say's Law proved to be inadequate). The only substantial accounts of Blake's economic work are to be found in Corry (1962) and *The New Palgrave* entry by Giancarlo De Vivo (Eatwell, Milgate, and Newman 1987, 1:251–52).

[56] See, for example, Trower's own plan (of 1822) for redeeming the debt in Bonar and Hollander's edition of Ricardo's *Letters to Trower*.

[57] See also the discussion of the Tory financial policy in the immediate postwar years in Hilton (1977, 33–35), where it is argued that Vansittart "abused the sinking fund" (33) to finance current expenditures on public services. Sidney Buxton was even more blunt on the subject of Vansittart; deploying Dr. Johnson's words, he described him as a man with a "mind as narrow as a vinegar cruet" (1888, 1:15). Ricardo himself seems to have been well aware of Vansittart's propensity in this direction; see, for example, his speech in the House of Commons, March 6, 1821 (1951–73, 5:79–80).

benefits to be derived from a sinking fund to deal with the problem of the national debt, maintaining that "no securities can be given by ministers that the sinking fund shall be faithfully devoted to the payment of the debt, and without such securities we should be much better without such a fund" (1816, 196).

Concluding Remarks

By structuring his argument about democratic reform of politics around a theoretical account of the operation of the market mechanism, by grounding the science of politics on the science of political economy in this way, Ricardo's economics and his politics are deeply interwoven, and it is for this reason that they are vulnerable precisely at that point. It is worth remembering, however, that in being vulnerable at its core, Ricardian politics finds itself in distinguished company. Utilitarian politics in general had to face up to the possibility that its particular account of human nature might be wildly inaccurate, while the older politics of civic virtue might well be accused of offering a no more viable alternative in its conception of the moral characteristics of the ruling classes. Nevertheless, Ricardo's assertions clearly led him to embrace a numerically expansive conception of the reasonable part of the country, and from this, in turn, he was led to advocate extensive democratic participation in the political process under the actual conditions that then prevailed in Britain.

Chapter Ten

UTOPIAS AND STATIONARY STATES

> The celebrated optimism of economic theory . . . has
> led to economists being looked upon as Candides,
> who, having left this world for the cultivation of their
> gardens, teach that all is for the best in the best of all
> possible worlds provided we will let well alone. . . . It
> may well be that the classical theory represents the way
> in which we should like our economy to behave. But
> to assume that it actually does so is to assume our
> difficulties away.
> —John Maynard Keynes, *General Theory*

WHEN THOMAS MORE punned on the Greek *eutopia* ($\varepsilon\dot{\upsilon}$ + $\tau\acute{o}\pi o\varsigma$) or "good place," to give us the word *utopia* ($o\dot{\upsilon}$ + $\tau\acute{o}\pi o\varsigma$) or "no place"—but a good no place nonetheless—he could scarcely have imagined the longevity it would enjoy. Whether his particular utopia charted the landscape of a secret inner life transcending actual life in the real states of the sixteenth century, or whether it was framed under the influence of an Augustinian dialectic between a depraved individualism and an ideal community of the city of God, is difficult to say. What is clear, however, is that More intended *Utopia* neither as a practical programme for society nor a blueprint on which to shape actual political practices or policies. By substantive designation, it could not be so. *Utopia* served instead as a touchstone against which prevailing ideas or conditions of the day might be brought into sharper relief. Utopias have functioned in much the same way ever since.

Utopias themselves are often wonderful no places. They are sometimes islands, like More's own *Utopia*, the *Isles of the Blessed* spoken of by the ancients, or Francis Bacon's *New Atlantis*. In twentieth-century utopias, distant planets often substituted for islands. They are sometimes magnificent cities, like Tommaso Campanella's *City of the Sun*. They are sometimes mythical countries, such as Harrington's *Oceana*, Samuel Butler's *Erewhon*, or William Dean Howells's *Altruria*. They sometimes bear striking resemblance to prelapsarian paradises like the Garden of Eden. They are sometimes worlds of a pure rustic simplicity, like an arcadia, Johan Eberlin's *Wolfaria*, or William Morris's future nowhere. Still others are undiscovered civilisations come on by chance, like

Charlotte Perkins Gilman's *Herland*. As George Kateb once nicely put it, "We can legitimately say that these old stories, together with more recent retellings of them, . . . are the repository of . . . immemorial longings" (1968, 268).

Wherever they are imaginatively located or in whatever wished-for time, there are some broad characteristics that all utopias seem to share. Harmony prevails: within and between individuals, the social orders, the sexes, and the ruled and the rulers. Perpetual peace reigns supreme (provided utopias remain uncontaminated by contact with any actual human society). Equality, tranquillity, knowledge, and sufficiency in some form are frequently to be found there.[1] Endowed with these properties, it is easy enough to see why utopias might have proved to be attractive devices to some economic and political thinkers.

If utopias are *imaginative* constructs set apart temporally and spatially from the actual worlds in which their creators live—if they are what Karl Mannheim called "situationally transcendent" constructs—then it can certainly be said that there are many utopias of political and economic thought. Into this tradition falls works as different as Plato's *Republic* and Rousseau's *Social Contract*. Yet it is important to remember that not all works of imaginative literature, or economic and political theory, should be called utopian.[2]

That utopian ideas were already at large in economic thinking by the eighteenth century may be concluded from the explicit and invariably negative comments made about them by the classical economists themselves. In the *Wealth of Nations*, Smith spoke of utopias as "useless and chimerical" (1776, 5.3:934).[3] And in another quite revealing context, he remarked that "to expect . . . that the freedom of trade should ever be restored in Great Britain, is as absurd as to expect that an Oceana or Utopia should ever be established in it" (1776, 4.2:471). In his monumen-

---

[1] Although not always. Guillaume Grivel's *L'Isle inconnue*, for example, is an absolutist utopia.

[2] On this crucial point, see the careful distinction drawn by Frank Manuel and Fritzie Manuel in their classic study of Western utopian thought (1979, 8ff). While we are broadly in agreement with the classification they provide, it should be noted that they also include certain theories of progress (for example, that of Turgot) that we exclude for our present purposes. The point worth emphasising, however, is that the mere presentation of a general "theory" of the working of the market mechanism (or political society) should not be confused, as it frequently has been, with the construction of a utopia.

[3] Here, as in so many places in Smith, one hears the voice of Hume in the background. When asserting that the idea of a perfect commonwealth was perhaps a subject worth exploring, Hume begged his reader's indulgence: for they would be "apt to regard such disquisitions as both useless and chimerical" (1777a, 514). He added that "all plans of government, which suppose great reformation in the manners of mankind, are plainly imaginary"—a charge made against both Plato and More. Interestingly, Harrington's *Oceana* was excused from this epithet.

tal *Rationale of Judicial Evidence* (composed between 1803 and 1812),
Bentham wrote mockingly of utopia as "a country that receives no visits"
(1827, 206) and warned of how the stamp "utopian," when once placed
on an argument, would render its acceptance "next to hopeless" (69).
Reviewing the second edition of McCulloch's *Discourse of Political Economy* in the *Westminster Review* for July 1825, John Stuart Mill had followed suit, and contrasted the speculations of "castle builders and Utopians" with the serious study of the science of political economy through
which, he claimed, "the road to happiness is discovered" (1825a, 758).
So widespread had this opinion become by the mid-nineteenth century,
the epithets "visionary" or "utopian" were enough to damn almost any
pronouncement.[4] By the 1820s, the *Edinburgh Review* was already speaking scathingly of "utopia mongers."

A small incident in the eventful life of Owen may serve to illustrate this
last point. In 1817, in the midst of widespread postwar economic distress,
Owen proposed a "Plan for Providing for the Poor"—a plan offered at
the deliberations of a committee of the great and the good chaired by the
then archbishop of Canterbury.[5] The proposal was to build "villages of
co-operation" up and down the country to provide employment for the
destitute. These artificial communities would be built to a geometric design, and spades would replace the horse and plough as the agricultural
technology of community (not competitive) choice. Such was Owen's no-
toriety and skill at self-publicity that his utopian plan commanded considerable public attention for a couple of years after its appearance.

The first classical writer to address the plan explicitly was Robert Torrens. After spending a considerable amount of time explaining the importance of applying sound principles of political economy to the existing
distress, Torrens was harsh in his assessment of Owen's performance:

> [Mr. Owen's plans] to divide the country into compartments, containing
> each a thousand acres; to erect on each of these a village in the form of a
> parallelogram . . . and to place in each village a thousand inhabitants . . .
> who, from the period of infancy, are to be placed in preparatory schools,
> and subjected to a regular system of instruction and moral training. Under
> these arrangements he promises that poverty and crime shall cease; and evil,
> physical and moral, be utterly banished from the earth! (1819, 463)

In a speech a little earlier that same year (reprinted in the *Scotsman* of
August 21, 1819), Torrens had damned Owen's scheme as being "in the

---

[4] Thomas Babbington Macaulay's comment to the effect that "an acre in Middlesex is
better than a principality in Utopia" (1852, 402) was no less scornful of utopias.

[5] Owen relates the genesis of the plan in his autobiography (1857, 1:121ff). A fuller
account of its contents, and Robert Torrens's reaction to it, can be found in De Vivo (2000,
i–vii) to whom we are indebted for having drawn it to our attention.

highest degree visionary." In the *Edinburgh Review* article just quoted, Torrens exclaimed that were Owen's plans actually to be based on sound principles of political economy, he "should be among the foremost to hail him as the deliverer of the people, as the saviour of his country" (1819, 464). But since those plans were unworkable, according to Torrens, he would "continue to regard him as an amiable, but mistaken enthusiast, who, had he the means of executing his plans, would aggravate the evils he dreams he could remove" (464). And as for the idea of "spade cultivation," it was plainly "incapable of working the miracles" that Owen expected of it (465). It was in large measure from this attack by Torrens that Owen's proposed communities came to be disparaged as "parallelograms of paupers."

When the plan came to Malthus's attention, he was likewise dismissive of its possibilities (and the economic argument behind it):

> It has lately been stated, that spade cultivation will yield both a greater gross produce and a greater neat produce. I am always ready to bow to well established experience; but if such experience applies in the present case, one cannot not sufficiently wonder at the continued use of plough and horses in agriculture. Even supposing that the use of the spade might, on some soils, so improve the land, as to make the crop more than pay the additional expense of the labour, taken separately; yet, as horses must be kept to carry out dressing to a distance and to convey the produce of the soil to market, it could hardly answer to the cultivator to employ men in digging his fields, while his horses were standing idle in his stables. As far as experience has yet gone, I should certainly say, that it is commerce, price and skill, which will cultivate the wastes of large and poor territories—not the spade. (1820, 263n)[6]

Ricardo was only a little less forthright in his criticism of the Owen scheme at a meeting in 1819 (the same meeting at which Torrens had been more direct). Ricardo is reported by the *Times* of June 28, 1819, to have

---

[6] It is worth observing that the economic argument that Malthus deployed to dispute the idea that both gross and net product might be augmented, was quite different from the one that Torrens used. Malthus and Torrens recognised that Owen's preference for spade cultivation required an increase in gross and net product, and Malthus held that this would not occur because "under these circumstances . . . there would be a great diminution in the quantity of corn produced . . . [and] . . . a great diminution in the whole value of the produce" (1820, 263). Both Malthus and Torrens (1819, 466) relied on arguing that even if gross product were to increase (a concession they made only grudgingly), net product might not follow suit. But the reasons net product might not increase were different for each. As Giancarlo De Vivo (2000, iv) has pointed out, this is of some interest given the famous change of opinion that Ricardo made in the third edition of his *Principles* on the subject of machinery, where net product might *rise* but gross product *fall*, hence creating unemployment, with the introduction of more mechanized techniques of production.

said that while in "a limited degree he thought the scheme likely to succeed," he did not think it capable of yielding "all the good anticipated from it by his sanguine friend" (1951–73, 5:467–68). Sanguine rather than visionary—faint praise indeed.[7]

These almost wholly negative attitudes towards utopias of economic and political thought are hardly surprising. At its eighteenth-century foundation, classical political economy was intended to be explanatory of the actual workings of the emerging market economy. Rather than developing an idealized picture of the market, Smith had proposed an enquiry into the *actual* nature and causes of the wealth of nations. What is more, that enquiry was to provide a practical guide to policymaking. Leslie Stephen went so far as to claim that Smith's readers listened because here was a man who had "all the available statistics at his fingers' ends, and was able to show them in black and white the mode in which the English commercial system had generated certain definite and assignable evils" (1902, 2:318).[8] One has only to recall Malthus's famous dictum that "the science of political economy is essentially practical, and applicable to the common business of human life" (1820, 11) to gauge the pervasiveness of that original intention.

Malthus, of course, had had a direct and decisive encounter with utopian speculation—an encounter we have already examined in the context of the principle of population. When he read Godwin, Malthus had found a "visionary" effort to offer a "principled" analysis of the very political and economic crises he too was observing in Britain. It is somewhat ironic, then, that in his great effort to avoid utopian elements entering into his own economic arguments—whether about population growth or general gluts—Malthus managed to weave into the heart of his account of the workings of the market over time an argument that would later prove quite useful to those who were interested in utopias. For with its aid, the

[7] But it would be Marx who would become the most trenchant critic of utopias of political and economic thought. Utopias for him were not just fantasies; they were dangerous delusions. For those who think Marx himself should be rendered with a utopian hue, there is not a little irony in this. But that, for now, is beside the point. The utopian socialists bore the brunt of Marx's attack in the *Communist Manifesto*. For utopian socialists, he claimed, "historical action is to yield to their personal inventive action, historically created conditions of emancipation to fantastic ones" (1848, 497–48). He went on to observe that the utopian socialists dreamed of the "experimental realization of their social Utopias, founding isolated "*phalanstères*," establishing "Home Colonies," setting up a "Little Icaria"—duodecimo editions of the New Jerusalem" (499). In fact, they dreamed so much of "castles in the air" that "by degrees," they sank into what Marx disparagingly called "the category of reactionary conservative Socialists" (499).

[8] Stephen contrasted this characteristic of Smith's writing with that of his French contemporaries (he mentions Turgot explicitly) whose writings, it was said by Stephen, "savoured of metaphysical refinement." We shall have cause to say more about this idea later.

principle of population was soon to enable others—and Owen, Charles Fourier, and Henri de Saint-Simon stand out—to present market capitalism as tending inexorably to *dystopia*.[9]

This principle of population effectively added a new dimension to an idea that had already existed in classical political economy—namely, the idea of a stationary state of society. A stationary state of society was now, however, not only one in which capital accumulation had ceased but also one in which population was pressing against available subsistence, thus driving wages to a bare minimum. Malthus summed up the point neatly in his *Principles of Political Economy*:

> [I] endeavoured to show in my Essay on the Principle of Population that, under circumstances the most favourable to cultivation which could possibly be supposed to operate in the actual state of the earth, the wages of the labourer would become more scanty, and the progress of population be finally stopped by the increasing difficulty of procuring the means of subsistence. (1820, 371)

The idea of a stationary state of society—or the stationary state, as it came to be called by subsequent classical writers—had been alluded to by Smith in the *Wealth of Nations*. It did not take many years for the classical stationary state, with its Malthusian dimension appended, to enter the conscious discourse of political economists. It did not take many more years for it to be transformed by degrees, first, into a vision of human degradation that gave a spur to utopian thought, and second, into an element of the very answer to those various utopias proposed as alternatives to it.

The Classical Stationary State

Smith's stationary state had two related but distinct manifestations. On the one hand, it was the condition in which an economy would find itself if all accumulation of capital had ceased, a state in which the growth of opulence had rendered the progress of wealth at a standstill. On the other hand, it was also the description of an actually existing historical condition in which one particular economy—that of China—was said to have found itself. While it did not occupy Smith for long, it is worth recalling what he had to say about it.

---

[9] Dystopia here is not the opposite of utopia. That is, it is not an imaginatively constructed, situationally transcendent, bad no place but a real (bad) place. The point is that the road to utopia is an imaginary mapping. Malthus had supplied an actual mapping to his dystopia.

Without any really convincing argument as to why it should necessarily be so (except some vague remarks about the "number of hands" multiplying "beyond their employment"), Smith's stationary state was not only a world of zero economic growth (with new investment only sufficient to maintain capital intact) but also a world of low real wages: "though the wealth of a country should be very great, yet if it has been long stationary, we must not expect to find the wages of labour very high" (1776, 1.8:89).[10] And Smith's reading led him to believe that he had found an actual case: "China has been long one of the richest, that is, one of the most fertile, best cultivated, most industrious, and most populous countries of the world. It seems however to have long been stationary" (1.8:89). Smith did not fail to recognise one feature of this stationary state of affairs: it was not immutable. For although China "had probably long ago acquired that full complement of riches which is consistent with the nature of its laws and institutions" (1.9:11), it was still possible to see room for improvement. To begin with, "this complement may be much inferior to what, with other laws and institutions, the nature of its soil, climate, and situation might admit" (1.9:111–12). In this context, Smith mentions the centrality of the laws of property and contract, the first of which he felt were wanting in China.

More important, however, Smith saw the expansion of foreign commerce as a way out. He repeats over and over again in the *Wealth of Nations* that China "never excelled in foreign commerce" (2.5:367; see also 1.3:35). In China, foreign trade was "every way confined within a much narrower circle than that to which it would naturally extend itself, if more freedom was allowed to it" (4.9:680).[11] Since the division of labour was limited only by the extent of the market, it is not difficult to see why Smith regarded foreign trade as an effective means of improvement. It did not merely expand demand (and yield cheaper sources of certain commodities) but fostered productivity growth and technological advancement as well.

Nevertheless, if Smith's readers might still have been feeling a little troubled over the picture he had painted of a stationary state in China (where, after all, he had reported that the practice of infanticide was widespread), he provided them with another picture: the situation in

[10] As Smith put it, "The lowest class of labourers . . . notwithstanding their scanty subsistence, must some way or another make shift to continue their race so far as to keep up their usual numbers" (90).

[11] A putative aversion to deal and/or trade with foreigners (and the associated opportunity costs of low rates of innovation, or more accurately, the opportunity costs of failing to bring innovation to market) has recently been deployed by David Landes (1998) as the basis for a whole explanation of "why some are so rich and some so poor."

eighteenth-century Holland.[12] Things were quite different there. As with China, which had arrived, Holland was approaching that stationary state of society where it "had acquired its full complement of riches" (1776, 1.9:113). But unlike China, the nature of Holland's laws, institutions, and habits made it "a richer country than England" (1.9:108). Wages were higher and profits were lower there. It was "unfashionable not to be a man of business there" (1.9:113). Its citizens, and the owners of "great capitals" in particular, had a direct and indirect stake in government. In Holland, those of both large and middling fortunes were therefore willing to invest their capital at home despite the lowness of the rate of profit to be had from it there (5.2.k:906).[13] In short, Holland was "by far the richest country in Europe" (2.5:373)—and if Holland was proximate to a stationary state of society, an arrival at such a destination offered a happier prospect.

What is apparent from all of this is that the classical stationary state, on its introduction at least, was by no means an ideal construct to be aimed at (or avoided) because it was (or was not) attractive. In this sense, it was neither a utopia nor a dystopia. When the principle of population was added to the classical repertoire by Malthus, however, the stationary state came to resemble a dystopia—a real (bad) place. Insofar as it represented the inevitable working out of the secular tendencies of market capitalism, things did not look at all good. In the Malthusian stationary state, wages would be at subsistence and grinding poverty would prevail; the mass of society would have nothing to expect from life but misery and degradation.[14] The horror stories that Smith had told of the drowning of

[12] The image of a stationary China was not infrequently used in this way in the age of the classical economists. In his review of its deployment in the second volume of Tocqueville's *Democracy in America*, for example, John Stuart Mill commented that "it would be an error to suppose that such could not possibly be our future" (1840, 197).

[13] "The residence of such wealthy people necessarily keeps alive, in spite of all disadvantages, a certain degree of industry in the country" (5.2.k:906). What would be recognised today as capital flight was also something that Smith was well aware of, and he was interested as far as possible in fostering home investment. Capitalists were "citizens of the world" (5.2.f:848) and were apt to abandon any country if the need arose (see also 5.2:927–28). "Vexatious laws" on taxation, for example, might compel them to depart without a second thought. As Smith saw it, the problem was that capital could not be said to "belong" to a country, and the wealth derived from it could not be fully "secure" until capital had "been spread as it were over the face of the country, either in buildings, or in the lasting improvement of lands" (3.4:426). In England, the relative merit of home versus foreign investment was to become the subject of a perennial debate, emerging once again in the late nineteenth century in the great debate over the role of the export of capital in Britain's relative slowdown.

[14] In *Commerce Defended*, James Mill had written only slightly less ominously that in a stationary state of society, wages would reach "the lowest rate consistent with common humanity" (1808a, 87).

babies in barrels (and the eating of the carcasses of dead dogs) in the stationary China of his mind's eye, were nothing compared to this.[15] Furthermore, this Malthusian stationary state of society was not one at which Holland had, as Smith had earlier suggested, almost arrived.

If the prospect of reaching this stationary state of society was worrying enough to contemporary readers of the *Essay on Population*, Malthus was soon to give them worse news. By the time that his *Principles of Political Economy* appeared in 1820, he had added to the scourge of mass poverty (arising from the pressure of population on limited food supplies) the spectre of economic stagnation.[16] According to Malthus, the latter would arise from what came to be called the possibility of a general glut. In more modern language, the emergence of a permanent problem of economic stagnation depended on being able to demonstrate that it was possible for aggregate effective demand to fall short of what was required to ensure economic prosperity, not just temporarily, but permanently.[17]

Malthus introduced two caveats: the possibility of prudential checks through moral restraint, and the possibility of technological progress and further accumulation. The dénouement of the operation of his principle of population might be postponed, perhaps indefinitely so, by moral (rather than strictly economic) reform: namely, by the strengthening of prudential checks to the reproductive behaviour of the poor.[18] He said as

[15] As a salutary warning, Malthus had also noted in the *First Essay* that "the wealth of China has long been stationary" (1798a, 325).

[16] Here is how Malthus saw it: "It has been fully stated and allowed, that a period of stagnation must finally arrive in every country from the difficulty of procuring subsistence. But an indisposition to consume in large quantities the goods produced at home . . . may occasion, and has often occasioned, a similar stagnation" (1820, 448).

[17] From a strictly analytical point of view, of course, whether the possibility of a permanent and general glut was admitted (or not) depended on the acceptance or rejection of Say's Law: namely, the acceptance or rejection of the proposition that it was impossible for savings not to find its way into productive investment. If "productions are always bought by productions," or for the sake of brevity, if "supply creates its own demand," then a general glut was certainly impossible. Say himself had summed up the claim nicely: "Where there is a supply of commodities . . . in the market . . . they will universally find the most extensive demand" (1826, 134). As Ricardo was quick to point out in private correspondence, since Malthus accepted all of the key assumptions that guaranteed the logical adequacy of these propositions, he was clearly in error in attempting to derive from those premises the conclusion that a general glut was possible. But whatever the faults of Malthus's logic, or whatever the niceties of the analytical debate, Malthus repeatedly asserted the contrary.

[18] A couple of years later, in 1823, the teenage John Stuart Mill was to eschew moral reform as a means of adequately securing this prudential check and he set about distributing birth control information to the poor, an act for which he was to find himself at odds with the law. The younger Mill's loss of faith in moral reform might have had something to do with the performance of his father, James, whose wife managed nine children despite the

much himself on more than one occasion, perhaps nowhere more succinctly than in his *Principles of Political Economy*:

> It is quite obvious . . . that the knowledge and prudence of the poor them-
> selves, are absolutely the *only* means by which any improvement in their
> general condition can be effected. They are really the arbiters of their own
> destiny; and what others can do for them is like the dust of the balance
> compared with what they can do for themselves. (1820, 306; see also 346)

Malthus also conceded that the continued accumulation of capital and
continued technological change might, although to a more limited (and
less permanent) degree than a change in the moral habits of the poor,
equally postpone the arrival of the stationary state (413). Unlike moral
restraint, however, Malthus saw these two routes as being ultimately constrained by the level of effective demand. Yet even a lack of effective demand was not without its remedies.

What is quite apparent is that many of Malthus's readers came away
with the distinct impression that nothing at all could be done.[19] Others
either emphasised that the stationary state was "yet far distant," or if they
felt it was near at hand, proposed utopian schemes of social reorganisa-
tion to replace the world in which they lived.

Ricardo was one of those who sought to affirm that the stationary state
was "yet far distant." Moreover, Ricardo's incorporation of Malthus's
population principle into his theory of distribution (to arrive at an exoge-
nously determined real wage) was also rather more nuanced than Malthus's had been, and led him to a technically different account of the
stationary state.[20]

---

elder Mill's full familiarity with (and broad adherence to) the intellectual niceties of Malthus's account of the evils of population growth. As Mill the younger put it in his *Autobiography*, his father simply failed to practice what he preached (1873, 2). A longer account of
this incident may be found in Milgate and Stimson (1991b, 117n), and the full story is told
in Michael St. John Packe's biography (1954, 57–59). The theologians were, of course,
outraged by the young philosophic radical's "diabolical handbills." They were entirely at
one with Malthus in urging moral restraint, not contraception. Among the best known of
these was Thomas Chalmers (a theologian and later a professor of divinity at Edinburgh),
who had urged the "moral preventative check" in his *Political Economy* (1832, 1:43; see
also 2:133).

[19] For those who had read only the anonymous *First Essay*, there was some excuse for
this feeling, as first impressions are often the longest lasting. At that time, Malthus had
written that the consequences of the operation of the principle of population were "of a
nature we can never hope to escape" (1798a, 346–47). This suggestion, as we have seen,
was significantly revised as subsequent editions of the *Essay* reached the press.

[20] In a letter to Trower in 1816, Ricardo had already remarked that "we are happily yet
in the progressive state, and may look forward with confidence to a long course of prosperity" (1951–73, 6:17). A couple of years later in his paper on the *Funding System*, he was to

But even if "yet far distant," what of the real wage in a Ricardian sta-tionary state of society? To answer this question adequately, it is necessary to say a little more about Ricardo's theory of wages itself. As an adherent of the Malthusian population model, Ricardo had argued in his *Principles* that "the natural price of labour is that price which is necessary to enable labourers, one with another, to subsist and perpetuate their race, without either increase or diminution" (1821, 91), and that it depended on "the price of the food, necessaries, and conveniences required for the support of the labourer and his family" (91). It is important to note the distinction Ricardo draws here between the subsistence wage as some bundle of "nec-essary" commodities and the price of those commodities—that is, be-tween the commodity composition of the subsistence wage and the natu-ral price of labour (or the value of a given bundle of wage goods). This distinction is critical to a proper appreciation of what Ricardo meant by both a stationary state of society and what its chief features would be.

With these preliminaries in place, Ricardo concluded in an almost Malthusian fashion:

> When the market price of labour exceeds its natural price the condition of the labourer is flourishing and happy, that he has it in his power to command a greater proportion of the necessaries and enjoyments of life, and therefore to rear a healthy and numerous family. When, however, by the encourage-ment which high wages give to the increase of population, the number of labourers increased, wages again fall to their natural price. (94)

But his point is not quite Malthusian. To begin with, it is apparent that this mechanism, determining as it did the value or price of the "subsis-tence" wage, determined it in *every* state of society rather than in only a stationary one. If there was something to be feared about wages being at their subsistence level, it was everywhere to be feared, not just in some possible future stationary state. Indeed, it was to the effect on the natural price of labour or, what comes to the same thing, the price of "necessar-ies" (wage goods) that Ricardo deferred in some of his most celebrated attacks on the effects of restrictions on the importation of corn (and

---

be more eloquent (and more precise) in print: "The richest country in Europe is yet far distant from that degree of improvement, but if any had arrived at it, by the aid of foreign commerce, even such a country could go on for an indefinite time increasing in wealth and in population, for the only obstacle to this increase would be the scarcity, and consequent high value, of food and other raw produce. Let these be supplied from abroad in exchange for manufactured goods, and it is difficult to say where the limit is at which you would cease to accumulate wealth and to derive profit from its employment" (1820a, 4:179). Similarly, in his notes on Bentham's *Sur la prix*, Ricardo had jotted down the observation that the stationary state was "far distant" (1951–73, 3:274).

bounties on its export). The Corn Laws, on his line of argument, artificially drove up the natural price of labour by raising the price of Ricardo's principal wage-good: corn.[21] The physical quantity of wage goods (or the commodity composition of the wage) was taken as given. For Ricardo, the consequence of this was a lowering of the rate of profit as well as a lowering of the rate of accumulation of capital (growth).

But a second and rather more intriguing departure from Malthus occurred in Ricardo's use of the idea of the subsistence wage itself—an old idea dating back at least to Smith.[22] On this subject, Ricardo worked a crucial modification on what Malthus had been able to say (and on much of what had gone before Malthus as well): "It is not to be understood that the natural price of labour, *estimated even in food and necessaries*, is absolutely fixed and constant. It varies at different times in the same country, and very materially differs in different countries. It essentially depends on the habits and customs of the people" (1821, 96–97; emphasis added).[23] The subsistence wage (that is, its commodity composition) was thus to be understood as a historically, socially, and culturally "given" quantity, rather than as some absolute level of physical necessity below which life itself would be threatened by famine, pestilence, or disease.[24]

---

[21] Ricardo's habit of thinking in terms of a single wage good—namely, corn—is something that did not go unnoticed by his contemporaries. Malthus and Torrens stand out among them. While Malthus was to use it to challenge Ricardo's whole theory of profits, however, Torrens recognised that it was simply an "assumption" that allowed the argument on profits to proceed without any loss of generality (see De Vivo 1984, 46–73).

[22] Here is how Smith put it: "A man must always live by his work, and his wages must at least be sufficient to maintain him. They must even on most occasions be somewhat more; otherwise it would be impossible for him to bring up a family, and the race of such workman could not last beyond the first generation" (1776, 1.8:85). Of course, the idea of subsistence had a long existence before its formal application in classical political economy. Sir William Petty had discussed it in his *Political Anatomy of Ireland* in 1691, and it appears in Locke's *Considerations of the Consequences of Lowering Interest* in 1692. This analytical preexistence, so to speak, was altered in the hands of Smith and the physiocrats. In Turgot's *Reflections*, one finds a clear early statement of it: "The wage of the Workman is limited to what is necessary in order to enable him to procure his subsistence" (1766, 122).

[23] Ricardo adds in footnote that the whole subject "is most ably illustrated by Colonel Torrens," who was perhaps the one classical writer to follow most closely the Ricardian theory of distribution. The reference is to Torrens's *External Corn Trade*.

[24] One is reminded of what Marx would have to say on this same subject a generation later in his *Contribution to the Critique of Political Economy*. For Marx, too, the starting point of modern political economy is the recognition that the value of labour power [viz., the real wage] is something given (1858). Later, in *Capital*, Marx recognised that "in a given country at a given period, the average amount of means of subsistence for the worker, is a known *datum*" (1867, 1.6:275). But this was not a subsistence wage in the Malthusian sense, for "even the most favourable situation for the working class, the most rapid possible growth of capital, however much it may improve the material existence of the worker, does

Nothing could be further from the picture that Malthus had painted of population being "kept equal to the means of subsistence by misery and vice" (1798a, 141), or the labouring poor suffering from "the want of proper and sufficient food," and living in "unwholesome habitations" (99). The stationary state of Ricardo could be odious for the worker, but it was by no means necessarily so: "The friends of humanity cannot but wish that in all countries the labouring classes should have a taste for comforts and enjoyments, and that they should be stimulated by all legal means in their exertions to procure them. There cannot be a better security against a superabundant population" (1821, 100). This is no more than just a reflection of the fact that for Ricardo, the subsistence wage was customary (socially determined), whereas for Malthus it represented the biological minimum necessary for life.

For Ricardo, then, it would seem that the problem with a stationary society was not the subsistence wage but rather the end of accumulation it heralded: a situation in which "the wealth and resources of a community will not admit of an increase" (1822, 4:234). It was the end of growth, not the subsistence wage, that led Ricardo to assert that such a state of society was "yet far distant" and argue that its arrival might readily be postponed into an indefinite future through the benefits of what today would be called globalisation and technological change: "By the extension of foreign trade, or by improvements in machinery, the food and necessaries of the labourer can be brought to market, at a reduced

---

not remove the antagonism between his interests and the interests of the bourgeoisie, the interests of the capitalists" (*Wage Labour and Capital*, 211). Nor was there really anything new in the idea that subsistence was to be understood in relation to place, culture, and time. Smith had made the same point in the *Wealth of Nations*:

> By necessaries I understand, not only the commodities which are indispensably necessary for the support of life, but whatever the custom of the country renders it indecent for creditable people, even of the lowest order to be without. A linen shirt, for example, is, strictly speaking, not necessary for life. The Greeks and Romans lived, I suppose, very comfortably, though they had no linen. But in the present times, through the greater part of Europe, a creditable day-labourer would be ashamed to appear in public without a linen shirt, the want of which would be supposed to denote that disgraceful degree of poverty, which, it is presumed, nobody can well fall into without extreme bad conduct. Custom, in the same manner, has rendered leather shoes a necessary of life in England. The poorest creditable person of either sex would be ashamed to appear in public without them. In Scotland, custom has rendered them a necessary of life to the lowest order of men; but not to the same order of women, who may, without any discredit, walk about bare-footed. In France, they are necessaries neither to men nor to women; the lowest rank of both sexes appearing publicly, without any discredit, sometimes in wooden shoes, and sometimes bare-footed. Under necessaries, therefore, I comprehend, not only those things which nature, but those things which the established rules of decency have rendered necessary to the lowest rank of people. (1776, 5.2:821–22)

price, profits will rise" (1821, 132).[25] But if this was the actual voice of the optimistic Ricardo, many of his audience were not cheered. To most, if not all, the subtleties of these arguments were lost, and a more pessimistic message was taken away—a message, in fact, that left most of Malthus's more dire warnings almost unaltered in the popular consciousness, and that opened the door to some famous utopias of economic thought.[26]

BUILDING UTOPIAS

The powerful threat of the stationary state, which had solidified itself in the discourse of political economy by the 1820s, combined with the use to which certain early nineteenth- century critics of the market had begun to put the idea of profits as a surplus and the antagonism of interests between classes, sponsored the introduction of utopian solutions to the difficulties they prefigured. These utopias, while often just as fantastical in conception as anything to be found in poetry or prose, were actually to be constructed. Owen, Fourier, Saint-Simon, and Etienne Cabet stand out among their architects.

Owen, in particular, had long been in the business of building actual utopias. By the 1820s, his model village at New Lanark, Scotland, established in 1800, had become almost a place of pilgrimage for philanthropic and socially responsible capitalists. Visits by royalty and religious leaders had even given it the official seal of approval. Despite a certain mismatch between rhetoric and reality, its reception had given a fillip to Owen's utopian zeal, and after 1820, he launched himself into an altogether more ambitious project: to create not just a model village but the society of the future. In this undertaking, however, he was to be markedly less successful.

In 1824, Owen purchased twenty thousand acres of land in Indiana, on the banks of the Wabash. For the not inconsiderable sum of three

[25] It is worth noting that while these stationary states are described in economic terms and the solutions to them conceived of in terms of economic factors (the expansion of trade, technological progress, or capital accumulation), in some earlier discussions, such solutions were seen to lie more directly in politics. For example, Ferguson's *Progress and Termination of the Roman Republic* contains a discussion of Rome's "stationary state" having been arrived at due to the ambition of its monarchs, and requiring (necessarily) a revolution "in order to preserve it in its former progressive state" (1783, 13).

[26] Another response, of course, was simply to declare Ricardo's reasoning "unworldly." Brougham's likening of him to someone who had "dropped from another planet" comes immediately to mind, and Arnold Toynbee codified that particular response in his *Lectures on the Industrial Revolution in England*. According to Toynbee, Ricardo's "powerful mind . . . never stopped to consider the world to which the argument implied"—a "world less

thousand pounds, he had secured the land from a community of followers of George Rapp, and in the little town of Harmony, Owen established New Harmony. Owen's son took charge, and in its first fortnight of existence, New Harmony received eight hundred new settlers (Cole 1930, 243). This utopia had cost Owen more than three-quarters of his personal wealth. Regrettably, New Harmony was soon confronted by a familiar problem that seems to plague such ventures: the disjunction between the imagined serenity and sufficiency of these otherworlds, and the insecurity and scarcity of this world.[27] Owen severed his connections with New Harmony in 1829 and came away a poorer, but not wiser man.[28]

Even less fortunate was to be the fate of other utopian attempts at escape from the world of capitalism. In 1848, Cabet tried with Icaria in Denton County, Texas. The venture was a comic tragedy. Of the sixty-nine Icarians who left Le Harve, France, for the United States, two died on the voyage, several defected on their arrival in New Orleans, and more died on their journey through the heat of the Louisiana swamps. Things only grew worse. When the surviving Icarians arrived in Texas, the land that they had expected to be free, turned out to cost a dollar an acre— and their utopia turned into a nightmare world of physical depravation, malarial infection, and despondency.[29]

For thirty more years, the ever optimistic Icarians travelled from disaster to disaster across the United States, from Louisiana, to Iowa, to Saint Louis (where Cabet died in 1858), back to Iowa, and finally to California. At every step of the way, they endured disease, hunger, natural disaster (tornados and fires), death, debt, and doctrinal schism.[30]

It would be remiss to leave a discussion of the failed attempts by these nineteenth-century utopians to actually build their own little heavens on earth without mentioning a striking parallel that exists between their arguments (and sometimes even some of their projects) and the position that had begun to emerge among the classical political economists on the

---

real than the island of Lilliput" (1884, 7). We have examined the adequacy of this opinion elsewhere (Milgate and Stimson 1991b, 3–5).

[27] A more sympathetic G.D.H. Cole observed: "The surprising fact is not that New Harmony collapsed, but that it lasted so long" (246–47).

[28] A decade later, in 1839, Owen tried again, this time in England. Queenswood, in Hampshire, was his last great venture in utopia building. It was an outright disaster and failed in 1845. It might be added that in the last decade of his life, Owen devoted his energy to his other great cause—the trade union movement. In this arena, he was to make contributions that were to have, unlike his utopia-building projects, a lasting impact on the future development of industrial capitalism.

[29] Such was the magnitude of the calamity that when a second contingent arrived later in the year, the Icarians determined to return to New Orleans forthwith. Nine more died on their way back.

[30] Ironically, the Icarian settlement in California was named Speranza, meaning "hope."

subject of colonies. Although it could hardly be said that colonies were utopias, they were in an important sense real-world substitutes for them. It came to be widely asserted that colonies might be a means of relieving the very economic distresses that had led the utopians to their endeavours in the first place. Owen's "home colonies" were to be replaced by "overseas" ones. Colonies were much like utopias in that they, too, were often distant islands. They differed, however, in that they actually existed— and in that they were the property of the Crown. Wakefield's celebrated advocacy of "systematic colonisation" and Torrens's support for it should perhaps be read in this light.

The position of the classical economists on colonies was ambivalent to say the least. The colonies were frequently seen in a quite negative light. Smith had two minds on the subject—and in this context it is worth remembering that the first edition of the *Wealth of Nations* is dated in the same year as the American Declaration of Independence. In 1793, Bentham had famously declared to the revolutionaries in France: "Emancipate your colonies!" Say had set out what he felt were the excessively burdensome economic costs of colonial territories in his *Treatise on Political Economy* (1826, 210), and had elsewhere lamented the monopolistic restrictions that were widely associated with a colonial trade still dominated by large trading companies (1821a, 129–31). In 1750, Turgot had even predicted the likelihood of costly wars of independence in colonies resulting from their economic exploitation and political subjugation by colonial powers. With important exceptions, the view that on the whole, colonies were liabilities rather than assets had become almost mainstream in classical circles by the early 1820s.[31]

This conventional wisdom is perhaps nowhere better illustrated than in Mill's article "Colony" for Napier's edition of the *Encyclopedia Britannica* in 1820. Mill had long been a convert to Bentham's earlier plea to the French republicans for colonial emancipation. In the *Edinburgh Review* for 1809, he had already written of the "advantages of a commercial nature" that "would assuredly spring from the emancipation of South America" (1809, 282), and had compared those benefits favourably with the beneficial effects that (he claimed) had followed from independence in North America. In the *Britannica* entry, he took the argument onto an altogether more general stage.

---

[31] When Ricardo turned to an examination of colonial trade in his *Principles*, he began by concurring with Smith, who had, thought Ricardo, shown "most satisfactorily, the advantages of a free trade, and the injustice suffered by colonies, in being prevented by their mother countries, from selling their produce at the dearest market, and buying their manufactures and stores at the cheapest" (1821, 338). Still, while he fully agreed that restrictions on colonial trade would unambiguously damage the interests of the colony, he took a differ-

For the *Britannica*, Mill subjected the case for colonies to a withering attack. It is difficult to come away from a reading of his entry without the feeling that there was nothing of substance to any of the then current arguments for colonisation. As a remedy for overpopulation, they were chimerical, drawing off more capital or means of employment than the pressure that the export of people was supposed to relieve (1820a, 262). As penal settlements, they were neither reformative, an effective deterrent, nor cost-effective. As a source of revenue for the colonial power, they were unreliable (264), either because a politically subjugated colony would resist the extraction of its surplus revenue or because a self-governing colony would cease to yield it voluntarily.

Deferring to Smith and "the profound work of Mr. Ricardo" (266), Mill maintained that it could "never be advantageous to a country to maintain colonies merely for the sake of their trade" (265). And this was not all. Colonies enriched the few at the expense of the many; they enhanced the political power of the ruling classes (through the multiplication of places, offices, and sinecures); they increased the likelihood of war (both between competing colonial powers and within disputatious colonies themselves); and they were the engines driving unjustified military expenditures and the increase in the public debt. These wholly negative views, and many others like them, dominated the mainstream classical thinking in the first two decade of the nineteenth century.

But this prevailing attitude towards colonisation was to change. By the early 1830s, after the appearance of Wakefield's writings on colonisation, which had given an altogether more sound economic argument about the advantages of colonisation without monopolistic restrictions, a sort of mass conversion seems to have taken place. Beginning with his *Letter from Sydney* in 1829, Wakefield embarked on a campaign to explain that it was not colonies but misguided colonial policy that was at the heart of earlier scepticism over a colonial solution to British difficulties. As Wakefield saw it, systematic colonisation could supply an outlet both for surplus population and surplus capital, provided only that colonial land was disposed of by the Crown at a certain "minimum" or "sufficient" price.[32] This price, or so the argument ran, would serve two functions at the same time. On the one hand, it would act as a deterrent to the habit of colonial wage labourers of immediately becoming landowners (thereby aggravating a shortage of wage labour in the colony). On the other hand, it would also act as a source of revenue against which to defray the cost of any

---

ent line to Smith in explaining that "the narrow policy adopted in the countries of Europe . . . is not less injurious to the mother countries themselves" (338).

[32] Until the Ripon Regulations of 1831, colonial policy had been either to provide land free (by grant) or at a nominal price.

state-sponsored programme of emigration. And if Wakefield's influence was not enough, Torrens added his not inconsiderable voice with the publication of his *Colonization of South Australia* in 1835, advocating an essentially similar system of colonisation.[33]

By the 1840s, however, the case for colonisation had become even more compelling to its supporters. Such was the economic and political condition of England in the "hungry forties" that Torrens, for one, saw the situation not only as being "pregnant with danger" (1844, 227) but also as signalling that the dreaded stationary state might actually have arrived. In 1843, Torrens wrote (and had published) a letter to Robert Peel in which he claimed that "our powers of production have outgrown the field of employment" (241), and he proceeded to sketch a picture of the condition of England in which population pressures had driven wages to a minimum and insufficient demand had led to "a general glut of capital, occasioning over-trading" (240).[34] To this problem, colonies presented themselves to Torrens as an almost (but not quite) providential solution.

Having demonstrated to his satisfaction that neither an extension of free trade nor the advance of more mechanized techniques of production could be counted on to relieve the economic condition of the country, Torrens imagined a "miraculous island" (of an acreage roughly the equivalent to that of twice the area of the British Isles) to have appeared and attached itself to England (1844, 287). This miraculous island of his "illustrative hypothesis" turned out to offer the solution to the present woes: "distress would vanish from the land, and a season of rapid progress and universal prosperity arise" (300). Moreover:

> The crown possesses in the colonies an extent of fertile and unappropriated territories equal, not to twice the area of the United Kingdom, but to ten times that area. The analogy is perfect between what might take place with respect to unappropriated land in extended England, and what may take

---

[33] Torrens had, in fact, long been enamoured of colonies. He had attempted (and failed) to gain appointment as the governor of New South Wales in 1816, and had tried (and failed) to do the same in South Australia in 1835. But this romance with what he called "the England of the Southern Cross" was not entirely unrequited—the quiet river running through the centre of Adelaide still bears his name.

[34] It will be apparent that Torrens was saying here something very close to what Malthus had said two decades earlier in his *Principles*—that both overpopulation and overtrading were possible "futures." Of course, as early as 1817, Torrens had advocated colonies as a means of relieving the poor (and reducing the burden of poor rates) in response to Owen's utopian plan for parallelograms of paupers (as Torrens called them). But he had not then fully subscribed to the argument on general gluts that appears in 1843. Compare Torrens (1817) and Torrens (1844). There is some inconsistency in Torrens's varying position on the possibility of a general glut, which at times he appears to support while at others he seems (following Ricardo) to deny.

place with respect to unappropriated land in the more distant dominions of the crown. (306)

No "miraculous interposition of Providence" (300) was called for here, no utopian imaginings of possible otherworlds. According to Torrens, this extension of territory was "not an hypothesis, but an existing fact" (300).

Colonies offered nonutopian solutions to the threat posed by an imminent stationary state of industry. And to writers like Wakefield and Torrens, that stationary state was *not*, as Ricardo had thought, far distant, but actually on them. Colonies were the rational and practical alternative to the visionary schemes of the utopians—schemes that had been driven by the very same fears over the onset of a stationary state.

THE CLASSICAL STATIONARY STATE AND UTOPIAS

Alongside these responses to the stationary state, the late 1840s saw another theme enter the discourse of political economy on the subject of the stationary state. Its architect was John Stuart Mill and its vehicle was his *Principles of Political Economy*. Although he did not intend it to be so, the effect of Mill's intervention was to change the classical stationary state into a construct essentially utopian in content and character.

Mill began the composition of his *Principles of Political Economy* in 1845 against the economic backdrop of the hungry forties. The finished manuscript went to the printers in December 1847 (although the book did not appear until April 1848). In the meantime, in February 1848, the citizens of Paris had attacked the Tuileries, François Guizot had been dismissed as prime minister, Louis Phillipe had abdicated, and a provisional government had been established in the name of the workers. The second edition of Mill's *Principles* appeared in 1849—and it was in this edition that the really substantial material on socialism was added. The third edition saw further significant recasting of this material, together with the material on "the probable futurity of the labouring classes." This turbulent backdrop, both in England and France, cannot be ignored in attempting to understand Mill's role and intentions in the transformation of the classical stationary state that was to take place in his hands.

For Mill, a recast picture of the stationary state presented a challenge to the critique of existing capitalist production offered by the utopian (and indeed all) socialists of his day. Mill, of course, agreed with many of the moral objections offered by socialist critics to the competitive "ramping up" of the market as it then existed. He accepted that the "intellectual and moral grounds of socialism deserve the most attentive study" (1879, 736). At the same time, however, Mill found the critical comparison of an actually existing market economy to an imagined utopian community too facile and beside the point. Furthermore, he rejected the general outlines of the socialist critique on economic grounds as being "exaggerated" and based on "errors of political economy" (727). In the fourth book of his *Principles of Political Economy*, he invented his own syndicalist-inspired, decentralized, competitive form of commodity production—a stationary state as it *might* operate within an ideal capitalism. Neither economic reformers nor economic theorists were persuaded of its practical possibilities.

Mill's critique of socialist alternatives was premised on the claim that rational debate demanded that one should compare an ideal capitalist society with an ideal socialist one rather than contrast actually existing capitalist society (which everyone knew was not perfect) with an ideal socialist society (as was being done, Mill felt, by the gainsayers of capitalism). Instead, Mill argued that "to make the comparison applicable, we must compare Communism at its best, with the regime of individual property not as it is, but as it might be" (1871, 2.1.§3:207). It was in the construction of this capitalism "as it might be" that the stationary state of Mill's mind's eye played such a vital part. But to see just how this was so, and appreciate the transformation of the classical stationary state that came about in the process, it is necessary to say a little more about the arguments Mill advanced on the subject of the socialist alternative.

Let us state at the outset that it would be difficult to prosecute the case that Mill was somehow temperamentally averse to socialism.[35] It might be more accurate perhaps to say that he was at least tolerant of its ideals.[36] Yet he did raise certain difficulties with the socialist alternative that were to figure prominently in later critiques of socialist society. Moreover, Mill saw no reason to eradicate capitalism simply because he felt that the system of private property *could* be much better than it actually was in his day. He put it succinctly in his *Principles of Political Economy*:

> The political economist, for a considerable time to come, will be chiefly concerned with the conditions of existence and progress belonging to a society founded on private property and individual competition; and that the object

[35] In fact, the reverse seems rather to have been the case. Here is how Mill reported his own attitude to the Saint Simonians in his *Autobiography*: "I felt that the proclamations of such an ideal of human society could not but tend to give a beneficial direction to the efforts of others to bring society, as at present constituted, nearer to some ideal standard" (1873, 117). It should also be said that Mill found this group "far superior" to Owen, and found their ideas to be "the work of altogether larger and more accomplished minds" than his (1963–91, 2.1.: 3–6, 981).

[36] Mill's toleration of socialism often resembles nothing so much as his well-known pleas for the toleration of alternative lifestyles that crop up in many of his political writings.

to be principally aimed at in the present stage of human improvement, is not the subversion of the system of individual property, but the improvement of it, and the full participation of every member of the community in its benefits. (1871, 2.1.§4)

It is no accident that Mill mounted this defence of capitalism in the second book of the *Principles*, which is concerned with distribution. It was on the question of the justness of the distribution of national wealth between labour and capital that many of the most serious criticisms of market society that had appeared since Smith had been grounded—criticisms that were articulated not only by intellectuals in print but also by workers (both at home and abroad) on the streets. While in less troubled times, perhaps, Smith could rest his case for advantages of commercial society primarily on an analysis of the *nature and causes* of the wealth of the nation—an analysis that broadly indicated to him the advantages of free competition—Mill was obliged to erect his case on the analysis of the *distribution* of wealth in capitalist society.

There appears to be two important strands in Mill's defence of what he sometimes calls the "institution of property" (1871, 2.2.§1) or the "régime of private property" (2.1.§2:124). The first was his consideration and critique of the charge that capitalism was inherently unacceptable because it produced an unjust distribution of income between labour and capital. The second was his consideration and critique of the claim that a socialist organisation of society would be a better one.

To reveal what we might call the acceptable face of capitalism, Mill's task was to cast off the notion that profits were an unjustly appropriated share of the product of labour accruing to capitalists simply by virtue of their ownership of stock.[37] To this end, it was necessary to claim instead that profits were not "the leavings of wages" but rather were a separate though similar kind of reward for the work, effort, or sacrifice put in by the owners of stock. In short, he set out to show that profits were *analogous* to wages.[38] This project is particularly evident when one finds Mill arguing that "industry and frugality cannot exist where there is not a preponderant possibility that those who labour and spare will be permitted to enjoy," and that "private property [is a means] to guarantee individuals the fruits of their own labour and abstinence" (1871, 2.1.§3:129). The active verbs "to spare" and "to abstain" are the key here. The idea

---

[37] It is worth remembering that the basis for such an idea had appeared in Smith when he had argued that "the whole product of labour does not always belong to the labourer . . . [he must] share it with the owner of the stock which employs him" (1776, 1.6:49).

[38] Notice the apparent deviation from Smith on this point: "The profits of stock, it may perhaps be thought, are only a different name for the wages of a particular sort of labour, the labour of inspection and direction. They are, however, altogether different" (1776, 1.6:48).

was that profits were the due return to owners of capital stock who in advancing it to their workers in the form of wages, materials, and tools, had abstained from its consumption. Like workers who toiled in the factory or field, capitalists too incurred a degree of "pain" for which a future "pleasure" was justly due to them. This is why one finds Mill speaking regularly of profits as "the remuneration of abstinence" (3.15.§1:245; see also 2.2.§5), or as being "an equivalent for abstinence" (4.4.§3) or the result of "abstinence, risk and exertion" (246), such that "for this forbearance he requires a recompense" (3.15.§1:245). While Mill seems to blur the distinction between real cost and opportunity cost here, his intention could not be more plain.

It is almost as if Mill himself drew the kind of conclusion that had been reached by Thomas de Quincey (and others) from too literal an application of Smith's view of profits:

> The foundation of the whole [institution of property] is, the right of producers to what they themselves have produced. It may be objected, therefore, to the institution *as it now exists*, that it recognises rights of property in individuals over things which they have not produced. For example (it may be said) the operatives in a manufactory create, by their labour and skill, the whole produce; yet, instead of its belonging to them, the law gives them only their stipulated hire, and transfers the produce to someone who has merely supplied the funds, without perhaps contributing anything to the work itself, even in the form of superintendence. The answer to this is, that the labour of manufacture is only one of the conditions which must combine for the production of the commodity. The labour cannot be carried on without materials and machinery, nor without a stock of necessaries provided in advance, to maintain the labourers during the production. All these things are the fruits of previous labour. (2.2.§1; emphasis added)

It was one thing to offer a new moral interpretation of profits along these lines, however; Smith's own tales about how, in commercial society, the whole product of labour was no longer owned by the worker (as it had been in "that early and rude state of society"), and of it having to be shared with the owner of stock, was after all just a different moral tale when it comes down to it. But it was quite another thing to show satisfactorily that the *magnitude* of the rate of profit was determined by, or bore any consistent and unambiguous relation to, the *quantity* of "abstinence" (if, that is, we could know the units in which it was measured) or "forgone consumption."

The analytical problem is to show that profits are apportioned strictly in accordance with the amount of abstinence—that is, to show how the quantity of capital "advanced" acts to determine the rate of profit. To this question, Mill had no convincing answer. He was left only with his moral tale.

On the great debate over the relative merits of capitalism versus socialism, which was seen by Mill as being essentially an argument about distributive justice, a two-pronged resistance was deployed: a positivist response, and a rationalist (logic-chopping) one.

According to the first, Mill claimed that the positive task of political economy was to explain what "is," not what "ought to be." The data (including the distribution of initial endowments) were a given, and not the subject of political economy. Moreover, Mill also claimed that the initial distribution of wealth was a matter of "human institution" or "societal consent,", and could be changed by an act of collective will, making greater income equality perfectly compatible with capitalism: "The Distribution of Wealth . . . is a matter of human institution solely. Things once there, mankind, either individually or collectively, can do with them as they like" (2.1.§1).

The idea that initial distribution is a matter of convention that could be changed is seen most clearly in Mill's discussion of the laws of inheritance, where he allows a wide latitude for redistribution.[39] Note that Mill distinguishes between what he calls bequests and other inheritances (from intestate estates). As to inheritance, he simply says "that the property of persons who have made no disposition of it during their lifetime, should pass first to their children, and failing them, to the nearest relations, may be a proper arrangement or not, but is no consequence of the principle of private property" (1871, 2.2.§3). As to bequests, which are part of the principle of private property, he nevertheless says that "the power of bequest may be so exercised as to conflict with the permanent interests of the human race" (2.2.§4). He thus concludes:

> The inequalities of property which arise from unequal industry, frugality, perseverance, talents, and to a certain extent even opportunities, are inseparable from the principle of private property, and if we accept the principle, we must bear with these consequences of it: but I see nothing objectionable in fixing a limit to what anyone may acquire by the mere favour of others,

---

[39] The idea that the "initial distribution" is a matter of human institution or societal consent contrasts sharply with the fact that it is also the product of a whole history of transition in the Western world—a history that when discussed by Smith in Book 3, looks more to be the result of an innate propensity to "rape, loot and pillage" than of societal consent (or even a propensity to truck, barter, and exchange). Marx would soon claim that the initial distribution is nothing more than the process of force and violence ("bloody legislation") that "freed" workers from ownership of their means of subsistence and turned them into "wage slaves."

without any exercise of his faculties, and in requiring that if he desires any further accession of fortune, he shall work for it. (2.2.§4)[40]

According to the second strand in Mill's consideration of the socialist alternative, in *rational* debate one should compare an ideal capitalist society with an ideal socialist one rather than an actually existing capitalist society with an ideal socialist one.[41] While he noted a number of problems with the socialist ideal—the unchecked growth of population and the problem of apportioning skills to rewards (via the market versus through the state)—he did not see any real grounds for rejecting the socialist alternative: "If . . . the choice were to be made between Communism with all its chances, and the present state of society with all its sufferings and injustices . . . all the difficulties, great or small, of Communism would be but as dust in the balance" (2.1.§3). The reason that Mill was sceptical of rejecting socialism on these grounds alone seems both straightforward and interesting. "Free-riding," for example, ignored the capacity of individuals for public virtue. Moreover, a rational population programme had become part of the socialist package. And while there were limits to the omniscience of socialist planners (they lacked the knowledge needed to plan skill matching and wage determination), the market itself could also fail in this arena.[42]

Unfortunately, however, even if the socialist idea might be a viable possibility, Mill claimed that "the principle of private property has never yet had a fair trial in any country; and less so, perhaps, in this country than in some others" (2.1.§3):

The laws of property have never yet conformed to the principles on which the justification of private property rests. They have made property of things

[40] The case of landed property is striking: "Whenever, in any country, the proprietor, generally speaking, ceases to be the improver, political economy has nothing to say in defence of landed property"' (1871, 2.2.§6), and that "when the 'sacredness of property' is talked of, it should always be remembered, that any such sacredness does not belong in the same degree to landed property. No man made the land. It is the original inheritance of the whole species" (1871, 2.2.§6).

[41] Note that for Mill, socialism entails the collective ownership of the means of production; communism goes a step further and requires also an equal distribution of wealth (1871, 1.2.§2).

[42] Mill's real insight into the grounds of the choice between socialism and capitalism is to be found not so much in the above kind of argument (though those arguments are interesting) but instead in a couple of less prominent speculations about the nature of a good society: "No society in which eccentricity is a matter of reproach, can be in a wholesome state" (2.1.§3). The question is: Which of "the two systems is consistent with the greatest amount of human liberty and spontaneity" (2.1.§3). This is where the socialist alternative fared less well.

which never ought to be property, and absolute property where only a qualified property ought to exist. They have not held the balance fairly between
human beings, but have heaped impediments upon some, to give advantage
to others; they have purposely fostered inequalities, and prevented all from
starting fair in the race. (2.1.§3)

Conveniently, Mill's own account of capitalism at its best, with wages
and profits being analogous and fair, came in handy.

ECONOMIC HARMONIES

In 1848, a book titled *The Harmony of Interests, Agricultural, Manufacturing, and Commercial* was published in Philadelphia. Its author was
Henry Carey, the son of the U.S. publisher and protectionist Matthew
Carey. In 1850, *Les harmonies économiques* by Frédéric Bastiat was published in Paris. These "harmonies" deserve a place in any account of utopias and stationary states as they represent another attempt to present
actually existing market societies as socially harmonious places.

On one level, of course, the idea of an inherent harmony in nature is a
deeply religious one—though it need not be so. Smith had employed a
language of harmony, especially in the *History of Astronomy* and the
Moral Sentiments, on a number of occasions. Smith regularly spoke of
the "harmony of society" in *Moral Sentiments*, and the "harmony of sentiments" (1759, 22, 25) arising from the intervention of the impartial
spectator in individual moral formation. He wrote also of harmonies engendered by economic development and economic policy: "The perfection of police, the extension of trade and manufactures, are noble and
magnificent objects. . . . They make part of the great system of government, and the wheels of the political machine seem to move with more
harmony and ease by means of them" (185). Smith wrote of the "regular
and harmonious movement of the system" and "the machine or oeconomy by means of which it is produced" (183). Smith chose to associate
the origin of this "immense system," or the "great machine," with "the
great Physician of Nature," "its all-wise Architect and Conductor," the
"great Superintendent of the universe as well as the "great plan of Jupiter," and just "Nature." In each of these cases, it is evident that harmony
flowed from the system (289). While these kinds of associations disappear
almost entirely in the *Wealth of Nations*, there appears to be some justice
in seeing in the early Smith such ideational (though not analytical) commitments to the notion of systemic harmony.

After such early remarks by Smith, though, that association in classical
political economy faded and the idea appeared only occasionally in rather

limited circles. In the work of Richard Whately, for example, who became the archbishop of Dublin in 1831 after leaving the Drummond chair of political economy at Oxford, its presence is clearly discernable. His opposition to the spread of Ricardian doctrines was due in part to the incompatibility perceived to exist between his underlying theological presuppositions and the idea of class conflict supposedly present in Ricardo's account of the distribution of income. It is said that on Whately's founding of a chair of political economy in Trinity College, Dublin, its occupants were "under pressure to present an optimistic or harmonious picture of how the market economy operates" (Moss 1976, 153). But these kinds of theologically inspired views always remained in a small minority in the circles of political economy, and appear to have had little lasting impact on its development. While a considerable debate over the precise meaning of the idea of "economic harmony" took place in the twentieth century and continues to this day, it is more clear what both Carey and Bastiat had in mind when we turn to their own works.[43] Carey was concerned to argue that a harmony rather than a necessary conflict of economic interest existed between the social classes. He took exception to Ricardo's idea that "profits depend upon wages," and was not impressed with his idea that "the interest of the landlord is always opposed to that of the consumer and manufacturer" (Ricardo 1821, 335). Carey claimed that "Mr Ricardo's system is one of discords. . . . [I]ts whole tends to the production of hostility among classes and nations. . . . His book is the true manual of the demagogue, who seeks power by means of agrarianism, war and plunder" (1851, 74–75). That Carey was writing in a United States that was riven at the time by accusation and counteraccusation from agrarian and industrial interests against each other—an antipathy that was to break out into open conflict a decade and a half later—may go some way towards explaining his own position. Yet it would also seem that Carey's idea that Ricardo's "system" must be wrong simply because it was suggestive of either implicit or actual conflict, could only have been derived from an assumption that any correct system of political economy should suggest only stability and social peace.[44]

Somewhat perversely for an author whose first work had been strongly free trade in character, Carey does not appear to have provided an alterna-

[43] Some see it nascent in Smith, Richard Cantillon, and Quesnay (see Halévy 1928, 89; Schumpeter 1954, 234), but this seems to involve nothing more than a confusion between the idea of harmony (absence of conflict) and the different idea of natural price (a contrasting case is made by Robbins 1961, 22–29). Others see it as present in the Bentham–James Mill discussions of "identity of interest," but this doctrinal effort seems to confuse an absence of conflict with an identity of interest.

[44] Since Carey had few resources to draw on to legitimate such an assumption either in his own theory or the work of other political economists, he advanced a "law of association" by

tive account of the market mechanism such as would show that it worked harmoniously or providentially for the good (as many others adhering to the doctrine of economic harmony were to do). He suggested instead an alternative "system" to Ricardo's—one based on the protection of trade though tariffs.[45] In this sense, economic harmony for Carey appears to have necessitated establishment through deliberate acts of government policy rather than through letting things alone.

This brings us to Bastiat. Here we encounter an entirely different view, and an uncompromising advocacy for leaving things alone. In the case of Bastiat, there was definitely a commitment to the idea that there existed an underlying harmony in the unhindered operation of markets. As a proselytising free trader, the founder of the Association for Free Trade in Paris in 1846 (modelled on Richard Cobden's Anti-Corn Law League in England), a vociferous antisocialist, a champion of the inviolable rights of private property, and someone whom Schumpeter could call "the most brilliant economic journalist who ever lived" (1954), Bastiat saw economic harmony everywhere. Not only were the interests of contracting parties harmoniously resolved by the market but so too were the national interests of countries engaging in free trade between themselves. An article for the *Journal des économistes* in 1844 on the latter subject, claiming to present the mutual benefits that might flow to France and England from free trade between them, caused a political stir.

In his introduction to Bastiat's *Selected Essays on Political Economy*, Hayek called him a "publicist of genius" (Bastiat 1964, 1.1). Hayek, it seems, was particularly taken by Bastiat (as are many modern libertarians) by virtue of what Hayek took to be the "more general significance" of his "central idea": namely, "that if we judge measures of economic policy solely by their immediate and concretely foreseeable effects, we shall not only not achieve a viable order but shall be certain progressively to extinguish freedom and thereby prevent more good than our measures will produce" (1.1). That Hayek should have glimpsed the antecedents of

---

virtue of which protectionism, not the Ricardian doctrine of free trade, was seen to promote harmony and balance.

[45] A warning here is in order. Carey is never easily interpreted on finer points, since he struck out in so many different (and often apparently contradictory) directions in his work. For example, he invented an account of rent that was the inverse of Ricardo's—namely, that *more* fertile lands were successively brought under cultivation (rather than *less*), so that rent appeared as the due return to landlords for this beneficial extension of cultivation. While this was a reasonable observation about how agriculture in the United States had expanded in the nineteenth century, it failed to grasp that in the analytical schema of Ricardo, "fertility" is *formally* defined in terms of the prevailing rate of profit and available techniques of production. Then again, it might also be said that Ricardo frequently slipped into a language where he seemed to be talking about "natural fertility."

his own assertions about "spontaneous orders" and "unintended consequences" in Bastiat is perhaps not surprising. Whether they are there, or whether this is what Bastiat thought himself to be doing, is dubious. Bastiat proceeds much more in the manner of a Mandeville by deploying ridicule against the targets of his pen. He does not appear to have deployed some subtle philosophical position—one, in fact, that was not even invented until the Austrian economists came on the scene some three or four decades later—to advance his case. Bastiat used his wit instead.

He was certainly good at ridicule. Bastiat's spoof petition from candle makers against competition from the sun is a case in point. While it wittily captures the dangers of allowing sectional interests to persuade governments that policies in the private interests of candle makers are in the public interest as well (the prohibition of windows in this case)—more cleverly than anything Smith could muster in his arguments against the mercantilists—it is scarcely more than wit. And his other recurring theme, that political economists need to look beyond the short-run effects of their proposals and consider their long-run consequences, is more a lesson in best practice rather than an application of a philosophical principle invented later by the Austrian school.

It would be incorrect to think that beyond these two cases that explicitly spoke of economic harmonies, other notions of economic harmony were not to some degree encountered elsewhere in the literature of classical political economy. Every claim about reaching a "balance" between economic forces, market prices gravitating towards their "natural" level, the "adjustment" of supply to effectual demand, or a "tendency" suggest an implicit language of harmony. When the neoclassical writers at the end of the nineteenth century spoke of "equilibrium" or "optimality," that language became more explicit.[46]

THE OTHERWORLD OF PERFECT COMPETITION

When we turn to the neoclassical economic theory that drives much of contemporary economic thinking, however, we encounter something quite different. A flavour of what is to be found in this new economic

---

[46] The tale of Walras's nomination for the Nobel Peace Prize in 1906, supported by the argument (penned by Walras himself) that understanding competitive equilibrium (and free trade) was a contribution to world peace, illustrates just how close to the surface not just the language of harmony but also a real commitment to it had once again become. An account of this episode may be found in Niehans (1990). It should also be said that John Bates Clark in the United States used the associated marginal productivity theory of distribution to maintain that the returns to different classes were equal to what they contributed to production.

arena may be gleaned from a comment that Lionel Robbins made at the beginning of his celebrated *Essay on the Nature and Significance of Economic Science*:

> We have been turned out of Paradise. We have neither eternal life nor unlimited means of gratification. Everywhere we turn, if we choose one thing we must relinquish others, in different circumstances, we would wish not to have relinquished. Scarcity of means to satisfy given ends is an almost ubiquitous condition of human behaviour. (1932, 15)

This new characterisation of economic life as involving a fall from paradise appears to evoke nostalgia for utopia. Yet when we draw back the veil of rhetoric surrounding it, the world we live in seems less problematic. The economic problem, according to Robbins, was the allocation of scarce resources among competing ends. But this was a problem that would be solved for the good (or with maximum efficiency) thanks to the rational action of individual agents operating in *perfectly competitive* markets. It would appear that we might merely have fallen from one paradise into another. In that world, on the neoclassical account of its operation, Vilfredo Pareto had convincingly shown that the working of the competitive market would produce results in which the condition of no one (in terms of their utility) could be improved on without making someone else worse off (again, in terms of their utility).[47] *Ophélimité*. As Hegel might have remarked, it is a fortunate fall indeed.

ROBINSON CRUSOE: THE CASTAWAY AS ECONOMIC MAN

If perfect competition provided neoclassical writers with one kind of otherworld in which to explore the outcome of the rational pursuit of self-interest by economic man, the island world of Daniel Defoe's *Robinson Crusoe* offered another one. The "Robinsonade is wedded to the utopian mode" (Manuel and Manuel 1979, 433). Crusoe supplied "a new utopian form with magnetic appeal" (433): the first thing that strikes economists about Crusoe is that he acts as a rational optimiser.

---

[47] Modern neoclassical economic analysis, which is still commonly (but inaccurately) supposed to be coterminous with classical political economy, is universally understood to be the study of choice in the face of scarcity. Its only real step forward has been to raise the question of whether that choice is made in the face of full or limited information. Today the most elementary textbooks of economics inculcate this fiction as a given fact of the world. The problem of constrained optimisation is thought to be all that is "really" going on behind any observable economic phenomenon—it provides those "microeconomic foundations"

In examining the neoclassical concept of rationality, Kenneth Arrow has given a useful exposition of its basically utopian character. He notes that "rationality is not in principle essential to a theory of the economy, and in fact, theories with *direct application* usually use assumptions of a different nature. . . . For classical political economists such as Smith and Ricardo, rationality had a basically limited meaning of preferring more to less" (1986, 204). As Arrow puts it, "Capitalists choose to invest in the industry yielding the highest rate of return, landlords rent their property to the highest bidder, while no one pays for land more than it is worth in product" (204).

Within classical political economy, of course, individuals were rational. But rationality for them was not understood to imply that economic agents were engaged in solving "constrained optimisation problems" in the way they are imagined to do by neoclassical writers. A conceptual transformation had taken place, in contrast, in neoclassical economic theory. "Rationality in application is not merely a property of the individual. Its useful and powerful implications derive from the conjunction of individual rationality and the other basic concepts of neoclassical theory: equilibrium, competition, and completeness of markets." Indeed, it seems evident that "we need not merely pure but perfect competition before the rationality hypotheses have their full power" (Arrow 1986, 203). In the real world of the market, as Arrow noted, "rationality assumptions become strained and possibly even self-contradictory. They certainly imply an ability at information processing and calculation that is far beyond the feasible" (203). So one leaves the real world for imagined ones.

The apogee of the treatment of Crusoe comes with Arthur Cecil Pigou, who devoted three whole chapters to "Robinson Crusoe Economics" in his *Economics of Stationary States*. Pigou was as unapologetic as he was assertive. Was this an "academic plaything without practical significance"? Was this the same as examining "imaginary individuals living solitary upon islands"? Was this like considering an Atlantic liner without paying attention to its length and breadth? For anyone who was tempted to answer "yes," Pigou had a surprise in store: "Nobody should object to an economist's resting for a time on Robinson's island" (1935, 33). The problem for Pigou, as with all other economists who sojourned for a time with Crusoe, is whether what they write about his behaviour as, say, a "representative" agent has any application whatsoever beyond that island. This has proved a problematic matter. Marshall was confident that

---

that are deemed indispensable to the very practice of the science. But how this has come about, and what its consequences have been, is a subject for some future work.

the formal balancing of economic costs and benefits, for example, was exactly the same whether one was talking of Crusoe or a modern business-man (1890, 69, 69n).

A CHANGE IN THE CONCEPT OF THE STATIONARY STATE

With the rise to dominance of perfect competition (and tales of Robinson Crusoe), the notion of a stationary state in economic thought changed again. The idea of the stationary state as the possible end point of an actual process of economic development disappeared, and it was replaced by the idea of the stationary state as a theoretical abstraction that provided a vehicle for the static analysis of price determination. But despite this radical redefinition, in which one might have expected Mill's utopian picture to have vanished, it actually surfaces in another form. For in the "thorough-going stationary state," resources are allocated efficiently and without waste, all individuals find their production and consumption plans to be realisable, and there are no tendencies to change.

Chapter Eleven

LABOUR DEFENDED

> One is almost tempted to believe that capital is a sort
> of cabalistic word, like Church or State, or any other of
> those general terms which are invented by those who
> fleece the rest of mankind to conceal the hand that
> shears them. It is a sort of idol before which men are
> called upon to prostrate themselves, while the cunning
> priest from behind the alter, profaning the God whom
> he pretends to serve, and mocking the sweet sentiments
> of devotion and gratitude, or those terrible emotions of
> fear and resentment, one or the other of which seems
> common to the whole human race, as they are enlight-
> ened and wise, or ignorant and debased, puts forth his
> hand to receive and appropriate the offerings which
> he calls for in the name of religion.
> —Thomas Hodgskin, *Labour Defended*

BY THE EARLY 1820s, the often violent mass agitations that had accompanied the years immediately following the conclusion of the Napoleonic
Wars had given way to a period of relative economic calm in Britain.
Under the stewardship of the then chancellor of the Exchequer Frederick
Robinson—or "Prosperity Robinson," as he came to be known—it appeared that the memory of events like the massacres at Peterloo in 1819
and the spectacle of the public execution of some of the Cato Street con-
spirators in 1820 had been eclipsed.[1] But it was only temporarily so, and
by the middle of the decade popular labour unrest had resumed.

In the mill towns across the north of England, workers were again in
direct conflict with both the owners of capital and the state. In April 1826,
at Chatterton near Ramsbottom, six Lancashire workers were gunned

---

[1] Robinson was a man who appears to have attracted nicknames. Soon after he introduced the Corn Laws into the House of Commons in 1815, his home was besieged by an
angry crowd, and in the ensuing disturbance two people were killed by security forces.
When speaking in the Commons of these events, Robinson broke down into tears and acquired the sobriquet "the blubberer." In 1818, he was appointed to the presidency of the
Board of Trade and then made the treasurer of the Navy. In 1823, he moved to the Treasury
as Chancellor of the Exchequer (succeeding Vansittart). During that term of office, he secured the funds for the founding of the National Gallery. In 1827, Robinson became Viscount Goderich and moved to the House of Lords (later being created Earl Ripon). He was

down by troops as they protested against the mechanisation of cotton spinning (through the introduction of the self-acting mule). In May 1829, cotton spinners rioted in Rochdale, Blackburn, and Manchester. That year, in Salford, troops shot ten protesters, and in London, Robert Peel's police force was first deployed. For more than twenty years, labour unrest along with economic and political conflict continued unabated. In the 1830s, the Chartists had taken to the streets, and their messages and tactics (especially those of the "physical force" faction) were directly antagonistic to the established economic and political order.[2] The words of the prominent Chartist firebrand Bronterre O'Brian, writing in the *London Mercury* in May 1837, give a flavour of just how sharp that division of opinion had become:

> What means a social revolution? I mean by it a radical reform in the relative duties and positions of the different classes of society. Political revolutions seldom go beyond the surface of society. They seldom amount to more than a mere transfer of power from one set of political chiefs to another. At best they only substitute one aristocratic form of government for another, and hence all political revolutions of which history makes mention have left the world pretty much as they found it—not wiser—not happier—not improved in any one essential particular. (O'Brian 1837, 161–2)[3]

In the 1840s, the condition of England continued to give trouble to the establishment.

---

briefly prime minister from late 1827 until early 1828 (after Liverpool's death). A full account of Robinson's career can be found in Jones (1967).

[2] It is worth remembering just how wide the Chartist appeal was. The National Charter Association claimed between 50,000 and 70,000 members by the early 1840s. Public meetings drew even larger crowds: 50,000 in Birmingham on June 19, 1837 (in 1841, Birmingham's population was 183,000); 150,000 in Glasgow on May 21, 1838 (its 1841 population was 275,000); 200,000 at Newhall Hill, Birmingham, on August 6, 1838; 250,000 at Kersal Moor, Manchester, in September 1838 (its 1841 population being 243,000); and 25,000 in Bradford on October 18, 1838 (its 1841 population was 67,000). Even the ill-fated Kennington Common meeting of April 10, 1848 drew 25,000 (watched over by an army of "special constables" of some 170,000, one of whom, incidentally, was none other than Louis-Napoléon).

[3] He continued: "Instead of a semi-feudal oligarchy of landowners [the revolution of 1688] gave us a mixed mongrel aristocracy of landowners and moneymongers to compose our future parliaments [. . .]. The American Revolution [. . .] and the French Revolution [. . .] were on a larger scale and of a more democratic character than any of the preceding ones. Nevertheless they were only political revolutions. The Constitution of 1791 was for the French Bourgeoisie of that epoch what the 'Bill of Rights' was for the English Shopocracy of 1688. It divided the government of France between the moneymongers and the landowners. The American Revolution [. . .] did not change the system of acquiring and transmitting property. It was [. . .] a mere political revolution. In leaving the institution of property where it found it, it left all the germs of social evil to ripen in the womb of time, and these germs remaining, it was of little consequence what the particular form of government was, or might be" (ibid).

Parallel to these events, in the twenty-five years following Ricardo's death in 1823, political economy was taken onto the streets, sometimes quite literally so. A group of writers, in the vanguard of which was Hodgskin, emerged as the popularisers of the doctrines of classical political economy. Their writings provided the intellectual artillery in an increasingly radicalised political struggle between the interests of capital and those of labour. A heady mixture of economic discontent, growing popular demand for parliamentary reform, and grand tournaments between political economists themselves (over the labour theory of value as well as the relation between the wage and the rate of profit) was to transform the landscape of political economy. The ideas and events of these decades were, in an important sense, to set the stage for the eventual replacement of classical political economy by an altogether more reassuring, legitimating version of economic science—one engineered by the neoclassical economists of the final quarter of the nineteenth century.

What is relevant for us is how these thinkers introduced a new and different dimension into the discourse of politics and political economy during that transition: namely, the idea that political economy, as a "science," might mandate a revolutionary transformation of capitalist society.

Variously called the "Ricardo Economists" (Read 1829, xxix, 282ff), the "Labour Writers" (Marx 1963, 3:14–15), the "Utopian Socialists" (Marx 1848, 497), the "Ricardian Socialists" (Foxwell 1899), or the "Pre-Marxians" (Gray 1946, 262), these writers were in fact quite a diverse group.[4] To the British establishment, of course, some of their work represented what Marx called "the unpleasant side of classical political economy" (1963, 3:502; emphasis omitted). While the precise membership of the group is rendered a little differently according to the preferences and purposes of the author discussing them, it included (in addition to Hodgskin) Charles Hall, William Thompson, Piercy Ravenstone (Richard Puller), John Francis Bray, John Gray, and Owen.[5]

---

[4] Samuel Read also included James Mill and McCulloch in the Ricardo Economists category since, for him, they too presented arguments suggesting an antagonism of interest between labour and capital—an opinion which Read set about attempting to dispel by showing the 'productiveness' of capital by hinting at what was to become known an abstinence theory of profit. In this enterprise, he was joined by George Poulett Scrope (1833) and, most famously, by Nassau Senior (1836). These early abstinence theories of profit (and some of the parallel remarks John Stuart Mill was to make in his *Principles of Political Economy*) were, of course, incomplete. For while they made a plausible enough argument that profits might be regarded as a reward for 'abstaining from consumption' (or 'waiting', as neoclassicals like Böhm-Bawerk and Marshall would later put it), they were unable to establish any relation between the amount of 'abstinence' and the magnitude of the rate of profit. We shall not be including McCulloch and James Mill in the present consideration of the group.

[5] We shall not have much more to say about Hall, not only because his work on the *Effects of Civilisation on the People in European States* is earlier (1805), but also because his is rather more an indictment of the lack of refinement in manufacturing activity and a

Although their writings all shared the common characteristic of being critical of the existing capitalist organisation of production, their work reveals two strands of thinking that are important for our purposes (a simple classification first suggested by Max Beer [1919]). On the one hand, there were those of a more "revolutionary" turn of mind who deployed their understanding of political economy to advocate the wholesale replacement of the existing social and political order. Hodgskin is preeminent here (along with Ravenstone).[6] On the other hand, there were those of a less revolutionary, more benevolent, and socially responsible turn of mind who used their understanding of political economy to advocate the establishment of workers cooperatives or experimental socialist communities. Owen stands out here (with Thompson, Gray, and Bray somewhat similarly disposed).

Schumpeter confidently dismissed these interventions; he conceded that they were "entitled to a great place in the history of socialist thought," yet he claimed that they offered "but little that is relevant to a history of economic analysis" (1954, 479).[7] These interventions appear to constitute, however, a decisive moment in the whole development of economic thought (and not just of its classical manifestations); no account of nineteenth-century developments can be complete without attending to them. The genealogy of these ideas, their content, the effects they had on the conceptual transformation of politics and political economy, and what they might owe to Smith or Ricardo (or their author's own imaginings) concern us here.[8]

---

paean of praise for agricultural pursuits (in which he is more in the line of Thomas Spence and William Ogilvie). Yet Hall does call attention to what Marx would later refer to as "the increasing misery of the proletariat," and he also sees the movement of workers from agriculture to industry as constituting the "forcible expropriation" of their means of subsistence. In general, as the Chartist movement grew in strength in the 1830s and 1840s, many of their number used arguments drawn from classical political economy to underpin their advocacy of either "moral force" or "physical force" Chartism.

[6] James Mill famously wrote to Brougham suggesting that Hodgskin's ideas threatened to overturn the whole of civilisation (see Robbins 1961, 135).

[7] For the present, we concentrate on the first group—namely, those who traced the source of economic malaise to something inherent in the operation of the capitalist system itself. Within that group, we shall focus almost exclusively on its most influential and theoretically sophisticated representative: Hodgskin.

[8] Much work has been done and much heated controversy has been generated in an attempt to establish the parenthood of their system of ideas. The literature on this subject is both large and of variable quality. Of those who seek to forge a link between them and Ricardo himself, there are different schools of thought. When Foxwell coined the term Ricardian Socialists in 1899, for example, it was designed to allow him to associate these writers with what he took to be (echoing both Jevons and Toynbee) Ricardo's fundamentally erroneous theory of political economy—and thereby to dismiss them. When Marx connected them (and most especially Hodgskin) to Ricardo, it was to make the point that

When it comes to Hodgskin, then, there is perhaps no better place to begin than with his view of the transformative role that the science of political economy had to play in the process of social and political change. Far from being simply an input into the speculative thinking of political philosophers or political theorists, or just a source of information to legislators as they went about the task of lawmaking, Hodgskin saw political economy as providing the basis for the elimination of the state and the "artificial" property rights prevailing in his day.

THE SCIENCE OF THE LEGISLATOR OR THE SCIENCE OF THE PEOPLE?

The London Mechanics Institution was formed at a public meeting in the Crown and Anchor Tavern (on the Strand) in 1823. The meeting was attended by nearly two thousand people. Hodgskin and J. C. Robertson had suggested the idea, and George Birkbeck (who had removed to London from Edinburgh, where he had set up a similar organisation) and Francis Place were instrumental in securing subscription funding. Similar institutes soon sprang up around the country and abroad (see Kelly 1957). The institution was the forerunner of what is now Birkbeck College in the University of London.

In 1825, Hodgskin opened his anonymous tract, *Labour Defended against the Claims of Capital,* with an attack on the parliamentary sessions that had generated the Combination Act of 1825.[9] This and other legislation, he contended, had placed the need to protect the interests of capital at the forefront of its concerns, to the detriment of the interests of labour. As far as Hodgskin was concerned, "The condition of the labourer can never be permanently improved till he can refute the theory, and is determined to oppose the practice, of giving nearly everything to capital" (1825, 19). From the outset, then, he set up his analytical project by arguing that a great contest existed between capital and labour—a contest

---

they had unearthed inconsistencies in Ricardo's theory of value and distribution that required correction.

[9] The Tory government of Lord Liverpool had defended the Combination Laws of 1799 in the face of a long-standing attack from Whig and radical reformers alike, and among the Tories, perhaps none defended them more staunchly than William Huskisson. External opposition to the laws was orchestrated by Place, and in Parliament, by Joseph Hume and Francis Burdett. The 1799 legislation was finally repealed in 1824. Perhaps unsurprisingly, there followed a spate of industrial disputes that led to the passing of a replacement Combination Act in 1825. The law of 1799 had made it illegal for workers to combine with the aim of securing higher wages or shorter hours; the law of 1825, while it allowed certain combinations, severely circumscribed their legality and, importantly from Hodgskin's point of view, made all collective action outside those defined limits a criminal conspiracy in restraint of trade.

in which workers must appeal to reason "to suggest some arguments in favour of labour against capital." To provide that scientific support was, he wrote, "my chief motive for publishing the present pamphlet" (22). In this way, so to speak, the "science of the legislator" was to become the "science of the people" in their struggle for economic and distributive justice.

Hodgskin's aim was also to reveal the "true" character of the structure of political power that supported and legitimated the claims of capital. While his claims about the political system as well as his antipathy towards it are better expressed in other works, *Labour Defended* argued that the legislature was composed exclusively of capitalists, clergy, and landlords, and represented no other interests. Thus, "all that we are compelled to suffer, all that we have inflicted on us, has been done for the advantage of capital" (24–25). Hodgskin stated unambiguously that his intention was to examine the claims of the capitalist to see how far they were supported by the theories of political economy; there was a necessity for labour both to comprehend as well as be able to refute the received notion of the nature and productivity of capital.

After asserting that he intended to reexamine some of the positive properties widely ascribed to the owners of capital, he quoted some "great men" (in this case McCulloch and James Mill) who, he said, looked merely to *explain* the existing order rather than ask whether it could be *improved*. He contended that these thinkers had mistakenly tried to argue that capital aided production, that the capitalist provided for the labourer by advancing their wages, and that capital combined with labour in the production of commodities in order to provide an economic justification for the profits they reaped. His intellectual project was to expose received ideas about capital in order to vindicate the claims of the labourer vis-à-vis those of the capitalist, and thereby to reveal the political and intellectual structure that supported the latter.

Importantly, in *Labour Defended*, Hodgskin also argued for the centrality of popular education, and in particular, a wider knowledge of the first principles of the science of political economy, as a means to promote social and political change. His claim was twofold: first, that such change was both impending and would actually occur; but second, that the spread of education among the labouring classes would accelerate the process. "It is not possible," he wrote, "that any large body of men who are acquainted with their rights will tacitly acquiesce in insult and injury" (99). This increasing knowledge among the labouring classes would, he claimed, make "impossible for the greatest visionary to suppose that any class of men can much longer be kept in ignorance of the principles on which societies are governed" (100).

Hodgskin was quite insistent on the role of the spread of knowledge among workers in the movement for social progress. The Mechanics Institutions, he claimed, taught men moral and physical sciences as well as to probe all things—convinced, as he seems to have been, that this would ensure both that "change will not be effected by violence" and that change "cannot be counteracted by force" (100). Nothing, he wrote, could put down that "insurrection" by which knowledge would "subvert whatever is not founded in justice and truth" (101).[10]

In a way that would become familiar after Marx's interventions some years later, Hodgskin held that his own work illustrated how (and why) capital had no just claim to the surplus product of labour (namely, profits), and that the system of capitalist production itself actually caused (and intensified) the poverty of the worker. Once workers knew this, it would be impossible that they would long acquiesce in such a state of things. In short, Hodgskin presents something like a rising contest between capital and labour from a scientific understanding of which all would be revealed. He held, for example, that as the formation of combinations of workers became more widespread, the only consequence would be stronger laws protecting the interests of capital, and that this, in its turn, would merely allow the cause of worker oppression to be more distinctly seen:

> The contest now appears to be between journeymen, or between one species of labour and another, but it will soon be displayed in its proper characters; and will stand confessed a war of honest industry against the idle profligacy which has so long ruled the affairs of the political world with undisputed authority. (104)

Hodgskin's idea that eventually labour would slough off its submissiveness and turn to subverting the very system that supported the oppressive exaction of profits, would appear again (in a different guise) in the *Communist Manifesto*. It is hardly surprising, then, that the ruling classes of the day took fright—or that Hodgskin chose to print *Labour Defended* anonymously.

In 1827, however, Hodgskin published *Popular Political Economy*, a work now appearing under his own name—and although it possessed a

---

[10] It should be noted that Hodgskin also claimed that the different classes of labour were at the time beginning to think and act as one body in opposition to other classes, and that they would not stop short of any ultimate truth: "By casting aside the prejudices which fetter the minds of those who have benefited by their degradation, they have everything to hope. On the other hand, they are the sufferers by these prejudices, and have everything to dread from their continuance" (102). This is a very different view of the political function and consequences of an education in political economy than anything entertained by Malthus, Ricardo, or James Mill.

slightly different focus from *Labour Defended* (and advanced some new ideas), the theme of promoting the cause of social and economic change through the spread of knowledge of the principles of political economy among the working classes was again very much at the forefront.[11] The book was based on a series of lectures delivered at the London Mechanics Institution (themselves resulting from the reception of *Labour Defended*). Once again, Hodgskin began by extolling the value of the science, but he now explicitly set up his work as an examination of its "natural laws" (something he had not done before). In the preface, for example, Hodgskin explained that he had chosen the term "popular" because the principles he was about to enunciate were "more agreeable to the popular prejudices than those which have been made prevalent, though still unpopular, by the writings of Mr. Malthus" (1827, preface). Although Hodgskin did state that *Popular Political Economy* had no pretensions to be practical, he immediately added that if the principles he advanced were correct (namely, that there existed a set of "natural" laws regulating and determining the production of wealth), then "to know [them], is to apply them."[12] In Hodgskin's hands, however, these "applications" were to amount to something quite different from the idea entertained by, say, Ricardo of "directing governments to right measures."

Popular Political Economy, then, like *Labour Defended*, sought to reveal the principles of political economy in order to facilitate a deeply critical stance over the contemporary organisation of society. Half a decade later, in *The Natural and Artificial Right of Property Contrasted* (1832), Hodgskin reprised the same theme. Although that book comprised a series of letters to Brougham (composed but not dispatched in 1829) on the subject of combinations of workers, Hodgskin reiterated that principles dictated practice: "By deductions from principles not here enunciated, the author has satisfied himself that all law making, except gradually and quietly to repeal all existing laws, is arrant humbug" (1832, i).

Although each book has a different focus, the theme is fairly consistent across all three works. If *Labour Defended* and *Popular Political Economy* respond more directly to theories of political economy (and are where Hodgskin presents the bulk of his economic analysis), *Popular Political Economy* also brings out what he sees as a contrast between the

---

[11] A fact attested to perhaps by noting that Hodgskin dedicated *Popular Political Economy* to Birkbeck.

[12] It is not without interest to note that Hodgskin argued that because "moral feeling and scientific truth must be in harmony with each other," he was somehow obliged to trace to its source the repugnance felt to some of the doctrines of political economy at the time: "Men turn away disgusted, not from truth, but from errors dogmatically enforced" (preface).

"natural" order of the economy (and society) and then existing character-istics of the current system. In *The Natural and Artificial Right of Prop-erty*, on the other hand, a contrast between the natural and the artificial takes centre stage—and Hodgskin's concern is less with the economy (and theories of political economy) than it is with theories of government and lawmaking. Hodgskin's argument here is complex, as he appears to want to contend that both the current system inflicts great misery on society by ignoring the natural right of property, *and* it is ineffective because the natural right of property is much stronger than the artificial order and is overcoming it.

In this way, Hodgskin's intellectual project shifted from an attack on existing theories of political economy (and the qualities attributed to the capitalist organisation of production), to the presentation of a theory of the natural economic order and production of wealth, and finally to an attack on the system of legislation and its propagation of an unjust and artificial system of property rights. It seems apposite to look at each of these in turn.

A CONTRIBUTION TO THE CRITIQUE OF CAPITALIST SOCIETY

In the introduction to *Popular Political Economy* (1827), Hodgskin as-serted that the science of political economy could ascertain the differences in the productive powers of people, and since there were some classes in society who did not labour, also explain the consequences of having al-lowed those few to throw off necessity and appropriate the product of the labour of others.[13] As we shall see, Hodgskin's answers to these two questions reveal all that is most characteristic of his thought. He estab-lished the "unproductiveness" of capital by claiming that since physical capital was nothing more than the privately accumulated product of "past" labour, only labour was truly "productive."[14] Accordingly, he claimed that if the product of this past labour happened to accrue to the owners of capital in the form of profit, it did so not because capital was productive but because of the legally enforceable, artificial property rights accorded to the owners of capital.

---

[13] Those few he named as capitalists, landowners, legislators, and clergy, and elsewhere, more lyrically, as the "rapacious landlord, the usurious capitalist, and the profligate de-pendants on, and profligate supporters of, profligate governments, [and] . . . idlers in soci-ety" (121).

[14] It is important to be clear about the meaning of Hodgskin's language here. Productive means for him productive of value—not productive of wealth. This is a very different use of this idea than is to be found in either Smith or the physiocrats. In addition, past means not labour in the historical past but in the labour used in other industries that produce

Hodgskin had opened *Labour Defended* with the claim that since wages varied inversely with profits, it was "profits, or the capitalists share of the national produce, which is opposed to wages, or the share of the labourers" (1825, 27–28).[15] The familiar Ricardian idea of an inverse relation between the wage and the rate of profits, rather than Smith's adding-up theory of value (which contained no inverse relation between wages and the rate of profits), thus seems to have formed the starting point for both his economic analysis and the deeply oppositional stance he adopted towards the existing social, legal, and political arrangements of his day. It was one of the twin pillars of his attack on the citadel of capital.[16] But just what was Hodgskin's understanding of the content of that key relation?

Having "gotten rid of rent" as a "component part of price," Ricardo had been able to speak interchangeably of that relation as being one between the *share* of wages and the rate of profits, between the wage *rate* and the rate of profits, and between the *value* of the wage and the rate of profits because he had assumed that commodities exchanged at labour-value prices.[17] His followers, however, notably McCulloch and James Mill, had been less clear, and by the middle of the 1820s, they had effectively abandoned all but the idea that relative *shares* varied inversely (see De Vivo 1984, 57–62).

Hodgskin seems to have struck out on a path much more in line with that of Ricardo. He began with a distinction between circulating capital (wage goods) and fixed capital (tools and machinery), both of which, he claimed, represented quantities of "co-existing labour" (1825, 38, 55). With respect to circulating capital, he wrote:

> As far as food, drink, and clothing are concerned, it is quite plain, then, that no species of labour depend on any previously prepared stock, for in

---

capital goods today. In an attempt to avoid confusion on this point, Hodgskin sometimes called it "concurrent" or "co-existing" labour (see, for example, 1825, 69).

[15] Hodgskin briefly discussed rent (the share of produce obtained on all but the least fertile land) and argued that the landlord's share "does not keep the labourer poor" (30–31). Thus, "labourers do only receive, and ever have only received, as much as will subsist them, the landlords receive the surplus produce of the more fertile soils, and all the rest of the whole produce of labour in this and in every country goes to the capitalist under the name of profit for the use of his capital" (31).

[16] The other being his attack on the idea of legally defined private property rights, a subject to which we shall return a little later.

[17] Indeed, on the assumption that capital consists entirely of wage goods, these are all the same as saying that the *shares* of wages and profits vary inversely with each other—an otherwise seemingly trivial observation. This is easy enough to see. Let us write R, W, L, and Q as total wages, total profits, total labour used, and total product, respectively (with lower case r and w denoting the *rates* of profits and wages, respectively). We then have: $R/Q \cdot Q/W \equiv R/W \equiv R/wL$ and $r \equiv R/W \equiv R/wL$.

fact no such stock exists: but every species of labourer does constantly, and at all times, depend for his supplies on the co-existing labour of some other labourers. (45)[18]

With respect to fixed capital, consisting of instruments and machines, Hodgskin maintained that while it was undeniable that these enabled workers to perform tasks that could not be performed without them (or at least to perform them better), they too were nothing other than the product of labour, so that "fixed capital does not derive its utility from previous, but present labour; and does not bring its owner a profit because it has been stored-up, but because it is a means of obtaining a command over labour" (55). What Hodgskin had done was to reduce the quantity of labour embodied in the production of commodities to quantities of "direct" *and* "indirect" labour embodied in their production—and profits were nothing other than the surplus labour accruing not to workers but to capitalists.

The same conclusion emerged from Hodgskin's discussion of the determination of commodity prices.[19] Here he started with Smith not Ricardo. Natural prices were determined by the quantity of labour nature required, directly and indirectly, in the production of commodities. When commodities exchanged at their natural prices (labour values), there was no profit. Hodgskin claimed that there was also something he called a "social" price, however—the price that obtained in society when the rights of private property (enshrined in English law) applied. In other words, the so-

---

[18] He goes on to identify the origin of profits as follows: "It is by the command that the capitalist possesses over the *labour of some men*, not by his possessing stock of commodities, that HE is enabled to *support* and consequently employ other labourers" (52).

[19] Hodgskin, like all the classical writers, excluded from the analysis at this point both nominal (money) prices and the "market" prices that prevailed when the market was disturbed by what Smith had called "fitful and irregular" causes. Interestingly, when Hodgskin turned to the question of money, he deployed the argument that money was nothing more than the instrument "for carrying on buying and selling, and the consideration of it no more forms a part of the science of political economy, than the consideration of ships or steam-engines" (1827, 179). When Hodgskin examined paper money, a variation of the real-bills doctrine seems to appear. He contended there were two species of paper money: the paper money regulated and controlled by government, and the paper money in circulation by the merchants. Paper money issued by government should be opposed, as it is valueless, unlimited, and "confers on the individuals who possess the government a boundless power of working mischief" (198). Hodgskin offered something of a brief history of paper money, claiming that it had long been in use, and "it never is issued but for the purpose of surreptitiously and fraudulently levying a tax on the people" (199). Yet he argued that commercial paper was quite different. He contended that promissory notes were probably the oldest form of commercial paper money and that they facilitated trade in the ancient world. Whether the state sanctioned it or not, paper money would form a principle part of the circulation in every economy; this was not a matter of theory, legislation, or the schemes of some "hot-brained projector" but rather of general agreement (204).

cial price was the price that obtained outside what Smith had called the "early and rude state of society," before the private accumulation of capital and the appropriation of land. The social price was therefore the natural price enhanced by the social regulations that prevailed in the form of the régime of private property: "natural price, thus increased to the labourer, is social price" (1827, 220).

With this distinction between the social and natural prices of commodities, we may begin to appreciate, perhaps for the first time, the important alterations to the labour theory of value that took place after Smith—and how, as a result, its significance to political thinking changed. The central problematic of the labour theory of value, conceived of as a theory of the determination of the relative prices of commodities by the quantity of labour embodied (directly and indirectly) in their production, had always been the domain of its application. When profits were positive, when the accumulation of capital in private hands characterised the conditions of production of commodities, the question was whether the labour theory of value had anything useful left to say about price determination.

Smith had thought not, and had settled on an adding-up approach to price determination as a result. Ricardo had disagreed, and had thought that the labour theory of value would suffice as an explanation (albeit with important exceptions that he recognised would take place with a *change* in the distribution of income between wages and profits). Hodgskin took another route. He appears to have recognised that when profits were positive, there would be a systematic *difference* between the relative prices of commodities and the relative quantities of labour embodied in their production (between his social price and natural price, respectively).[20] At a stroke, the labour theory of value also took on a new politi-

---

[20] It does not seem possible to say with any certainty how Hodgskin reached this (analytically correct) conclusion. It is always possible that he did so by way of Ricardo (and a critique of the first chapter of Ricardo's *Principles*), but there is no convincing evidence to support that possibility. More likely, he reached the conclusion by way of Smith, and there are two reasons to think that this might have been the case. First, Smith had written that "the produce of labour" constituted its "natural recompense" (1776, 1.8:82)—something that a subscriber to a Lockean notion of property rights like Hodgskin would have found appealing. Smith had also written that "as soon as stock has accumulated in the hands of particular persons" (1.6:65), the value that "workmen add to . . . materials . . . resolves itself . . . into two parts, of which one pays their wages, the other the profits of their employer" (1.6:66)—an argument likely to strike someone like Hodgskin (with his Lockean commitments) as a departure from the natural right of property. Second, Smith had also understood that when that was the case, the relative prices of commodities were no longer determined by the relative quantities of labour *embodied* in their production (1.6:67), or as Hodgskin put it, the social price no longer corresponded to the natural price. Combining this with his Lockean conception of property rights, it may be that Hodgskin simply put one and one together to get two: the capitalist system was unnatural and unjust, and needed

cal significance, since it was to be used by Hodgskin, as we shall see, to challenge both the justness of the social relations of capitalist production and the legitimacy of the political arrangements that supported them.[21]

Since Hodgskin had asserted that it was by the labourers' labour and nothing else that natural price was measured—and that labour did not obtain all the commodities it produced—he could then maintain that in the present state of society, price was not naturally but socially determined. Natural price was, as it were, the limit (in one direction) for the social price; its attainment would be through the elimination of those pernicious social regulations (the right of private property) that kept the social price above its natural level:

> The power now possessed by idle men to appropriate the produce of labourers, seems to me the great cause of bloated and unhappy weariness in the former, who, having their natural wants provided for, necessarily live having no useful aim and object,—and of poverty and wretchedness in the latter, who being obliged to subsist many more than their own families, have no time and no thought, but how to obtain the means of preserving an existence so filled with toil and care as to seem scarcely worthy of preservation. (1827, 235)

Removing the legislative barriers that kept the social price above its natural level, though, would mean a social revolution. Not a few of Hodgskin's readers took fright.

But Hodgskin was no superficial critic of capitalist society, and thus did not fail to attempt to anticipate some of the attacks to which he would be subjected and address them in advance. We shall return later to his defence against those who would charge him as being a danger to civilisation itself. Yet for the present, let us focus on his defence against one other such criticism: the question of whether there would remain any motive to save if there were to be no profits from capital (254). This was a question that Hodgskin clearly took seriously.

When Hodgskin examined the effects of an increase in the reward to labour, in consequence of the elimination of profits, he believed that it would be accompanied by improved productivity. Rather than it leading to a decline of industry, Hodgskin thought it would herald its renaissance. Productivity growth would be attendant on both the greater incentive higher wages would give to workers to apply themselves to the immediate

---

to be replaced. But whether his political commitments held primacy over his economic views, or vice versa, is not easy to determine.

[21] Marx, of course, was later to strike out in a different political direction from his own rendition of the labour theory of value.

task at hand and the encouragement they would give for workers to acquire greater skills.

Furthermore, by claiming that it was necessary to remember that savings—or what for him amounted to the same thing, investment—was in any case nothing more than the putting aside of durable commodities for future use, Hodgskin was able to construct an argument that saving did not require the incentive of profits. Saving would continue unimpeded after the social transformation of society he proposed. The incentive to saving arose, he thought, from a relation between filial affection and population growth, together with the physical properties of durable commodities (256—57), rather than from the profit motive. Hodgskin was not especially sanguine about the profit motive, since not all capitalists invested their profits productively in any case.

Interestingly, Hodgskin's antipathy towards the capitalist class did not, it seems, extend to private bankers. Hodgskin in fact argued that private bankers were of great utility to society—a conclusion, he contended, that might be confirmed simply by observing their existence in every part of Europe. But while private banking was a necessary part of the great natural system of cooperative production, "it would be difficult to find a single scientific principle" to support the government issue of paper money (210). According to Hodgskin, who used traditional quantity-theory presuppositions, if banks were to be permitted freely to issue banknotes, their mutual oversight and competition would provide a natural check against that overissue that would generate fluctuations in the general level of prices. While he conceded that money had "been productive of incalculable mischief" in his day (and the past), he strongly held that all this mischief had been due to "government tampering." Although the "present generation" attributed these problems "to the instrument itself," in point of fact, Hodgskin claimed, currency depreciations and monetary disturbances had uniformly been caused by the manner in which the currency had "been abused by the venerated governments of Europe" (214; emphasis omitted).

One could scarcely find a language more congruent with the doctrines of the so-called Free Banking school than this. Parallel to the disappearance of the state in the arena of property rights, it seems, would be its disappearance in the arena of currency and finance. Hodgskin summed this up as follows:

> Banking . . . never let us never forget, with the issuing of bank notes, is altogether a private business, and no more needs to be regulated by meddling statesmen, than the business of paper making. In fact, the impertinent interference of law-makers, their pretended wise regulations, but in reality their tricks and frauds, with the currency, have been the causes of all the evils we

have suffered within the last century from variation in the value of metallic and paper money; and nothing can rescue mankind from such desperate fluctuations in prices, as have of late afflicted all the countries in Europe, but allowing, both the coining of metallic and the issuing of paper money, to find, under the controlling influence of natural circumstances, their proper course and just level. (215)

This, then, completes Hodgskin's economic critique of capitalist society. The crux of Hodgskin's argument is that fixed and circulating capital exist only as the products of labour, and do not possess any productive power independent of that labour; that the capitalist class enters between the actual producers of commodities (wage goods and capital goods) until gradually workers come to believe they are indebted to capital for their subsistence. But for Hodgskin, while the capitalist was not unlike the English middleman in Ireland, private bankers performed an essential service to the economic machine.[22]

An Unpleasant Side of Classical Political Economy

When Marx spoke of an "unpleasant side of classical political economy" (1963, 3:502), he had in mind writers like Hodgskin. Hodgskin had argued that since political economists loudly proclaimed the necessity of the security of property, they should scarcely hesitate to agree that whatever labour produced ought to belong to it. In saying this, however, he was not just taken as being witty; he was seen by the party of order to be a threat to civilisation itself. If political economy was the science of wealth, as Smith had told us, then for Hodgskin "all wealth is *created* by labour, and there is no wealth that is not the produce of labour" (1827, 19). Even more unpleasant would be the implications that Hodgskin was to draw from this concerning distributive justice.

According to Hodgskin, the distribution of income was determined by two sets of circumstances: natural circumstances (or laws not dependent on or derived from government) and social regulations (these are the creation of government). Moreover, only natural circumstances could be productive of just outcomes. To the extent that social regulations altered the natural outcomes, they should be swept away. In the exchange between labour and capital, which determined the distribution of income between the classes, Hodgskin perceived a disfiguring injustice. Had not "Dr. Smith" told us that the wages of workers were held at subsistence level,

---

[22] Hodgskin could not resist pointing out the irony of the fact that while the middlepeople of Ireland were stigmatized as oppressors by the economists, political economy portrayed capitalists as benefactors.

while the profits of capital grew? Had not "Mr. Malthus" and "Mr. Ricardo" told us that the natural operation of the principle of population was all that was at work to keep wages at their subsistence level? Hodgskin disagreed:

> This is so palpable a violation of the natural principle . . . it is so completely the principle of slavery, to starve the labourer unless his labour will feed his master as well as himself, that we must not be surprised if we should find it one of the chief causes, wherever it exists, and it exists almost universally, of the poverty and wretchedness of the labouring classes. (52)

Thus, Hodgskin rejected the Malthus-Ricardo idea that wages were kept at subsistence level through the operation of the principle of population—it was not natural in any sense. He instead located the problem squarely in the domain of social regulation.

In fact, Hodgskin's treatment of population was rather novel and involved a rejection of Malthus. He observed that political economy had correctly defined the limits of the division of labour by "the extent of the market," but that the extent of the market was an ambiguous phrase. Yet what if the extent of the market was intimately connected to the number of labourers and their productive power? In that event, Hodgskin argued, the growth of population and the demographic changes that went with it, created not only new demands (and needs) but also gave an incentive to improved efficiency in the production of wealth. Such a mechanism would widen the extent of the market and would create wealth sufficient to keep wages from falling: "There would be more to be mutually exchanged by and amongst labourers, and a proportionate extension of the market and the division of labour" (117). Hodgskin gave an example to illustrate his point. Comparing England, Russia, and the United States, he asserted that the fact that England was more densely populated, that its division of labour was more advanced, and that its annual production was greater clinched his case.[23] In suggesting that rapid technical progress could forestall the effects of population growth, Hodgskin introduced a criticism of Malthus's formulation of the principle of population that was to become de riguer.

---

[23] And he mustered other evidence:

The immense revenue levied by our government, augmenting from year to year; the enormous and increasing amount of the sums annually paid to the pretended servants of a benevolent Deity; the increased wealth of the capitalist and the yearly augmenting revenue of the owners of land,—all arising from the annual produce of labour, are indisputable proofs of that vast increase in productive power, the natural well-head of which is an increase in the number of labourers. (121)

If it is not the natural operation of demographic change on economic circumstance that keeps wages at their subsistence level, what is it? Hodgskin's answer is straightforward: "not a part, but the whole of the poverty" of workers is caused by "*vexatious regulations*" (139)—an unpleasant side indeed.

THE ROLE OF GOVERNMENT

It was in the *Natural and Artificial Right of Property* that Hodgskin most fully developed his antipathy towards government and governing institutions—an antipathy that had been present in a more scattered form elsewhere.[24] It is here that one encounters arguments, despite Hodgskin's protestations to the contrary, with a distinctly anarchistic flavour. It is the "maxim of the masters of mankind," he said, to let the people perish but to let the law live (1832, 45).[25] The problem, as he articulated it, was that "the great object of the law and of government has been and is, to establish and protect a violation of that natural right of property they are described in theory as being intended to guarantee" (48).

[24] *The Natural and Artificial Right of Property* was a series of unsent letters to Brougham. Hodgskin was none too fond of Brougham. In his postscript to the book, Hodgskin presented a ninth letter to Brougham that opens with the observation that Brougham's actions as lord chancellor in setting forth the sword of the law against "the poor victims of the system of misgovernment" and taking "the jurors of London to task on September 8, 1831 for violating the words of ministers" for executing the cruel criminal code, had convinced him that Brougham's "love of liberty and humanity" was a pose—a mere stepping-stone to power (1832, 165). He also took this opportunity to hold Brougham responsible for a Whig publication that had criticised *Labour Defended* (1825, 168).

It is worth remembering that Hodgskin had published *The Natural and Artificial Right of Property* in light of the events that occurred after the completion of his eighth letter, and that the events in Europe leading up to his 1832 publication had prompted him to do so. In the book, he noted that even before the current problems, the Saint-Simonians had risen up in France, and the legal right of property was being questioned in the United States (170). Private property was now the subject of nearly universal controversy, and the agitation had been made more manifest by the expulsion of Charles X in France. As these political changes could not bring the expected benefits, he continued, people would turn to enquire into the sources of evil and would come to the great source—the opposition between the legal and natural right. Hodgskin argued that the whole of the doctrines of the distribution of wealth, as they use principles of rent and profit, are founded on an understanding of the artificial, legal right of property, and thus on a false basis (171).

[25] Hodgskin maintained that it was ridiculous to say that society would collapse into anarchy without the law, since "self-preservation" was the first duty of animals. Hodgskin felt that society would not be left to confusion and anarchy; instead, the power that overruled the legislator would establish a social order far superior to anything the legislator had ever contemplated. Hodgskin never described in any detail why this be would an ordered state of society.

The "crime of the legislator," as he called it, was artificially to protect the wealth of the "legislative classes" against the natural claims of labour. Legislatures protected the landed aristocracy by investing in them the right to alienate land; they protected the religious establishment by exchanging with it part of the annual production for the support of the religious classes in inculcating respect for authority; they protected the private property of capitalists despite their having, he contended, no natural right to the large share of the annual production that the law secured them (53).[26] This kind of argument was not new for Hodgskin; in *Labour Defended*, he had already stated abruptly that the members of the legislature "profess liberal principles" but "make laws to keep the labourer in thraldom" (1825, 106).

Hodgskin's deep antipathy to the state (or perhaps better, the capitalist state) stemmed from his philosophical precommitment to the notion that there existed a "natural order" of things that could be discovered by the science of political economy. To him, at least, the science of political economy revealed that this order had been deformed and distorted by the laws and institutions of his day.[27] When Hodgskin spoke of a natural course of things that was carried forward by "natural passions," he therefore saw this course as having been diverted by legal and political institutions that acted in the interests of the legislative classes. Thus, he maintained, if the human race was carried on a current that it could not stem, those statesman "who pretend to direct the march of nations," and "continue to look on human society as a machine put together and regulated in all its movements by the politician" (1832, 37), were at best simply beguiled by appearances.

The account that Hodgskin provided of the "natural progress" of society illustrates what he had in mind. In some original state of things, he argued, people could appropriate commodities from nature without wronging other people. In this stage, the techniques of appropriation (and production) were compatible with a harmonious and natural set of social relations that stood alongside them. But this very act of initial appropriation changed the original relation of humans to nature. As new commodities and new means of producing them were invented (and as population grew), techniques of production and appropriation changed—and the original relation between nature to property rights ceased to exist. For Hodgskin, the right of property *protected by law* thus arose as an artificial

---

[26] Hodgskin maintained that even though conflicts might exist between the interests of capitalists and those of landowners, both classes were formed in an intimate union against the interests of labour.

[27] Tracing his lineage back to Smith in the familiar way of writers after Smith, he held that humankind had remained ignorant of these laws until Smith had first outlined those that determined the wealth of nations.

rather than a natural right. It could never be, and it never ought to be, protected by law *as if* it were a natural right (55). If nature determined all, including the present suffering arising from a present violation of its fundamental and original principles, as Hodgskin thought he had shown, then people could be excused for believing that nature was a better judge of how things should be—better, to be sure, than was either the existing law of property or existing social institutions (58). With such "natural rights" went political and economic justice:

> While each labourer claims his own reward, let him cheerfully allow the just claims of every other labourer; but let him never assent to the strange doctrine that the food he eats and the instruments he uses, which are the work of his own hands, become endowed, by merely changing proprietors, with productive power greater than his, and that the owner of them is entitled to a more abundant reward than the labour, skill, and knowledge which produce and use them. (1825, 90)

It is easy enough to see how Hodgskin concluded that the best way to secure social progress was to do "justice" by allowing "labour to possess and enjoy the whole of its produce" without the artificial constraints imposed by the (capitalist) state.

Not only was this conclusion at odds with the idea (attributed to Bentham) that government was *necessary* to both create and secure the rights of property, but it also differed, he claimed, from the understandings of Rousseau and Owen who had, like him, presented the problems of economic society as stemming from *any* individual right of property (and who favoured their abolition).

Not surprisingly perhaps, Hodgskin chose to draw on Locke to legitimate this way of thinking. It was Locke, he claimed, who had argued that nature had given to each individual their body and labour—and it was Locke who had shown that what an individual could obtain by their own labour "naturally" belonged to them. The motive to labour, the power to labour, and the product of labour all existed exclusive of legislation (1832, 27) so that antecedent to all legislation, nature bestowed on every individual what their labour produced, just as it gave them their body. While Hodgskin suggested that all this was perfectly in line with what Locke had had to say, however, he appears to have wanted to make an even stronger case: that nature had created not only a right of property but also a law of appropriation, when it bestowed on labour the right to the product of labour.

Since nature had provided humankind with motives to respect this property right, Hodgskin argued that it was part of the natural constitution of human beings to respect those property rights.[28] Of course, Hodgs-

---

[28] Hodgskin contended that a mutual sufferance or forbearance arises among people for each person's property, and this, rather than the law, is what protects the rights and enjoy-

kin warned his readers that this was not to say that there were any natural motives to respect the existing legal (or artificial) rights of property (32), nor were there were any moral grounds for supporting their continuance—what was natural was moral, and what was artificial was not. It is little wonder that James Mill saw him as an avatar of the end of civilisation as they knew it.

RECEPTION AND REACTION

It is perhaps one of those little ironies of life that Hodgskin, probably the most reviled of the anticapitalist writers of the years immediately following Ricardo's death, turned to a journalistic career with the *Economist* in 1848. Even more ironic still is the fact that he has become a favoured son of libertarians, who see his distinctly antigovernment turn of mind as akin to their own.[29] That Hodgskin could not possibly have had any of *their* central tenets in mind is reasonably clear, especially since it was the end of capitalist society as he knew it that required the eclipse of the state, rather than the preservation of its essence without more than a night watchman state to enforce property rights. A better description perhaps is given by Esther Lowenthal, who portrayed Hodgskin's as an "extreme statement of the individualist platform: self-interest, competition, laissez-faire, natural rights and natural law" (1911, 82).

---

ments of all. Hodgskin rejected those who distinguished sufferance and right; he claimed that laws themselves depend on sufferance. He argued that if we look into the greater part of our rights, they are not guaranteed by any law, "and have no other security but the mutual respect of man for man, or the moral feelings of individuals" (136). Hodgskin offered many examples: the mutual regard for rights between landlords and tenants illustrates that this respect occurred without the law (137); the mutual confidence between different tribes and trading nations involving new rights of property is not protected by law (because they exist across geographic and jurisdictional boundaries); and in domestic relations, where husbands, wives, and children do not need the law to guarantee their possessions from each other (142). As to what the law guarantees, Hodgskin was scathing: "It guarantees the rights of the land-owner as far as it can, it protects the possessions of the clergy, it gives the tax eater his bread, but that it protects or guarantees the possessions and enjoyments of the industrious classes, is only true if it be found prescribing our domestic duties and protecting all our individual possessions" (143). What is interesting about Hodgskin's discussion here is not just that he denies that the law can protect property but that he links the motive to produce and respect property back to the same moral principles.

[29] The Online Library of Liberty has even added *Popular Political Economy* and *The Natural and Artificial Right of Property* to its full-text service.

Chapter Twelve

INDIVIDUAL LIBERTY AND THE LIBERTY OF TRADE

The so-called doctrine of Free Trade . . . rests on
grounds different from, though equally solid with, the
principle of individual liberty asserted in this Essay. . . .
As the principle of individual liberty is not involved in
the doctrine of Free Trade, so neither is it in most of
the questions which arise respecting the limits of
that doctrine.
—John Stuart Mill, *On Liberty*

HAYEK ONCE DREW a sharp distinction between what he called a "false" rationalistic individualism, as exemplified (he claimed) by the English utilitarians and the French physiocrats, and a "true" antirationalistic individualism that he associated with Ferguson, Smith, Burke, and Tocqueville. To false individualism, Hayek attributed illiberal political tendencies, while to true individualism he attributed genuine political liberty. What is interesting about Hayek's dichotomy is that it located John Stuart Mill in both camps (1946, 11, 28) and accurately recognised the existence of a disjuncture in Mill's discussion of liberty. Of course, according to Hayek, Mill's opinions were to be understood as a confusing mixture of earlier contrasting traditions, so that they had the dual consequence of obscuring from view the true character of individualism (26) and giving individualism a bad name (11).

In another influential reading of Mill, Gertrude Himmelfarb highlighted the same disjuncture in Mill's argument. Like Hayek, Himmelfarb seems to have been interested in recovering from Mill what she took to be a more "temperate, humane, capacious liberalism" (1974, xxii) whose luminaries included Montesquieu, Burke, Tocqueville, and the founding fathers (337). The strategy she deployed to arrive at essentially the same conclusion as Hayek, however, was rather different. Himmelfarb held that Mill had never intended to extend "the one very simple principle" in *On Liberty* to all forms of social action, and she called attention instead to the other Mill whose thoughts on liberty were expressed in different works. This other Mill, she argued, placed significant weight on the positive functions of society, government, and the state in enforcing moral values (336). On Himmelfarb's reading, then, Mill's discussions were less a misleading mixture of opposing traditions than two quite separable claims about liberty between which contemporary liberals must choose.

While it is true that there are two arguments (at least) about liberty in Mill's work, it can be asserted that their sources and implications are different from those either Himmelfarb or Hayek would have us believe. They should be seen neither as a confusing mixture nor an inconsistency requiring us to choose between opposed and incompatible views.[1] Instead, Mill's arguments appear to originate, in part, in a distinction he drew within both his science of politics and science of political economy between what might usefully be called "matters of opinion" and "matters of fact," and the methods of analysis appropriate to each. This distinction runs deep in Mill's thinking. Once it is recognised, it becomes possible to understand and account for many of Mill's complex commitments to liberty.

This distinction helps to explain, for example, his praise of laissez-faire, on the one hand, and his sympathies with socialism, on the other. It clarifies why he valued free competition in the marketplace for ideas, but warned of the destructive effects of competition on character and culture in the marketplace for commodities. It reconciles his fear of the encroachments of a paternalist state with his advocacy of expansive government as an enabler of both economic and moral progress. In short, the key to understanding the complexities of Mill's contentions about liberty appears to turn on tracing the differing scope of his science of politics and political economy, respectively, and revealing the qualitatively different character of the argumentation and conclusions of each.[2]

INDIVIDUAL FREEDOM, THE FREEDOM OF TRADE, AND THE "FACTS" OF ECONOMIC LIFE

The grounds on which Mill felt that it was possible to draw so clear a distinction between the discussion of the two liberties are bound up with

---

[1] This view owes something to Alan Ryan, who proposed to take at face value Mill's self-conscious statement that the case for the two liberties—that is, nonintervention in political/moral and economic life, respectively—might rest on different principles (1970, 250–55). Our argument, however, follows a different analysis of the origins and role of the two liberties in Mill's thought. There is a vast secondary literature on Mill's discussion of liberty, and prominent within that literature have been disputes about how to interpret Mill's substantive positions on liberty in a kaleidoscope of differing political, moral, and economic frameworks. See, for example, Ashcraft (1998), Donner (1991), Hamburger (1965, 1999), Hollander (1985), Riley (1998a, 1998b), Skorupski (1989), and Thompson (1976). We are concerned only with the narrower question of how the conceptual context of Mill's political economy and his politics figured in his use of these two understandings of liberty.

[2] Our interest here is neither in evaluating varieties of liberalism, nor in determining whether it is better to treat ideas about economic liberty and individual liberty as being closely connected or disjointed. Instead, our intention is to consider how, and how effectively, Mill was able to develop his arguments about liberty, to reveal the lineages of thought

his particular conception of the relation between the sciences of politics and political economy as well as with his vision of the distinctive character of the science of political economy itself. While political economy and the science of politics were both moral sciences, they differed significantly in their reach. Political economy was to be conceived narrowly as a science that studied the acquisitive behaviour of wealth-seeking individuals. Mill described it as one concerned exclusively with a person "as a being who desires to possess wealth, and who is capable of judging of the comparative efficacy of means for obtaining that end" (1836, 137).

This should not be taken to imply that when Mill examined the determination of the relative prices of commodities (or the distribution of income between social classes) that emerged from such behaviour, he did so by taking as *given* people's preferences and then deriving the outcome of a constrained optimisation process along lines that were to become familiar to twentieth-century economists. Instead, what Mill appears to have done is better understood as a halfway house towards this position. On most occasions, especially in the theory of value and distribution, he was content to follow Ricardo (or at least his version of Ricardo)—an approach that involved the determination of the relative prices of commodities from the *given* technological conditions of production and a historically *given* real wage. There are instances, though, not least in his discussion of exceptions to laissez-faire, where that more modern approach does seem to have been deployed.

The importance of this point for an understanding of Mill's political economy should not be underestimated. It is one thing to see the market as being populated by rational, self-interested, acquisitive individual agents. It is quite another to develop a theory of value and distribution by translating that general characterisation of economic man into a formal model of constrained optimisation. Almost no political economist of any period would have been troubled by adopting the general characterisation. But it was not until the advent of the marginalist approach to the determination of relative prices that this general idea was reformulated so as to become the basis of a theory of value. So ingrained has this model become that it is sometimes difficult to see beyond it when one looks back to writers of the past. It is often the case that when the idea of self-interested behaviour is encountered in earlier works, an interpretation is cast in these terms—an interpretation thus framed in a conceptual and theoretical language that would not have been available to the thinker concerned.[3]

---

from which they might have derived, and to show how his arguments were altered by political economists not long after his death.

[3] This is simply to note what may be obvious. For example, while one might be able to claim that uncertainty is an all-pervasive aspect of economic life, this would not be the same

Furthermore, according to Mill, the predictions of political economy involved only those "phenomena of the social state as take place in consequence of the pursuit of wealth," or what amounts to the same thing, the economic behaviour of individuals in a *competitive market*. In this manner, Mill was able to claim that political economy abstracted from "every other human passion or motive; except those that may be regarded as perpetually antagonizing to the desire of wealth, namely aversion to labour and desire of the present enjoyment of costly indulgences" (1836, 137–38; see also 1872, 6.9.§3).

It was for this reason Mill maintained that "with respect to those parts of human conduct of which wealth is not even the principle object, . . . Political Economy does not pretend that its conclusions are applicable" (1836, 139). In so describing economic man, Mill was insistent on its status as an abstract construct—one that was instrumental to the analysis of market behaviour, but that nevertheless remained "an arbitrary definition of man" (144).[4] While necessary to the science of political economy, this model of man was far too attenuated to form the basis of a broader science of politics. For Mill, that science was concerned with the larger and "permanent interests of man as a progressive being" (1859, 16), rather than with man as a "trampling, crushing, elbowing" market participant (1871, 4.6.§2). In this way, the science of politics, which embraced "every part of man's nature, in so far as influencing the conduct or condition of man in society" became for Mill the "foundation of practical politics, or the art of government, of which the art of legislation is a part" (1836, 136).[5]

When making his argument for political liberty, then, there seems to be little doubt that Mill deployed a formal utilitarian approach in much the same way as his father had done in his essay on *Government*. Of course, the younger Mill's approach was more nuanced, avoiding interpersonal comparisons of utility, understanding how institutional contexts might impact on rational choices, and maintaining steadfastly that "pushpin was not as good as poetry." In the assertion for free trade, however, the positive case is made by drawing on what Mill called the "theory of international values" (later to become known as the theory of com-

---

as saying that either Aristotle or Mill, whenever they discussed problems of uncertainty, can be understood as precursors or adherents to, say, the von Neumann–Morgenstern approach to choice under uncertainty.

[4] As far as economic man was concerned, Mill believed that no "political economist was ever so absurd as to suppose that mankind are really thus constituted" (139). Whether Mill was quite accurate in his assessment of what other political economists might or might not have thought will not be considered here.

[5] Mill uses the terms science of politics, speculative politics, and social economy interchangeably (see 1836, 135, 136).

parative advantage). It was only in the negative case, where he considered exceptions to free trade, that a model resembling the one he used in *On Liberty* entered the picture—and even then not in all of those exceptional cases (*vide* the infant industry case). This is why, for Mill, the doctrine of free trade was "not involved in" and "rests on grounds different from" arguments pertaining to individual liberty drawn from his science of politics.

Mill's claim was that the laws of the market take on the character of the laws of the natural sciences (1872, 6.9.§3; see also 1836, 125). They are "abstract truths" (1836, 4:329), and "errors in political economy" are not in any simple sense "the rejection of any practical rules of policy which have been laid down by political economists" but rather demonstrate "ignorance of economic facts, and of the causes by which the economic phenomena of society as it is, are actually determined" (1879, 5:727). Just as the principle of gravitation deals with the facts of the physical world, for Mill the principles of political economy deal in the facts of the economic world. Politics, however, does not share this particular feature with political economy. The marketplace for political ideas is not governed by abstract laws or principles. It is governed by opinion—and the only principle operative in it, Mill holds, is that no opinion should remain unchallenged. In this latter science, where Mill considers man in his largest sense as a progressive being, the principles to be derived from politics are of a qualitatively different character from those drawn from political economy.[6]

Mill's own examples in this regard illustrate the distinction he had in mind. In *On Liberty*, while repeating the refrain that "restrictions on trade [are] restraints" and "all restraint, *qua* restraint, is an evil" (1859, 116), Mill was clear that legitimate limitations to economic liberty existed. For instance, regulations of product quality as well as those affecting health and safety at work were legitimate, because they "affect only that part of conduct which society is competent to restrain, and are wrong solely because *they do not really produce the results which it is desired to produce by them*" (116–17; emphasis added). Of course, Mill warned that it was necessary not to mistake questions putatively concerning economic liberty for ones that were instead "essentially questions of liberty [itself]" (1859, 117). He cited as examples of such confusion the Maine

---

[6] In his theory of political economy, then, Mill narrowed the science of society. Certainly, he did not invent the famous fiction of *homo economicus* or economic man, but in focusing on the competitive system that alone gives content to that fiction, his work provided the basis from which Jevons, Walras, Marshall, and others would put it to its now familiar use.

prohibition law, restrictions on the importation of opium, and laws restricting the sale of poisons.

In these cases, interference clearly had a moral rather than an economic purpose. The real subject of such restrictions was not the seller but the buyer. The action restricted was not purchasing but consuming alcohol, and hence became the restriction of a personal not a social action. Therefore, according to Mill, if such restrictions were thought to diminish economic liberty, it was not because they interfered with free trade but because they could not produce the results intended (e.g., temperance). Yet Mill also clearly believed that such restrictions raised larger moral questions of individual liberty of "how to make the fitting adjustment between individual independence and social control" (9–10).

Two criteria now came to legitimate government intervention in the economic sphere: its desirability as a matter of fact (the subject of the science of political economy) rather than opinion, and whether the results of such intervention could actually be achieved through government agency. These two criteria served to separate the arena of those individual and political liberties protected from intrusion on moral grounds in *On Liberty*, from that larger sphere of social and market life. In this latter sphere, however, Mill could also envisage—and actually proposed—state intervention on economic grounds, *even in matters of moral life.*

While it is true that almost everything Mill wrote in *On Liberty* demonstrates his desire to protect the individual from the accretion of state power, it is also true that the principal liberties at stake for Mill were limited to ones of personal belief, opinion, and the conceptually difficult category of purely self-regarding action (110). In the case of economic life and the inherently other-regarding actions of market exchange, Mill deployed a different kind of argument concerning the legitimacy of state action. The limits to government intervention in economic affairs were not established simply by an appeal to an ideological presupposition against it but also by consulting the facts (an appeal to the laws of political economy) and the efficacy of intervention. If consistent with the "facts" and efficacious, Mill maintained that even state intervention in the moral sphere could be justified.

For example, while it might at first glance seem surprising for the author of *On Liberty* to propose state regulation restricting early marriage and regulating family size, Mill had no hesitation in doing so:

> In a country either over-peopled, or threatened with being so, to produce children, beyond a very small number, with the effect of reducing the reward of labour by their competition, is a very serious offence against all who live by the remuneration of their labour. The laws which, in many countries on the Continent, forbid marriage unless the parties can show that they

have the means of supporting a family, do not exceed the legitimate powers of the State. (133)

Mill saw the procreative aspects of marriage as falling not only within the purview of other-regarding social action but also, decisively, within the domain of political economy. He called the production of children in excess of the means of supporting them a "mischievious act," injurious to others (132), and treated the activity as being one of a special kind—the subject of a science—and thus governed by Malthusian "scientific" principles. The basis of this view, Mill argued, was to be found in the "facts" about population growth revealed by Malthus in his abstract theory of population and wages. The Malthusian principle of population was therefore assumed by Mill to have the status of "fact," and convinced of the effectiveness of the remedy, Mill was not prepared to reject it on grounds of noninterference in the moral sphere of the family or the private sphere of sexual practice.[7] Indeed, restrictions on marriage or the denial of additional poor relief in support of children beyond a number supportable at subsistence were "not objectionable as violations of liberty" (1859, 133). State interference in the moral sphere could be legitimated on the grounds of fact and remedial effectiveness alone.

The converse argument was not employed. Economic interference was not legitimated on moral grounds—a feature apparent in Mill's controversial and evolving stance towards socialism.

It is often suggested that Mill's later political and economic thought was inspired by some variant of socialism. Frequently cited in such assertions are passages from Book 4 of the *Political Economy* in which Mill outlines a syndicalist-inspired, decentralized, and competitive socialist form of commodity production. In earlier writings, Mill had attacked socialism, in part on Malthusian grounds—as a removal of the demand to prudential restraint. Yet in a set of papers on socialism written in 1869 but only published posthumously, this reservation seems to be significantly modified without embracing it as the necessary solution to the Malthusian dilemma that utopians such as Godwin had proposed:

It is of course open to discussion what form of society has the greatest power of dealing successfully with the pressure of population on subsistence, and

---

[7] Critics of Mill have sometimes held this argument to be inconsistent with his position on freedom of action in sexual matters that would have left both prostitution and homosexuality as activities within the protected sphere of private "self-regarding" liberty (see, for example, the anonymous review of *On Liberty* in the 1859 *National Review*). Yet it is clear that Mill drew a distinction between extramarital sex (in which he encouraged young women in the use of prophylactics), and the production of children within the recognised family unit subject to the benefits and restrictions of the New Poor Law.

on this question, there is much to be said for Socialism; what was long
thought to be its weakest point, will, perhaps, prove to be one of its strongest.
But it has no just claim to be considered as the sole means of preventing the
general and growing degradation of the mass of mankind through the peculiar tendency of poverty to produce over-population. (1879, 729)

Both his *Autobiography* (1873) and these final chapters on socialism
shared the concerns implicit in the moral objections offered by socialist
reformers to the competitive market as it then existed: "the greed of rapid
gain substitutes itself for the modest desire to make a living"; "more and
more of the gambling spirit is introduced into commerce"; "the simplest
maxims of prudence disregarded"; and "all, even the most perilous, forms
of pecuniary improbity receive a terrible stimulus" (731). This unhealthy
"ramping up" of competition—particularly that between workers—that
formed a part of "the meaning of what is called the intensity of modern
competition" (731) could not be conceived as an analogue of the competition of ideas urged in *On Liberty*. Still, Mill was not prepared to reject
what he continued to believe were the beneficial aspects of competition
to the productive process. That is, he accepted that the "intellectual and
moral grounds of socialism deserve the most attentive study" (736), but
rejected the general outlines of the socialist critique on economic grounds,
as being "exaggerated" and based on "errors of political economy"
(727).[8] Mill recognised the moral objections of socialists, but was not
prepared to intervene in the economy on moral grounds alone. Rather, it
had to be shown that such an intervention could be based on a factual
science of political economy (and that it could indeed achieve the effects
proposed), and this Mill believed socialists could not demonstrate.

Utility in the Science of Politics and Political Economy

Another way to understand Mill's rationale for treating the two liberties
in so contrasting a fashion is to recognise that the utilitarian model of
man played a different role in each context. While this model clearly informed Mill's argument in *On Liberty*, its role in Mill's model of the

---

[8] Mill continues in a reiteration of an argument contained in the *Political Economy*
(1871, 476–77):

The present system is not, as many Socialists believe, hurrying us into a state of general
indigence and slavery from which only Socialism can save us. The evils and injustices
suffered under the present system are great, but they are not increasing; on the contrary,
the general tendency is towards their slow diminution. Moreover the inequalities in the
distribution of the produce between capital and labour, however they may shock the
feeling of natural justice, would not by their mere equalisation afford by any means so

market mechanism is negligible. Indeed, the only role it plays in the economic model is that of providing the underlying rationale for competition. This does not preclude the fact that one may understand Mill's economics as being utilitarian in the informal sense that the goal of economic policy was the maximisation of the wealth of the nation (and thus with what could be termed the greatest happiness). Nevertheless, this is distinct from the formal model of utilitarianism from which Mill derived the presumption in favour of individual liberty.

The formal logic of that model involves certain presuppositions about the character and behaviour of individual agents. They must have well-defined interests and act rationally, in any given environment and within any given set of constraints, to secure the greatest individual utility possible from their choices. Since the premise of the model is that the aim of individual action is the greatest degree of utility possible, two conditions need to be satisfied: it must be the case that the utility associated with any given action *ex ante* will be realised *ex post*, and that an individual's *ex ante* ranking of the degrees of utility associated with different actions is arrived at under the assumption that information is fully available to all agents. In Mill's language, the first requirement was that of "security"; the second was that of "knowledge." It was the necessary function of government to ensure that the society is one in which both requirements are met. It is in the application of these premises of the principle of utility that many of the most characteristic features of Mill's case for individual liberty emerge.

The argument that if utility was the ultimate end of human action, then liberty was the appropriate means through which it was to be secured, logically entailed a general presumption that individual liberty should be the rule, and interference with it justified only "so long as we do not attempt to deprive others of theirs, or impede their effort to obtain it (1859, 18). This formal property of the theory, which allowed such exceptions to the rule, created for Mill a significant area for government activity. Security of person and property became a paramount responsibility of the state since "insecurity of person and property, is as much to say, uncertainty of the connexion between all human exertion or sacrifice, and the attainment of the ends for which they are undergone" (1871, 5.8:1).

The fact that it is necessary for individuals to know in what degree utility is embodied in actions, led Mill to admit further areas for the legitimate state restriction of individual liberty. To begin with, the doctrine of individual liberty when grounded in utilitarian theory "is meant to apply

---

large a fund for raising the lower levels of remuneration as Socialists, and many besides Socialists, are apt to suppose. (1879, 736)

only to human beings in the maturity of their faculties" so that "those who are still in a state to require being taken care of by others, must be protected against their own actions as well as against external injury" (1859, 15). This category included children (101), those without "the ordinary amount of understanding" (93), and "barbarians" (16). In such cases, incomplete knowledge of the consequences of actions mandated another potentially extensive arena of state intervention. For example, it became for Mill almost a "self-evident axiom, that the State should require and compel the education, up to a certain standard, of every human being who is born its citizen" (129).[9]

In addition to these activities, there exists another class of measures designed to ensure the availability of suitable *means* through which to achieve the maximisation of utility. While this is a class of cases somewhat different from those earlier considered (which derived more from a consideration of *ends* than means), certain measures allowed under the first heading would also be of service in this domain—most obviously security of person and property. The real target of Mill's discussion, however, was the necessary function of the government in eliminating what he called "bad social institutions" (116), which impeded individuals in the pursuit of their own interests.[10]

Having admitted these qualifications to an absolute doctrine of liberty, Mill then necessarily and immediately entered into one of the more perilous regions of utilitarian theory. In such cases, where inevitably one agent may gain and another agent may lose, the question arises as to how the principle of utility is to be applied: "As soon as any part of a person's conduct affects prejudicially the interests of others, society has jurisdiction over it, and the question of whether the general welfare will or will not be promoted by interfering with it, becomes open to discussion" (1859, 92–93). Put in more modern terminology, the question concerns interpersonal comparisons of utility, this time raised in the specific context of Mill's utilitarianism.

Reverting for a moment to Benthamite utilitarianism, the answer to this question appears to have been genuinely unambiguous. Interpersonal comparisons were permissible for Bentham, since the principle of utility as a criterion for judging the merits of state intervention was interpreted

---

[9] Of course, the same logic could be seen to mandate the institutionalization of lunatics and despotic regulation of "backward societies." Yet it is worth remembering that Mill firmly stated he was "not aware that any community has a right to force another to be civilized" (113).

[10] While the problem of monopoly is probably the one Mill had most in mind in this context, in other contexts, such "problem institutions" were thought to include the established church, marriage without the possibility of divorce, and indentured servitude (1871, 5.11:11; 1869, 285, 293, 298).

as referring to the sum total of utilities of individuals in a given society. Thus, or so Bentham claimed, intervention "may be said conformable to . . . the principle of utility when . . . the tendency which it has to augment the happiness of the community is greater than any which it has to diminish it" (1789, 1.7). It is worth noticing that Bentham had been led into this particular formulation of the principle of utility by a rather crude and direct analogy between the well-being of an individual and that of the community. Bentham simply applied the core utilitarian proposition— that an individual could be said to be better off if and only if the sum total of that individual's utility increased consequent on some action—to social utility as a whole (see, for example, 1.2–4). It was in consequence of making this hypothesis that Benthamite utilitarianism was led into some of its more celebrated difficulties over the provision of a cardinal index of utility. But the notion of measurable utility, though essential to it, does not appear to be primary in explaining the source of the Benthamite formulation of utilitarianism.

In Mill's case, the question of the role of interpersonal comparisons is not quite so easily resolved. In this area, though, there is a certain sense in which Mill's arguments represent a considerable advance over those of Bentham. If we consider in isolation Mill's discussion of the harm principle, say, there appears to be evidence to support the contention that Mill neither used nor sanctioned interpersonal comparisons of utility.[11]

In contrast to the systematic application of utilitarian theory to the discussion of individual liberty was the line of argument followed by Mill in the discussion of market exchange. There, utilitarian theory fell into the background and an essentially different model of the market took centre stage.[12] In this model, value, distribution, and accumulation were not determined by utilitarian calculation but rather by the requirement that given available technology, commodities that are inputs into the production process were returned to those branches of industry so as to ensure their continued reproduction. That is, natural prices were determined by what Smith, Ricardo, and Mill thought of as the "difficulty and facility" of their production, rather than by the relationship between their utility and scarcity.[13] According to that account of the economic machine, interferences with economic liberty were not to be determined by appeal to utilitarian theory but instead were to be based on whether the economic

[11] This aspect of the utilitarian model was later reformulated by Pareto to unambiguously exclude interpersonal comparisons.

[12] That is, while every individual in market exchange might well be a utilitarian calculator, the outcomes produced by their interaction (namely, relative prices and the distribution of income) are not explained in terms of those individual actions.

[13] See, however, Samuel Hollander (1985), who takes the opposite view.

model confirms or rejects the hypothesis that the effects of any interference are indeed the ones intended. On this line of argument, Mill was led inevitably to acknowledge not only that "the admitted functions of government embrace a much wider field than can easily be included within the ring-fence of any restrictive definition" but also that "it is hardly possible to find any ground of justification common to them all ... nor to limit the interference of government by any universal rule" (1871, 5.1.3).

Mill's economic theory contains, then, several familiar features of the classical mode of thought: the idea of a conventionally determined subsistence wage, the separability between the study of value and distribution, and the dependence of accumulation on the distribution of income between classes.[14] Although lacking the logical accuracy and precision of Ricardo, the absence of homogeneity between the elements of cost in this model (Mill 1945) still meant that for Mill (just as it had been for Ricardo), the natural prices of commodities (in contrast to their market prices) were not determined by the mutual interaction of supply and demand. That is, they were not determined by reference to the subjective conditions of their consumption but rather by reference to the objective conditions of their reproduction.[15] For this reason, natural prices could not possess the property of ensuring an "optimal outcome" in any significant sense of that phrase. The absence of demand—that is, the absence of the idea that in the long run, prices are determined solely by reference to the actions of individual utility and profit-maximising agents—signals the lack of a formal utilitarian model of action at the core of Mill's theory.

Thus, for example, on the question of the governmental regulation of wages, Mill did not defer to considerations of individual liberty in order to oppose restraint. Instead, his argument was a simple and straightforward application of his particular version of classical wage theory. Claiming that the "rate of wages which results from competition distributes the whole existing wages-fund among the whole labouring population," Mill maintained that even if the government succeeded in "fixing wages above this rate," some labourers would be unable to find employment. Therefore, he concluded that that it was "nothing to fix a minimum of wages, unless there be a provision that work, or wages at least, be found for all who apply for it" (1871, 2.12.1).[16]

[14] We set aside here the question of the status of Mill's economic theory in the history of economic thought (on this point, see Hollander 1985).

[15] Of this property of the Ricardian theory of value, Mill declared that "there [was] nothing in the laws of Value which [remained] for the present or any future writer to clear up"; indeed, that the "theory of the subject" as Ricardo had it left, was "complete" (1871, 3.1.1).

[16] It should be mentioned that this passage was written after Mill's reconsideration (sometimes said to be a recantation) of an earlier statement of the wages-fund theory in his review of Thorton's On Labour in 1869.

Similarly, in almost all of the other areas of his political economy in which Mill was led into extensive analysis of the merits of economic liberty (or legitimate departures from it), he utilised arguments derived exclusively from his science of political economy. This helps to explain why the framework of concepts informing his discussion of individual liberty is nowhere to be found in his discussions of government loan expenditure, combinations among workers, direct government support to private industry, the provision of public goods, and the national debt.

THE TWO LIBERTIES IN CLASSICAL POLITICAL ECONOMY

The obvious place to begin tracing the lineage of John Stuart Mill's arguments is with his utilitarian forebears, Bentham and James Mill. After all, despite Mill's famous second thoughts about Bentham's formulation of utilitarianism (Mill 1838), he retained throughout his life a commitment to utility as "the ultimate appeal on all ethical questions" (1859, 16; see also 1861b, 254). Moreover, despite his youthful rejection of his father's philosophy, he never denied his parent's intellectual influence (1873, 143). To the extent that a version of the utilitarian argument permeates almost every sentence that James Mill or Bentham wrote on questions of political liberty, there can be little doubt that the younger Mill was indebted to them not only for the basic logic of the argument of *On Liberty* but also for the axiomatic assumption—the ability of people to judge correctly their own interest and to act on it—which underpinned the claim. Indeed, Mill's own argument on this subject may be regarded as a sophisticated restatement of Bentham's famous dictum that "each counts for one."

At the level of individual liberty, then, while Mill's contribution undoubtedly represents a significant advance on that of his father (not least in his distinction between the higher and lower pleasures) and Bentham, there is equally little doubt that it is linearly descendant from them. As to whether the younger Mill was likewise following his immediate predecessors in distinguishing the discussion of individual liberty from that concerning the liberty of trade, everything hinges on the character of the assertions offered for freedom of trade by the elder Mill and Bentham.

In the case of James Mill, the argument for the liberty of trade was relatively straightforward. It depended on whether intervention or freedom of trade secured the most profitable employment of capital. As he maintained in the *Elements of Political Economy*, "If it should appear, that production and exchange fall into the most profitable channels, when they are left free to themselves; it will necessarily follow that, as often as they are diverted from those channels, by external interpositions of any sort, so often the industry of the country is made to employ itself less advantageously" (1826a, 197). Like the contention of the younger Mill, this argument does not recur to the formal utilitarian one for individual liberty but rather relies on a model of the operation of the market mechanism, which makes intervention contingent.[17]

In contrast, in his *Manual of Political Economy*, Bentham quite expressly employed the utilitarian argument of "appropriate knowledge" in order to cast doubt on the state's capacity ever to "employ the power of government" in directing economic activity (1793–95, 1:231). In doing this, he drew on the essentially utilitarian position that such intervention was uncalled for because each economic agent was the best custodian of his own material interests. It would appear that unlike the Mills, Bentham did not distinguish between the character of the argument to be made for individual liberty and the liberty of trade. This contrast with the younger Mill is not particularly surprising since Bentham's view of the nature of humans presumed a universally acquisitive model equally as applicable to questions of political liberty as it was to economic liberty.

If the foregoing argument accurately captures the contribution of early utilitarian thinking to the position that John Stuart Mill subsequently came to adopt, the extent to which there may also have been a Smithian element in that claim is worth examining. After all, it is in Smith that one finds the first statement of the classical economists' argument for liberty of trade. There is, of course, no doubt that Smith anticipates Mill's belief that "all restraint, *qua* restraint, is an evil." Yet in much the same way as Mill, Smith did not allow this belief to take the form of an unqualified principle on which to determine his position on questions of the liberty of trade. On that subject, Smith turned to his economic model. Thus, for example, when considering the merits of any given interference with the liberty of trade (whether it be bounties, drawbacks, excise duties, or the granting of exclusive privileges), Smith recognised the stimulus that such restrictions would give to particular sectors of the economy, but opposed them on the grounds that it did not "increase the general industry of society, or . . . give it the most advantageous direction" (1776, 4.2:453).[18]

---

[17] It should be noted, however, that when writing about the physiocratic argument for free trade, Mill ascribed to them a version of the claim for the liberty of trade that applied the formal utilitarian model in a manner suggesting his agreement with it (1818a, 713–14). This ascription must be weighed against Mill's own presentation of the free trade argument in his *Elements*.

[18] The logic of Smith's economic argument is relatively straightforward. He investigated the effect of any given restriction on the pattern of relative prices and the extent to which these prices deviated from their natural level as a result of the interference. Where such deviations occurred, the return to capital invested in different lines of production would differ, resulting in an intersectoral flow of investment. The restraint was judged "undesirable" to the extent that such flows failed to reestablish long-period natural prices (and the general rate of profit).

Despite the fact that Smith and Mill shared the logic of the case for liberty of trade, Smith was patently less willing to permit state intervention into economic affairs to anything like the extent that Mill would later propose. This difference might be traced to the degree to which the so-called doctrine of unintended consequences coloured all of Smith's discussions of social action. This doctrine, together with a nearly required optimism that such consequences would be uniformly good, profoundly circumscribed for Smith the admissible range of state activity to just three "plain and intelligible" duties: defence, justice, and public works (1776, 4.9:687–88).

Yet in having had the advantage of witnessing some of the unintended consequences of capitalist development (many of which Smith himself could not have imagined), Mill was perhaps understandably more amenable to the possibility that direct and intentional collective action for the improvement of the economic condition of the individual was consonant with his model of economic liberty.

This is not to say that there were no strands at all in Smith's contentions that could be linked to the positions subsequently developed by John Stuart Mill. The moment one considers Smith's *Moral Sentiments*, a precursor can be found to many of Mill's more characteristic arguments concerning the moral value of self-regarding action that distinguished him from Benthamite utilitarianism (see Semmel 1984, 48–49). The *Moral Sentiments* consisted essentially of a sustained attempt to demonstrate the ethical character of self-interested action. Indeed, there is a sense in which Smith's task was even more wide-ranging than this way of putting it might suggest. He actually contrived to show that *all* ethically praiseworthy qualities of character—propriety, virtue, honour, duty, prudence, valour, and the like—had their basis in self-interest. Mill was to repeat the performance more than a century later in *Utilitarianism*.

By resting his model of human nature on the idea that individuals have a capacity for sympathy, an ability to see themselves as others do, and judge their actions in accordance with the approbation or disapprobation of an impartial spectator, Smith transmitted a potentially powerful political as well as economic message. Thus, when Smith introduced the metaphor of the invisible hand in the *Moral Sentiments*, its effect was not so much to assert that the socially constructed self of that book acts ethically as it was to indicate that the uncoordinated actions of autonomous individuals "tend to promote the public welfare" (1759, 5.2.10). Leaving aside the question of whether Smith himself chose to do so, this identification of virtue and self-interest in the hands of others proved sufficient to sustain an argument for liberty in any context.

An argument for economic liberty derived exclusively from the principles of political economy finds, of course, its archetypal expression in the work of Ricardo. Ricardo's insistence that restrictions on the free importation and exportation of corn were detrimental to the national interest rested entirely on his focus on the net product, and its distribution between profits and rent. He held that any increase in the price of corn caused by the restriction of free trade would have the effect of driving agricultural production to marginal land, raising rents at the expense of profits, and therefore retarding economic growth. Mill's position on the necessity of freedom of international trade, while an advance on Ricardo's position in some aspects, is essentially the same. Indeed, Mill suggested at one point in the *Principles* that his own position was directly derivative of that of Ricardo (1871, 3.17.2).

Hence, it becomes apparent that while classical economists focused almost exclusively on the development of the economic theory in the *Wealth of Nations* and its application to practical affairs, utilitarian social and political thought developed along different but parallel lines. On this broader front, arguments for expanding individual liberty were being carried forward under the banner of utilitarian theory, and its prophet was Bentham rather than Smith. Despite the fact that the two liberties came into consideration in each context, the character and formal content of the utilitarian argument for individual liberty was quite unlike anything being deployed by the classical economists for free trade.

The distinctive feature of the dual development which took place in this period is that it culminated in different conclusions concerning the conditions for state intervention in economic life as opposed to individual moral life. If one begins with utilitarian theory, a general presumption against state intervention could be readily derived, as we have seen, that the model of individual liberty was the means through which to secure the "greatest good." The argument of the classical economists for liberty of trade, however, involved no such general presumption. They proceeded by considering individual cases and judging the merits of intervention or nonintervention in each case according to whether they advanced or retarded the wealth of the nation—a judgment that depended on the model of the market mechanism rather than the formal application of the utilitarian theory of constrained maximisation. In some cases they did and in some cases they did not, but no general rule can be derived from an assertion of this kind.[19] Of course, it is true that on some of the most

---

[19] This is not to say that the classical economists failed to share certain sentiments concerning the proper limits to state action. Indeed, they all subscribed to a broad consensus that held that state intervention was in some general sense an unnecessary interference with the freedom of individuals to pursue their own interests. Such views were in fact common to the whole school of classical economists and not just to those who were members of its British branch. Jean-Charles-Léonard Simonde de Sismondi, for example, who drew from his economic theory nothing resembling the general presumption in favour of laissez-faire,

controversial questions of the day, they favoured laissez-faire—a preference from which their reputation as free traders largely derives. Yet their positions even on such important practical questions do not generate a general presumption in favour of laissez-faire, and certainly not one based on the priority of individual liberty.[20]

Without wishing to cast this dual development in an excessively rigid mould, since innumerable crosscurrents acted to complicate the picture, what seems to have transpired was that the two strands of thought developed in the late eighteenth century by Smith and Bentham, were carried forward into the first decades of the nineteenth century by two closely associated, but nevertheless distinct schools of thought whose membership in some cases overlapped. One consisted of the classical economists, and the other of utilitarians or philosophic radicals. A failure to recognise this dual development appears to have obscured the clear line of demarcation between the classical economists' case for the liberty of trade and the utilitarian argument for individual liberty. Leslie Stephen's claim that "utilitarian theory was embodied in [classical] political economy" might be considered one example of the failure to appreciate this distinction (1900, 2:138).

The Conjunction of Individual Liberty and Laissez-Faire

Up to this point, we have considered the separation made by Mill between the two liberties, the ways in which Mill's mode of reasoning concerning these liberties reflected the differences between the moral sciences of politics and political economy, and the extent to which his reasoning was prefigured in the literature of classical political economy. To complete an understanding of Mill's treatment of the two liberties, however, it is necessary to consider a significant instance in Mill's account of economic liberty where this separation was not maintained. A recognition of this fact serves to illuminate the subsequent development in political economy whereby Mill's distinction between the two liberties was collapsed. This instance arises in that part of the fifth book of his *Political Economy* where Mill addressed in the most general sense the question of the role

---

had argued in the quite general context of civil policy that the duty of the state was to ensure for each of its citizens "the benefits of liberty, virtue and knowledge" (1814, 39).

[20] There can be little doubt that it is in the social and political ideas of the utilitarians, and not in the economic theory of the classical school, that one first encounters an argument capable of providing the basis for a general presumption in favour of laissez-faire. Not only is the work of the self-styled philosophical radicals exemplary of that contention but it was also the aspect of the early development of the doctrine of laissez-faire that played a decisive role in its subsequent movement in economics circles.

of the state in economic affairs, and where the argument appears utilitarian in character.

Mill began with an attempt to enumerate the "general functions of government" in a customarily utilitarian fashion. He claimed that such an investigation aimed to determine how far and into "what departments of human affairs" the state should extend its authority under the supposition "that individuals are the proper guardians of their own interests" (1871, 5.1.1–2). The same problematic, "the nature and limits of the power which can be legitimately exercised by society over the individual," would later become the starting point of On Liberty. The formal basis of Mill's analysis of the scope for governmental intervention in Book 5 of the Political Economy derives from an application of the same utilitarian theory of action that he uses in On Liberty.[21] It is in the application of this principle of utility that one finds the singular instance in which there is a conjunction of the two liberties.

Just as in On Liberty, in Book 5 of the Political Economy, the protection of person and property was a necessary function of the state. This function arose, however, not simply because such security underlies the contractual order of society but also because of the formal requirement of utilitarian theory that there be an unambiguous link between utility foregone and the attainment of the ends for which it was foregone (1871, 5.8.1). This distinction in On Liberty hinged on the relationship between the anticipated and realised utility. It was in this context that Mill was led into that lengthy discussion of combination, free association, and voluntary contract that occupies two full chapters of the Political Economy, and where he drew a sharp distinction between the "authoritative" interference of government and government "agency" (5.11.1). This is the hallmark of utilitarian theory proper. By restructuring incentives rather than restricting the freedom of individual action, Mill's preference here for agency is clearly of wider import to the question of liberty than anything that could be derived from purely economic arguments.[22]

Furthermore, in this context, one finds Mill basing the extent of economic liberty (the doctrine of laissez-faire) on utilitarian considerations concerning appropriate knowledge: laissez-faire could "never be applicable to any persons but those who are capable of acting in their own be-

---

[21] Although On Liberty appeared in 1859 (the first edition of the Principles having appeared in 1848), John M. Robson suggests that "from the end of 1854 on, manuscripts were either written or drafted containing material later published as On Liberty" (1968, 56–57).

[22] In this section of the Political Economy, Mill's determination to secure "some space in human existence . . . sacred from authoritative intrusion" (1871, 5.11.2) reappeared without alteration in On Liberty.

half," so that where "the individual may be an infant, or a lunatic, or fallen into imbecility," it would be necessary for the state to "look after the interests of such persons" (1871, 5.1.2; see also 5.11.9). Similarly, education as a means of providing information about the consequences of actions in terms of utility was "one of those things which it is admissible that a government should provide" (5.11.8). Here, the education of consumers so that they may correctly judge "the goodness of the commodity" was also a required characteristic of the economy (5.11.9).

Finally, Mill introduced a class of exceptions to laissez-faire designed to ensure the availability of *means* through which to achieve the maximisation of utility, which paralleled the arguments of *On Liberty*. Competitive markets were adduced on these grounds to be essential to economic well-being, leading Mill to advocate the elimination of monopoly, the regulation of externalities, and the provision of public goods. Having admitted an exception to the maxim of laissez-faire in the case of external effects, Mill also entered into an analysis of the question of interpersonal comparisons of utility in *Political Economy* in a way analogous to his discussion of the harm principle.

These arguments seem to stand as the exceptions to Mill's general practice of separating the discussions of individual liberty and the liberty of trade, and his explicit assertions for doing so as expressed in *On Liberty*. Such arguments, indicative of the possibilities of collapsing that separation by the application of the utilitarian model of rational choice to economic theory, were to become the rule, however, for others. The elimination of this separation in the name of a "reductionist" conception of individual liberty more familiar in certain branches of contemporary economic theory took root almost immediately after Mill's death in the work of the neoclassical economists.

Jevons's *Theory of Political Economy*, which appeared in 1871, exemplified this next generation of neoclassical economists, and contained a withering attack on Mill's political economy. Jevons declared the whole trend of classical economic thinking after Ricardo to have developed along the wrong tracks, and for Jevons, Mill's economic theory stood as representative of the errors of the classical school. What is significant for the present discussion about this intervention is that it rejected the very part of Mill's claim on which his separation of the two liberties largely rested.

In establishing what he took to be the "true system of economics," Jevons simply borrowed the utilitarian model of humans and utilised it as the exclusive basis of a new theory of the market mechanism. By establishing homogeneity between the elements of cost (interpreted as disutility), Jevons was able to show that the relative prices of commodities were determined by their final degree of utility. In a way open neither to Mill nor the classical school, this equilibrium condition would soon be shown by other neoclassical economists to involve the proposition that the market mechanism produced an efficient or optimal allocation of resources. Jevons declared his theory to be "entirely based on a calculus of pleasure and pain," which he described as "the mechanics of utility and self-interest" (23, 21). Thus Jevons rejected classical economic theory, but wholeheartedly embraced the utilitarian theory of humans, and applied that mode as the basis of a new economic theory.[23]

According to neoclassical economics, free exchange became the means through which to secure the most efficient allocation of social resources. The immediate implication of this revolution for the theory of state intervention was that this new economic theory now provided a general presumption (indeed a scientific basis) for the "doctrine" of laissez-faire. The conception of the role of the state in economic affairs, on this presumption, is identical to the conception of its role in questions of individual liberty. That is, interference or noninterference in either context is dependent on the extent to which it infringes on the ability of individuals to pursue their own interests in their own way.

Of course, this does not mean that neoclassical economics completely closed the space for government intervention. For exactly the same reasons as such intervention was admitted by Mill in his discussion of individual liberty, intervention would be required in the case of this vision of economic liberty. Strategically, Jevons's innovation amounted to little more than a reproduction of the manner in which Mill discussed the liberty of trade in the single instance in which he conjoined it with the case for individual liberty.

Concluding Remarks

A general presumption that would seem to follow from the separability of the two liberties is that Mill's separation of the two liberties meant for him, that economic intervention might be justified without reference to individual liberty. This theme (although submerged by early neoclassical writers such as Jevons) returned to prominence in those varieties of liberalism associated with Keynesian and New Deal interventionist strategies that sprang up in the interwar years in the United States and Britain. The logic of an argument within which a strong separability between the two liberties is central implies that the domain of individual liberty would not

---

[23] On the continent, the marginal revolution was simultaneously carried forward by Menger and Walras. Their strategy was exactly the same as Jevons: reject Mill's economic theory and embrace the formal model of utilitarianism.

be compromised by a much enlarged role for government in the coordination and control of economic activity. Of course, others were to suggest exactly the opposite. The influential criticisms formulated by Schumpeter and Hayek suggested that this kind of interventionism was effectively no different from collectivist economic planning, and that as such, it constituted the greatest threat to liberty. The doubts these two writers cast on any form of intervention in the name of individual liberty (doubts that have proven to be so influential) obscured from view the existence of an alternative liberal agenda—namely, that state action in the economy neither necessarily nor automatically threatened individual freedom.

Chapter Thirteen

TWO CRITIQUES OF CLASSICAL POLITICAL ECONOMY

When at length a true system of economics comes to be
established, it will be seen that the able but wrongheaded man, David Ricardo, shunted the car of economic science on to a wrong line.
—William Stanley Jevons, *Theory of Political Economy*

[Smith] sometimes confuses . . . the determination of
the value of commodities by the quantity of labour
required for their production with . . . the quantity of
commodities with which a definite quantity of living
labour can be bought. . . . This contradiction in Adam
Smith and his passing from one kind of explanation to
another is based upon something deeper, which
Ricardo, in exposing this contradiction, overlooked
or did not rightly appreciate, and therefore also did
not solve.
—Karl Marx, *Theories of Surplus Value*

Why should we persist in using everyday language to
explain things in the most cumbrous and incorrect way,
as Ricardo has often done and as John Stuart Mill does
repeatedly in his *Principles of Political Economy*, when
these things can be stated far more succinctly, precisely
and clearly in the language of mathematics.
—Léon Walras, *Elements of Pure Economics*

THE CONDITION in which Mill had left politics and political economy in
the middle of the nineteenth century was somewhat unsatisfactory. But
this state of affairs did not owe its existence to the fact that Mill had
admitted exceptions (often numerous) to almost every principle of his
political economy—not least to the general presumption in favour of
laissez-faire. It instead arose from the unequal weight that Mill had given
to political as opposed to economic considerations in supporting it. As far
as laissez-faire had a theoretical foundation at all in Mill, it was located in
a quite sophisticated application of utilitarian political theory. Looking

back at Mill, it is not hard to imagine how his critics could have formed the view that economic analysis proper seemed to have had nothing *systematic* to contribute to the task of providing an answer to the question of the appropriate limits to state intervention.

In this context, the outstanding contribution of the recasting of the mainstream of political economy undertaken in the closing decades of the nineteenth century was that it provided, for the first time, an account of the workings of market exchange under conditions of perfect competition that was capable of sustaining a general presumption in favour of laissez-faire. The question of just how this reconciliation between the conclusions of utilitarian political theory and those of economic theory was effected is a simple one to answer: the calculus of pleasure and pain was systematically applied to an analysis of market exchange and a full-fledged utilitarian economic theory was the result. The differences between the political and economic case for laissez-faire that had existed previously were eliminated at a stroke.

Two critiques of classical political economy appeared in the second half of the nineteenth century, however. The implications of these critiques for the subsequent development of politics and political economy could not have been more different or profound; they had the effect of directing economic thought and its substantive implications for politics onto entirely new paths. One was the critique of classical political economy embarked on by the early marginalist writers Menger, Jevons, and Walras in the 1870s. The other was the contribution to the critique of classical political economy launched by Marx in the late 1850s and early 1860s.

In the case of Menger, Jevons, and Walras, they and others who followed them were to engineer a new conceptual understanding of the operation of the market mechanism and its implications for the efficacy of political action as well as individual welfare and freedom that within a generation of the first appearance of their critiques, had become the conventional wisdom of the discipline of economics—and it has remained so ever since. In the case of Marx, he and those who followed him generated a repository of ideas and arguments concerning the alienating and exploitative character of capitalism, and the limited efficacy of social and political reform, that inspired revolutionaries and radical critics alike.

THE BASIS OF THE CRITIQUES

Despite the ideological divide that separated Marx from the early marginalists, and each from that version of classical political economy presented by John Stuart Mill, the basis of their critiques of the classical tendency does not seem easily to be resolved into one of a difference in political persuasion or programme. Instead, the basis of their critiques—or better, the basis they explicitly set out in their original publications—concerned a charge of logical inadequacy directed towards the classical solution to the problem of price determination.

Jevons put it succinctly. A new approach to political economy was called for because, it was maintained, Ricardo's theory of value contained a formal or analytical error.[1] According to Jevons, the simple equation "produce = profit + wages" of the classical writers was "radically fallacious" because it involved *the attempt to determine two unknown quantities from one equation*" (1871, 256). Writing in 1874, independently and almost simultaneously, Walras made the same point in a slightly different but somewhat clearer way.[2]

Walras proceeded much as Jevons had done, by writing down an equation explicitly relating price (P) to wages (S), profits (I) and rent (F)—his version of the so-called adding-up theory of value: $P = S + I + F$. This, he argued, represented the "English Theory," and he repeatedly cited John Stuart Mill as its leading exponent. Walras then recognised two things concerning the classical development of this equation about which Jevons had been less explicit. First, that the English Theory then constructed "a theory of rent according to which rent is not included in the expenses of production" (1874, 425).[3] Second, that they took the real wage (S) as

---

[1] Although we wish to make no claim that this is the single or only cause of the marginal revolution, it is perhaps worth noting that the existence of doubt as to the formal (logical) adequacy of an existing theory is a necessary precondition set out by Thomas Kuhn for the emergence of a new "normal science" (see, for example, 1970, 62, 75, 92).

[2] There are other avenues or traditions of thought through which Jevons or Walras might have arrived at their own personal positions with respect to Ricardo or Mill. On that subject, one might usefully consult Meek (1956, 247) and Keynes (1933, 110–11, 117). Our focus here is on their published efforts explicitly to renounce and set aside several of the presuppositions of both Mill's and Ricardo's individual contributions to classical political economy.

[3] In Smith's adding-up theory of value, rent was a separate component part of price. But, according to Ricardo, this formulation was incorrect since "price is everywhere regulated by the return obtained by this last portion of capital, for which no rent whatever is paid" (1821, 329; also 77–78). It was from this proposition that Ricardo's famous position that high rent is not a *cause*, but rather an *effect*, of a high price of corn was reached—explaining why landlords might be interested in preserving the Corn Laws. For Ricardo, rent was a kind of transfer payment from capitalists to landlords, made possible by the existence in production of a scarce resource (fixed in supply). Rent derived from the 'diminished return' to capital last invested on the land: "It is only, then, because land is not unlimited in quantity and uniform in quality, and because in the progress of population, land of an inferior quality, or less advantageously situated, is called into cultivation, that rent is ever paid for the use of it" (1821, 70). It was this conception that allowed Ricardo to get rid of rent: "By getting rid of rent [. . .] the distribution between the capitalist and the labourer becomes a

given. The equation then becomes $P = S + I$, and "one equation cannot be used to determine two unknowns" (425).

To appreciate the similarity of each of these positions, it is only necessary to deploy some uniform notation. Let p = price, q = level of output, l = quantity of labour required, k = quantity of capital, w = real wage rate, and r = rate of profit. If the available techniques of production are known (that is, k, l, and q are all given), then Jevons suggested that the classical approach required $q = wl + (1 + r)k$ (that is, one equation to determine the two unknowns, w and r), whereas Walras presented the requirement as $pq = wl + (1 + r)k$ (that is, one equation to determine the two unknowns, p and r). The only difference seems to be that Walras worked with the *value* of the product (while Jevons worked with its *quantity*), and that he recognised (unlike Jevons) that the classical writers also took w as given.

According to the early marginalists, then, the perceived problem involved in the classical argument was that given the available techniques of production and the real wage rate, it was necessary to know the rate of profit in order to determine the value of the product, but to determine the rate of profit it was necessary to know the value of the product. Marx made the same analytical criticism of the classical writers' approach to the determination of prices. Although the language of Marx (and his method of proceeding) was very different from anything to be found in Jevons or Walras, the analytical problem identified by Marx was much the same.

Marx observed that Ricardo began "with the determination of the magnitude of value of the commodity" as the quantity of labour required (directly and indirectly) for its production, and that he then examined "whether the other economic relations and categories contradict this determination . . . or to what extent they modify it" (1963, 2:164). The whole of Marx's formal criticism of classical political economy can be summed up by saying that he recognised the existence of a systematic *difference* between labour values and the prices of commodities whenever there was a positive rate of profit rather than, as Ricardo had thought, that there might simply be exceptions to this rule when the distribution between wages and profits *changed*. Marx's argument is perhaps stated most clearly in his *Theories of Surplus Value*:

[Ricardo] asks himself what effect the rise or fall of wages will have on the respective profits on capitals with different periods of turnover and con-

---

much more simple consideration" (1951–73, 8:194). Of course, Ricardo's debt to Malthus on the theory of rent should not be forgotten.

taining different proportions of the various forms of capital. And here of course he finds that . . . a rise or fall of wages must have a very different effect on capitals. . . . Thus in order to equalise again the profits in the different spheres of production . . . the prices of commodities . . . must be regulated in a different way. . . . Hence he should have said: these average cost-prices are different from the values of commodities. . . . He would [then] have found that, even if wages are assumed to remain constant, the difference exists and therefore is quite independent of the rise or fall of wages. (1963, 2:174–76; emphasis omitted)

It is not difficult to see what is going on here (especially if a few simplifications are made). Imagine for the moment that the only form of capital is that advanced in production as wages. We could then present the central message of the classical approach to distribution as saying that profits were given by output *minus* wages (that is, capital advanced), or alternatively, that the rate of profit is equal to output *minus* wages (the surplus) *divided by* advanced wages.[4] That is, using the notation introduced earlier, and remembering that "wages" here means the wage bill (wl), we could present the classical view as being that $r = (pq - wl)/wl = (pq/wl) - 1$. Even if we knew the real wage rate (w), output (q), and the available techniques of production (l), all would not be well; we could not get both price and the rate of profit from this equation.

But what if prices *were* equal to labour values? Then things would be more tractable. This was how Ricardo had proceeded. He began with what he called Smith's "original error respecting value" and claimed to show that the quantity of labour embodied in the production of commodities was the only circumstance that regulated their exchangeable value—and this not only in the "early and rude state of society" allowed by Smith but also after capital had been accumulated (positive profits) and land had been appropriated. The reasoning that Ricardo employed to demonstrate this is interesting and crucial. He considered relative prices, and thought that the only source of *change* in those prices was an alteration in their difficulty or facility of production—that is, a change in the quantity of labour directly and indirectly embodied in their production:

In estimating, then, the causes of the *variations* in the value of commodities . . . in the subsequent part of this work . . . I shall consider all the great *variations* which take place in the relative value of commodities to be produced by the greater or less quantity of labour which may be required from time to time to produce them. (1821, 36–37; emphasis added)

---

[4] That is to say, the rate of profit equals the value of output *minus* the value of capital advanced *divided by* the value of capital advanced.

As before, given the real wage, the level of output, and the available techniques of production, as long as the labour theory of value held, the rate of profit would now be determined by "the proportion of the annual labour of the country . . . devoted to the support of the labourers" (49).

Ricardo, however, next noticed what he called *modifications* or *exceptions* to the labour theory value by admitting that there were some sources of price *variation* due to *changes* in the distribution between wages and profits that did not entail a change in the relative quantities of labour embodied. These exceptions, Ricardo stated, were due to three factors: unequal proportions of labour to the means of production, unequal periods of production, and the use of fixed capital in production (22, 38, 30). Marx later recognised that these exceptions are in fact the rule not the exception, thus taking us back to the original problem: in order to determine the value of the product it was necessary to know the rate of profit, but to determine the rate of profit rendered it necessary to know the value of the product.[5]

THE MARXIST SOLUTION

Having made the point that commodities do not exchange at prices that are equal to labour values—that Ricardo had mistaken "values" for "prices," "surplus value" for "profits," and "the rate of surplus value" for "the rate of profit"—Marx explicitly rejected the labour theory of value as a theory of price determination. Marx now made an analytical promise, so to speak: "The progress of the investigation will lead us back to exchange value as the necessary mode of expression, or form of appearance, of value—for the present however we consider the nature of value independently of its form of appearance" (1867, 1:128). That promise, to which the ensuing (and long) debate on the "transformation problem" provides ample evidence, was not followed through, however.

Analytically, it did transpire that one could determine prices of production from the given data of the real wage, the available techniques of production, and the structure and level of output that Marx had deployed.[6] Moreover, that solution did not revive the labour theory of value in the way Marx had expected. Whenever the value of capital depends on the rate of profit, the labour theory of value will not explain the relative

---

[5] Malthus, of course, had made exactly this point to Ricardo himself in their correspondence over the theory of value (see De Vivo 1984, 100–101).

[6] That solution had to await the appearance of Sraffa's *Production of Commodities by Means of Commodities* (1960).

prices of commodities. Only when the two are *independent*—that is, when the relationship between the wage and the rate of profit is *linear*—will the labour theory of value suffice. Interestingly, this very assumption turned out to be required by the marginalist approach to value and distribution as outlined by its early practitioners.

The Marginalist Solution

If the Marxian approach was to be treated as analytically unsound and unscientific economics, the marginalist approach fared better. It became the new mainstream of the discipline, and we now know it as neoclassical economics. If the statements by Jevons and Walras quoted at the outset of this chapter are indicative of the attitude adopted by the majority of the early writers of the marginalist school towards classical political economy, then it is incumbent on us to ask exactly what elements of this new approach to political economy, now called "economics," marked such a decisive movement away from the central organising concepts of the classical writers.[7] On this question, there is little doubt that such a movement is best captured in the opposing stand taken by each on the question of deciding how best to commence an analysis of the theory of value. The whole of the classical tendency was to examine value in the context of what has come to be called the "objective conditions of production" under competitive conditions, whereas the marginalist writers argued vigorously that it was only from an investigation of the "subjective conditions of consumption" under *perfectly* competitive conditions that meaningful results could be obtained.

Jevons and Walras returned to the celebrated water-diamonds paradox of the *Wealth of Nations* (1776, 1.4:44–45) and started again. Smith, they maintained, had confused total utility with marginal utility—or what comes to the same thing, had ignored the relationship between scarcity and utility—when he had observed that things with great utility (water) might have little value in exchange, while things with little utility (diamonds) often had a high exchangeable value. This confusion, they further claimed, had led Smith (wrongly) to reject "utility" as relevant to the

---

[7] Eugen von Böhm-Bawerk expressed a sentiment similar to the majority of the early writers of the marginalist school as well. He wrote of "the *peculiar turn* taken by the economic doctrine of value after Smith" (1884, 1:242; emphasis added). Given this hostility to Ricardo, it is worth remembering that two other prominent marginalist writers of a later time, Marshall and Knut Wicksell, claimed a strong analytical link with Ricardo, and were more forgiving of his errors. By the time that Jevons came to publish the second edition of his *Theory of Political Economy* in 1879, he had substituted the term economics for the older term political economy in everything but the title of his book. It should be noted that

determination of exchangeable value, and turn instead to the "difficulty or facility of production" for that explanation.[8] For the marginalists, it was from the relationship between "wants" and scarce "things"—that is, the subjective conditions surrounding the consumption of commodities— that those things derived their exchangeable value. Exchange was to be viewed as a process of reallocation and transformation of a (given) set of initial endowments of privately owned scarce commodities according to the (given) wants of individuals and (given) techniques of production.[9]

In this altered framework of concepts, it was maintained that the application of the theory of marginal utility to market exchange would render irrelevant all of the problems in the theory of value that had occupied the minds of the classical writers, and that had led to their analytical error. Jevons, for instance, argued forcefully that it was "impossible to have a correct idea of the science of economics without a perfect comprehension of the theory of exchange," and that it was "both possible and desirable to consider this subject before introducing any notions concerning labour or the production of commodities" (1871, 126).

THE IMPOTENCY OF POLITICS

If it is interesting that the critiques of classical political economy presented by Marx and the early marginalists should have amounted, at a formal level, to very much the same thing, then it is striking that their new systems of political economy and economics, respectively, also shared a com-

---

Jevons, of course, traced his lineage back to Cantillon and Smith via the work of Nassau Senior (see Jevons 1871, 72).

[8] Exchangeable value is, then, rigidly independent of utility, a premise that distinguished Smith's enquiry (and those of later classical writers) from the marginalists writers who stressed the importance of utility in the determination of relative prices. It is worth observing that while Ricardo had also opened his *Principles* where Smith had started, he had deployed a different argument to sustain the relevance of the objective conditions of production to the determination of exchangeable value. Ricardo introduced a distinction between scarce and produced commodities: "Possessing utility, commodities derive their exchangeable value from two sources: from their scarcity, and from the quantity of labour required to obtain them" (1821, 12). This distinction allowed Ricardo to be quite precise: "In speaking then of commodities, of their exchangeable value, and of the laws which regulate their relative prices, we mean always such commodities only as can be increased in quantity by the exertion of human industry, and on the production of which competition operates without restraint" (12). Only for scarce commodities, that is those not entering directly or indirectly into the production of other commodities, was there a role for the "wealth and inclinations" of those desiring them to affect their price.

[9] Philip Wicksteed remarked that the early marginalists "were erecting a theory of value upon this obvious but strangely neglected principle, which bases economic thought on . . . the psychology of choice between alternatives" (1910, 2).

mon feature—namely, a deep challenge to the efficacy of political action in the economic sphere. Their understandings of the market mechanism of capitalist society suggested that the economy constrained politics in important and fundamental ways.

To begin with, the narrowing of the conceptual focus of neoclassical economics to the question of how the market mechanism resolves problems of allocating given resources between competing ends within its abstract model of perfect competition effectively distanced the understanding of economic life from political life. Yet it did so at the cost of producing a science that tended to adopt a certain studied indifference towards the political and social institutions and structures within which markets function.[10] Furthermore, while divorcing the understanding of the market mechanism from either its historical or social context, it made possible an economic science claiming to offer valid truths irrespective of the constraints of time or location, and there have been attendant costs to this conceptual adjustment.[11] Those costs lay not so much in the commonly observed conceptual elision of economic and political liberty in the marginalist model, although certainly the influence of its subjectivist model of constrained optimisation operated to render possible a view of political actors as reducible to a caricature, say, of voters acting rationally to maximise their expected utility (Downs 1957) or interest groups acting as rent seekers (Tullock 1967).[12] Instead, there was another, potentially

[10] One example was George Stigler's statement that in the area of monopoly, no economist had "any professional knowledge on which to base recommendations that should carry weight with a sceptical legislator," and he continued by arguing that economists imported unexamined, normative policy commitments into the advice they offered legislators on the subject: "Our present support for pro-competitive policies is due in good part to the strong virtues we attach to competitive markets and industries" (1982, 6, 9). A second example is James Coleman's observation that "markets function differently and give different equilibrium prices, depending on the institutions through which exchange is organized. . . . Social institutions and social networks which are not completely, but are largely, ignored in neoclassical theory can make differences in outcomes without any change at all in the model of rational action" (1987, 183–84). A great deal of Buchanan's motivation for the introduction of constitutional economics was prompted by this feature of mainstream neoclassical economics.

[11] For example, Winch has noted that "marginalism enabled neoclassical economists to go further towards excluding historical and institutional categories from pure economics, so that even if the idea of drawing a clear boundary between pure and applied science was shared with the classical economists, there remain differences as to where the boundaries of pure science itself should be drawn." Winch continued: "The best-known exclusion was a theory of population. It would be difficult to imagine classical political economy, with its concern for the problems of growth and macro distribution, without some version of the population doctrine" (1972, 70).

[12] The explanatory adequacy of such views has not wanted for either theoretical or empirical criticism. Two of the widely known assaults on the efficacy of identifying economic with political man made in the mid-twentieth century still retain some critical edge. The first, of

more constraining political legacy of the neoclassical understanding of the operation of the market mechanism. And in one sense, it curiously returns us to some of the political conundrums of Smith.[13]

Smith had imagined the market as the aggregate activity of self-interested individuals working within well-defined social groupings—landowners, workers, and capitalists—each pursuing in a more or less unrestricted manner their own interest such that the composite wealth produced would be overwhelmingly beneficial to all. Writing as he did at the outset of systematic thinking about the market, his political considerations of the scope for free trade or government action to allay some of the more obvious problems of distributive justice of actual commercial life were, not surprisingly, tenuous, equivocal, and open-ended as historical occasion or wise leadership might dictate. The political impetus of the neoclassical view, starting from a model that begins "let us assume," would seem quite otherwise.[14]

The implication of this effort was to guide thinking about the operation of the market (under the constraints of scarcity) into narrow channels of possibility. For example, if the starting point of every economy was to be "the goods directly available to economic subjects"—and if the goal of all economy was to assure the satisfaction of our "direct needs"—then for any given theory of navigating the route from aim to outcome (that

---

course, was Macpherson's critique of the testability of those hypotheses that can be derived from the economic theory of politics, and the limitations of marginalism as an adequate theory of economic as well as political reality (1973, 185). The other (and perhaps more pertinent) was Brian Barry's critique of the logical "defects" in Downs's version of interparty competition and its "unfruitful" understanding of voting behaviour (1970, 13–22, 99–125). It is interesting that Macpherson elided Smith's understanding of political and economic life with that of the neoclassicals. He applied *one* critique to both. In this work, our aim has been to resist just such conflations.

[13] In surprising ways, the concept of the free individual (agent) has seemed to shrink out of sight in later expressions of the neoclassical market mechanism. The notion of the market has nearly expanded to mean destiny—that is, the market understood as a system that directs the individual to his "true" interests. Such market imperatives—even if only assertoric hypothetical imperatives—should not be identified with liberty, though. The place given to the invisible hand in Smith's own conception of the market remains debated. Yet irrespective of the answer to that historical question, it might still be argued that in some conceptual transformations of it after Smith, the market came to be thought of as less guided by Providence than *as* Providence. This rendering brings us uncomfortably close to one of the market as our fate.

[14] Of course, though it may be trivial to say so, a problem for any such model built on assumptions arises as soon as those assumptions are questioned. While it may be true that in differing ways, the classical economists focused almost completely on trying to explain actual circumstances, the neoclassicals simply assumed many of them away at the outset of their investigations—but ended up having to explain them in "real life" later on, as either imperfections or short-run deviations from the norm.

is, from a described starting point to a presumed goal) would require, as Menger put it, that individuals act "in as *suitable* a way as possible, *i.e.* in our case, in as *economic* a way as possible" (1883, 119). Menger argued that under any given circumstances, "only one road can be the most suitable," so that "if economic humans under given conditions want to assure the satisfaction of their needs as completely as possible, only one road prescribed exactly by the economic situation leads from the strictly determined starting point to the just as strictly determined goal of economy" (216–18).[15]

The model of the market mechanism that neoclassical economic theory thereby bequeathed to modern politics was not one claiming that the market was indestructible or unstoppable, or even that it was always beneficial to all, though some expressions have made this seem to be the case. Instead, given homo economicus as they assumed him to be, it was one in which his political expectations should be decidedly small.

That none of this is to be found in Smith, or rather, that none of it could possibly have been part of his decidedly eighteenth-century intentions, should be clear enough. But that it is certainly the product of conceptual transformations in the development of politics and political economy that took shape *after* Smith is equally clear. If our efforts in this volume were to have the effect of stimulating a return to a consideration of *those* transformations, we should judge them to have been worthwhile.

[15] Similar statements might also be found in Jevons. A much more extensive discussion of these can be found in Meek (1972).

REFERENCES

Andriopoulos, Stefan. 1999. The invisible hand: Supernatural agency in political economy and the gothic novel. *English Literary History* 66 (3): 739–58.

Annas, Julia. 1993. *The Morality of Happiness*. Oxford: Oxford University Press.

Aristotle. 2000. *Nicomachean Ethics*. Trans. and ed. Roger Crisp. Cambridge: Cambridge University Press.

Arrow, Kenneth J. 1986. Rationality of self and others in an economic system. *Journal of Business* 59 (4): 210–15. (Reprinted in *Rational Choice: The Contrast between Economics and Psychology*, ed. Robin M. Hogarth and Melvin W. Reader [Chicago: University of Chicago Press, 1987].)

Arrow, Kenneth, and Frank Hahn, H. 1971. *General Competitive Analysis*. Edinburgh: Oliver and Boyd.

Ashcraft, Richard. 1998. John Stuart Mill and the theoretical foundations of democratic socialism. In *Mill and the Moral Character of Liberalism*, ed. Eldon J. Eisenbach. University Park: Pennsylvania University Press.

Bagehot, Walter. 1855. The first Edinburgh reviewers. *National Review* 1 (October): 253–84. (Reprinted in Walter Bagehot, *Collected Works*, of Walter Bagehot, ed. Norman St. John Stevas [London: Economist, 1965–86], 1:309–41.)

———. 1881. *Biographical Studies*. London: Longmans, Green. (Orig. pub. 1867.)

———. 1965–86. *The Collected Works of Walter Bagehot*. Ed. Norman St. John Stevas. 15 vols. London: Economist.

[Bailey, Samuel]. 1821a. *An Inquiry into Those Principles Respecting the Nature of Demand and the Necessity of Consumption Lately Advocated by Mr Malthus*. London: R. Hunter. Repr., London: Frank Cass and Company, 1967. The brackets indicate that the attribution of this work to Bailey is doubtful.

———. 1821b. *Observations on Certain Verbal Disputes in Political Economy, Particularly Relating to Value, and to Demand and Supply*. London: R. Hunter. Repr., London: Frank Cass and Company, 1967. The attribution of this work to Bailey is doubtful.

———. 1825. *A Critical Dissertation on the Nature, Measures, and Causes of Value & Etc.* London: R. Hunter. Repr., London: Frank Cass and Company, 1967.

———. 1826. *A Letter to a Political Economist: Occasioned by an Article in the Westminster Review on the Subject of Value*. London: R. Hunter. Repr., London: Frank Cass and Company, 1967.

Bain, Alexander. 1882. *James Mill: A Biography*. London: Longmans, Green and Company.

Barry, Brian M. 1970. *Sociologists, Economists, and Democracy*. London: Collier-Macmillan.

Bastiat, Frédéric. 1850. *Les harmonies économiques*. Trans. W. H. Boyers. Repr., Princeton, NJ: Van Nostrand, 1964.

Bastiat, Frédéric. 1964. *Selected Essays on Political Economy*. Ed. and trans. Seymour Cain, with preface George B. de Huszar, and introd. Friedrich A. Hayek. Repr., Irvington-on-Hudson, NY: Foundation for Economic Education, 1995.

Beer, Max. 1919. *A History of Socialism*. London: Allen and Unwin.

Bentham, Jeremy. 1776. *A Fragment on Government or a Comment on the Commentaries & Etc*. In *The Works of Jeremy Bentham*, ed. John Bowring, 1:221–95. Repr., New York: Russell and Russell, 1962.

————. 1789. *An Introduction to the Principles of Morals and Legislation*. London: T. Payne and Son. Ed. J. H. Burns and H.L.A. Hart (rev. ed). Repr., London: Athlone Press, 1970.

————. 1793–95. *Manual of Political Economy*. Reprinted in *Economic Writings*, I, pp.219–274.

————. 1797. Pauper management improved. *Annals of Agriculture*. In vol. 2 of *The Collected Works of Jeremy Bentham: Writings on the Poor Laws*, ed. Michael Quinn. Oxford: Oxford University Press.

————. 1802. *Theory of Legislation*. Trans. C. M. Atkinson (1914). Oxford: Clarendon Press.

————. 1817. *A Plan for Parliamentary Reform in the Form of a Catechism & Etc*. In *The Works of Jeremy Bentham*, ed. John Bowring, 3:533–57. Repr., New York: Russell and Russell, 1962.

————. 1827. *Rationale of Judicial Evidence, Specially Applied to English Practice*. In vol. 6 of *The Works of Jeremy Bentham*, ed. John Bowring. Repr., New York: Russell and Russell, 1962.

————. 1830. *Constitutional Code*. In *The Collected Works of Jeremy Bentham: First Principles Preparatory to Constitutional Code*, ed. Philip Schofield. Repr., Oxford: Oxford University Press, 1989.

————. 1838–43. *The Works of Jeremy Bentham*. Ed. John Bowring. 10 vols. Repr., New York: Russell and Russell, 1962.

————. 1952. *Jeremy Bentham's Economic Writings*. Ed. W. Stark. 3 vols. London: George Allen and Unwin.

————. 2001. *Writings on the Poor Laws*, ed. M. Quinn. Vol. 1 of *The Collected Works of Jeremy Bentham*, ed. F. Rosen and P. Schofield. Repr., Oxford: Oxford University Press, 1983.

Berg, Maxine. 1980. *The Machinery Question and the Making of Political Economy: 1815–1848*. Cambridge: Cambridge University Press.

Black, Eugene C., ed. 1969. *British Politics in the Nineteenth Century*. New York: Harper and Row.

Blake, William. 1823. *Observations on the Effects Produced by the Expenditure of Government during the Restriction of Cash Payments*. London: John Murray.

Blaug, Mark. 1958. *Ricardian Economics: A Historical Study*. New Haven, CT: Yale University Press.

Böhm-Bawerk, Eugen von. 1884. *Kapital und Kapitalzins*. Trans. from 4th ed. (1921) as *Capital and Interest* (vol. 1). Repr., South Holland: Libertarian Press, 1959.

Bonar, James, ed. 1894. *A Catalogue of the Library of Adam Smith, Author of the "Moral Sentiments" and the "Wealth of Nations."* New York: Augustus M. Kelley.

Bonar, James, and Jacob H. Hollander, eds. 1899. *Letters of David Ricardo to Hutches Trower and Others: 1811–1823.* Oxford: Clarendon Press.

Booth, William James. 1993. *Households: On the Moral Architecture of the Economy.* Ithaca, NY: Cornell University Press.

Bray, John Francis. 1839. *Labour's Wrongs and Labour's Remedy or, the Age of Might and the Age of Right.* Leeds: D. Green. Repr., New York: Augustus M. Kelley, 1968.

———. ca. 1840. *A Voyage from Utopia.* Ed. and introd. M. F. Lloyd-Prichard. Repr., London: Lawrence and Wishart, 1957.

Briggs, Asa. 1956. Middle-class consciousness in English politics, 1780–1846. *Past and Present* 9 (April): 65–74.

Brinton, Crane. 1949. *English Political Thought in the Nineteenth Century.* Cambridge, MA: Harvard University Press.

Brougham, Henry. 1804. Lord Lauderdale on public wealth. *Edinburgh Review* 4, no. 8 (July): 343–77.

———. 1871. *The Life and Times of Henry, Lord Brougham, Written by Himself.* 3 vols. Edinburgh: William Blackwood and Sons.

Brown, Vivienne. 1991. Signifying voices: Reading the Adam Smith problem. *Economics and Philosophy* 7:187–220.

———. 1994. *Adam Smith's Discourse: Canonicity, Commerce, and Conscience.* London: Routledge.

———. 2008. Agency and discourse: Revisiting the Adam Smith problem. In *Elgar Companion to Adam Smith*, ed. Jeffrey Young. Aldershot: Edward Elgar.

Buchan, James. 2006. *Adam Smith and the Pursuit of Perfect Liberty.* London: Profile Books.

Buchanan, James M. 1989. Constitutional economics. In *The New Palgrave: The Invisible Hand*, ed. John Eatwell, Murray Milgate, and Peter Newman, 79–87. London: Macmillan.

Buckle, Henry T. 1873. *History of Civilisation in England.* 3 vols. London: Longmans, Green and Company. (Orig. pub. 1858.)

Burke, Edmund. 1791a. *An Appeal from the New to the Old Whigs & Etc.* In *Works*, III, pp.331–457.

———. 1791b. *Letter to a Member of the National Assembly & Etc.* In *The Works of Edmund Burke*, 9: 287–329. Boston: Little and Brown, 1839.

———. 1795. *Thoughts and Details on Scarcity.* In *The Works of Edmund Burke*, 4:249–80. Repr., Boston: Little and Brown, 1839.

———. 1839. *The Works of Edmund Burke.* 9 vols. Boston: Little and Brown.

Burrow, J. W. 1988. *Whigs and Liberals: Continuity and Change in English Political Thought.* Oxford: Clarendon Press.

Buxton, Sydney. 1888. *Finance and Politics: An Historical Study, 1783–1885.* London: John Murray. Repr., New York: Augustus M. Kelley, 1966.

Cannan, Edwin. 1894. Ricardo in Parliament: I & II. *Economic Journal* 4, no. 14 (June): 249–61 and 4, no. 5 (September): 409–23.

Carey, Henry. 1851. *The Harmony of Interests, Agricultural, Manufacturing, and Commercial*. Philadelphia: H. C. Baird.

Carpenter, Kenneth E. 2002. *The Dissemination of* The Wealth of Nations *in French and in France, 1776–1843*. New York: Bibliographical Society of America.

Carr, Wendell Robert. 1971. James Mill's politics reconsidered: Parliamentary reform and the triumph of truth. *Historical Journal* 14 (3): 553–80.

Chalmers, Thomas. 1832. *On Political Economy, in Connexion with the Moral State and Moral Prospects of Society*. Glasgow: William Collins.

Claeys, Gregory. 1987. *Machinery, Money, and Millennium*. Cambridge: Polity Press.

———. 1989. *Citizens and Saints: Politics and Anti-Politics in Early British Socialism*. New York: Cambridge University Press.

Clark, John Bates. 1899. *The Distribution of Wealth*. London: Macmillan.

Clive, John L. 1956. *Scotch Reviewers: The Edinburgh Review, 1802–1815*. London: Faber and Faber.

Coats, A. W. 1967. The classical economists and the labourer. In *The Classical Economists and Economic Policy*, ed. A. W. Coats, 144–79. Repr., London: Methuen, 1971.

———, ed. 1971. *The Classical Economists and Economic Policy*. London: Methuen.

———, ed. 1983. *Methodological Controversies in Economics: Historical Essays in Honour of T. W. Hutchison*. New York: JAI Press.

Cockburn, Henry. 1852. *The Life of Lord Jeffrey, with a Selection from His Correspondence*. 2 vols. Edinburgh: Adam and Charles Black.

———. 1856. *Memorials of His Time*. Abridged and ed. W. Forbes Gray. Repr., Edinburgh: Robert Grant and Sons, 1946.

Cole, G.D.H. 1930. *The Life of Robert Owen*. 2nd ed. London: Macmillan. (Orig. pub. 1925.)

Coleman, James. 1987. Psychological structure and social structure in economic models. In *Rational Choice: The Contrast between Economics and Psychology*, ed. Robin M. Hogarth and Melvin W. Reder. Chicago: University of Chicago Press.

Collini, Stefan, Richard Whatmore and Brian Young (eds). 2000. *Economy, Polity, and Society: British Intellectual History, 1750–1950*. Cambridge: Cambridge University Press.

Collini, Stefan, Donald Winch, and John Burrow. 1983. *That Noble Science of Politics: A Study in Nineteenth-century Intellectual History*. Cambridge: Cambridge University Press.

Collison-Black, R. D. 1976. Smith's contribution in historical perspective. In *The Market and the State: Essays on Adam Smith*, ed. Andrew W. Skinner and Thomas Wilson. 1976. Oxford: Clarendon Press.

Corry, Bernard A. 1962. *Money, Saving, and Investment in English Economics: 1800–1850*. New York: St. Martin's Press.

Cropsey, Joseph. 1957. *Polity and Economy: An Interpretation of the Principles of Adam Smith*. The Hague: Martinus Nijhoff.

————. 1976. Adam Smith and political philosophy. In *The Market and the State: Essays on Adam Smith*, ed. Andrew S. Skinner and Thomas Wilson, 132–53. Oxford: Clarendon Press.

————. 1979. The invisible hand: Moral and political considerations. In *Adam Smith and Modern Political Economy: Bicentennial Essays on the Wealth of Nations*, ed. Gerald P. O'Driscoll Jr., 165–76. Ames: Iowa State University Press. Davidson, William L. 1916. *Political Thought in England: The Utilitarians from Bentham to J.S. Mill*. New York: Henry Holt and Co.

Davie, George Elder. 1961. *The Democratic Intellect: Scotland and Her Universities in the Nineteenth Century*. Edinburgh: Edinburgh University Press.

Deane, Phyllis. 1989. *The State and the Economic System: An Introduction to the History of Political Economy*. Oxford: Oxford University Press.

De Marchi, Neil. 1983. The case for James Mill. In *Methodological Controversies in Economics: Historical Essays in Honour of T. W. Hutchison*, ed. A. W. Coats, 155–84. New York: JAI Press.

De Vivo, Giancarlo. 1984. *Ricardo and His Critics: A Study of Classical Theories of Value and Distribution*. Modena: Università degli studi di Modena.

————. 2000. Introduction to Torrens's article "Mr Owen's plan for relieving the national distress." In vol. 8 of *The Collected Works of Robert Torrens*. Bristol: Thoemmes Press.

Dickey, Laurence. 1986. Historicizing the "Adam Smith problem": Conceptual, historiographical, and textual issues. *Journal of Modern History* 58, no. 3 (September): 579–609.

Dictionary of National Biography. 1885–1901. Ed. Leslie Stephen and Sidney Lee. 66 vols. and suppl. London: Smith, Elder and Company.

Dijksterhuis, Eduard J. 1959. *The Mechanization of the World Picture: Pythagoras to Newton*. Trans. C. Dikshoorn, foreword D. J. Struik. Repr., Princeton, NJ: Princeton University Press, 1986.

Dixon, William. 2008. Ricardo: Economic thought and social order. *Journal of the History of Economic Thought* 30, no. 2 (June).

Dobb, Maurice H. 1973. *Theories of Value and Distribution since Adam Smith; Ideology and Economic Theory*. Cambridge: Cambridge University Press.

Donner, Wendy. 1991. *The Liberal Self: John Stuart Mill's Moral and Political Philosophy*. Ithaca, NY: Cornell University Press.

Downs, Anthony. 1957. *An Economic Theory of Democracy*. New York: Harper and Row.

Duncan, G. C. 1973. *Marx and Mill: Two Views of Social Conflict and Social Harmony*. Cambridge: Cambridge University Press.

Dunn, John. 1990. What is living and what is dead in the thought of John Locke. In *Interpreting Political Responsibility: Essays 1981–1989*. Princeton, NJ: Princeton University Press.

Eatwell, John. 1996. International financial liberalization: The impact on world development. *UNDP/ODS Discussion Paper* 12. New York.

Eatwell, John, Murray Milgate, and Peter Newman, eds. 1987. *The New Palgrave: A Dictionary of Economics*. 4 vols. London: Macmillan.

Eden, Frederick Morton. 1797. *The State of the Poor*. 3 vols. London: J. Davies.

Ekelund, Robert B., Jr., and Robert F. Hébert. 1990. *A History of Economic Theory and Method*. New York: McGraw-Hill.

Empson, W. 1837. Life, writings, and character of Mr. Malthus. *Edinburgh Review* 64, no. 130 (January): 469–506. (Reprinted in Bernard Semmel, ed., *The Occasional Papers of T.R. Malthus* [New York: Burt Franklin, 1963].)

Engels, Friedrich. 1844. *Outlines of a Critique of Political Economy*. In *Collected Works*, by Karl Marx and Friedrich Engels, 3:437. Repr., New York: International Publishers, 1975.

Fenn, Robert A. 1992. Review of Ricardian politics. *American Political Science Review* 86, no. 4 (December,): 1046–47.

Ferguson, Adam. 1767. *An Essay on Civil Society*. Ed. Duncan Forbes. Repr., Edinburgh: Edinburgh University Press, 1966.

———. 1783. *The History of the Progress and Termination of the Roman Republic*. Repr., Philadelphia: Thomas Wardle.

Fetter, Frank Whitson. 1965. *Development of British Monetary Orthodoxy: 1797–1875*. Repr., Fairfield, NJ: Augustus M. Kelley, 1978.

———. 1975. The influence of economists in parliament on British legislation from Ricardo to John Stuart Mill. *Journal of Political Economy* 83, no. 5 (October): 1051–64.

———. 1980. *The Economist in Parliament: 1780–1868*. Durham, NC: Duke University Press.

Finley, Moses. 1987. Aristotle. In *The New Palgrave: A Dictionary of Economics*, ed. John Eatwell, Murray Milgate, and Peter Newman. Vol. 1. London: Macmillan.

———. 1989. *The Ancient Economy*. Berkeley: University of California Press.

Fitzgibbons, Athol. 1995. *Adam Smith's System of Liberty, Wealth, and Virtue: The Moral and Political Foundations of the Wealth of Nations*. Oxford: Clarendon Press.

Fleischacker, Samuel. 2004. *On Adam Smith's Wealth of Nations: A Philosophical Companion*. Princeton, NJ: Princeton University Press.

Fontana, Biancamaria. 1985. *Rethinking the Politics of Commercial Society: The Edinburgh Review, 1802–1832*. Cambridge: Cambridge University Press.

Fontenelle, Bernard le Bovier de. 1728. *A Week's Conversation on the Plurality of Worlds*. Trans. William Gardiner. 2nd ed. London: Bettesworth.

Forbes, Duncan. 1966. Introd. to *An Essay on Civil Society*, by Adam Ferguson. Ed. Duncan Forbes. Edinburgh: Edinburgh University Press.

———. 1975. *Hume's Philosophical Politics*. Cambridge: Cambridge University Press.

———. 1976. Sceptical whiggism, commerce, and liberty. In *The Market and the State: Essays on Adam Smith*, ed. Andrew S. Skinner and Thomas Wilson. Oxford: Clarendon Press.

Force, Pierre. 2003. *Self-Interest before Adam Smith: A Genealogy of Economic Science*. Cambridge: Cambridge University Press.

Forman-Barzilai, Fonna. 2000. Adam Smith as globalization theorist. *Critical Review* 14 (4): 391–419.

———. 2005. Sympathy in space(s): Adam Smith on proximity. *Political Theory* 33:189–217.

Fox, Charles James. 1808. *A History of the Early Part of the Reign of James II*. London: W. Miller.

Foxwell, Herbert Somerton. 1899. Introduction and bibliography. In *The Right to the Whole Produce of Labour*, by Anton Menger. Repr., New York: Augustus M. Kelley, 1968.

Friedman, Milton. 1962. *Capitalism and Freedom*. Chicago: University of Chicago Press.

Garnsey, Peter, and Richard Saller. 1987. *The Roman Empire: Economy, Society, and Culture*. Berkeley: University of California Press.

Gay, Peter. 1984. *Education of the Senses*. Vol. 1 of *The Bourgeois Experience: Victoria to Freud*. Oxford: Oxford University Press.

George, Henry. 1926. *Progress and Poverty*. New York: Garden City Publishing.

Glanvill, J. 1661. *The Vanity of Dogmatizing: or, Confidence in Opinions. Manifested in a Discourse of the Shortness and Uncertainty of Knowledge, and Its Causes; with Some Reflexions on Peripateticism; and an Apology for Philosophy*. London: H. Eversden.

Godwin, William. 1793. *An Enquiry concerning Political Justice and Its Influence on Modern Morals and Happiness*. 2 vols. London: G. G. and J. Robinson.

———. 1797. *The Enquirer: Reflections on Education, Manners, and Literature*. London: G. G. and J. Robinson.

———. 1798. *An Enquiry Concerning Political Justice and Its Influence on Modern Morals and Happiness*. 2nd ed. 2 vols. London: G. G. and J. Robinson. (Orig. pub. 1793.)

———. 1820. *Of Population: An Enquiry Concerning the Power of Increase in the Numbers of Mankind, Being an Answer to Mr. Malthus's Essay on that Subject*. London: Longman.

Gordon, Barry. 1964. Aristotle and the development of value theory. *Quarterly Journal of Economics* 78:115–28.

———. 1976. *Political Economy in Parliament, 1819–1823*. London: Macmillan.

Grampp, William D. 1948. On the politics of the classical economists. *Quarterly Journal of Economics* 62 (5): 714–47.

Gray, Alexander. 1946. *The Socialist Tradition: Moses to Lenin*. London: Longmans, Green and Company.

Greig, J.Y.T. 1931. *David Hume*. London: Jonathan Cape.

———, ed. 1932. *The Letters of David Hume*. 2 vols. Oxford: Oxford University Press.

Haakonssen, Knud. 1981. *The Science of a Legislator: The Natural Jurisprudence of David Hume and Adam Smith*. Cambridge: Cambridge University Press.

———. 1984. From moral philosophy to political economy: The contribution of Dugald Stewart. In *Philosophers of the Scottish Enlightenment*, ed. Vincent Hope, 211–32. Edinburgh: Edinburgh University Press.

———. 1985. James Mill and Scottish moral philosophy. *Political Studies* 33, no. 4 (December): 628–36.

———, ed. 2006. *The Cambridge Companion to Adam Smith*. Cambridge: Cambridge University Press.

Haakonssen, Knud, and Donald Winch. 2006. The legacy of Adam Smith. In *The Cambridge Companion to Adam Smith*, ed. Knud Haakonssen. Cambridge: Cambridge University Press.

Halévy, Elie. 1903. *Thomas Hodgskin*. Ed. and introd. A. J. Taylor. Eng. ed. Repr., London: Ernest Benn Ltd., 1956.

———. 1913–32. *A History of the English People in the Nineteenth Century*. 2nd English ed. Trans. E. I. Watkin and D. A. Barker. 6 vols. Repr., London: Ernest Benn, 1960–61.

———. 1928. *The Growth of Philosophic Radicalism*. London: Faber and Faber. (Orig. pub. France 1900–1904.)

Hamburger, Joseph. 1962. James Mill on universal suffrage and the middle class. *Journal of Politics* 24, no. 1 (February): 167–90.

———. 1963. *James Mill and the Art of Revolution*. New Haven, CT: Yale University Press.

———. 1965. *Intellectuals in Politics: John Stuart Mill and the Philosophic Radicals*. New Haven, CT: Yale University Press.

———. 1999. *John Stuart Mill on Liberty and Control*. Princeton, NJ: Princeton University Press.

Hamilton, William, ed. 1855. *The Collected Works of Dugald Stewart, Esq. FRSS*. 11 vols. Edinburgh: Constable.

Hargreaves, E. L. 1930. *The National Debt*. London: Edward Arnold and Co.

Harris, Jose, ed. 2004. *Civil Society in British History: Ideas, Identities, Institutions*. Oxford: Oxford University Press.

Hayek, Friedrich A. 1935. *Prices and Production*. 2nd ed. London: George Routledge and Sons. (Orig. pub. 1931.)

———. 1946. Individualism: True and false. In *Individualism and Economic Order*. Repr., Chicago: University of Chicago Press, 1948.

———. 1948. *Individualism and Economic Order*. Chicago: University of Chicago Press.

———. 1967. *Studies in Philosophy, Politics, and Economics*. London: Routledge and Kegan Paul.

Heckscher, Eli Filip. 1931. *Mercantilism*. Trans. Mendel Shapiro. 2 vols. Repr., London: George Allen and Unwin, 1935. (Rev. ed. 1955.)

Hill, L. 2001. The hidden theology of Adam Smith. *European Journal of the History of Economic Thought* 8, no. 1 (Spring).

Hilton, Boyd. 1977. *Corn, Cash, Commerce: The Economic Policies of the Tory Governments, 1815–1830*. Oxford: Oxford University Press.

———. 1988. *Age of Atonement: The Influence of Evangelicalism on Social and Economic Thought, 1795–1865*. Oxford: Clarendon Press.

Himmelfarb, Gertrude. 1974. *On Liberty and Liberalism: The Case of John Stuart Mill*. New York: Knopf.

———. 1983. *The Idea of Poverty: England in the Early Industrial Age*. New York: Random House.

Hirschman, Albert O. 1977. *The Passions and the Interests: Political Arguments for Capitalism before Its Triumph*. Princeton, NJ: Princeton University Press.

———. 1986. *Rival Views of Market Society and Other Recent Essays*. New York: Viking.

———. 1991. *The Rhetoric of Reaction: Perversity, Futility, Jeopardy*. Cambridge, MA: Belknap Press.

Hodgskin, Thomas. 1825. *Labour Defended against the Claims of Capital; or, the Unproductiveness of Capital Proved with Reference to the Present Combinations amongst Journeymen*. Ed. and introd. G.D.H. Cole. Repr., London: Labour Publishing Company, 1922.

———. 1827. *Popular Political Economy: Four Lectures Delivered at the London Mechanics' Institution*. London: Charles Tate. Repr., New York: Augustus M. Kelley, 1966.

———. 1832. *The Natural and Artificial Right of Property Contrasted*. Repr., Clifton, NJ: Augustus M. Kelley, 1973.

———. 1843. *A Lecture on Free Trade, in Connexion with the Corn Laws; Delivered at the White Conduit House, on January 31, 1843*. London: G. J. Palmer.

Hollander, Jacob H. 1928. The founder of a school. In *Adam Smith, 1776–1926: Lectures to Commemorate the Sesquicentennial of the Publication of "The Wealth of Nations."* Chicago: University of Chicago Press.

Hollander, Samuel. 1973. *The Economics of Adam Smith*. Toronto: University of Toronto Press.

———. 1985. *The Economics of John Stuart Mill*. 2 vols. Toronto: University of Toronto Press.

———. 1987. *Classical Economics*. Oxford: Basil Blackwell.

———. 1989. Malthus and utilitarianism with special reference to the *Essay on Population*. *Utilitas* 1 (November): 170–210.

Holmes, Stephen. 1995. *Passions and Constraint: On the Theory of Liberal Democracy*. Chicago: University of Chicago Press.

Hont, Istvan. 1994. Review of Ricardian politics. *Political Theory* 22, no. 2 (May): 339–43.

———. 2005. *Jealousy of Trade: International Competition and the Nation State in Historical Perspective*. Cambridge, MA: Harvard University Press.

Hont, Istvan, and Michael Ignatieff, eds. 1983. *Wealth and Virtue: The Shaping of Political Economy in the Scottish Enlightenment*. Cambridge: Cambridge University Press.

Hope, Vincent, ed. 1984. *Philosophers of the Scottish Enlightenment*. Edinburgh: Edinburgh University Press.

Horne, Thomas. 1978. *The Social Thought of Bernard Mandeville: Virtue and Commerce in Early Eighteenth-century England*. London: Macmillan.

Horner, Francis. 1803a. Canard's Principes d'économie politique. *Edinburgh Review* 1 (2): 431–50. (Reprinted in Francis Horner, *The Economic Writings of Francis Horner in the Edinburgh Review, 1802–6*, ed. and introd. F. W. Fetter [New York: Kelley and Millman, 1957], 57–76.)

———. 1803b. Lord King on bank restriction. *Edinburgh Review* 2 (4): 402–21. (Reprinted in Francis Horner, *The Economic Writings of Francis Horner in the Edinburgh Review, 1802–6*, ed. and introd. F. W. Fetter [New York: Kelley and Millman, 1957], 77–95.)

———. 1843. *Memoirs and Correspondence of Francis Horner M.P.* Ed. Leonard Horner. 2nd ed. with additions. Repr., Boston: Little, Brown and Company, 1853.

Horner, Francis. 1957. *The Economic Writings of Francis Horner in the Edinburgh Review 1802–6.* Reprints of Scarce Works on Political Economy 13. Ed. and introd. F. W. Fetter. New York: Kelley and Millman.

Hume, David. 1739–40. *A Treatise of Human Nature.* Ed. L. A. Selby-Bigge. 2nd rev. ed. P. H. Nidditch. Repr., Oxford: Clarendon Press, 1978.

———. 1741–42. *Essays, Moral and Political.* In *Essays: Moral, Political, and Literary,* by David Hume. Ed. Eugene F. Miller. Repr., Indianapolis: Liberty Classics, 1777.

———. 1748. *An Enquiry Concerning Human Understanding.* Ed. L. A. Selby-Bigge. 3rd rev. ed. P. H. Nidditch. Repr., Oxford: Clarendon Press, 1975. (Referred to herein as *Enquiry 1.*)

———. 1751. *An Enquiry Concerning the Principles of Morals.* Edited by L.A. Selby-Bigge. 3rd edition revised by P.H. Nidditch. Oxford: Clarendon Press, 1975. Referred to herein as *Enquiry 2.*

———. 1752a. Of money. Originally published in *Political Discourses* and reprinted in *David Hume: Writings on Economics,* edited by Eugene Rotwein, 1955.

———. 1752b. Of the independency of parliament. In *Essays: Moral, Political, and Literary,* by David Hume. Ed. Eugene F. Miller. Repr., Indianapolis: Liberty Press, 1985.

———. 1752c. *Political Discourses.* Nine of the twelve essays in this volume are collected by Eugene Rotwein in Hume's *Writings on Economics* (1955) and all are reprinted in *Essays* (1777b).

———. 1754–62. Six volumes. *History of Great Britain from the Invasion of Julius Caesar to the Revolution of 1688.*

———. 1775. *My Own Life.* As reprinted in *Essays* (1777b).

———. 1777a. *Essays: Moral, Political, and Literary.* Ed. Eugene F. Miller. Indianapolis: Liberty Classics.

———. 1777b. *Two Essays* [Of suicide; Of the immortality of the soul]. In *Essays: Moral, Political, and Literary,* ed. Eugene F. Miller. Indianapolis: Liberty Classics.

———. 1955. *Writings on Economics.* Ed. Eugene Rotwein. Madison: University of Wisconsin Press.

Hundert, E. J. 2000. Sociability and self-love in the theatre of the moral sentiments: Mandeville to Adam Smith. In *Economy, Polity, and Society: British Intellectual History, 1750–1950,* ed. Stefan Collini, R. Whatmore, and B. Young, 31–47. Cambridge: Cambridge University Press.

Hutchison, Terence W. 1953. James Mill and the political education of Ricardo. *Cambridge Journal* 7, no. 2 (November): 81–100.

———. 1967. Review of James Mill: Selected economic writings. *Economic Journal* 77, no.306 (June): 398–400.

———. 1988. *Before Adam Smith.* London: Basil Blackwell.

———. 1994. *The Uses and Abuses of Economics: Contentious Essays on History and Method.* London: Routledge.

James, Patricia. 1979. *Population Malthus: His Life and Times.* London: Routledge and Kegan Paul.

Jeffrey, Francis. 1809. Parliamentary reform. *Edinburgh Review* 14, no. 28 (July): 276–306.

———. 1819. State of the country. *Edinburgh Review* 32, no. 64 (October): 293–309.

Jevons, William Stanley. 1871. *The Theory of Political Economy.* Reprinted from 2nd ed. (1879). Repr., New York: Augustus M. Kelley, 1965.

Johnson, W. E. 1899. Goods; classification of. In vol. 1 of *Dictionary of Political Economy,* ed. R.H.I. Palgrave. London: Macmillan.

Jones, G. S. 2001. Hegel and the economics of civil society. In *Civil Society: History and Possibilities,* ed. S. Kaviraj and S. Khilnani. Cambridge: Cambridge University Press.

———. 2004. *An End to Poverty? A Historical Debate.* London: Profile Books.

Jones, Peter. 1983. The Scottish professoriate and the polite academy. In *Wealth and Virtue: The Shaping of Political Economy in the Scottish Enlightenment,* ed. Istvan Hont and Michael Ignatieff, 89–117. Cambridge: Cambridge University Press.

Jones, Peter, and Andrew S. Skinner, eds. 1992. *Adam Smith Reviewed.* Edinburgh: Edinburgh University Press.

Jones, W. D. 1967. *"Prosperity" Robinson: The Life of Viscount Goderich, 1782–1859.* London: Macmillan.

Kateb, George. 1968. Utopias and utopianism. In *International Encyclopedia of the Social Sciences,* ed. David Sills, 16:267–70. New York: Macmillan.

Kaviraj, S., and S. Khilnani, S. 2001. *Civil Society: History and Possibilities.* Cambridge: Cambridge University Press.

Keane, John. 1988. Despotism and democracy. In *Civil Society and the State: New European Perspectives,* ed. John Keane London: Verso.

Kelly, T. 1957. *George Birkbeck: Pioneer of Adult Education.* Liverpool: Liverpool University Press.

Kennedy, Gavin. 2005. *Adam Smith's Lost Legacy.* London: Palgrave.

Keynes, J. M. 1933. *Essays in Biography.* London: Macmillan. (Reprinted in vol. 10 of *Collected Writings,* ed. D. Moggridge [London: Macmillan].)

———. 1971–89. *Collected Writings.* Ed. D. Moggridge. London: Macmillan.

Kuhn, Thomas. 1970. *The Structure of Scientific Revolutions.* 2nd ed. Chicago: University of Chicago Press.

Kurke, Leslie. 1999. *Coins, Bodies, Games, and Gold: The Politics of Meaning in Archaic Greece.* Princeton, NJ: Princeton University Press.

Lal, Deepak. 2006. *Reviving the Invisible Hand: The Case for Classical Liberalism in the Twenty-first Century.* Princeton, NJ: Princeton University Press.

Landes, David S. 1998. *The Wealth and Poverty of Nations: Why Some Are So Rich and Some So Poor.* London: Abacus.

Laski, Harold J. 1920. *Political Thought in England from Locke to Bentham.* New York: Henry Holt Company.

Lauderdale, Eighth Earl [James Maitland]. 1804. *An Inquiry into the Nature and Origin of Public Wealth, and into the Means and Causes of Its Increase.* Edinburgh: Archibald Constable and Company. (2nd ed. 1819.) Repr., New York, Augustus M. Kelley, 1967.

Lauderdale, Eighth Earl [James Maitland]. 1805. *Thoughts on the Alarming State of the Circulation, and on the Means of Redressing the Pecuniary Grievances in Ireland*. Edinburgh: A. Constable and Company.

———. 1812. *The Depreciation of the Paper Currency of Great Britain Proved*. London: Longman, Hurst, Rees, Orme, and Brown.

———. 1813. *Further Considerations on the State of the Currency; in Which the Means of Restoring Our Circulation to a Salutory State Are Fully Explained, and the Injuries Sustained by the Public Treasury, as well as by the National Creditor from Our Present Pecuniary System, Are Materially Established*. Edinburgh: A. Constable and Co.

Lindgren, J. R. 1969. Adam Smith's theory of inquiry. *Journal of Political Economy* 77 (6): 897–915.

Lloyd-Prichard, M. F. 1957. Introduction to J.F. Bray, *A Voyage from Utopia*. London: Lawrence and Wishart.

Long, Anthony A. 1996. *Stoic Studies*. Cambridge: Cambridge University Press.

———. 2006. Stoic philosophers on persons, property-ownership, and community. In *From Epicurus to Epictetus: Studies in Hellenistic and Roman Philosophy*. Oxford: Oxford University Press.

———. 2007. Stoic communitarianism and normative citizenship. *Social Philosophy and Policy* 24, no. 2 (Summer): 241–61.

Long, Douglas. 2002. Men, merchants, and citizens: Unity and plurality in Adam Smith's thought. Paper presented at the Eighteenth Century Scottish Studies Society meetings on Union and Cultural Identities in Eighteenth Century Scotland, Edinburgh, July 3–7.

———. 2003. A host of Scotch sophists: Jeremy Bentham and Scottish moral philosophy. Unpublished manuscript.

Lowenthal, Esther. 1911. *The Ricardian Socialists*. Columbia: Columbia University Press. (Repr., New York: Augustus M. Kelley, 1972.)

Lowry, S. Todd. 1979. Recent literature on ancient Greek economic thought. *Journal of Economic Literature* 17, no. 1 (March): 65–86.

———. 1998. The economic and jurisprudential ideas of the ancient Greeks: Our heritage from Hellenic thought. In *Ancient and Medieval Economic Ideas and Concepts of Social Justice*, ed. Barry Gordon and S. Todd Lowry. New York: Brill.

Luhmann, Niklas. 1986. *Ökologische Kommunikation: Kann die moderne Gesellschaft sich auf ökologische gefährdungen einstellen*. Oplade: Westdeutcher Verlag.

Macaulay, Thomas Babington. 1829. Mill's Essay on Government: Utilitarian logic and politics. *Edinburgh Review* 49, no. 97 (March): 159–89. (Reprinted in Macaulay's *Miscellaneous Writings*, 1:388–419.)

———. 1852. *Lord Bacon*. London: Longman, Brown, Green, and Longmans.

Mackintosh, James. 1818. Universal suffrage. *Edinburgh Review* 31, no. 61 (December): 165–203.

———. 1820. Parliamentary reform. *Edinburgh Review* 34, no. 68 (November): 461–502.

———. 1832. *A General View of the Progress of Ethical Philosophy & Etc*. Philadelphia: Carey and Lee.

———. 1836. *Memoirs of the Life of the Right Honourable Sir James Mackintosh.* 2nd ed. Ed.Robert James Mackintosh. 2 vols. Repr., Boston: Little, Brown and Company, 1853. (Orig. pub. 1835.)

Macpherson, C. B. 1962. *The Political Theory of Possessive Individualism: Hobbes to Locke.* Oxford: Oxford University Press.

———. 1973. *Democratic Theory: Essays in Retrieval.* Oxford: Oxford University Press.

Malthus, Thomas Robert. 1796. The Crisis, a view of the present state of Britain, by a friend to the constitution. Surviving paragraphs of unpublished pamphlet. In *The Occasional Papers of T.R. Malthus,* ed. Bernard Semmel, 241–46. Repr., New York: Burt Franklin, 1963.

———. 1798a. *An Essay on the Principle of Population, as It Affects the Future Improvement of Society & Etc.* London: J. Johnson. (Reprinted as *First Essay on Population, 1798,* for the Royal Economic Society, with notes by James Bonar [London: Macmillan, 1926].)

———. 1798b. *An Essay on the Principle of Population as It Affects the Future Improvement of Society with Remarks on the Speculations of Mr. Godwin, M. Condorcet, and Other Writers.* London: J. Johnson. (Reprinted in E. A. Wrigley and D. Souden, eds., *The Works of Thomas Robert Malthus,* vol. 1 [London: W. Pickering, 1986].)

———. 1800. Investigation of the Cause of the Present High Price of Provisions. In *The Works of Thomas Robert Malthus,* ed. E. A. Wrigley and D. Souden, 7:9. Repr., London: W. Pickering, 1986.

———. 1803. *An Essay on the Principle of Population or a View of Its Past and Present Effects on Human Happiness; with an Inquiry into Our Prospects Respecting the Future Removal or Mitigation of the Evils Which It Occasions* (with the variora of 1806, 1807, 1817, and 1826). Ed. Patricia James. 2 vols. Repr., Cambridge: Cambridge University Press, 1989.

———. 1820. *Principles of Political Economy.* (Vol. 1 of the Variorum edition.) Ed. John Pullen. 2 vols. Cambridge: Cambridge University Press.

———. 1823. *The Measure of Value.* In *The Works of Thomas Robert Malthus,* ed. E. A. Wrigley and D. Souden, 7:179. Repr., London: W. Pickering, 1986.

———. 1824. Review of J.R. McCulloch's "Essay on Political Economy" in the *Supplement to the Encyclopedia Britannica. Quarterly* Review 30, no. 60, article 1, 297–334. (Reprinted in E. A. Wrigley and D. Souden, eds., *The Works of Thomas Robert Malthus,* vol. 7 [London: W. Pickering, 1986].)

———. 1826. *An Essay on the Principle of Population as It Affects the Future Improvement of Society with Remarks on the Speculations of Mr. Godwin, M. Condorcet, and Other Writers.* London: J. Johnson. (Reprinted in E. A. Wrigley and D. Souden, eds., *The Works of Thomas Robert Malthus,* vol. 1 [London: W. Pickering, 1986].)

———. 1836. *Principles of Political Economy.* In *The Works of Thomas Robert Malthus,* ed. E. A. Wrigley and D. Souden, 5:8. Repr., London: W. Pickering, 1986.

Malynes, Gerard de. 1601. *A Treatise of the Canker of England's Commonwealth.* London: Richard Field for William Johnes. (Reprinted [in part] in Richard H. Tawney and Eileen Power, eds., *Tudor Economic Documents: Being*

Selected Documents Illustrating the Economic and Social History of Tudor England [New York: Barnes and Noble, 1963].)

Mandeville, Bernard. 1714. *Fable of the Bees*. Ed. P. Harth. Repr., Baltimore: Penguin Books, 1970.

Manuel, Frank, and Fritzie Manuel. 1979. *Utopian Thought in the Western World*. Cambridge, MA: Harvard University Press.

Marcet, Jane. 1821. *Conversations on Political Economy, in Which the Elements of That Science Are Familiarly Explained*. 4th ed. London: Longman, Hurst, Rees, Orme, and Brown. (Orig. pub. 1816.)

Marshall, Alfred. 1890. *Principles of Economics*. 8th ed. Repr., London: Macmillan, 1920.

Marshall, Alfred, and Mary Paley Marshall. 1881. *The Economics of Industry*. 2nd ed. London: Macmillan. (Orig. pub. 1879.)

Marx, Karl. 1846. *Letter to P. V. Annenkov*. In *The Marx-Engels Reader*, ed. Robert C. Tucker, 136–42. 2nd ed. Repr., New York: W. W. Norton, 1978.

———. 1848. *Manifesto of the Communist Party*. In *The Marx-Engels Reader*, ed. Robert C. Tucker, 469–500. 2nd ed. Repr., New York: W. W. Norton, 1978.

———. 1849. Wage labour and capital. In *The Marx-Engels Reader*, ed. Robert C. Tucker, 2nd ed. Repr., New York: W. W. Norton, 1978.

———. 1858. *Contribution to the Critique of Political Economy*. Repr., London: Lawrence and Wishart, 1948.

———. 1859. *Groundwork of the Critique of Political Economy*. Repr., Harmondsworth, UK: Penguin, 1993.

———. 1867. *Capital*. Vol. 1. Ed. E. Mandel. Repr., New York: Vintage, 1977.

———. 1963. *Theories of Surplus Value*. 3 vols. Moscow: Progress Publishers.

McCulloch, John Ramsay. 1818. Ricardo's political economy. *Edinburgh Review* 30, no. 59 (June): 59–87.

———. 1827. *Principles of Political Economy*. Edinburgh.

McLean, Ian. 2006. *Adam Smith, Radical and Egalitarian: An Interpretation for the Twenty-first Century*. Edinburgh: Edinburgh University Press.

Meek, Ronald L. 1956. *Studies in the Labour Theory of Value*. London: Lawrence and Wishart.

———. 1967. *Economics and Ideology and Other Essays: Studies in the Development of Economic Thought*. London: Chapman and Hall.

———. 1972. Marginalism and Marxism. *History of Political Economy* 4 (2). (Reprinted in Ronald L. Meek, *Smith, Marx, and After: Ten Essays in the Development of Economic Thought* [London: Chapman and Hall, 1977].)

———, ed. 1973. *Turgot on Progress, Sociology, and Economics*. Repr., Cambridge: Cambridge University Press, 1973.

———. 1976. New light on Adam Smith's Glasgow lectures on jurisprudence. *History of Political Economy* 8:439–77.

———. 1977. *Smith, Marx, and After: Ten Essays in the Development of Economic Thought*. London: Chapman and Hall.

Meikle, S. 1979. Aristotle and the political economy of the polis. *Journal of Hellenic Studies* 99:57–93.

Menger, Carl. 1871. *Grundsätze der Volkswirtschaftslehre*. Trans. as *Principles of Economics*, introd. Friedrich A. Hayek. Repr., New York: New York University Press, 1981.

———. 1883. *Untersuchungen über die Methode der Socialwissenschaften und die politischen Ökonomie insbesondere*. In *Investigations into the Method of Social Sciences with Special Reference to Economics*. Trans. F. J. Nock, introd. L. H. White. Repr., New York: New York University Press, 1985.

Mercier de la Riviere, Pierre-Paul. 1767. *The Natural and Essential Order of Political Societies*. In *Source Readings in Economic Thought*, ed. Phillip C. Newman, A. D. Gayer, and M. H. Spencer. Repr., New York: W. W. Norton, 1954. (Reprinted in Phillip C. Newman, A. D. Gayer, and M. H. Spencer, eds., *Source Readings in Economic Thought* [New York: W. W. Norton, 1954].)

Milgate, Murray. 1982. *Capital and Employment*. London: Academic Press.

Milgate, Murray, and Shannon C. Stimson. 1991a. Economic opinion on parliamentary reform: The case of Ricardo. *Contributions to Political Economy* 10:21–45.

———. 1991b. *Ricardian Politics*. Princeton, NJ: Princeton University Press.

Mill, James. 1804. Lord Lauderdale on public wealth. *Literary Journal* 4, no. 1 (July): 1–18.

———. 1806a. Colquhoun's system of education for the labouring poor. *Literary Journal* 2 (2nd series): 528–39.

———. 1806b. Craig on Millar. *Literary Journal* 1, no. 6, 2nd series (June): 624–29.

———. 1806c. Filangieri on the science of legislation. *Literary Journal* 2, no. 3, 2nd series (September): 225–42.

———. 1806d. Sir James Steuart's works. *Literary Journal* 1, no. 3, 2nd series (March): 225–35.

———. 1808a. *Commerce Defended*. Repr., New York: Augustus M. Kelley, 1965.

———. 1808b. [Thomas] Smith on money and exchange. *Edinburgh Review* 13, no. 25 (October): 35–68.

———. 1809. Emancipation of Spanish America. *Edinburgh Review* 13, no. 26 (January): 277–311.

———. 1812. *Schools for All, in Preference to Schools for Churchmen Only*. Orig. pub. in the *Philanthropist*. (Reprinted in W. H. Burston, ed., *James Mill on Education* [Cambridge: Cambridge University Press, 1969].)

———. 1813. Education of the poor. *Edinburgh Review* 21, no. 41 (February): 207–19.

———. 1814. Corn laws. *Eclectic Review* 2, new series (July): 1–17.

———. 1815. Stewart's Philosophy of the Human Mind. *British Review and London Critical Journal* 6 (August): 170–200.

———. 1817a. *Banks for Savings*. Orig. pub. in *Encyclopedia Britannica* (1816–24), suppl., 4th, 5th, and 6th eds., 2:91–101.

———. 1817b. *Benefit Societies*. Orig. pub. in *Encyclopedia Britannica* (1816–24), suppl., 4th, 5th, and 6th eds., 2:263–69.

———. 1817c. *Colony*. Orig. pub. in *Encyclopedia Britannica* (1816–24), suppl., 4th, 5th, and 6th eds., 3:257–73.

Mill, James. 1818a. *Economists*. Orig. pub. in *Encyclopedia Britannica* (1816–24), suppl., 4th, 5th, and 6th eds. , 3:703–24.

———. 1818b. *Education*. Orig. pub. in *Encyclopedia Britannica* (1816–1824), suppl., 4th, 5th, and 6th eds. (Reprinted in W. H. Burston, ed., *James Mill on Education* [Cambridge: Cambridge University Press, 1969].)

———. 1820a. *Government*. Orig. pub. in *Encyclopedia Britannica* (1816–24), suppl., 4th, 5th, and 6th eds. (Reprinted in James Mill, *Essays on Government, Jurisprudence, Liberty of the Press, and Law of Nations* [London: J. Innes, 1825].)

———. 1820b. *Jurisprudence*. Orig. pub. in *Encyclopedia Britannica* (1816–24), suppl., 4th, 5th, and 6th eds. (Reprinted in James Mill, *Essays on Government, Jurisprudence, Liberty of the Press, and Law of Nations* [London: J. Innes, 1825].)

———. 1821. *Liberty of the Press*. Orig. pub. in *Encyclopedia Britannica* (1816–24), suppl., 4th, 5th, and 6th eds. (Reprinted in James Mill, *Essays on Government, Jurisprudence, Liberty of the Press, and Law of Nations* [London: J. Innes, 1825].)

———. 1824a. Periodical literature: *Edinburgh Review*. *Westminster Review* 1, no. 1 (January): 206–49.

———. 1824b. Periodical literature: *The Quarterly Review*. *Westminster Review* 2, no. 3 (October): 463–503.

———. 1826a. *Elements of Political Economy*. 3rd ed. London: Baldwin, Cradock and Joy. (Orig. pub. 1821; reprinted in James Mill, *James Mill: Selected Economic Writings*, ed. Donald Winch [Edinburgh: Oliver and Boyd, 1966], 203–366.)

———. 1826b. Formation of opinions. *Westminster Review* 6, no. 11 (July): 1–23.

———. 1826c. On the nature, measure, and causes of value. *Westminster Review* 5, no. 9 (January): 157–72.

———. 1826d. State of the nation. *Westminster Review* 6, no. 12 (October): 249–78.

———. 1826e. Summary review of the conduct and measures of the Seventh Imperial Parliament. *Parliamentary History and Review*. London.

———. 1827. Constitutional legislation. *Parliamentary Review*, sessions of 1826–27 and 1827–28, 335–74. London: Baldwin and Cradock.

———. 1829. *An Analysis of the Phenomena of the Human Mind*. 2 vols. Ed. with additional notes John Stuart Mill (1869). Repr., New York: Augustus M. Kelley, 1967.

———. 1830. The ballot. *Westminster Review* 13, no. 27 (July): 1–39.

———. 1835a. The ballot: A dialogue. *London Review* 1, no. 1 (April): 201–53.

———. 1835b. *A Fragment on Mackintosh: Being Strictures on Some Passages in the Dissertation by Sir James Mackintosh, Prefixed to the Encyclopedia Britannica*. London: Baldwin and Cradock.

———. 1835c. Law reform. *London Review* 2, no. 3 (October): 1–51.

———. 1835d. The state of the nation. *London Review* 1, no. 1 (April): 1–24.

———. 1836a. Aristocracy. *London Review* 2, no. 4 (January): 283–306.

———. 1836b. Whether political economy is useful? A dialogue. *London Review* 2 (4): 553–72.

———. 1966. *James Mill: Selected Economic Writings*. Ed. Donald Winch. Edinburgh: Oliver and Boyd.

———. 1992. *James Mill: Political Writings*. Ed. Terence Ball. Cambridge: Cambridge University Press.

Mill, John Stuart. 1824. War expenditure. *Westminster Review* 2 (July): 27–48.

———. 1825a. McCulloch's discourse on political economy. *Westminster Review* 4 (July). (Reprinted in John Stuart Mill, *Collected Works of John Stuart Mill*, ed. J. M. Robson et al. [Toronto: University of Toronto Press, 1963–91], 5:757–60.)

———. 1825b. The Quarterly Review: Political Economy. *Westminster Review* 3, no. 5, article 9 (January): 213–32. Reprinted in *The Occasional Papers of T.R. Malthus*, ed. Bernard Semmel. Repr., New York: Burt Franklin, 1963.

———. 1835. Tocqueville on democracy in America. Vol. 1. *London and Westminster Review* (October). In *Essays on Politics and Culture: John Stuart Mill*, ed. Gertrude Himmelfarb, 173–213. Repr., Gloucester: Peter Smith, 1972. (Also in John Stuart Mill, *Collected Works of John Stuart Mill*, ed. J. M. Robson et al. [Toronto: University of Toronto Press, 1963–91], 18:47–90.)

———. 1836. On the definition of political economy; and on the method of philosophical investigation in that science. *London and Westminster Review* 4, no. 26 (October): 1–29. (Reprinted *in Essays on Some Unsettled Questions*, under the title "On the definition of political economy; and the method of investigation proper to it," 120–64; also in John Stuart Mill, *Collected Works of John Stuart Mill*, ed. J. M. Robson et al. [Toronto: University of Toronto Press, 1963–91], 4:309–39).

———. 1838. Bentham. *London and Westminster Review* 31 (August). In *Essays on Politics and Culture: John Stuart Mill*, ed. Gertrude Himmelfarb, 77–120. Repr., Gloucester, MA: Peter Smith, 1972. (Also in John Stuart Mill, *Collected Works of John Stuart Mill*, ed. J. M. Robson et al. [Toronto: University of Toronto Press, 1963–91], 10:75–115).

———. 1840. Tocqueville on democracy in America (volume 2). *Edinburgh Review*, October 1840. In *Essays on Politics and Culture: John Stuart Mill*, ed. Gertrude Himmelfarb, 214–17. Repr., Gloucester, MA: Peter Smith, 1972. (Also in John Stuart Mill, *Collected Works of John Stuart Mill*, ed. J. M. Robson et al. [Toronto: University of Toronto Press, 1963–91], 18:153–204.)

———. 1845. Review of Arthur Helps: *The Claims of Labour: An Essay on the Duty of the Employers to the Employed*. *Edinburgh Review* 81 (April): 498–525. (Reprinted in John Stuart Mill, *Dissertations and Discussions* [1859], 2:181–217.)

———. 1859. *On Liberty*. In *Three Essays & Etc.*, 1–141. Repr., Oxford: Oxford University Press, 1975. (Also in John Stuart Mill, *Collected Works of John Stuart Mill*, ed. J. M. Robson et al. [Toronto: University of Toronto Press, 1963–91], 18:213–310.)

———. 1861a. *Considerations on Representative Government*. In *Three Essays & Etc.*, 143–423. Repr., Oxford: Oxford University Press, 1975. (Also in

John Stuart Mill, *Collected Works of John Stuart Mill*, ed. J. M. Robson et al. [Toronto: University of Toronto Press, 1963–91], 19:371–577.)

———. 1861b. *Utilitarianism*. Ed. and introd. Mary Warnock, 251–321. Repr., New York: Meridian, 1974. (Also in John Stuart Mill, *Collected Works of John Stuart Mill*, ed. J. M. Robson et al. [Toronto: University of Toronto Press, 1963–91], 10:203–326.)

———. 1863. *Utilitarianism*. 2nd ed. First published in three parts in *Fraser's Magazine* (1861). Repr., London: George Routledge and Sons, 1895.

———. 1869. *On the Subjection of Women*. In *Essays on Equality, Law, and Education*, 259–340. (Vol. 21 of the *Collected Works of John Stuart Mill*.

———. 1871. *Principles of Political Economy, with Some of Their Applications to Social Philosophy*. Ed. J. M. Robson and introd. V. W. Bladen. (Vols. 2 and 3 of the *Collected Works of John Stuart Mill*.)

———. 1872. *A System of Logic Ratiocinative and Inductive, Being a Connected View of the Principles of Evidence and Methods of Scientific Investigation*. Ed. J. M. Robson, introd. R. F. McRae. (Vol. 8 of the *Collected Works of John Stuart Mill*.)

———. 1873. *Autobiography of John Stuart Mill*. Preface John Jacob Coss. Repr., New York: Columbia University Press, 1924. (Also in John Stuart Mill, *Collected Works of John Stuart Mill*, ed. J. M. Robson et al. [Toronto: University of Toronto Press, 1963–91], 1:4–290.)

———. 1874. *Essays on Some Unsettled Questions of Political Economy*. 2nd ed. (Orig. pub. 1844.) London: Longmans, Green, Reader, and Dyer. (Also in John Stuart Mill, *Collected Works of John Stuart Mill*, ed. J. M. Robson et al. [Toronto: University of Toronto Press, 1963–91], 4:229–341.)

———. 1879. Chapters on socialism. *Fortnightly Review* 25 (February–April). In vol. 2 of *Essays on Economics and Society*, ed. Lionel Robbins. (Vol. 5 of *Collected Works of John Stuart Mill*, 705–63.)

———. 1945. Notes on N.W. Senior's Political Economy, by F.A. Hayek. *Economica* 12, no. 47 (new series): 134–39.

———. 1963–91. *Collected Works of John Stuart Mill*. Ed. J. M. Robson et al. Toronto: University of Toronto Press.

Millett, Paul. 1983. Maritime loans and the structure of credit in fourth-century Athens. In *Trade in the Ancient Economy*, ed. Peter Garnsey, Keith Hopkins, and C. R. Whittaker. London: Chatto and Windus.

Mirabeau, Victor Riquetti, Marquis de. 1763. *Philosophie Rurale*. In *The Economics of Physiocracy: Essays and Translations*, ed. Ronald L. Meek. Repr., London: George Allen and Unwin., 1962.

Misselden, Edward. 1622. *Free Trade*. Repr., New York: Augustus M. Kelley, 1971.

Mitchell, B. R. 1988. *British Historical Statistics*. Cambridge: Cambridge University Press.

Mitchell, B. R., and Phyllis Deane. 1962. *Abstract of British Historical Statistics*. Cambridge: Cambridge University Press.

Montesquieu, Charles-Louis de Secondat. 1748. *Spirit of the Laws*. Repr., New York: Macmillan, 1949.

Moore, James. 1977. Hume's political science and the republican tradition. *Canadian Journal of Political Science* 19:809–39.

Moss, L. S. 1976. *Mountifort Longfield: Ireland's First Professor of Political Economy*. Ottowa, IL: Green Hill.

Mun, Thomas. 1664. *England's Treasure by Forraign Trade*. London: Thomas Clarke. (Repr., Oxford: Blackwell, 1949.)

Muthu, Sankar. 2008. Adam Smith's critique of international trading companies: Theorizing "globalization" in the age of enlightenment. *Political Theory* 36, no. 2 (April): 185–212.

Naim, Moisés. 2004. Globalization: Passing fad or permanent revolution? *Interventionism* 26, no. 1 (Spring).

Napier, Macvey. 1879. *Selections from the Correspondence of the Late Macvey Napier Esq*. Ed. his son. London: Macmillan.

Nelson, Eric. 2004. *The Greek Tradition in Republican Thought*. Cambridge: Cambridge University Press.

Nesbitt, George L. 1934. *Benthamite Reviewing: The First Twelve Years of the Westminster Review, 1824–1836*. New York: Columbia University Press.

Newman, Phillip C, A. D. Gayer, and M. H. Spencer, eds. 1954. *Source Readings in Economic Thought*. New York: W. W. Norton and Co.

New Palgrave: A Dictionary of Economics. 1987. Ed,. John Eatwell, Murray Milgate, and Peter Newman. 4 vols. London: Macmillan.

Nicole, Pierre. 1675. *The Grounds of Sovereignty and Greatness*. London.

Niehans, Jürg. 1990. *A History of Economic Theory: Classic Contributions, 1720–1980*. Baltimore: Johns Hopkins University Press.

Nozick, Robert. 1974. *Anarchy, State, and Utopia*. New York: Basic Books.

———. 1994. Invisible-hand explanations. *American Economic Review, Papers, and Proceedings* 8, no. 2 (May): 314–18.

O'Brian, Bronterre. 1837. Article for the *London Mercury*. In *From Cobbett to the Chartists*, ed. Max Morris. Repr., London: Lawrence and Wishart, 1948.

O'Brien, D. P. 1975. *The Classical Economists*. Oxford: Clarendon Press.

O'Driscoll, Gerald P., Jr. ed. 1979. *Adam Smith and Modern Political Economy: Bicentennial Essays on the Wealth of Nations*. Ames: Iowa State University Press.

Oldfield, T.H.B. 1816. *The Representative History of Great Britain and Ireland: Being a History of the House of Commons & Etc*. 6 vols. London: Baldwin, Cradock, and Joy.

Oncken, August. 1897. The consistency of Adam Smith. *Economic Journal* 7, no. 27 (September): 443–50.

Owen, Robert. 1816. *A New View of Society or Essays on the Formation of the Human Character & Etc*. Introd. John Saville. Repr., London: Macmillan, 1972.

———. 1857. *The Life of Robert Owen by Himself*. 2 vols. London: E. Wilson.

Paine, Thomas. 1776. *Common Sense*. In *The Debate on the American Revolution, 1761–1783*, ed. Max Beloff, 229–64. Repr., Dobbs Ferry, NY: Sheridan House, 1989.

Paley, William. 1802. *Natural Theology; or, Evidences of the Existence and Attributes of the Deity, Collected from the Appearances of Nature.* London: Longman, Brown, Green, and Longmans.

Parliamentary Debates from the Year 1803 to the Present Time: Forming a Continuation & Etc. Various years. London: T. C. Hansard.

Pascal, Roy. 1938. Property and society: The Scottish contribution of the eighteenth-century. *Modern Quarterly* 1:167–79.

Paul, Ellen Frankel. 1979. *Moral Revolution and Economic Science: The Demise of Laissez-faire in Nineteenth-Century British Political Economy.* Westport, CT: Greenwood Press.

Phillips, M. S. 1996. Reconsiderations on history and antiquarianism: Arnaldo Momigliano and the historiography of eighteenth-century Britain. *Journal of the History of Ideas* 57 (2): 297–316.

Phillipson, Nicholas. 1981. The Scottish enlightenment. In *The Enlightenment in National Context*, ed. Roy Porter and Mikulas Teich, 19–40. Cambridge: Cambridge University Press.

———. 1987. Adam Ferguson. In *The New Palgrave: A Dictionary of Economics*, ed. John Eatwell, Murray Milgate, and Peter Newman, 2:301. London: Macmillan.

———. 2000. Language, sociability, and history: Some reflections on the foundations of Adam Smith's science of man. In *Economy, Polity, and Society: British Intellectual History, 1750–1950*, ed. Stefan Collini, Richard Whatmore, and Brian Young. Cambridge: Cambridge University Press. Pigou, Arthur Cecil. 1935. *The Economics of Stationary States.* London: Macmillan.

Place, Francis. 1822. *Illustrations and Proofs of the Principle of Population & Etc.* Ed. and introd. Norman Himes. Repr., London: George Allen and Unwin, 1930.

Plant, R. 1977. Hegel and political economy: I and II. *New Left Review* 103–4:79–92, 103–13.

Pocock, J.G.A. 1975. *The Machiavellian Moment: Florentine Political Thought and the Atlantic Republican Tradition.* Princeton, NJ: Princeton University Press.

———. 1983. Adam Smith as civic moralist. In *Wealth and Virtue: The Shaping of Political Economy in the Scottish Enlightenment*, ed. Istvan Hont and Michael Ignatieff. Cambridge: Cambridge University Press.

———. 1985. *Virtue, Commerce, and History: Essays on Political Thought and History, Chiefly in the Eighteenth Century.* Cambridge: Cambridge University Press.

Polanyi, Karl. 1944. *The Great Transformation: The Political and Economic Origins of Our Time.* New York: Farrar and Rinehart.

Pomeroy, Sarah B. 1994. *Xenophon, Oeconomicus: A Social and Historical Commentary.* New York: Oxford University Press.

Pope, Alexander. 1733. *An Essay on Man.* In *The Poems of Alexander Pope*, ed. John Butt. Vol. 3 (ed. Maynard Mack). Repr., London: Methuen, 1950.

Porter, Roy, and Mikulas Teich, eds. 1981. *The Enlightenment in National Context.* Cambridge: Cambridge University Press.

Poynter, J. R. 1969. *Society and Pauperism.* London: Routledge.

Pribram, Karl. 1983. *A History of Economic Reasoning*. Baltimore: Johns Hopkins University Press.

Quesnay, François. 1765. Observations sur le droit naturel des hommes réunis en société. *Journal de l'agriculture, du commerce & des finances* (September): 4–35.

Rae, John. 1895. *The Life of Adam Smith*. London: Macmillan.

Rashid, Salim. 1982. Adam Smith's rise to fame: A re-examination of the evidence. *Eighteenth Century: Theory and Interpretation* 23:64–85.

Rasmussen, Dennis C. 2006. Does "bettering our condition" really make us better off? Adam Smith on progress and happiness. *American Political Science Review* 100, no. 3 (August): 309–18.

Ravenstone, Piercy [Richard Puller]. 1824. *Thoughts on the Funding System and Its Effects*. London: J. Andrews. Repr., New York: Augustus M. Kelley, 1966.

Rawls, John. 1971. *A Theory of Justice*. Cambridge: Cambridge University Press.

Read, Samuel. 1821. *General Statement of an Argument on the Subject of Population, in Answer to Mr Malthus's Theory*. Edinburgh: Macredie, Skelly, and Company. Repr., New York: Augustus M. Kelley, 1976.

———. 1829. *Political Economy: An Inquiry into the Natural Grounds of Right to Vendible Property or Wealth*. Edinburgh: Oliver and Boyd. Repr., New York: Augustus M. Kelley, 1976.

Report from the Select Committee on the High Price of Gold Bullion [The Bullion Report]. 1810. In *The Paper Pound of 1797–1812*, 3–72. Repr., New York: A. M. Kelley, 1969.

Ricardo, David. 1810. *The High Price of Bullion, a Proof of the Depreciation of Banknotes*. In *The Works and Correspondence of David Ricardo*, ed. Piero Sraffa with Maurice H. Dobb, 3:47–127. Repr., Cambridge: Cambridge University Press, 1951–73.

———. 1815. *An Essay on the Influence of a Low Price of Corn on the Profits of Stock*. In *The Works and Correspondence of David Ricardo*, ed. Piero Sraffa with Maurice H. Dobb, 4:1–42. Repr., Cambridge: Cambridge University Press, 1951–73.

———. 1816. *Proposals for an Economical and Secure Currency*. In *The Works and Correspondence of David Ricardo*, ed. Piero Sraffa with Maurice H. Dobb, 4:43, 141. Repr., Cambridge: Cambridge University Press, 1951–73.

———. 1820a. *Funding System*. In *The Works and Correspondence of David Ricardo*, ed. Piero Sraffa with Maurice H. Dobb. Repr., Cambridge: Cambridge University Press, 1951–73.

———. 1820b. *Notes on Mr Malthus's work "Principles of Political Economy, Considered with a View to Their Practical Application."* In *The Works and Correspondence of David Ricardo*, ed. Piero Sraffa with Maurice H. Dobb. Repr., Cambridge: Cambridge University Press, 1951–73.

———. 1821. *The Principles of Political Economy and Taxation*. 3rd ed. (Vol. 1 of Ricardo's *Works and Correspondence*, 1817.)

———. 1822. *On Protection to Agriculture*. In *The Works and Correspondence of David Ricardo*, ed. Piero Sraffa with Maurice H. Dobb, 4:207–70. Repr., Cambridge: Cambridge University Press, 1951–73.

Ricardo, David. 1823. *On Blake's "Observations on the Effects Produced by the Expenditure of Government."* In *The Works and Correspondence of David Ricardo*, ed. Piero Sraffa with Maurice H. Dobb, 4:323–56. Repr., Cambridge: Cambridge University Press, 1951–73.

———. 1824a. *Defence of the Plan of Voting by Ballot*. In *The Works and Correspondence of David Ricardo*, ed. Piero Sraffa with Maurice H. Dobb, 5:504–12. Repr., Cambridge: Cambridge University Press, 1951–73.

———. 1824b. *Observations on Parliamentary Reform*. In *The Works and Correspondence of David Ricardo*, ed. Piero Sraffa with Maurice H. Dobb, 5:495–503. Repr., Cambridge: Cambridge University Press, 1951–73.

———. 1824c. *Plan for the Establishment of a National Bank*. In *The Works and Correspondence of David Ricardo*, ed. Piero Sraffa with Maurice H. Dobb, 4:275–97. Repr., Cambridge: Cambridge University Press, 1951–73.

———. 1951–73. *The Works and Correspondence of David Ricardo*. 11 vols. Ed. Piero Sraffa with Maurice H. Dobb. Cambridge: Cambridge University Press.

Riley, Jonathan. 1998a. *Mill on Liberty*. London: Routledge.

———. 1998b. Mill's political economy: Ricardian science and liberal utilitarian art. In *The Cambridge Companion to Mill*, ed. John Skorupski. Cambridge: Cambridge University Press.

Robbins, Lionel Charles. 1932. *An Essay on the Nature and Significance of Economic Science*. London: Macmillan.

———. 1961. *The Theory of Economic Policy in English Classical Political Economy*. London: Macmillan.

Robertson, John. 1983. Scottish political economy beyond the civic tradition: Government and economic development in the *Wealth of Nations*. *History of Political Thought* 4, no. 3 (Winter): 451–82.

———. 1997. The enlightenment above national context: Political economy in eighteenth-century Scotland and Naples. *Historical Journal* 40 (3): 667–97.

———. 2000. The Scottish contribution to the enlightenment. In *The Scottish Enlightenment: Essays in Re-Interpretation*, ed. Paul Wood, 37–62. Rochester, NY: University of Rochester Press.

———. 2005. *The Case for Enlightenment: Scotland and Naples, 1680–1760*. Cambridge: Cambridge University Press.

Robson, John M. 1968. *The Improvement of Mankind: The Social and Political Thought of John Stuart Mill*. Toronto: University of Toronto Press.

Robson, John M., and Michael Laine, eds. 1976. *James and John Stuart Mill: Papers of the Centenary Conference*. Toronto: University of Toronto Press.

Rodrik, Dani. 1997. *Has Globalization Gone Too Far? The Parameters of Desirable Integration*. Washington, DC: Institute for International Economics.

———. 1998. Symposium on globalization in perspective: An introduction. *Journal of Economic Perspectives* 12, no. 4 (Fall): 3–8.

———. 2007. The cheerleaders' threat to global trade. *Financial Times*, March 27.

Rosenberg, Nathan. 1979. Adam Smith and laissez faire revisited. In *Adam Smith and Modern Political Economy*, ed. Gerald O'Driscoll, 19–34. Iowa: Iowa State University Press.

Ross, Ian S. 1995. *The Life of Adam Smith*. Oxford: Clarendon Press.

Rothschild, Emma. 1992. Adam Smith and conservative economics. *Economic History Review* 16 (1): 74–96.

———. 1999. Globalization and the return of history. *Foreign Policy* 115 (Summer): 106–16.

———. 2001a. *Economic Sentiments: Adam Smith, Condorcet, and the Enlightenment.* Cambridge, MA: Harvard University Press.

———. 2001b. The politics of globalization circa 1773. *OECD Observer* 228 (September): 12–14.

———. 2004. Global commerce and the question of sovereignty in the eighteenth-century provinces. *Modern Intellectual History* 1 (1): 3–25.

Rothschild, Emma, and Amartya Sen. 2006. Adam Smith's economics. In *The Cambridge Companion to Adam Smith*, ed. Knud Haakonseen. Cambridge: Cambridge University Press.

Rotwein, Eugene, ed. 1955. *David Hume: Writings on Economics.* Repr., Madison: University of Wisconsin Press, 1970.

———. 1987. David Hume. In *The New Palgrave: A Dictionary of Economics*, ed. John Eatwell, Murray Milgate, and Peter Newman, 2:692–95. London: Macmillan.

Ryan, Alan. 1970. *John Stuart Mill.* New York: Pantheon Books.

———. 1972. Two concepts of politics and democracy: James and John Stuart Mill. In *Machiavelli and the Nature of Political Thought*, ed. Martin Fleisher, 72–113. New York: Atheneum.

———. 1984. *Property and Political Theory.* Oxford: Basil Blackwell.

Samuelson, Paul. 1948. *Economics.* New York: McGraw-Hill.

———. 1978. The canonical classical model of political economy. *Journal of Economic Literature* 18:1415–34.

Say, Jean-Baptiste. 1821a. *A Catechism of Political Economy.* In *Letters to Mr Malthus on Several Subjects of Political Economy & Etc*, trans. J. Richter. Repr., New York: Augustus M. Kelley, 1967.

———. 1821b. *Letters to Mr Malthus on Several Subjects of Political Economy & Etc.* Trans. J. Richter. Repr., New York: Augustus M. Kelley, 1967.

———. 1826. *A Treatise on Political Economy.* Trans. C. R. Prinsep. 5th ed. Repr., Philadelphia: Claxton, Ramsen and Haffelfinder, 1834. (Orig. pub. 1803.)

Schofield, Malcolm. 1991. *The Stoic Idea of the City.* Cambridge: Cambridge University Press.

Schofield, R., and E. A. Wrigley, eds. 1986. *Population and Economy: Population and History from the Traditional to the Modern World.* Cambridge: Cambridge University Press.

Schumpeter, Joseph A. 1954. *History of Economic Analysis.* Oxford: Oxford University Press.

Scrope, George Poulett. 1833. *Principles of Political Economy.* London: Longman. Repr., New York: Augustus M. Kelley, 1969. (A second edition was published in 1873 under the title *Political Economy for Plain People.*)

Semmel, Bernard. 1963a. Malthus and the reviews. In *Occasional Papers of T.R. Malthus*, ed. Bernard Semmel. New York: Burt Franklin.

Semmel, Bernard, ed. 1963b. *The Occasional Papers of T.R. Malthus*. New York: Burt Franklin.

———. 1965. Malthus's "Physiocracy" and the commercial system. *Economic History Review* 17: 522–35.

———. 1984. *John Stuart Mill and the Pursuit of Virtue*. New Haven, CT: Yale University Press.

———. 1993. *The Liberal Ideal and the Demons of Empire: Theories of Imperialism from Adam Smith to Lenin*. Baltimore: Johns Hopkins University Press.

Senior, Nassau William. 1827. *An Introductory Lecture on Political Economy*. In *Selected Writings on Economics: A Volume of Pamphlets, 1827–1852*. Repr., New York: Augustus M. Kelley, 1965.

———. 1836. *An Outline of the Science of Political Economy*. Repr., New York: Augustus M. Kelley.

Shelley, Percy Bysshe. 1819–20. *A Philosophical View of Reform*. In *The Complete Works of Percy Bysshe Shelley*, ed. Roger Ingpen and Walter E. Peck, 7:1–55. Repr., London: Ernest Benn.

———. 1965. *The Complete Works of Percy Bysshe Shelley*. Ed. Roger Ingpen and Walter E. Peck. 10 vols. London: Ernest Benn.

Sherwood, J. M. 1985. Engels, Marx, Malthus, and the machine. *American Historical Review* 90, no. 4 (October): 837–65.

Sismondi, Jean-Charles-Léonard Simonde de. 1814. *Political Economy*. Repr., New York: Augustus M. Kelley, 1966.

Skidelsky, R. 1992. *John Maynard Keynes: The Economist as Savior, 1920–1937*. London: Macmillan.

Skinner, Andrew S. 1974. *Adam Smith and the Role of the State*. Glasgow: University of Glasgow Press. (Reprinted in Andrew S. Skinner, *A System of Social Science: Papers Relating to Adam Smith* [Oxford: Oxford University Press, 1979].)

———. 1978. Introd. to *The Wealth of Nations: Books I–III*, ed. Andrew S. Skinner. Harmondsworth, UK: Penguin. (Orig. pub. 1970.)

———. 1979. *A System of Social Science: Papers Relating to Adam Smith*. Oxford: Oxford University Press.

———. 1990. The shaping of political economy in the enlightenment. *Scottish Journal of Political Economy* 37 (2): 145–65. (Reprinted as "Political Economy: Adam Smith and His Scottish Predecessors," in Peter Jones and Andrew S. Skinner, eds., *Adam Smith Reviewed* [Edinburgh: Edinburgh University Press, 1992], 217–43).

Skinner, Andrew S., and Thomas Wilson. 1976. *The Market and the State: Essays on Adam Smith*. Oxford: Clarendon Press.

Skinner, Quentin. 1969. Meaning and understanding in the history of ideas. *History and Theory* 8 (1): 3–53.

———. 1972. Motives, intentions and the interpretation of text. *New Literary History* 3:393–408. (Revised and reprinted in Quentin Skinner, *Visions of Politics: Regarding Method*, vol. 1 [Cambridge: Cambridge University Press, 2002].)

———. 1988. Interpretation and the understanding of speech acts. In *Meaning and Context*, ed. James Tully. Cambridge: Cambridge University Press. (Revised and reprinted in Quentin Skinner, *Visions of Politics: Regarding Method*, vol. 1 [Cambridge: Cambridge University Press, 2002].)

———. 1998. *Liberty before Liberalism*. Cambridge: Cambridge University Press.

———. 2002. Interpretation and the understanding of speech acts. In *Visions of Politics*, 1:103, 127. Cambridge: Cambridge University Press.

Skorupski, John. 1989. *John Stuart Mill*. London: Routledge.

Smith, Adam. ca. 1750. *The Principles Which Lead and Direct Philosophical Enquiries Illustrated by the History of Astronomy*. In W.P.D. Wrightman and J. C. Bryce (eds) *Essays on Philosophical Subjects*, ed. W.P.D. Wrightman and J. C. Bryce. (Vol. 3 of D. D. Raphael and Andrew S. Skinner, eds., *The Works and Correspondence of Adam Smith* [Oxford: Clarendon, 1980].)

———. 1759. *The Theory of Moral Sentiments*. Ed. A. L. Macfie and D. D. Raphael. (Vol. 1 of the Glasgow edition of Smith's *Works and Correspondence*.)

———. 1762–66. *Lectures on Jurisprudence*. Ed. Ronald L. Meek, D. D. Raphael, and Peter Stein. Repr., Indianapolis: Liberty Classics, 1982.

———. 1776. *An Inquiry into the Nature and Causes of the Wealth of Nations*. Ed. R. H. Campbell and Andrew S. Skinner (from 4th ed., 1786). 2 vols. (Vol. 2 of the Glasgow edition of Smith's *Works and Correspondence*.)

———. 1795. *Essays on Philosophical Subjects*. Vol. 3 of *The Works and Correspondence of Adam Smith*, ed. W.P.D. Wightman and J. C. Bryce. Repr., Oxford: Oxford University Press, 1976–85.

———. 1976–85. *The Works and Correspondence of Adam Smith*. The Glasgow edition. 6 vols. Oxford: Oxford University Press.

———. 2007. *An Inquiry into the Nature and Causes of the Wealth of Nations*. Ed. Jonathan Wright. Hampshire: Harriman House Publishers.

Soudek, J. 1952. Aristotle's theory of exchange: An inquiry into the origin of economic analysis. *Proceedings of the American Philosophical Society* 96:45–75.

Spengler, Joseph. 1975. Adam Smith and society's decision-makers. In *The Market and the State: Essays on Adam Smith*, ed. Andrew S. Skinner and Thomas Wilson. Oxford: Clarendon Press.

Spiegel, Henry William. 1983. *The Growth of Economic Thought*. Rev. ed. Durham, NC: Duke University Press. (Orig. pub. 1971.)

Sraffa, Piero. 1960. *Production of Commodities by Means of Commodities*. Cambridge: Cambridge University Press.

Stark, Werner. 1943. *The Ideal Foundations of Economic Thought: Three Essays on the Philosophy of Economics*. London: Kegan Paul.

Stephen, Leslie. 1878. The first Edinburgh reviewers. *Cornhill Magazine* 38 (August). (Reprinted in Leslie Stephen, *Hours in a Library* [G. P. Putnam's Sons, 1894], 1:241–69.)

———. 1894. *Hours in a Library*. New ed. in 3 vols. New York: G. P. Putnam's Sons. (Orig. pubc. 1874–79.)

———. 1900. *The English Utilitarians*. 3 vols. Repr., New York: Peter Smith, 1950.

———. 1902. *English Thought in the Eighteenth Century*. 3rd ed. 2 vols. London: John Murray. (Orig. pub. 1876.)

Steuart, James. 1767. *An Inquiry into the Principles of Political Economy.* Ed. Andrew S. Skinner. 2 vols. Repr., Edinburgh: Oliver and Boyd, 1966.

Stewart, Dugald. 1792–1827. *Elements of the Philosophy of the Human Mind.* In vols. 2, 3, and 4 of *The Collected Works of Dugald Stewart*, Dugald Stewart, ed. William Hamilton. Repr., Edinburgh: Thomas Constable and Company, 1854–60.

———. 1793. *An Account of the Life and Writings of Adam Smith LL.D.* From *The Transactions of the Royal Society of Edinburgh*, and reprinted in *The Collected Works of Dugald Stewart*, Dugald Stewart, ed. William Hamilton. Repr., Edinburgh: Thomas Constable and Company, 1854–60, 10:5–98. (This volume was reprinted with the same pagination under the title *Biographical Memoirs of Adam Smith, William Robertson, and Thomas Reid* [New York: Augustus M. Kelley, 1966].)

———. 1801. Critical examination of a late *Essay on the Principle of Population as it Affects the Future Improvement of Society.* In *The Collected Works of Dugald Stewart*, by Dugald Stewart, ed. William Hamilton, 8:203, 207. Repr., Edinburgh: Thomas Constable and Company, 1854–60.

———. 1809–10. *Lectures on Political Economy.* Vols. 8 and 9 of *The Collected Works of Dugald Stewart*, Dugald Stewart, ed. William Hamilton. Repr., Edinburgh: Thomas Constable and Company, 1854–60.

———. 1811. *Notes on the Bullion Report.* (Six notes sent to Lord Lauderdale.) In *The Collected Works of Dugald Stewart*, by Dugald Stewart, ed. William Hamilton, 8:431, 452. Repr., Edinburgh: Thomas Constable and Company, 1854–60.

———. 1815–21. *Dissertation Exhibiting the Progress of Metaphysical, Ethical, and Political Philosophy since the Revival of Letters in Europe.* In vol. 1 of *The Collected Works of Dugald Stewart*, Dugald Stewart, ed. William Hamilton. Repr., Edinburgh: Thomas Constable and Company, 1854–60.

———. 1854–60. *The Collected Works of Dugald Stewart.* Ed. William Hamilton. 11 vols. Edinburgh: Thomas Constable and Company.

Stewart, M. A. 1991. The stoic legacy in the early Scottish enlightenment. In *Atoms, Pneuma, and Tranquility: Epicurean and Stoic Themes in European Thought*, ed. Margaret Osler. Cambridge: Cambridge University Press.

Stigler, George, J. 1982. The economists and the problem of monopoly. *American Economic Review* 72, no. 2 (May): 1–11.

Stimson, Shannon C. 2004. From invisible hand to moral restraint: The transformation of the market mechanism from Smith to Malthus. *Journal of Scottish Philosophy* 2, no. 1 (Spring): 22–47.

Stimson, Shannon C., and Murray Milgate. 1993. Utility, property, and political participation: James Mill on democratic reform. *American Political Science Review* 87, no. 4 (December): 901–11.

Syme, Ronald. 2002. *The Roman Revolution.* Oxford: Oxford University Press. (Orig. pub. 1939.)

Thomas, B. 1986. Escaping from constraints: The industrial revolution in Malthusian context. In *Population and Economy: Population and History from the Traditional to the Modern World*, ed. R. Schofield and E. A. Wrigley. Cambridge: Cambridge University Press.

Thomas, William. 1969. James Mill's politics: The "Essay on Government" and the movement for reform. *Historical Journal* 12 (2): 249–84.

———. 1979. *The Philosophic Radicals: Nine Studies in Theory and Practice: 1817–1841.* Oxford: Clarendon Press.

Thompson, Dennis F. 1976. *John Stuart Mill and Representative Government.* Princeton, NJ: Princeton University Press.

Thompson, E. P. 1971. The moral economy of the English crowd in the eighteenth century. *Past and Present* 50 (February): 76–136.

———. 1963. *The Making of the English Working Class.* Harmondsworth, UK: Penguin.

Thompson, Noel W. 1984. *The People's Science: The Popular Political Economy of Exploitation and Crisis, 1816–34.* Cambridge: Cambridge University Press.

———. 1987. John Bray. In *The New Palgrave: A Dictionary of Economics,* 1:274. London: Macmillan.

———. 1988. *The Market and Its Critics: Socialist Political Economy in Nineteenth Century Britain.* London: Routledge.

Tocqueville, Alexis de. 1848. *Democracy in America.* Trans. George Lawrence, ed. J. P. Mayer. 2 vols. in one. Repr., New York: Anchor, 1969.

———. 1858. *The Old Régime and the French Revolution.* Trans. S. Gilbert. 4th ed. (French ed.). Repr., New York: Anchor, 1955. (Orig. pub. 1856).

Tooke, Thomas. 1848. *A History of Prices and of the State of Circulation, from 1839 to 1847 & Etc.* London: Longman, Brown, Green, and Longmans.

Torrens, Robert. 1817. On the means of reducing the poor rates & etc. *Pamphleteer,* no. 20. In vol. 4 of *The Collected Works of Robert Torrens,* ed. Giancarlo De Vivo. Repr., Bristol: Thoemmes Press, 2000.

———. 1819. Mr Owen's plans for relieving the national distress. *Edinburgh Review* 32 (October): 453–77. (Reprinted in vol. 8 of *The Collected Works of Robert Torrens,* ed. Giancarlo De Vivo [Bristol: Thoemmes Press, 2000].)

———. 1821. *An Essay on the Production and Distribution of Wealth & Etc.* In vol. 3 of *The Collected Works of Robert Torrens,* ed. Giancarlo De Vivo. Repr., Bristol: Thoemmes Press, 2000.

———. 1844. *The Budget. On Commercial and Colonial Policy & Etc.* London: Smith, Elder and Company. (Reprinted in vol. 5 of *The Collected Works of Robert Torrens,* ed. Giancarlo De Vivo [Bristol: Thoemmes Press, 2000].)

———. 2000. *The Collected Works of Robert Torrens.* Ed. Giancarlo De Vivo. 8 vols. Bristol: Thoemmes Press.

Toynbee, Arnold. 1884. *Lectures on the Industrial Revolution in England.* London: Rivingtons.

Trentman, Frank. 2000. *Paradoxes of Civil Society: New Perspectives on German and British History.* New York: Berghahn Books.

Tucker, G.S.L. 1960. *Progress and Profits in British Economic Thought.* Cambridge: Cambridge University Press.

Tullock, Gordon. 1967. The welfare costs of tariffs, monopolies, and theft. *Western Economic Journal* 5:224–32.

Turgot, Anne Robert Jaques. 1751. *On Universal History.* In *Turgot on Progress, Sociology, and Economics,* trans. Ronald Meek. Repr., Cambridge: Cambridge University Press, 1973.

Turgot, Anne Robert Jaques. 1766. *Reflections on the Formation and Distribution of Wealth*. In *Turgot on Progress, Sociology, and Economics*, trans. Ronald Meek (1788 ed.). Repr., Cambridge: Cambridge University Press, 1973.

van Gelderen, Martin, and Quentin Skinner. 2005. *Republicanism: A Shared European Heritage*. Volume 2 (vol. 1: 2002). Cambridge: Cambridge University Press.

Veitch, John. 1860. *Memoir of Dugald Stewart*. In *The Collected Works of Dugald Stewart*, by Dugald Stewart, ed. William Hamilton, 10:i–clxii. Edinburgh: Thomas Constable and Company. (This volume was reprinted with the same pagination under the title *Biographical Memoirs of Adam Smith, William Robertson, and Thomas Reid* [New York: Augustus M. Kelley, 1966].)

Viner, Jacob. 1927. Adam Smith and laissez faire. *Journal of Political Economy* 35 (April): 198–232. (Reprinted in Jacob Viner, *The Long View and the Short* [Glencoe, IL: Free Press, 1958].)

von Reden, Sitta. 1995. *Exchange in Ancient Greece*. London: Duckworth.

Wallas, Graham. 1925. *The Life of Francis Place*. 4th ed. London: George Allen and Unwin. (Orig. pub. 1898.)

Walpole, Spencer. 1889. *The Life of Lord John Russell*. 2 vols. London: Longmans, Green and Co. Repr., New York: Greenwood.

Walras, Léon. 1874. *Elements of Pure Economics*. Trans. and annotated William Jaffé. Repr., London: Allen and Unwin, 1954.

Waszek, Norbert. 1984. Two concepts of morality: A distinction of Adam Smith's ethics and its stoic origin. *Journal of the History of Ideas* 45 (4): 591–604.

———. 1988. *The Scottish Enlightenment and Hegel's Account of Civil Society*. Dordrecht: Kluwer Academic Publishers.

Waterman, A.M.C. 1991. *Revolution, Economics, and Religion: Christian Political Economy, 1798–1833*. Cambridge: Cambridge University Press.

Wellesley Index to Victorian Periodicals. 1966–89. Ed. Walter E. Houghton (vol. 5 ed. J. H. Slingerland). 5 vols. Toronto: University of Toronto Press.

Whatmore, Richard. 2002. Adam Smith's role in the French Revolution. *Past and Present* 175 (1): 65–89.

Wicksteed, Philip Henry. 1910. *The Common Sense of Political Economy*. 2nd ed. Ed. Lionel Robbins. 2 vols. Repr., London: Routledge and Kegan Paul, 1933.

Winch, Donald. 1972. Marginalism and the boundaries of economic science. *History of Political Economy* 4:325–43.

———. 1976. Comment. In *The Market and the State*, ed. Andrew W. Skinner and Thomas Wilson, 67–72. Oxford: Clarendon Press.

———. 1978. *Adam Smith's Politics: An Essay in Historiographic Revision*. Cambridge: Cambridge University Press.

———. 1983. Science and the legislator: Adam Smith and after. *Economic Journal* 93 (September): 501–20.

———. 1985a. The Burke-Smith problem and late eighteenth-century political and economic thought. *Historical Journal* 28 (1): 231–47.

———. 1985b. Economic liberalism as ideology: The Appleby version. *Economic History Review* 38:287–97.

———. 1988. Adam Smith and the liberal tradition. In *Traditions of Liberalism: Essays on John Locke, Adam Smith, and John Stuart Mill*, ed. Knud Haakonssen, 83–104. St. Leonards: Centre for Independent Studies.

———. 1990. Not just the saint of free enterprise. *Guardian*, July 16, 21.

———. 1993. Robert Malthus: Christian moral scientist, arch-demoralizer, or implicit secular utilitarian? *Utilitas* 5 (2): 239–54.

———. 1996. *Riches and Poverty: An Intellectual History of Political Economy in Britain, 1750–1834*. Cambridge: Cambridge University Press.

———. 2001. That disputatious pair: Economic history and the history of economics. Unpublished paper.

———. 2006. Scottish political economy. In *The Cambridge History of Eighteenth-Century Political Thought*, ed. Mark Goldie and Robert Wokler. Cambridge: Cambridge University Press.

Wolff, Robert Paul. 1965. Beyond tolerance. In *A Critique of Pure Tolerance*, 3–52. Boston: Beacon Press.

Wolin, Sheldon. 1960. *Politics and Vision: Continuity and Innovation in Western Political Thought*. Princeton, NJ: Princeton University Press.

Wrigley, E. A. 1989. The limits to growth: Malthus and the classical economists. In *Population and Resources in Western Intellectual Traditions*, ed. M. S. Teitelbaum and J. M. Winter, 30–48. Cambridge: Cambridge University Press.

Wrigley, E. A., and R. S. Schofield. 1981. *The Population History of England, 1541–1871*. London: Edward Arnold.

Wrigley, E. A., and D. Souden, eds. 1986. *The Works of Thomas Robert Malthus*. 8 vols. London: W. Pickering.

Xenophon. [1968–80]. *Works of Xenophon*. 7 vols. London: W. Heinemann.

INDEX

The letter *n* following a page number indicates a note on that page.

adding-up theory of value: Smith and, 102, 162n1, 226, 260n3; Walras and, 260
Analysis of the Phenomena of the Human Mind (J. Mill), 148
Annas, Julia, 28n38
Aristotle, 61–62; *Nichomachean Ethics*, 63, 64; *Politics*, 63
Arrow, Kenneth, 89, 215
Autobiography (J. S. Mill), 205n35, 244
"Avarice and Profusion" (Godwin), 125

Bank Restriction Act, 112–13
Banks for Savings (J. Mill), 157
Bastiat, Frédéric, 212–13; *Les harmonies économiques*, 210–12
Beer, Max, 220
Bentham, Jeremy, 112; economic and political life and, 73–74; franchise and, 163; liberty of trade and, 250; pauperism and, 124n10; *Rationale of Judicial Evidence*, 188; utilitarianism and, 246–47; utopianism and, 188; *Writings on the Poor Laws*, 73
Berkeley, George, 112
Birkbeck, George, 221
Blackstone, William, 16
Blake, William, 183–84; *Observations on the Expenditure of Government*, 183
Böhm-Bawerk, Eugen von, 264n
Booth, James, 63
Boyle, Robert, 77
Britain, demographics of, 153
Brougham, Henry, 102–3, 169n22, 174n; Hodgskin and, 233n24; on Ricardo, 56
Brown, Vivienne, 28n38
Buchan, James, 90; on Smith, 10n1, 14
Buchanan, James, 74–75
Bullion Controversy, 177
Bullion Report (Horner), 112
Burke, Edmund, 14, 155n34

Cannan, Edwin, 12, 95
Capital (Marx), 3n, 62, 197n24
Carey, Henry, 211–12; *Harmony of Interests*, 210
Case for Enlightenment (Robertson), 27n34
Chalmers, Thomas, 136
Chartists, 218
China as stationary state, 191–93
civil society, 33–34; allocation of social resources and, 59; economic aspects of, 5–6; history, political economy and, 41–49; institutions and, 59; Jevons and, 57–58; as machine, 46; marginalisation of, 56–59; mercantilism and, 34–39; political economy, intentions of statesmen and, 39–41; Ricardian political economy and capitalist society and, 50–56, 159; Smith and, 49–50
Clark, John Bates, 73
classical political economy, 1, 3n, 68–70; critiques of, 259–63; economic and political life and, 68–70; harmony and, 210–11; Jevons and, 260; market economy and, 190–91; Marx and, 8, 263–64; modern neoclassical analysis and, 214n; Newtonism and, 77–78; parliamentary reform and, 163n6; rationality and, 215; unpleasant side of, 231–33; Walras and, 260
Colbert, Jean-Baptiste, 34, 38n3, 39, 67
colonies: Bentham and, 201; mercantilism and, 38; J. Mill and, 201–2; Owen and, 201; Ricardo and, 201; Smith and, 201; Torrens and, 203–4
Colonization of South Australia (Torrens), 203
Common Sense (Paine), 38–39
Condorcet, Marquis de, 122
constitutional economics, 74–76, 266n10
constrained optimisation, 6, 214n, 215, 239, 266